TEXTS AND STU

Contributions to
Biblical and Patristic Lite

THIRD SERIES

Edited by
D.C. PARKER & D.G.K. TAYLOR

Volume 1

STUDIES IN THE EARLY TEXT OF THE GOSPELS AND ACTS

STUDIES IN THE EARLY TEXT OF THE GOSPELS AND ACTS

The Papers of the First Birmingham Colloquium on the Textual Criticism of the New Testament

EDITED BY
D.G.K. TAYLOR

THE UNIVERSITY
OF BIRMINGHAM

UNIVERSITY PRESS

First published in the United Kingdom by The University of Birmingham Press, Edgbaston, Birmingham, BI5 2TT, UK.

ISBN 0-902459-03-2

British Library Cataloguing in Publication data
A CIP catalogue record for this book is available from the British Library

Printed in Great Britain by Alden Press Limited

CONTENTS

FOREWORD

D.C. PARKER

This volume represents a double inauguration. First, it is the first in the revival of an old name. A hundred years ago, Texts and Studies was a proof of the vigour of scholarship in the generation that succeeded Westcott and Hort. Armitage Robinson, Rendel Harris, M.R. James, Kirsopp Lake, Alexander Souter, and above all F.C. Burkitt, are names to be revered. They produced monographs to which we continue to return. The Second Series, under the editorship of Dodd, was somewhat briefer, but no less glorious. We launch the Third Series with a reputation to be sustained, in the conviction that there is no shortage of scholars able to make equally valuable contributions to biblical and patristic literature.

The first two series were published by Cambridge University Press. The association was natural for the editors – Robinson at Christ's College and Dodd at Jesus College. The association with Birmingham is equally natural for the new series. The choice of font (Baskerville) seeks to recognise the series' connection with the two cities. John Baskerville lived and worked in Birmingham, where most of his work was done. He was also at one stage printer to Cambridge University Press, for whom he produced his famous printings of the Book of Common Prayer.

Secondly, this volume contains the papers of the First Birmingham Colloquium on the Textual Criticism of the New Testament, held at the University of Birmingham, England, 14-17 April 1997.[1]

Birmingham's association with New Testament textual criticism is a long one. As A.A.M. Bryer, our Professor of Byzantine Studies, reminded us at the colloquium's final dinner, Rendel Harris, who moved to Birmingham in 1905, is an abiding presence with us. It was through him that the Mingana Collection was formed at Selly Oak,

[1] It has been pointed out that there was in fact an earlier conference (held at Queen's College, Birmingham, in 1987), but that was a singular event, while this was the first in a series.

and largely through him that there came to be a Department of Theology in the university in which textual criticism could be pursued. Once that had happened, textual scholars have been regular patrons: H.F.D. Sparks was at one point Edward Cadbury professor of Theology; S.P. Brock taught here; and Neville Birdsall, Professor Emeritus of New Testament and Textual Criticism, is the name that readers will first associate with Birmingham in this regard. As this century draws to a close, with Gerard Norton for the Hebrew Bible and Septuagint, David Parker for the New Testament, and David Taylor for matters Syriac and Patristic, the tradition continues.

The First Colloquium was planned with only the broadest theme. The main speakers were offered topics that complemented one another; and the topics selected by those who offered titles were many and varied. What has emerged may suitably be called a celebration of the discipline, for it presents such a range of subjects, interests and approaches. In fact, the papers may be roughly divided between theoretical issues (Part One) and more specific studies, either of witnesses or of passages (Part Two).

Part One opens with a balanced pair of papers. The first is a retrospective, an account of a debate held a century almost to the day before our colloquium (the year, as it happens, of three volumes in the First Series).[2] Against this is set an account of the present state, and possible future direction, of the discipline. The following three studies approach different issues: the use of evidence that is both patristic and versional in reconstructing a hypothetical version of John's gospel earlier than the text known from the manuscript tradition; an analysis of the development of letter ratings used by the UBS editors; and the light cast by probability theory on stemmatics.

Part Two turns first to witnesses. It begins with a new look at some valuable material which has been overlooked, and then proceeds to a re-examination of a document which caused great excitement when it was first published over sixty years ago. This paper developed from a seminar held in Birmingham in 1995-96.[3] From witnesses the collection then turns to passages: several

---

[2] M.R. James, *Apocrypha Anecdota. Second Series* (TSt V.1); P.M. Barnard, *Clement of Alexandria: Quis dives salvetur* (TSt V.2); A.A. Bevan, *The Hymn of the Soul* (TSt V.3).

[3] In addition to the three named authors of the paper, the Revd Robert Parkinson was an active member of this seminar.

problems in Mark, then one in the Beatitudes, then the text of Codex Bezae in Luke 24, and finally Acts 2:14-21 in the B and D text forms.

Several contributions to the colloquium, projected or real, are absent from the volume. David Taylor gave a seminar on pre-Peshitta citations in the Syriac tradition of Basil, and W.J. Elliott spoke on abbreviations in Greek manuscripts. Neville Birdsall was to deliver a presidential address comparing the text-critical study of classical and biblical texts. Sadly, his wife's illness prevented his attending. Finally, the present writer gave a paper on the contents of the earliest 'complete' New Testament manuscripts.

W. Hutton, in *An History of Birmingham*,[4] described Baskerville as 'the true Birmingham model', in that he did everything, or could do everything. In producing camera-ready copy, David Taylor has shown that this tradition is alive and well. But many other people have made the colloquia, the revival of the series and this book possible. We wish to record our thanks to Cambridge University Press for graciously surrendering their rights to the title, to the University of Birmingham Press and especially to Vicki Whittaker, the editor, for taking it on; to Mrs Sue Bowen for administering the colloquia so efficiently and pleasantly; to our colleagues for support and encouragement, and especially to successive Heads of the Theology Department, without whom none of this could have happened: Frances Young, Hugh McLeod and Denys Turner.

[4] Birmingham, 1781.

ABBREVIATIONS

AAWG.PH	*Abhandlungen der Akademie der Wissenschaften in Göttingen. Philologisch-historische Klasse*
AJT	*American Journal of Theology*
AMC	C. Wessely, *Les plus anciens monuments du christianisme écrits sur papyrus*, II (PO 18.3; 1924)
AnBib	Analecta Biblica
ANRW	Aufstieg und Niedergang der römischen Welt
ANTF	Arbeiten zur Neutestamentlichen Textforschung
BDR	F. Blass, A. Debrunner, & F. Rehkopf, *Grammatik des neutestamentlichen Griechisch* (Göttingen: Vandenhoeck & Ruprecht, [16]1984)
Bib	*Biblica*
BibOr	Biblica et Orientalia
BR	*Biblical Research*
BT	*The Bible Translator*
CBM	Chester Beatty Monographs
CBQ	*Catholic Biblical Quarterly*
Colwell, *Studies*	E.C. Colwell, *Studies in Methodology in Textual Criticism of the New Testament* (NTTS 9; Leiden: E.J. Brill, 1969)
CQR	*Church Quarterly Review*
CSCO	Corpus Scriptorum Christianorum Orientalium
CSEL	Corpus scriptorum ecclesiasticorum Latinorum
DACL	*Dictionnaire d'archéologie chrétienne et de liturgie*
DJD	Discoveries in the Judaean Desert
ÉBib	Études Bibliques
Editio	*Editio. Internationales Jahrbuch für Editionswissenschaft - International Yearbook of Scholarly Editing - Revue Internationale des Sciences de l'Edition Critique*
Ehrman & Holmes	B.D. Ehrman & M.W. Holmes (eds), *The Text of the New Testament in Contemporary Research: Essays on the Status Quaestionis. A Volume in Honor of Bruce M. Metzger* (SD 46; Grand Rapids: Eerdmans, 1995)

Ehrman, *Orthodox Corruption*	B.D. Ehrman, *The Orthodox Corruption of Scripture: The Effect of Early Christological Controversies on the Text of the New Testament* (New York/Oxford: Oxford University Press, 1993)
EKKNT	*Evangelisch-katholischer Kommentar zum Neuen Testament*
Elliott, *Language*	J.K. Elliott (ed.), *The Language and Style of the Gospel of Mark. An Edition of C.H. Turner's 'Notes on Marcan Usage' Together with Other Comparable Studies* (NovT Suppl 71; Leiden/New York/Köln: E.J. Brill, 1993)
Elliott, *Studies*	J.K. Elliott (ed.), *Studies in New Testament Language and Text: Essays in Honour of George D. Kilpatrick on the Occasion of his Sixty-Fifth Birthday* (Leiden: E.J. Brill, 1976)
Epp & Fee, *Studies*	E.J. Epp and G.D. Fee, *Studies in the Theory and Method of New Testament Textual Criticism* (SD 45; Grand Rapids: Eerdmans, 1993)
ExpTim	*Expository Times*
FGNK	Forschungen zur Geschichte des neutestamentlichen Kanons und der altkirchlichen Literatur
Fil Neotest	*Filologia Neotestamentaria*
Fornberg & Hellholm	T. Fornberg & D. Hellholm (eds), *Texts and Contexts: Biblical Texts in their Textual and Situational Contexts. Essays in Honor of Lars Hartman* (Oslo/Copenhagen/Stockholm/Boston: Scandinavian University Press, 1955)
GCS	Die Griechischen christlichen Schriftsteller der ersten Jahrhunderte
Gospel Traditions	W.L. Petersen (ed.), *Gospel Traditions in the Second Century. Origins, Recensions, Text, and Transmission* (Christianity and Judaism in Antiquity 3; Notre Dame: University of Notre Dame Press, 1989)
GRBS	*Greek, Roman, and Byzantine Studies*
HTB	Histoire du texte biblique
HTR	*Harvard Theological Review*
ICC	International Critical Commentary

IGNT, *Luke* — *The New Testament in Greek: The Gospel according to St. Luke*, ed. the American and British Committees of the International Greek New Testament Project (2 vols.; Oxford: Clarendon Press, 1984, 1987)
JBL — *Journal of Biblical Literature*
JR — *Journal of Religion*
JRS — *Journal of Roman Studies*
JSNT — *Journal for the Study of the New Testament*
JSNT Suppl — Journal for the Study of the New Testament Supplements
JSP — *Journal for the Study of the Pseudepigrapha*
JTS — *Journal of Theological Studies*
LQ — *Lutheran Quarterly*
Metzger, *Textual Commentary I* — B.M. Metzger, *A Textual Commentary on the Greek New Testament* (London/New York: United Bible Societies, 1971)
Metzger, *Textual Commentary II* — B.M. Metzger, *A Textual Commentary on the Greek New Testament* (Stuttgart: Deutsche Bibelgesellschaft/United Bible Societies, ^{2}1994)
MIO — *Mitteilungen des Instituts für Orientforschung*
NA^{26} — *Novum Testamentum Graece*, ed. K. Aland & B. Aland (Stuttgart: Deutsche Bibelstiftung, 1979)
NA^{27} — *Novum Testamentum Graece*, ed. K. Aland & B. Aland (Stuttgart: Deutsche Bibelstiftung, 1993)
Neot — *Neotestamentica*
NovT — *Novum Testamentum*
NovT Suppl — Novum Testamentum Supplementum
NTS — *New Testament Studies*
NTTS — New Testament Tools and Studies
OCA — Orientalia Christiana Analecta
OrChr — *Oriens Christianus*
Parker & Amphoux — D.C. Parker & C.-B. Amphoux (eds), *Codex Bezae. Studies from the Lunel Colloquium June 1994* (Leiden: E.J. Brill, 1996)
PBA — Proceedings of the British Academy
PG — J.-P. Migne (ed.), *Patrologia Graeca*
PL — J.-P. Migne (ed.), *Patrologia Latina*
PO — *Patrologia Orientalis*
QR — *Quarterly Review*

RB	*Revue Biblique*
SBLNTGF	Society of Biblical Literature. The New Testament in the Greek Fathers
SBLSCS	Society of Biblical Literature. Septuagint and Cognate Studies
SC	Sources Chrétiennes
SD	Studies and Documents
SJT	*Scottish Journal of Theology*
StPatr	Studia Patristica
Stud. Pal.	Studien zur Paläographie und Papyruskunde
TLG	Thesaurus Linguae Graecae
TS	*Theological Studies*
TSK	*Theologische Studien und Kritiken*
TSt	Texts and Studies
TU	Texte und Untersuchungen
Turner, *Syntax*	J.H. Moulton, W.F. Howard, & N. Turner, *A Grammar of New Testament Greek*, Vol. 3, *Syntax*, by N. Turner (Edinburgh: T&T Clark, 1963)
TWNT	G. Kittel & G. Friedrich (eds.), *Theologisches Wörterbuch zum Neuen Testament* (Stuttgart: Kohlhammer, 1933-1973)
UBS[3]	*The Greek New Testament*, ed. K. Aland, M. Black, C.M. Martini, B.M. Metzger, & A. Wikgren (United Bible Societies, 1975)
UBS[4]	*The Greek New Testament*, ed. B. Aland, K. Aland, J. Karavidopoulos, C.M. Martini, & B.M. Metzger (Deutsche Bibelgesellschaft/United Bible Societies, 1993)
VC Suppl	Supplements to Vigiliae Christianae
Westcott & Hort	B.F. Westcott & F.J.A. Hort (eds.), *The New Testament in the Original Greek*, Vol. 1, *Text*, Vol. 2, *Introduction* (Cambridge/London: Macmillan, 1881)
WUNT	Wissenschaftliche Untersuchungen zum Neuen Testament
ZAW	*Zeitschrift für die alttestamentliche Wissenschaft*
ZNW	*Zeitschrift für die neutestamentliche Wissenschaft*
ZPE	*Zeitschrift für Papyrologie und Epigraphik*

PART ONE

STUDIES

THE OXFORD DEBATE ON THE TEXTUAL CRITICISM OF THE NEW TESTAMENT, HELD AT NEW COLLEGE ON MAY 6, 1897: AN END, NOT A BEGINNING, FOR THE TEXTUS RECEPTUS[1]

J.L. North

Over breakfast on the morning of Thursday 6 May 1897 six Oxford men read their London Times, contemplated the events of the previous day and perhaps those of the day just beginning. The paper reported the latest phase in the Graeco-Turkish War, a disastrous fire at a charity function in Paris and an unfortunate accident at Christ Church. A young man visiting his brother there was now fighting for his life with a gun shot wound to the head. After lunch five of the six men would walk to New College and take part in the Debate which is our theme today. In order to understand the proceedings of what F.C. Conybeare a few weeks later was to call 'almost a historical occasion',[2] we must go back nearly 50 years or, as one protagonist recognized, probably back to 1831. (As we shall see, this Debate is best understood backwards.) In 1831 Carl Lachmann (1793-1851), the Berlin classical philologist and Germanist, had produced an edition of the Greek New Testament which was the first to abandon the Textus Receptus in favour of the earliest attainable, viz. that current in the fourth-century Eastern church. The introductions to the two volumes which comprise the second edition (1842-50) explain Lachmann's principles, and his text puts into practice the principle that it is early rather than late manuscripts to

[1] Versions of this article have been read as public lectures in Birmingham, Durham, Leeds and Oxford.

[2] 'The Growth of the Peshitta Version of the New Testament, illustrated from the Old Armenian and Georgian Versions', *AJT* 1 (1897) 883-912, at 884.

which recourse should be had in editing.[3] He died on 13 March 1851 and within two years his mantle had been assumed by two young

[3] Lachmann's text had a mixed reception amongst English commentators. The first edition of the first volume of Henry Alford's *The Greek Testament* (London, 1849), on the gospels, followed 'in the main the text of Lachmann and Buttmann'; cf. *Life, Journals and Letters of Henry Alford, D.D., Late Dean of Canterbury, edited by his Widow* [F. Alford] (London etc., ³1874), 147. 'In the main' is clarified in the Prolegomena to this volume, where Alford calls his text 'a *provisional* text only', 'an experiment' (70), a pastorally cautious 'middle course' between Lachmann's concern with 'older', 'primary' manuscripts and the popular Textus Receptus (69). Without naming *any* names or going into *any* details, W.J. Conybeare & J.S. Howson appear to follow Alford's lead; cf. *The Life and Epistles of St. Paul* (first in second edition of 1856, i.xxv). In the commentaries that B. Jowett and A.P. Stanley published in 1855 on the Pauline epistles, it was Lachmann's text once again that they used. They had met Lachmann in Dresden in 1844: 'There was Lachmann', Stanley informed a correspondent, 'with long, streaming yellow hair, the editor of the Greek Testament which you have often seen in my rooms'; cf. R.E. Prothero, *The Life and Correspondence of Arthur Penrhyn Stanley, D.D.* (London, 1893), i. 329, 473; Jowett, *The Epistles of St. Paul to the Thessalonians, Galatians, Romans* (London, 1855), i.v-viii; E. Abbott & L. Campbell, *The Life and Letters of Benjamin Jowett, M.A., Master of Balliol College, Oxford* (London, ³1897), i.89-91: 'Various others, ... Lachmann's Greek Testament, who [sic] were formerly supposed to be myths, also sprang up into life and reality' (91). But two reviewers criticized Jowett and Stanley for adopting Lachmann's text. J.B. Lightfoot, 'Recent Editions of St Paul's Epistles', *Journal of Classical and Sacred Philology* 3 (1856) 81-121, at 88-9: 'To accept Lachmann's text as final therefore would be to use it for a purpose, which the great critic himself would probably have been the first to reprobate.' Lightfoot also criticized Stanley's inaccurate description of textual authorities (90-91). In *QR* 98 (1856) 148-89, at 152 and note, an anonymous critic chose Jowett as the target for strident assault, for 'maintaining [Lachmann's text] with a servile adherence' and not establishing an independent text. Was this critic Alford, who had rewritten the last quarter of the first volume of his first edition (see above) in the light of the newly published second edition of Tischendorf's Greek New Testament (1849)? For Alford's change of mind, see his Prolegomena, 68, 71, and F. Alford (above), 197, 203-5 (where the first edition's text is called 'a very lame affair', 'a crude and ill-digested production'), 209, 506-7. Or was Jowett's anonymous reviewer Ellicott himself, who in his 1854 commentary on Galatians, after some indecision, had expressed his preference for Tischendorf over Lachmann? After all, Tischendorf was still alive, 'still learning, still gathering, still toiling'; cf. xvii-xviii, ²1859, = xxi-

Cambridge dons, both still in their twenties, F.J.A. Hort (1828-92) and B.F. Westcott (1825-1901), who were determined to produce a new text of the Greek New Testament which presented 'exactly the original words of the New Testament, so far as they can now be determined from surviving documents'.[4] The similarity with Lachmann's aim, as well as their greater confidence, is clear from this statement. But there were other influences which contribute to our understanding of Westcott and Hort and therefore of the Debate. If Lachmann was the revolutionary theoretician, it was the assiduous searchers after new manuscripts, men like Tischendorf (1815-74) and Tregelles (1813-75), who put into the hands of Westcott and Hort the materials which largely confirmed Lachmann's text by amplifying its base. Tischendorf and Sinaiticus (א) are legendary, but it is not mere jingoism which urges at least parity of respect for the self-taught Tregelles.[5] So, before Westcott

---

xxiii, [3]1863. It was certainly Ellicott who had already inflicted a stinging eighty-page attack on Alford's first two cautious volumes, not least on their text, 'disfigured by the inaccuracies' of Lachmann's edition; cf. *Christian Remembrancer* 22 (1851) 61-101, esp. 81-5; 26 (1853) 125-64, esp. 143-9. Ellicott's general accusations of plagiarism are specifically echoed by Tischendorf, whom he quotes: *Tamen editionem meam recentissimam ubi primum* [Alford] *nactus erat, omni modo, neque vero sine mala fide, suam in rem convertit* (81). Later, after Alford's death, Ellicott apologized to Mrs Alford for 'the crudities and ungentle comments that disfigured that article'; cf. her biography (above), 501-2. Perhaps a man who as a schoolboy had been taken by his headmaster to stand on the very scaffold to observe the hanging of a condemned man had been traumatized against life's gentler emotions; cf. *The Victoria History of the County of Rutland*, (ed.) W. Page (London, 1908) 277.

[4] *The New Testament in the Original Greek*, vol. 2, *Introduction* (London, 1907) *Appendix* 1; cf. 288.

[5] In fact S.P. Tregelles deserves to be placed alongside other stalwarts of nineteenth-century criticism such as Tischendorf. In the time he could spare from labouring in an iron works he began working on the textual criticism of the New Testament in the early 1830s when he was c. 20 and, in complete ignorance of Lachmann's methods and results, reached similar conclusions to the German professor's but on better grounds; cf. his *An Account of the Printed Text of the Greek New Testament* (London, 1854), 151-3. Secondly, the Miller–Sanday Debate in the 90s had been anticipated not only by Burgon's attack on Westcott and Hort in the 80s but also by the 'energetic, though amicable' disagreements between Tregelles and Scrivener in the 50s and

and Hort commenced their work in 1853, there had been twenty years and more of innovation, theory and discovery, together encouraging the abandonment of the Textus Receptus and the elaboration of a text based on better foundations than those enjoyed by what Hort called 'that vile [earlier, 'villainous'] *Textus Receptus*'.[6]

After eighteen years of work Westcott and Hort made available the first instalment, the gospels, to 'the Members of the Company of Revisers of the English New Testament' and to a few other scholars.[7] Over the next five years, 1871-76, the whole New Testament would be in their hands, but already in the 50s, in 1859, C.J. Vaughan had expressed his indebtedness to Westcott, his colleague at Harrow, for the Greek text accompanying his commentary on Romans. In a note in this book, Westcott states: 'It has been our object to give a text which contains what appears to be the exact words of the Apostle, even in points of orthography, simply from the consideration of the evidence, without paying any regard to the *textus receptus* or to any other standard'.[8] Similarly, the Greek text of J.B. Lightfoot's *Galatians* (1865) was largely the work of Westcott and Hort, his old Cambridge friends.[9] And so, though not finally published till May and September 1881, Westcott and Hort's text and principles had

---

60s, not least over Syriac matters, esp. the significance of Sy^{c} apropos Sy^{p}. Sy^{c} had been available to scholars since 1848. We need a monograph on Tregelles as textual critic.

[6] Cf. A.F. Hort, *Life and Letters of Fenton John Anthony Hort* (London, 1896), i.211 (letter dated 29 and 30 December 1851). G.A. Patrick, *F.J.A. Hort, Eminent Victorian* (Sheffield, 1987), devotes pp.76-87 to Hort's share in Westcott and Hort and the Revised Version New Testament.

[7] Cp. *The New Testament in the Original Greek*, vol. 2, *Introduction* (London, 1907), 18; Hort, *Life and Letters*, ii.137; and A. Westcott, *Life and Letters of Brooke Foss Westcott* (London, 1903), i.237, 430.

[8] *St Paul's Epistle to the Romans, with Notes* (London, ^{4}1874), xiii-xiv; also his *The Epistle to the Hebrews, with Notes* (London, 1890), viii. R.R. Williams claimed that Vaughan's '*Romans* is interesting too as the occasion of the first publication of any part of the Westcott–Hort text of the New Testament'; cf. 'A Neglected Victorian Divine, Vaughan of Llandaff', *CQR* 154 (1953) 72-85, esp. 80.

[9] *St Paul's Epistle to the Galatians, a Revised Text with Introduction, Notes, and Dissertations* (London, ^{5}1876), viii. For Lightfoot's own views on the need for a new Greek text, see *On a Fresh Revision of the English New Testament* (London, ^{2}1872), 19-32.

been more or less common property in academic circles for over twenty years. In the same week that Westcott and Hort's text was published, the Revised Version New Testament was published, and the close link between Greek text and the revision was immediately noticed. After all Westcott and Hort had been members of the Revision Company from the beginning and, as we have seen, the Revisers had had access to the Greek text as its several parts were finished. Though it is not true to say that the Revised Version New Testament is a translation of Westcott and Hort, they are sufficiently close for criticism of the one to be seen as criticism of the other.

Since we now begin to talk of criticism, it is time to introduce the name of J.W. Burgon (1813-88). He is the man who provides the link between Westcott and Hort, the Revised Version New Testament in the early 80s and the 1897 Debate. Further back, he it was who saw 1831 as the date of the beginning of the decline in textual criticism as applied to the New Testament.[10] He it was who became the sternest, perhaps the most vituperative, critic of Westcott and Hort and the Revised Version New Testament. It was his views that Edward Miller (1825-1901), his self-constituted champion, maintained at the Debate, nine years after Burgon's death. Burgon turned to serious textual criticism relatively late in life. It is true that while in Rome in the spring of 1860 as a *locum* chaplain to the English congregation he had inspected enough of codex Vaticanus (B) to be able to describe it as 'one of the most vicious extant',[11] but he had other windmills at which to tilt before he began to prepare his first textual work on *The Last Twelve Verses of the Gospel according to S. Mark vindicated against Recent Objectors*, published in 1871 when he was fifty-eight. I suspect that it was the relegation of Mark 16:9-20 to the status of an appendix in the editions of Tregelles (1857) and Tischendorf (^{8}1864) that obliged him to pick up his lance on its behalf. It was in the following year, 1872, that he committed the rest of his life to a defence of what he called the Traditional Text. I say 'committed' deliberately, because he speaks of the challenge and his

---

[10] E.M. Goulburn, *John William Burgon, Late Dean of Chichester* (London, 1892), ii.277: 'Ever since 1831, the Text of the N.T. has been like a storm-tossed barque, drifting along without captain, chart, or compass.'

[11] *Letters from Rome to Friends in England* (London, 1862), 13-35 (entirely on B), at 33. Burgon's visit to the Vatican Library is also described in Goulburn, *op. cit.*, i.256-8.

decision in terms almost of an evangelical conversion.[12] But like all good conversions, there had been preparation; there is evidence that five or six years earlier he had already begun to think along these lines.[13] The provisional draft of the gospels that Westcott and Hort made available to the Revision Company in July 1871, with the Longer Ending of Mark in double square brackets, would have only confirmed Burgon in the rightness of the immense task he was undertaking.[14] Burgon could have gained sight of this draft from F.H.A. Scrivener (1813-91), one of the Revisers and one who shared Burgon's views about the history of the text. So, for at least twenty years before his death Burgon had been at his task, corresponding with and visiting foreign libraries in search of New Testament manuscripts[15] and, chiefly, collecting patristic quotations of the New Testament and assembling them into sixteen huge portfolio volumes, now in the British Library. These were to provide the basis of what he called 'my book', viz. *True Principles of the Textual Criticism of the New Testament*. The latter was never written in that form,[16] though Miller, his literary executor, was to compile two books from his accumulated materials. Of the former, the patristic quotations, only a small portion saw the light, 118 pages on Matthew 1-14, edited by Miller in 1899. His biographer tells us that as Burgon lay dying, he asked that his portfolios 'on which he had spent so many laborious days and nights' be 'brought upstairs and placed upon' a bed 'where he could see them'. 'I won't read them, or open them', he said, 'I only want to look at them'.[17] How sad! He had started too late in life and he had allowed himself to be distracted by the appearance of the Revised Version New Testament, on which he had mounted a ferocious attack, and by other literary work. But, as I have noted, in addition to his work on the fathers he was an indefatigable traveller

[12] Goulburn, *op. cit.*, ii.274.

[13] Goulburn, *op. cit.*, ii.277-9, 274.

[14] Lightfoot's book *On a Fresh Revision*, first published in 1871, may have been another factor in Burgon's decision to devote himself to resisting the 'Revisionists'' attacks on the Traditional Text.

[15] Goulburn, *op. cit.*, ii.58-9, 82-4, 198-200, 277.

[16] Goulburn, *op. cit.*, ii.82 and n.7; F.H.A. Scrivener, *Adversaria Critica Sacra* (Cambridge, 1893), v-vi and note, comments on projects interrupted by death, including Burgon's.

[17] Goulburn, *op. cit.*, ii.300-1; cf. *ibid.* 82, n.7, 374.

to foreign libraries. Like Tischendorf and Tregelles before him, his great work which will stand the test of time was his discovery and collation of hundreds of New Testament manuscripts.

Given Burgon's combative temperament we should also note, however briefly, other theological and ecclesiastical factors that made him fear for the Ark of God and compelled him to gird himself for its defence. In addition to the revelations of Charles Darwin and T.H. Huxley, there was the monstrous *Essays and Reviews* (1860), every one of whose contributors Burgon regarded as an infidel. The early 60s also saw the publication of the first five horrifying contributions which J.W. Colenso was making in distant South Africa to the problems of the Hexateuch. The debate about the continued use of the Athanasian Creed in the liturgy was under way in the late 60s; in 1871 the disestablishment of the Irish church came into force. Perhaps most painfully, in 1870 'Soapy Sam' Wilberforce, the bishop of Winchester, had proposed the revision of the Authorized Version to the Convocation of Canterbury. Salt was rubbed into the wound by the impious appointment of a Unitarian scholar to the New Testament Company and the invitation to him to share in the Communion Service with which the Revisers started their work that June. Burgon's world was collapsing.[18]

The principles that Burgon elaborated and defended and that Miller was to champion are summarized by Miller under five heads; the essential characteristics of the True Text are:

> (a) It must be grounded upon an exhaustive view of the evidence of Greek copies in manuscript in the first place; and in all cases where they differ so as to afford doubt, of Versions or Translations into other languages, and of Quotations from the New Testament made by Fathers and other early writers.

[18] For this paragraph see O. Chadwick, *The Victorian Church* vol. ii (London, 1970), chs. 1-3, 8. E.B. Pusey also knew which way the text-critical wind was blowing. Writing on 12 February 1870, just two days after the proposal to revise the Authorized New Testament had been made, he said to Wilberforce: 'I fear that evil will result [from revision], from the state of criticism as to the text of the New Testament'; cf. H.P. Liddon, *Life of Edward Bouverie Pusey* vol. iv (London, 1897), 230; and cp. 367-9 for his fears realized (as he thought).

(b) It must have descended from the actual composition of Books of the New Testament, and must thus possess the highest possible antiquity.

(c) It must be the outcome, not of one stem of descent, but of many. Consentient copies, made by successive transcription in the different countries where the Holy Scriptures were used, revered, and jealously watched, must confirm and check one another.

(d) The descent must be continuous, without break or failure, or it would be no real descent, but a fragmentary or stunted line of genealogy, broken up or prematurely closed.

(e) The Readings, or Text, must be such as to commend themselves to the enlightened judgement of Christendom.[19]

As applied to editions currently available, while the Traditional Text, a pure form of the Textus Receptus, embodied these principles perfectly, the editions of Lachmann, Tregelles, Tischendorf, and Westcott and Hort did not. Burgon's criticism of them was threefold and simple. They attached overriding importance to a few documents while he saw no reason to ignore the vast majority of Greek witnesses. The early dates of their few witnesses, which Burgon did not contest, was more than outweighed by the very early date of the Syp, second century if not earlier.[20] Thirdly, it was unthinkable that God's truth had been left so uncertain for so long, until a pair of scholars in the nineteenth century brought it to light. The pastoral consequences of allowing the contrary were all too clear to the churchman in Burgon. As Dean Goulburn of Norwich, his sympathetic biographer whom I have already quoted, said, with reference to the marginal comment on the Lord's Bloody Sweat in

---

[19] E. Miller, *The Oxford Debate on the Textual Criticism of the New Testament, held at New College on May 6, 1897* (London, 1897), xii.

[20] For recent summaries of the materials for and the study of the Syriac New Testament, which is an important element in the background to the Debate, cf. S.P. Brock, 'Versions, Ancient (Syriac)', *Anchor Bible Dictionary* (New York etc., 1992), vi.796-9, and J.H. Charlesworth, 'Sinaiticus, Syrus', *ibid.* 49-50; W.L. Petersen, 'The Diatessaron of Tatian', T. Baarda, 'The Syriac Versions of the New Testament', S.P. Brock, 'The Use of the Syriac Fathers for New Testament Textual Criticism', all in Ehrman & Holmes, 77-96, 97-112, 224-36 respectively. All five articles have rich bibliographies.

the Revised Version of Luke 22:43-4, following its double bracketing in Westcott and Hort: 'The Revisers ... make our voices falter, and our hearts to have misgivings, while we pray in words which the Church has put into our mouths; – "By thine Agony and bloody Sweat, Good Lord, deliver us"'.[21]

It is something of a puzzle that Westcott and Hort did not respond to Burgon's theories and attacks. We know that Hort was tempted to, but Lightfoot persuaded him not to reply, presumably on the principle 'Truth will out'.[22] As we shall see, there were defenders of their principles in abundance, but nothing from Westcott and Hort themselves. All we have in print is Westcott's quiet statement in the preface to the second edition of their Introduction and Appendix (1896): 'No arguments have been advanced against the general principles maintained in the Introduction and illustrated in the Notes, since the publication of the first Edition, which were not fully considered by Dr. Hort and myself in the long course of our work and in our judgement dealt with adequately'.

Before at last we proceed to the Debate itself, there are two more factors we must mention. First, just as Burgon was influenced by his cultural and ecclesiastical environment (how could it be otherwise?), so was Miller. Between Burgon's death in 1888 and the Debate, the notorious essays published as *Lux Mundi* had appeared in 1889 and Sy^{s}, which we shall meet again, in 1894. In the month after the Debate, the Queen would celebrate her Diamond Jubilee at the age of 78. Though this would be a happy event, it would inevitably provoke questions about her health and the uncertain future. In other words, I hope that I do not overpress the impact of non-theological factors in seeing in *fin de vie* and *fin de siècle* fears and feelings something of Miller's personal attitude before the Debate. Was his world collapsing as well? Secondly, the Debate was conducted by the Epigoni, the successors, of the Titans who had

---

[21] Goulburn, *op. cit.*, ii.212-3.

[22] Cf. Chadwick, *op. cit.*, 54. Privately, it was different. Writing to Hort on 28 October 1881, Westcott was gnomic: 'His [viz. Burgon's] violence answers himself' and three months later Hort commented on another attack: 'poor, sorry, acrid stuff, duller than the last article, and no better ... nonsense.' Cf. Westcott, *op. cit.*, i.404; Hort, *op. cit.*, ii.289. Twenty years or so later Julius Wellhausen was to apply to Burgon the proverb '... dass Alter nicht vor Torheit schuetzt'! Cf. *Einleitung in die drei ersten Evangelien* (Berlin, [2]1911), 4.

hammered out the fundamental positions. Most of them were now beyond reach, either dead or on the episcopal bench. Burgon and Scrivener and, on the other side, Lightfoot and Hort, were dead; the latter's colleague, Westcott, and Ellicott, the Chairman of the New Testament Revisers' Company and Westcott and Hort's staunchest supporter, were now the bishops of Durham and of the united see of Gloucester and Bristol. This does not mean that the six participants in the Debate were insignificant. As we shall see, they were no mean scholars, especially on the Hortian side (for example, William Sanday [1843-1920]), but, as we have said, they chiefly represent a discussion that had taken place yesterday and that can only be understood backwards, with reference to Burgon and Hort. A confrontation between *them* would have been a veritable Titanomachia!

So let us proceed to the participants. First, Edward Miller, the prime mover of the Debate.

Like Burgon, Miller had turned to textual criticism late in life. He had published a primer popularizing Burgon's views in 1886 when he was sixty-one (*A Guide to the Textual Criticism of the New Testament*), and produced a valuable revision of Scrivener's useful *A Plain Introduction to the Criticism of the New Testament for the Use of Biblical Students* (1894). In 1896 he had prepared two books[23] for publication from the materials that Burgon had left, the generally hostile reaction to which led to his seeking an opportunity to explain 'the system of Textual Criticism advocated by the late Dean Burgon and myself, in order to the removal of misconceptions of it'.[24] Sanday offered a debate and the date was fixed. Perhaps Miller saw this as almost an evangelistic opportunity. When he died in August 1901, eleven days after Westcott, his obituary in the London *Times* spoke of his willingness to carry 'the war as far as he could through the country. Wherever he could get clergy and others together, he was ready to address them on what he considered the absurdities of the Westcott-Hort principles'.[25] The Debate was another such occasion, and one conceded by the enemy! This brings us to Sanday. As the Lady Margaret Professor of Divinity in the University of Oxford and

[23] *The Traditional Text of the Holy Gospels Vindicated and Established* and *The Causes of the Corruption of the Traditional Text of the Holy Gospels* (both London, 1896).

[24] *The Oxford Debate*, v.

[25] The London *Times* for 9 August 1901, 5e.

particularly as a distinguished editor of manuscripts of the Old Latin New Testament and vigorous defender of Westcott and Hort in a series of articles in the *Expositor* and *Contemporary Review* in 1881,[26] Sanday had been the obvious man for Miller to approach. Realising the centrality of the evidence of Sy^{p}, and wanting to dispel the significance of Sy^{s}, published less than three years before, Miller engaged the support of two champions of the Traditional Text who were also eminent Syriacists. G.H. Gwilliam (1846-1913), who had also been Burgon's curate 1875-77,[27] was presently editing the Sy^{p} gospels for the Clarendon Press. Albert Bonus (1854-1936) had published the previous year a collation of the Sy^{c}, Sy^{s} and Sy^{p}

---

[26] *Expositor* 2.2 (1881) 11-18, 241-78, 372-98, 401-18; *Contemporary Review* 40 (1881) 985-1006. Later, Sanday was also gently to qualify G.H. Gwilliam's high assessment of Sy^{p}; cf. *Studia Biblica et Ecclesiastica* ii (Oxford, 1890), 272; cf. n.36. (It is a little known fact that in 1891 Sanday had been preparing an *Introduction to the Textual Criticism of the New Testament* 'for some time'; cf. *ibid.* iii (Oxford, 1891), 235 n.2. It was probably never finished, but I wonder if the manuscript still survives?) But note that in October 1881, at the Newcastle Church Congress, and in April 1882, Sanday was also expressing some doubts about the premature adoption of Westcott and Hort and serious reservations about the style of the Revised Version New Testament; cf. S. Hemphill, *A History of the Revised Version of the New Testament* (London, 1906), 102-3, 110-12; Sanday in *The Official Report of the Church Congress held at Newcastle-on-Tyne on October 4th, 5th, 6th, and 7th, 1881*, ed. W.P. Swaby (London, 1882), 493-8, at 494-5, and in *Expositor* 2.3 (1882) 249-68 – Westcott and Hort should not yet be regarded as final ('I could have wished that a few more years had elapsed, so that the question might have received a thorough discussion' [254]), but as far as the Revised Version New Testament is concerned, Sanday's sympathies are with – Burgon (263, n.2)! One of Sanday's colleagues at Christ Church, C.L. Dodgson (= Lewis Carroll), was to speak out even more strongly about the Revised Version. In 1891-92 he suggested to two authors whose books he was reading and enjoying that any new edition of their works should have the Revised Version's quotations replaced by the Authorised Version! Cf. *The Letters of Lewis Carroll*, (ed.) M.N. Cohen (London, 1979), ii.843, 895. In the former letter he writes in italics: '*I hate* [the Revised Version]'.

[27] Goulburn, *op. cit.*, ii.110-12, 144, 304. Along with H.W. Yule, Gwilliam contributed an article on 'John William Burgon' to the *Expository Times* which came out in the same month as the Debate. Was this a coincidence? Cf. *ExpTim* 8 (1896-97) 344-8; cp. *ExpTim* 4 (1892-93) 345, 347, for earlier comments about Westcott and Hort and Sy^{p}.

gospels[28] and both had written on Sy^s in the *Expository Times* for 1895 and Gwilliam in the *Critical Review* for 1896.[29] Miller's supporters were very capable men. On the Hortian side, Sanday was to be joined by A.C. Headlam (1862-1947) and W.C. Allen (1867-1953). Headlam had already been Sanday's colleague in their famous commentary on Romans (published in the ICC series in 1895) and in other textual work where his knowledge of Coptic had been brought into play. He had been appointed the Rector of Welwyn the previous year and his biographer says that he used to lecture his Sunday School teachers on textual criticism![30] Willoughby Allen was a Semitist as well as a New Testament scholar, who published the Matthew volume in the same ICC series in 1907. As it happens, he was obliged to be absent from the Debate and his contribution was read by Sanday. Allen was also a member of Sanday's famous New Testament Seminar, and, though idle, it is interesting to speculate who else could have been present at the New College Debate that Thursday afternoon. From the Seminar and elsewhere there could have been Vernon Bartlett, R.C. Charles, Conybeare, W.R. Inge, Kirsopp Lake (of whom more anon), Walter Lock, D.S. Margoliouth, R.C. Moberly, C.H. Turner and H.J. White. F.C. Burkitt, J. Rendel Harris and J.O.F. Murray might have come across from Cambridge, to see how their heroes, Westcott and Hort, would be treated. Perhaps F.G. Kenyon came down from London and Bishop Ellicott from Gloucester. 'Truly there were giants in the earth in those days.'

And so the afternoon began. The chair was taken by Dr. William Ince (1825-1910), the Regius Professor of Divinity. One telling plea he entered was that there should be no 'imputation of motives'! This

---

28 *Collatio Codicis Lewisiani rescripti Evangeliorum sacrorum Syriacorum cum Codice Curetoniano (Mus. Brit. Add. 14,451)* (Oxford, 1896). When it was reviewed in *ExpTim* 8 (1896-97) 19-20, the reviewer, aware of the significance of Sy^s (cp. *ExpTim* 6 [1894-95] 97-8, 228, 389), invited comment on Bonus's collation: 'Now we should like to hear Mr. Gwilliam's or Mr. Miller's thoughts upon it'.

29 *ExpTim* 6 (1894-95) 157-61, 380-2; *Critical Review* 6 (1896) 14-22.

30 See R. Jasper, *Arthur Cayley Headlam* (London, 1960), 37-8, 337-8, for his textual and Coptic interests; 44-5 for the commentary on Romans; 46 for Headlam's part in Sanday's election to the Lady Margaret Chair; 63 for Headlam's classes in textual criticism. Cp. *Appendices ad Novum Testamentum Stephanicum iam inde a Millii Temporibus Oxoniensium Manibus tritum,* (ed.) W. Sanday (Oxford, 1889), 94, 182, n.1.

was clearly directed at Miller. He did behave himself that afternoon, unlike Burgon before him and his own sarcasm and petulance later on. In fact his Times obituarist, already quoted, said in this regard: 'The mantle of Dean Burgon had fallen on him so completely that he sometimes did his cause harm by his intemperate criticism of his opponents'. Miller opened the proceedings, which I shall deal with in more detail later on, with a statement of familiar points: the contrast between many witnesses, very largely in agreement with each other, and a few witnesses disagreeing with the majority. Here, of course, Bℵ are in mind. He vigorously disputed Westcott and Hort's notions about third- and fourth-century revisions ('phantom revisions', as they were called), quite without any basis in history, revisions which produced standardized texts, thereby denying to the many manuscripts any numerical ascendancy; finally the idea of 'conflation' was warmly scouted. But, as I have stated, all that was set in a framework of defending the two books he had published the previous year and defending their real author, Burgon, from misconceptions. He mentioned particularly the accusation that Burgon did not care for the 'value' or 'character' or 'weight' of manuscripts but only counted heads; that his scholarship deferred to the 1500 years' reign of the Traditional Text. He concluded with a plea for whatever degree of co-operation the fundamental difference of principle allowed: 'What I should hope very much is, that some plan may be set on foot from this time by which those who are on different sides on this question may find some sort of agreement and may co-operate one with another in threshing out this great question'.[31]

Sanday was known as a reconciler and his reply begins pacifically by listing the four points where he agreed with Miller.[32] But the peacemaker in him could see no room even for the co-operation Miller sought. His main criticism of Burgon–Miller concerned their method. Instead of beginning with the Textus Receptus, they should attempt a history of manuscripts: group manuscripts into families;

[31] *The Oxford Debate*, 18-9.

[32] Cf. A. Plummer's appreciation of 'William Sanday and his Work', in *ExpTim* 32 (1920-21) 151-5, 199-203, 247-52, at 153: Sanday as 'large-minded and fair and conciliatory'; M.D. Chapman, 'The Socratic Subversion of Tradition: William Sanday and Theology, 1900-1920', *JTS* 45 (1994) 94-116, esp. 94-5; see n.26.

work out the families' archetypes and from the archetypes go back to hyparchetypes and ultimately if possible to autographs. While he admits that Sy^{p} is the sheet-anchor of their position, he could not agree that Origen in the third century was the scholar responsible for the Bℵ text. Miller and Sanday were followed by their four supporters who concentrated mainly on the various relationships held to exist between the Sy^{c}, Sy^{s} and Sy^{p} gospels. Gwilliam and Bonus defended the priority of Sy^{p} and saw in the other two manuscripts later degeneration from it; Headlam and Allen reversed the order and saw in the Sy^{p} an edition of the Old Syriac, represented by Sy^{s} and Sy^{c}, revised in the light of fourth-century Greek manuscripts.

The proceedings appear to have been curtailed by the advent of dinner time at New College, and so our five Oxford men returned home to contemplate the day, and Miller to begin to prepare the report of the Debate, with transcripts of the six speeches, that I have summarized today. It appeared three months later.[33] What had it all amounted to? What did it lead to? In brief, very little. It had been a debate with no future. Sanday had refused any co-operation apart from what he called friendly meetings for the discussion of 'particular points, perhaps somewhat more limited in character than the very broad issue' discussed that afternoon.[34] Perhaps irritated and frustrated by this and the refusal to answer his defence of Burgon, Miller carried on the fight in the four years left to him, especially in two more pamphlets, 'printed for private circulation' and undated, but appearing one probably in 1899 and the other certainly in 1901.[35] We shall look at these in a moment. Gwilliam lived to publish the Sy^{p} gospels in 1901 and died in 1913.[36] Bonus

[33] Reviewed in *ExpTim* 8 (1896-97) 385, 532-6, and very briefly in *London Quarterly Review* 89 (1898) 155. An extensive report of the Debate had already appeared within a week, in the *Guardian* for 12 May 1897, 747, almost certainly contributed by Miller. It is here that Allen's absence from the Debate is mentioned.

[34] *The Oxford Debate*, 19.

[35] The innumerable, often single word, quotations from Miller's 1899(?) and 1901 pamphlets in the second part of this paper have not been referred to their appropriate pages. This was done to avoid overloading the footnotes. They are easily found.

[36] The review of this book by J.R. Harris, another Syriacist, shows that Harris sided with Headlam and Allen, as he already had with Robinson and Burkitt

passes completely out of the academic picture, quietly preparing a concordance to the Sy^{p} New Testament, which is still extant, unpublished, in Australia.[37] Perhaps as light relief, from semi-retirement near Exeter, he sent nearly twenty articles, notes and reviews to the *Expository Times* 6-37 (1895-1925), usually on Syriac matters. Sanday and his team were men of many parts. Headlam went on to other New Testament, theological, ecumenical and episcopal duties, Allen to various church callings in Lancashire and Norfolk,[38] and Sanday himself, though always retaining an interest in textual criticism, especially in the New Testament text of Irenaeus, moved into other parts of New Testament study.

About two years after his report of the New College proceedings, Miller produced another short statement: *The Present State of the Textual Criticism respecting the Holy Gospels*. In it he picked up certain points made by Sanday in the Debate. He welcomed Sanday's admission that Hort had claimed too much for 'Conflation', but when he moved on to what he called 'the Syriac Question', he makes no concession to the points made by Headlam and Allen nor (and this is much more culpable) to the argument published only a few months after the Debate in the *American Journal of Theology* by Conybeare. Conybeare had examined the texts of the Armenian and Georgian New Testaments and concluded that in the gospels they resembled Sy^{s} and not Sy^{p}. Since we know the dates when the Armenian and Georgian translations were made (between 325 and 400), Conybeare concluded that Sy^{p} was not used because it was not yet in existence

(see n.40). It develops into a review of the Debate as a whole; cf. *London Quarterly Review* 97 (1902) 99-107. Having contributed three papers on Sy^{p}, ancillary to this 1901 publication, in *Studia Biblica* (Oxford, 1885), 151-74, *Studia Biblica et Ecclesiastica* ii (Oxford, 1890), 241-71, *ibid*. iii (Oxford, 1891), 47-104, Gwilliam wrote a fourth and final paper in *Studia Biblica et Ecclesiastica* v (Oxford, 1903), 189-237. Here he responds to F.C. Burkitt's monograph, *S. Ephraim's Quotations from the Gospel* (TSt 7.2; Cambridge, 1901), which in the eyes of most commentators had finally proved that Sy^{p} was posterior to Sy^{s} Sy^{c}. Gwilliam *seems* very grudgingly to concede; cf. 221-2, 230, 236. But he does not mention or respond to Robinson or Conybeare (see n.40).

[37] Cf. B.M. Metzger, *Reminiscences of an Octogenarian* (Peabody, MA, 1997) 157-8.

[38] Cf. *Who was Who*, vol. 5, 1951-60 (London, 1961), 19.

and therefore must be later still.[39] Miller attempted to turn this point (which if true destroyed an important pillar of the defence of the Traditional Text) with an unlikely analogy from the Synoptic Problem. Incidentally, the bearing of the Armenian and Georgian versions could and should have been raised at the Debate itself because already in 1895 J.A. Robinson had said as much in his study of the Euthalian material, and in his review of this monograph Conybeare also had drawn attention to this point in February 1896.[40]

---

39 Cf. n.2.

40 J.A. Robinson, *Euthaliana: Studies of Euthalius, Codex H of the Pauline Epistles, and the Armenian Version* (TSt 3.3; Cambridge, 1895), 72-98; esp. 75-91; Conybeare, *Academy* 49 (1896) 98-9, confirming Robinson's use of the Armenian New Testament and adding Georgian evidence for good measure. (These conclusions were worked out in the article cited in n.2.) Robinson's *Euthaliana* was also mentioned later that year in *CQR* 43 (1896-97) 248 (see n.43). So there had been plenty of opportunity for all participants in the 1897 Debate to see that the axe was already 'laid unto the root of the trees'. But a great deal more had been missed, or at least had not been exploited, by the participants. In addition to Robinson, two of his Cambridge colleagues were working on the problem of the relationship of Sy^{c} and now Sy^{s} to Sy^{p} from a patristic point of view. Following the discovery of Sy^{s} by Mrs Lewis in 1892, along with R.L. Bensly, Harris and Burkitt had both been closely involved in its decipherment, editing and publication in 1894 (see nn.44-7). In a lecture delivered on 19 January 1894 on 'The Old Syriac Text of Acts' and printed in *Four Lectures on the Western Text of the New Testament* (London, 1894), 14-34, esp. 16-19, Harris takes it for granted that along with Sy^{c} and Aphraat, Ephraem is pre-Sy^{p} and shows that Ephraem's quotations from Acts are akin to D. In the *Contemporary Review* 68 (1895) 271-87, 'The Diatessaron: A Reply' [to W.R. Cassels], expanded in *Fragments of the Commentary of Ephrem Syrus upon the Diatessaron* (London, 1895), he showed that Ephraem's quotations from the gospels had used the Diatessaron, and so by implication not Sy^{p}. His unspoken assumption is that preference for D and Tatian implies not only non-use of Sy^{p} but the non-existence of Sy^{p}. This is more explicit in *London Quarterly Review* (n.36), 106. Burkitt signalled his views about the relative lateness of Sy^{p} and about Ephraem's quotations in the *Guardian* for 31 October 1894, 1707-08: 'the quotations found in Ephraim Syrus gave at best an uncertain sound'. So, all in all, 1894-95 had been a busy time for the second Cambridge triumvirate. Burkitt was to work out his views in an article in *JTS* 1 (1900) 569-71, 'On S.Ephraim's Quotation of Matt. xxi 3', and at greater length in his famous 1901 monograph (see n.36). This was the final nail in Sy^{p}'s coffin that had been seven years in the making. Miller must be referring to the 1900 article

Even Sanday, who read everything, had missed this. A great deal more than an uncertain analogy was needed. Finally, in this second pamphlet Miller gave a modified welcome to the short book of George Salmon, the elderly and distinguished Provost of TCD, published in London in 1897, *Some Thoughts on the Textual Criticism of the New Testament*. Although he does not pull his punches over Salmon's own shortcomings and can be unbelievably patronizing about his lack of deep acquaintance with the field, he is happy to use any ally against Hort. The last pamphlet, *The Textual Controversy and the Twentieth Century*, probably Miller's last publication before his death, opens on an optimistic note. He believes that the 'Hortists' have been 'rumbled'. A new generation of young scholars feels 'that the leaders in the immediate past were not so infallible as they were supposed to be'. The credit for this reversal Miller modestly claims for Burgon and himself. Salmon's now four-year-old critique of Westcott and Hort is again deployed as another exposé of their absurdities. Miller proceeds to a criticism of Salmon's own suggestions for the history of the text. Salmon had rechristened Hort's families with their 'question-begging' names but Miller saw no improvement in the new names. He attempted to show that such entities were valuable only for classification purposes, but they could make no contribution to the history of the text. In particular he devoted thirteen pages to the Western text because it was that which more and more was occupying the attention of scholars after Westcott and Hort, in Germany of men like Blass, Nestle and Wellhausen, in England of men like Burkitt and Harris, Sanday and Turner. Even Allen, who had been one of Sanday's supporters, could say ten years later in his 1907 commentary on Matthew: 'I am unable to assume that the edition of Westcott and Hort gives us a final text in either Gospel [sc. of Matthew and Mark]. In particular, I am inclined to believe that the second century readings, attested by the

---

rather than to the monograph which appeared after his death, when he lamely dismissed it with 'I hear that Mr. Burkitt impugns the conclusion of Mr. Woods [the reference is to Woods in *Studia Biblica et Ecclesiastica* iii (Oxford, 1891) 105-38]. It is a question of balance in favour of one or the other'. So it remains a puzzle why Sanday and his team failed to mention at the Debate what had been public property for over three years and which counted so much in their favour, and why Miller and his followers failed to acknowledge it, let alone recognize its force.

ecclesiastical writers of that century, and by the Syriac and Latin versions, are often deserving of preference' (lxxxvii). Miller's swan song concludes with a statement of his views about the history of the study of the text in the nineteenth century:

> The nineteenth century has presented us with quite enough views on Textual Criticism. It is now the duty of Textual students to buckle more closely to an exhaustive examination as far as can be of all the facts and evidence in the case, to cast away inveigling theories, and to work out conclusions, if in a less vainglorious, yet in a truly business-like way.

Although Miller took some note of later developments in New Testament textual criticism in the two later pamphlets, they also repeat so many points made earlier in his report of the Debate that the degree of overlapping quite justifies our taking the three documents together and combining from all three their chief features. This consolidated approach leaves one with the abiding impression that the pamphlets take part in a scholarly debate in an unscholarly manner. Let me specify. First, Miller's treatment of his opponents, notably Hort, and of their materials, notably Codex Vaticanus, is overly personalized. His opponents are called 'Hortists'. Westcott, still alive and the venerable bishop of Durham, is hardly mentioned by name. However, along with Hort, he can still be discerned behind the references to the 'one or two' or 'few individuals', clever modern critics, 'theorists', 'innovators', typical products of the nineteenth-century itch for change. Because of their reputation for learning, which Miller called 'subjective scholarship', 'shallow and delusive sciolism', Westcott and Hort were attended by a 'retinue'. Miller speaks of its excessive submission to them. Even the old Oxford–Cambridge rivalry is drawn in. 'Hero-worship which has prevailed in his own University, where his impressive presence was so long to be found, has no place in Oxford.' Worse follows: he speaks of 'the condemnation of any independent thought in the ranks of his followers' and 'of moral terrorism which they inspired at Cambridge amongst those who did not quash or conceal their difficulties'! This hostility to Hort and his Cambridge successors is extended, in part at least, to George Salmon, whom we have already mentioned, in whose book Miller found both things to praise and things to criticize. But if Miller's pen did not spare one of the country's best New Testament and patristic scholars of the century and at eighty older than even Miller, he certainly was not going to spare Kirsopp Lake, a stripling in his twenties and a third his own age. In 1896 Lake had had the audacity to criticize Miller's revision of Scrivener's *Introduction* and his own *Traditional Text of the Holy Gospels* in the pages of the prestigious *Classical Review*.[41] Miller mentions him but once in the 1899 pamphlet, where he speaks of the encouragement he had given Lake to follow up the manuscripts which we now speak of as Family1.[42] Acrimony was reserved for the third pamphlet of 1901. By that time Lake had added to his criticisms in the *Classical Review* his short classic, *The Text of the New Testament*, which appeared in London in 1900, and Miller was not slow to attack it. Neither Salmon nor Lake accepted the whole of Westcott and Hort's theory but they did accept their argument that what they called the Syrian text was secondary. That was enough for Miller. He calls Lake's treatment of the Western text 'a fine specimen of a fog in which the main issue of Textual Criticism is undiscoverable'. Lake wrote modestly but 'mistily'; he is condemned for accepting the Bezan reading at Luke 6:4; for accepting the idea that there was one 'common document lying behind at least much of the common tradition of the three Gospels'; he is chided for not acknowledging a debt to Miller, for 'crude representations and

---

[41] *Classical Review* 10 (1896) 263-5, 395-7. Also cf. his *The Text of the New Testament* (London, 1900), 68-9.

[42] Lake published the results of this investigation in *Codex 1 of the Gospels and its Allies* (TSt 7.3; Cambridge, 1902). Though he did not acknowledge Miller in this study – did he really need to? – after his death Lake generously spoke of Miller as 'a vigorous but courteous controversialist'; cf. *JTS* 3 (1902) 299. Several years earlier, Miller had invited the attention of H.C. Hoskier to these manuscripts and Hoskier published an excellent collation of one of them (157) in *JTS* 14 (1913) 78-116, 242-93, 359-84. Cf. Miller's revision of Scrivener's *A Plain Introduction to the Criticism of the New Testament* (London, 1894), i.398*. (Miller added two new appendices to some but, confusingly, not to all copies of this revision. In vol. i there is a new appendix, 'F', paged as 391*-398*, placed between 390 and 391. In vol. ii there is a new appendix, 'C', paged as 417*-418*, placed between 416 and 417. Apparently these appendices were also made available separately; cf *Academy* 46 (1894) 514ab; cf. 217a, 559ab.) Hoskier had already given Scrivener 'most friendly help'; cf. *Adversaria*, vii.

unsound views', for 'dogmatic misstatements'. Miller prefers Nestle's *Introduction* which is 'infinitely better and more trustworthy' than Lake's. With these explicit attacks on young Mr Lake, curate at St. Mary's (where, ironically, Burgon had been vicar twenty years earlier with Gwilliam as curate), the other attacks on nameless youthful tyros can easily be construed as more attacks on Lake. In replying to an anonymous reviewer in the *Church Quarterly Review*[43] he tartly responds: 'From various indications, it would seem that the reviewer had not then lost the happy infallibility which is apt to beset early manhood'. He speaks of 'youthful minds fresh from the lecture room and eager to set past ages right', of 'younger men whose history and philosophy lack the lengthened familiarity essential to sound judgement'. This is ageism in reverse! There is almost an accusation of laziness induced by the sheer bulk of material available for criticism. This is almost bound to result in 'partial' and therefore 'partizan' choices.

The materials the Hortists did choose are also criticized, particularly Bℵ and the two Syriac manuscripts, Sy^s Sy^c, alleged to precede Sy^p and therefore demote it. Over against the huge majority (nineteen out of twenty) of later Greek manuscripts, Bℵ are called a 'small oligarchy' and, with a new understanding of the word Catholic, they were dismissed as 'dissident' and 'sectarian'. Their very earliness in the fourth century is used to condemn them. That century was a time when church life and theology were 'at a low ebb', which witnessed the rise of Arianism, and, following Burgon, Miller was not slow to detect 'semi-Arian', 'sceptical' tendencies in these two products of that period. As for the attitude of Westcott and Hort towards them, Miller speaks of their 'very high estimate' and 'admiration' of Bℵ, of 'extreme adulation', 'veneration', even 'idolatry', with Westcott and Hort, presumably following Francis Bacon, as 'inveterate worshippers of the idols of the study'. The two Syriac manuscripts fared no better. Both were 'corrupt' and had 'low readings'. Of the two it was Sy^s, unknown to Burgon,[44] which drew

[43] *CQR* 43 (1896-97) 238-54. If the reviewer was not Lake, another candidate is Conybeare, who was thirty-nine at the time.

[44] Though Burgon died nearly four years before Sy^s was found, his great antagonist Hort had at least heard about it from Harris's announcement of the discovery, posted in the *Academy* 42, 110b (= *Athenaeum* 196b), both for 6 August 1892. Within three days of publication of the *Academy* in London,

Miller's heaviest fire. It was partially heretical, no doubt because of its omission of Mark 16:9-20 and its famous or infamous reading at Matthew 1:16 ('Joseph ... begot Jesus'). It had been the occasion of an academic spat in the winter of 1894-95, conducted largely in the columns of the *Academy*,[45] and it would have still been fresh in Miller's mind five years later. Even the physical condition and the palaeography of these four manuscripts were grist to Miller's criticism. The fact that Sy^{c} and Sy^{s} were incomplete fragments was a drawback, and the fact that Sy^{s} was a palimpsest rendered it doubly suspect: it had deserved to be overwritten and used for hagiography. As for Bℵ, they displayed a Greek text with no breathings, accents or punctuation; this helped to condemn them. Given this level of discussion, one is surprised that Miller did not point out the significance of the fact that B had been in the Vatican for 400 years and Sy^{s} had been discovered by a woman, from Cambridge![46]

Not only did Miller conduct his side of the controversy in much too personal a manner, striking out wherever and whenever he could, he was also unscholarly in his inconsistencies. Three examples come to mind. Firstly, he speaks of the providential preservation of the Traditional Text but only of the 'perhaps fortuitous' 'accident' of preservation of Bℵ, forgetting that Bℵ were also Holy Writ for some Christian communities somewhere. Providence and accidental preservation cannot be invoked to suit the demands of one's critical doctrines. Secondly, very properly and very frequently Miller contrasts the overriding claims of 'argument', 'evidence' and 'facts'

Hort was writing to his old pupil Harris from Switzerland for 'some few salient particulars about your new Old Syriac MS'. Cf. Hort, *op. cit.*, ii.449. Hort died less than four months later. I do not know if he received a reply from Harris.

[45] The fact that the *Academy* was a weekly journal meant that the give and take of debate could flow back and forth very easily. Between 10 November 1894 and 16 February 1895, there were thirty-six contributions on Sy^{s} from fourteen contributors. Two of these, Conybeare and R.C. Charles, contributed twelve. The main cause of discussion was Sy^{s}'s reading at Matthew 1:16. We have noted Gwilliam's and Bonus's discussions above (n.29), but see now J. Nolland, 'A Text-Critical Discussion of Matthew 1:16', *CBQ* 58 (1996) 665-73, esp. n.8.

[46] Reviewers had already drawn attention to Mrs A.S. Lewis's sex; cf. *CQR* 40 (1895) 102-32, at 103: the discovery of Sy^{s} by a woman was 'a sign of our times'; *ExpTim* 6 (1894-95) 389.

with 'false logic', 'neglect of witnesses', 'speculation', 'assumption', 'mere opinions', 'suspicions', 'presuppositions', 'conjectures', 'the wild, unrestrained play of youthful minds', etc. etc. The fact that this latter list is part of his description of the theories of Westcott and Hort and possibly Lake is beside the point. The contrast itself is absolutely correct. Miller's unscholarly inconsistency emerges in his own employment of opinions, suspicions, presuppositions and conjectures no less hypothetical and fanciful. One thinks of his reconstruction of the history of the text and his attempt to turn Conybeare's use of the Armenian and Georgian New Testaments to show that Sy^{p} could not have been in existence when they were prepared. One knows when Miller is hypothesizing when we come across 'must have' or 'must have been'. Again, I do not say that he is always wrong. I point out that he is doing what he criticizes in Westcott and Hort and Lake. He is inconsistent. The third case of inconsistency specifies the general point I have just made. One of the features of Westcott and Hort's theory was the idea that the Greek text was revised in the third and fourth centuries. Miller was correct in showing that there is no evidence from the church historians for this. Apart from the silence of history, there was of course another reason for Miller's unwillingness to countenance revision. To accept it would be to undermine the numerical preponderance of manuscripts containing the Traditional Text. Since no reading exclusively read by the Traditional Text predates the fourth century, a fourth century revision could be a sufficient explanation of its sudden emergence and popularity. Then Bא, which do predate the fourth century, going back, on Miller's own showing, to Origen and Caesarea, would be left holding the field. This lack of evidence was one of Miller's reasons for the charge about Westcott and Hort's 'unauthorized insertions into history', 'fine-drawn speculation', 'imaginary invention'. So far, so good. The inconsistency occurs because Miller, denying 'phantom revisions', uses language that appears to be virtually synonymous. The hateful word and the idea it represents are avoided; the reality seems to be conceded. He speaks of a 'settlement' or 'resettlement', of the text in the fourth century, the 'assertion' or 'reassertion' of the traditional text; corruption was 'purged' or 'ousted' or 'cast out'; the texts were 'verified', 'checked', 'corrected'; readings were 'adopted', 'established', 'ratified'.

In less than 100 pages all told Miller had done his intemperate best to represent and defend the views of Burgon. But, as we have seen, the future did not belong to them. Miller's theories were duly noted twice in the year he died. In his *Handbook to the Textual Criticism of the New Testament* (1901),[47] F.G. Kenyon dealt with Burgon and Miller in his discussion of what they called the Traditional Text, Westcott and Hort the Syrian, but what he preferred to call, less question-beggingly, the α-text. He summed up his opinion of Miller in a footnote he added to the second edition:[48] 'In spite of [his] devotion to the task he had taken up, his scholarship and judgement were not equal to the demands made on them'. Another critic was J.O.F. Murray of Cambridge. In a major but little known contribution to the fifth supplementary volume of Hastings' *A Dictionary of the Bible* (1904 but completed in 1901) he patiently dealt with the points raised by Miller and again had little difficulty in undermining them. Incidentally, it was through Murray that Hort made his reply to Burgon and Miller. For the last eight years of his life Hort and Murray had been members of the same Cambridge college, Emmanuel, and Kenyon claimed that in this contribution to Hastings, Murray had been able to make use of Hort's notes, which had been left to the college.[49] He, though dead, still spoke.

Miller's work was overtaken not only by his critics. Unresolved questions and new materials drew researchers to other investigations. We have already mentioned the attention the Western text attracted. Lake and von Soden isolated groups of manuscripts within the Traditional Text and showed it was not homogeneous. New discoveries however, as so often, made possible new perspectives and

---

[47] 262-3, 269-79 (= ^{2}1912, 307-8, 315-27).

[48] 308, n.1.

[49] Cf. *Dictionary of the Bible* (Edinburgh, 1909), (eds) J. Hastings *et al.*, 928: Murray's article (v.208-36) is 'an elaborate vindication of Westcott and Hort's position, based largely upon the materials left behind by Hort'; cf. also Hort, *op. cit.*, ii.458. Murray also edited and/or wrote prefaces for at least four of Hort's posthumous books. In his commentary on Ephesians (Cambridge, 1914), Murray speaks of 'a long apprenticeship to Dr. Hort' (iii) and includes an independent analysis of that epistle's Greek text (xcii-cii), especially of von Soden's edition and of the readings of Bא. C.F. Shepherd's *John Owen Farquhar Murray, D.D.* (London [Central Readers' Board], 1963) is only a sketch of twenty-five pages, but Hort is mentioned twice, on 4, 20.

new progress. In addition to the famous uncials W and Θ, undoubtedly the chief development of the twentieth century has been the discovery of nearly 100 papyri, several of which do allow us to penetrate into the dark pre-fourth century period. In particular, 𝔓75's amazing coincidence with B definitely brings Westcott and Hort's 'neutral' text back into the second century. Paradoxically, an earnest of the new century was already being printed off in Oxford even as the New College Debate was taking place. Grenfell and Hunt's *Logia Iesou, Sayings of our Lord,* found on papyrus scraps in Egypt, were being run off by the university's printer and would astonish the learned world ten weeks later in the middle of July. Though these sayings are not from a New Testament gospel manuscript, they anticipate the famous Chester Beatty and Bodmer finds that would revolutionize the world of New Testament text-critical scholarship.

To conclude: since the personal equation is part of the fun of scholarship, I have not tried to conceal its personal elements in telling this story, particularly Miller's manner of attacking his opponents. As we have just seen, Kenyon felt that neither Miller's scholarship nor his judgement were up to the demands of the task he had undertaken. My own conclusion, reached with some surprise and unwillingness, is similar. But there is more to it than that. When in 1861 Burgon published the sermons which represented his response to *Essays and Reviews,* an anonymous reviewer spoke of Burgon's 'screams of fear, rage and hate'.[50] Strong words, and *odium theologicum* has not been better defined, but again it is not difficult to understand why and agree that Burgon's later work on textual criticism could be similarly diagnosed. Like orthodox theology, an infallible Bible was a matter of life and death and excused any amount of bad temper and violence of language. But that is Burgon. What about Miller? One cannot escape the feeling that here is an old man, angry, perhaps unbalanced, petulant, outraged that fellow-Christians could write about the New Testament in the way they did. Perhaps he felt overwhelmed by the volume of material Burgon had left him and the volume of evidence accumulating in Cambridge against it. Perhaps he felt disappointed that Kirsopp Lake was

---

[50] *Westminster Review* NS 20 (1861) 543-60, at 545. Cp. Murray (n.49), 209: 'it is strange, but it is none the less true, that the study of Textual Criticism seems to have a peculiarly disastrous effect upon the temper'!

turning out not to be the kind of protégé and successor he might have been looking for. I find Miller an extremely sad and saddening man, and sadly conclude that 'fear, rage and hate' may apply to him no less than to Burgon.[51]

[51] Although I have added the clause 'an End, not a Beginning, for the Textus Receptus' to my title, to serve as a judgement on the Debate, I am not unaware that there has been a revival of Burgon's views in the last forty years and that scholars continue to 'Burgonize', a word coined by Harris; cf. Harris (n.36), 103; id., *Side-Lights on New Testament Research* (London, 1908), 91. Daniel B. Wallace has documented this resurgence in his contributions to Ehrman & Holmes, 297-320, and to *NTS* 41 (1995) 280-5 (on Scrivener and Hoskier). The evidence which Wallace adduces to underline the need for a re-evaluation of Scrivener can be augmented. See Scrivener's disagreement with Burgon over the latter's 'wholesale disparagement' of Vaticanus (Goulburn, *op. cit.*, ii.229) and his caution about supporting Burgon precisely in the way the latter had requested (Scrivener, *Adversaria*, ciii). Now see the printed but unpublished *Autobiography of a Biblical Student* (1888), 50, where Scrivener is speaking of either Westcott and Hort or the Revised Version New Testament, probably the latter: 'Within the last few years, however, the work has been judged of more dispassionately. The conscientious care, the varied learning, occasionally too the happy skill expended upon it, by the eminent persons who willingly spent the best they had to give, are becoming more highly appreciated than they were at the first hasty survey' (MS. 4908d8, by permission of the British Library). C.R. Gregory, *Canon and Text of the New Testament* (Edinburgh, 1907), 461-2, had said as much as long as ninety years ago.

BEYOND THE INTERLUDE? DEVELOPMENTS AND DIRECTIONS IN NEW TESTAMENT TEXTUAL CRITICISM

L.W. HURTADO

In the 1973 meeting of the Society of Biblical Literature, Eldon Epp presented a lecture, now famous among New Testament text critics, characterising twentieth-century New Testament textual criticism as an 'interlude', by which term Epp meant a period of significant activity but insufficient progress, particularly with regard to developing a persuasive theory of the early history of the New Testament text.[1] In the years that followed this lecture, Epp reiterated his critical appraisal (specifically interacting with Kurt Aland's complaints and claims)[2] and even offered a funereal warning about the general health of New Testament textual criticism in America.[3] It is not my purpose here to engage the specifics of Epp's analysis of twentieth-century textual criticism. I happen to think that he was essentially correct in his analysis of things then. But, whatever one may think of his judgements about the field, it has now been nearly a quarter-century since the 'Interlude' lecture and so it is

---

[1] This W.H.P. Hatch Memorial Lecture was published as 'The Twentieth Century Interlude in New Testament Textual Criticism', *JBL* 93 (1974) 386-414, and is now re-published in Epp & Fee, *Studies*, 83-108. Citations of the essay in this paper (hereafter 'Interlude') refer to the *JBL* page numbers.

[2] E.J. Epp, 'A Continuing Interlude in New Testament Textual Criticism', *HTR* 73 (1980) 131-51, re-published in Epp & Fee, *Studies*, 109-23, responding to K. Aland, 'The Twentieth-Century Interlude in New Testament Textual Criticism', in E. Best, R.M. Wilson (eds), *Text and Interpretation: Studies in the New Testament Presented to Matthew Black* (Cambridge/New York: Cambridge University Press, 1979), 1-14. For further interaction with Aland, see also Epp, 'New Testament Textual Criticism Past, Present, and Future: Reflections on the Alands' *Text of the New Testament*', *HTR* 82 (1989) 213-29.

[3] 'New Testament Textual Criticism in America: Requiem for a Discipline', *JBL* 98 (1979) 94-8 (cited hereafter as 'Requiem').

appropriate to assess where things stand now as we near the end of this century. I cannot attempt here the rather more daring coverage offered by Epp (the whole of twentieth-century work to his date of writing!), and instead shall focus on some encouraging signs of interest and activity and particular scholarly developments in the years since his lecture.[4] Essentially, I propose that these developments, valuable in their own right, may also indicate the directions New Testament textual criticism will (or should) be going.

I. *Renewed Interest and Activity*

Toward the end of his 'Interlude' lecture, after pointing to a few promising developments (especially more sophisticated quantitative analysis of manuscript relationships), Epp lamented the decline in interest in New Testament textual criticism, especially in North America; and in a subsequent essay he openly expressed fear that the discipline was in danger of vanishing from the American academic scene.[5] It is therefore very much worth noting that in the years since these anxieties were expressed there has been a modest upswing in interest and activity in New Testament textual criticism, especially in English-speaking scholarship and particularly (though by no means exclusively) in North America.

Surely one of the more significant developments in the North American scene has been the renewal of the prestigious monograph series 'Studies and Documents', founded by Kirsopp and Silva Lake and subsequently edited by Jacob Geerlings but which thereafter sank into inactivity for a number of years. Beginning with Harry Gamble's study of the textual history of Romans in 1977, this series was resurrected as an important vehicle for text-critical studies, and to date five volumes have appeared in this new phase of the only English-language monograph series devoted to the manuscript

---

[4] I have not attempted here a state-of-the-question coverage of the full spectrum of New Testament text-critical work, and several major areas are thus not treated, such as the important study of the versions and lectionaries. Readers interested in such wider-ranging surveys of the many specialised areas of work should consult the recent volume, Ehrman & Holmes.

[5] Epp, 'Interlude', 414; *id.*, 'Requiem'.

tradition of the New Testament.[6] Obviously, for such a monograph series to function there must be appropriate scholarly work to publish, and the mere existence of this series will not itself suffice to stimulate this work. But the re-appearance of this distinguished series gives us again a dedicated English-language outlet for high-quality volumes in New Testament textual criticism, and seems thus far to have succeeded sufficiently as a publishing venture to suggest both its viability and a readership for such publications. This may well thereby provide some encouragement to scholars (perhaps especially newer/younger ones) to conduct research in the field in the hope of publication and an interested readership.

More recently, we have another significant American publishing venture in textual criticism, a new monograph series analysing patristic evidence and sponsored by the Society of Biblical Literature: 'The New Testament in the Greek Fathers'.[7] To date, seven volumes have appeared since the inception of the series in 1986, and it has proven to be a valuable avenue of publication for this very specialised but important area of research.[8] In addition, the guidelines for the series reflect the more sophisticated and careful procedures for handling patristic evidence developed in recent years, particularly by Fee, involving requirements that studies be based only on critical editions of a Father's writings, that there be a

[6] The series is now published by Eerdmans Publishing Co. (Grand Rapids) and the volumes published in the period since the re-appearance of the series are the following: H.Y. Gamble, *The Textual History of the Letter to the Romans* (SD 42, 1977); L.W. Hurtado, *Text-Critical Methodology and the Pre-Caesarean Text: Codex W in the Gospel of Mark* (SD 43, 1981); F.W. Wisse, *The Profile Method for the Classification and Evaluation of Manuscript Evidence as Applied to the Continuous Greek Text of the Gospel of Luke* (SD 44, 1982); E.J. Epp, G.D. Fee, *Studies in the Theory and Method of New Testament Textual Criticism* (SD 45, 1993); B.D. Ehrman, M.W. Holmes (eds), *The Text of the New Testament in Contemporary Research: Essays on the Status Quaestionis* (SD 46, 1995). For vols. 42-5 Irving Alan Sparks led the editorial board, succeeded for vol. 46 by E.J. Epp.

[7] The series (SBLNTGF) is published by Scholars Press (Atlanta). Gordon Fee was the founding editor and the series is now edited by Bart Ehrman.

[8] The inaugural volume was Bart D. Ehrman, *Didymus the Blind and the Text of the Gospels* (SBLNTGF 1; Atlanta: Scholars Press, 1986). The most recent volume is Roderic L. Mullen, *The New Testament Text of Cyril of Jerusalem* (SBLNTGF 7; Atlanta: Scholars Press, 1997).

full presentation of the evidence, and that a full collation be made against selected representatives of previously identified textual groups.[9]

There is also a very promising French-language monograph series launched in recent years, 'Histoire du texte biblique', edited by C.-B. Amphoux and Bernard Outtier, which is intended to feature studies on a variety of topics relevant to New Testament textual criticism, including use of the Bible in the Church Fathers and studies of ancient lectionary texts.[10] This series is another encouraging indication of what may be a renewal of interest and effort in research related to text-critical questions.

If in the 'Studies and Documents' series we can speak of a resurrection of sorts, then with another project, this one of international nature, we can perhaps refer to a long-awaited birth after an unexpectedly long gestation period: the two-volume critical apparatus on the Gospel of Luke from the International Greek New Testament Project.[11] Having begun in 1952, the project has suffered a number of setbacks and the mortality of some of its founding members. But the volumes on Luke offer not only the fullest and most accurate apparatus on this New Testament writing, they also incorporate advances in methods (e.g., the Claremont Profile Method for categorising the mass of medieval manuscripts) and represent the high standards of collation and presentation of data that we must now demand for the future. Moreover, the membership of the project committees has been renewed through the readiness of newer American and British scholars to carry forward this historic work. There are now plans to proceed with an equivalent apparatus for the Gospel of John, and already we now have the excellent

---

[9] Note the statement of series parameters by G.D. Fee, 'The Use of the Greek Fathers for New Testament Textual Criticism', in Ehrman & Holmes, 198-200. See also the programmatic discussion of proper method by Fee, 'The Use of Greek Patristic Citations in New Testament Textual Criticism: The State of the Question', in Epp & Fee, *Studies*, 344-59 (also printed in ANRW 2.26/1 [1992] 246-65).

[10] The inaugural volume was *La lecture liturgique des Épîtres Catholiques dans l'Église ancienne*, eds C.-B. Amphoux & J.-P. Bouhot (HTB 1; Lausanne: Éditions du Zèbre, 1996).

[11] IGNT, *Luke*. On the project see now E.J. Epp, 'The International Greek New Testament Project: Motivation and History', *NovT* 39 (1997) 1-20.

volume on the papyri evidence edited by W.J. Elliott and David Parker.[12]

Perhaps the most innovative publishing venture, however, at least with regard to the medium of publication, is the new electronic journal on textual criticism launched in 1996, *TC: A Journal of Biblical Textual Criticism*, edited by James Adair and published at the Scholars Press World Wide Web site (TELA).[13] This journal is intended to feature articles on textual criticism of the Hebrew Bible as well as the Greek Bible (Old Testament and New Testament), a combination I regard as commendable.[14] Though it is as yet too early to judge the success of this project, it may well represent an important future medium for publication of scholarly research in a wide variety of disciplines.[15] In whatever medium, the launching of a new journal specifically designed to include New Testament textual criticism in its focus is certainly an encouraging indication of the health and prospects of the field.

---

[12] W.J. Elliott, D.C. Parker (eds), *The New Testament in Greek IV: The Gospel according to St. John, Volume One: The Papyri* (NTTS 20; Leiden: Brill, 1995). The volume is edited by Elliott and Parker on behalf of the IGNT project committees.

[13] The journal can be accessed by going to the TC Web site (http://purl.org/TC). There is also an unmoderated discussion list intended to facilitate discussion of articles appearing in *TC* (tc-list, subscribed to by e-mail at majordomo@shemesh.scholar.emory.edu). The editorial board includes Bart Ehrman, Michael Holmes, Larry Hurtado, David Parker, William Petersen, James Tauber, and Klaus Wachtel, to mention now familiar New Testament textual critics.

[14] Occasional conversations with scholars in Hebrew Bible/Old Testament have suggested to me that there is too much isolation of text-critical work on the Greek New Testament and the Hebrew Bible. Even familiar words have very different connotations. In Hebrew Bible studies, for example, an 'eclectic' text is one produced by selecting most likely readings from various witnesses, as distinguished from printing the text of one witness accompanied by a critical apparatus of readings from other witnesses. But what Hebrew Bible scholars call an 'eclectic' text would simply be called a 'critical edition' in New Testament studies, and 'eclectic' would designate a particular approach toward determining original readings (see G.D. Fee, 'Rigorous or Reasoned Eclecticism – Which?', in Epp & Fee, *Studies*, 124-40).

[15] For excellent discussions of relevant issues, see Robin Peek, Gregory Newby (eds), *Scholarly Publishing: The Electronic Frontier* (Cambridge: MIT Press, 1996).

These newer publishing ventures also reflect another encouraging development – the modestly resurgent numbers of scholars involved in New Testament textual criticism. Given Epp's fear that this field of study might disappear in North America, it is particularly interesting to note the growth in the number of scholars making contributions to the field in that continent, especially those whose work has begun to appear since Epp's dire warning in his 1979 'Requiem' essay: Bart Ehrman, Michael Holmes, Carroll Osburn, Jeffrey Childers, James Royse, Thomas Geer, William Petersen, and Daniel Wallace.[16]

This resurgence of scholarly numbers is not entirely limited to North America. As illustrations, I point to European scholars such as Christian-B. Amphoux (France), Eberhard Güting (Germany), and David Parker (U.K.), and, on the other side of the world, Stuart Pickering (Macquarie University, Australia).

In addition to an apparent growth in scholarly contributors, there also appears to be at least a modest renewal of interest in the results of their work. One might point to the impressive numbers who now attend the sessions devoted to New Testament textual criticism in the annual meetings of the Society of Biblical Literature. When I made my first SBL presentation in 1971 while still a Ph.D. student, I appeared before an imposing but very small group of about a dozen scholars in the field. More recently, the SBL program unit on New Testament textual criticism tends to draw an attendance that ranges between forty to eighty and now includes an interesting spectrum of established and emergent textual critics, scholars outside the speciality, and aspiring scholars (graduate students).

As another indication of interest in New Testament textual criticism beyond the circle of contributors to the field, I point to the *New Testament Textual Research Update*, a bi-monthly bulletin produced by Stuart Pickering that summarises developments in the field for specialists and other interested readers.[17] To cite another

[16] I hope I shall be permitted to include myself as well, at least for the purpose of indicating those seriously interested in textual criticism, though my contributions to the work have been only occasional.

[17] This bulletin began appearing in 1993 and is published in co-operation with the Ancient History Documentary Research Centre, Macquarie University, by Textual Research Publications, 38 Tintern Rd, Ashfield, NSW 2131, Australia.

phenomenon, the impressive level of interest in New Testament textual criticism reflected in the volume of exchanges on the Internet discussion list devoted to textual criticism (TC-List) is worth noting.[18] A number of those participating on this list are technically 'amateurs' (in that they do not hold academic posts in New Testament), but clearly show a strong interest and sometimes an impressive investment of effort in the field.

One of the matters that most concerned Epp in his 'Interlude' lecture, and even more sharply in his 'Requiem' essay, was the recruitment and training of future New Testament textual critics.[19] Owing to retirements of major figures (e.g. Bruce Metzger) and other career developments affecting other scholars, Epp feared that there might be diminishing opportunities (especially in North America) for graduate students to pursue Ph.D. work in New Testament textual criticism under the supervision of a scholar with demonstrated interest and competence in the field. With relatively recent appointments in universities in the U.K. and the U.S., however, the situation looks somewhat more assured.[20] Moreover, I note with appreciation that a number of the contributions to the more recent Metzger *Festschrift* include helpful indications to future researchers about unresolved questions and insufficiently investigated matters, reflecting a forward-looking attitude and perhaps even an increased hope for the future of the discipline.[21] The massive work of the Münster Institut goes on, now under the capable leadership of Barbara Aland, with valuable publications and

---

[18] As with most unmoderated Internet discussion lists, one finds among contributors (especially those from the 'general public') a wide variety in competence and a sometimes disappointing frequency of poorly informed dogmatism in point of view.

[19] Epp, 'Interlude', 414; *id.*, 'Requiem', esp. 97-8.

[20] In the U.S., Bart Ehrman's appointment at the University of North Carolina, and in the U.K. the appointment of David Parker at Birmingham and my own appointment at Edinburgh, in addition to J.K. Elliott at Leeds, provide assurance of continuing opportunities for Ph.D. work in the field in English-language universities. Moreover, scholars such as Michael Holmes (Bethel Theological Seminary, St. Paul, Minnesota) and Carroll Osburn (Abilene Christian University), though not in Ph.D.-granting programmes, are major textual critics able to recruit newer researchers.

[21] Ehrman & Holmes.

a team of scholars, but it is always well for a field of inquiry to have various centres where research can be promoted.

The preceding brief notices will perhaps suffice to support the view that the interest shown in New Testament textual criticism in the last couple of decades is encouraging. It is still unfortunately the case that many New Testament scholars seem to regard the subject as arcane and tedious, and far too many new Ph.D. graduates in New Testament and Christian origins seem ill-equipped even to navigate the textual apparatus of the Nestle-Aland Greek New Testament or to make an informed judgement on textual variants (though such matters should be of obvious prior importance for exegesis). Nevertheless, there are the sorts of more positive phenomena I have listed which may, for those of us so inclined, provide some reason for a more sanguine outlook for New Testament textual criticism than observers such as Epp might have entertained in the 1970s.

II. *Work that Points Ahead*

If the foregoing paragraphs illustrate in general a somewhat more encouraging level of interest and activity in the face of earlier concerns about the health of New Testament textual criticism, in what follows I should like to highlight recent scholarly contributions that point to the sort of future work that can and should characterise the field in coming years. The traditional aim of New Testament textual criticism has been to establish the 'original' text of the New Testament writings by determining original readings wherever there is evidence of textual variation. In addition to this task, scholars have also advocated tracing of the history of the transmission of the text and the relationship of this history to the history of early Christianity as a worthy aim in its own right. I want to affirm the validity of both aims and also assert that each is logically related to the other. In the attempt to establish the original readings of the New Testament writings, for example, even if one's approach is a 'radical eclecticism' that emphasises transcriptional probability over the evaluation of individual witnesses, claims about transcriptional probability are only as good as our knowledge of how scribes actually worked in copying the text. And our knowledge of scribal practices depends upon us becoming closely familiar with the history of the text, the nature of the manuscript tradition, and the wider forces in early Christianity that may have helped shape this tradition. For my own part, I side with those textual critics who advocate a combination of internal and external evidence in making judgements about readings, which makes the history of the textual tradition perhaps even more obviously important.[22] I shall therefore emphasise developments that point us toward a more thorough knowledge of the early history of the New Testament text. Whatever approach one takes to the practice of assessing variants, I trust that advances toward a more soundly based theory and history of the New Testament text will be welcome.

1. *Thorough Examination of Important Witnesses*

The first matter I wish to highlight is a more thorough knowledge of important textual witnesses. Several recent scholarly contributions demonstrate the sort of more thorough study of important evidence that ought to characterise the future of the field. With reference to individual manuscripts, David Parker's multi-faceted analysis of Codex Bezae seems to me a model for the sort of work that could be done on a good many more of the important, major witnesses that we all invoke but probably know less about than we should.[23] As Parker shows, there is a great deal of information to be garnered from a study of the palaeography, scribal features, corrections, and textual complexion of key manuscripts (though it will be difficult for many individual scholars to acquire the breadth of expertise that Parker demonstrates to make such an investigation on their own!). Certainly, his complaint seems fair that even textual critics have dealt with textual evidence with insufficient attention to the actual witnesses, and that we have thus dealt with textual evidence 'disembodied' from the documents and all that they have to tell us. If

---

[22] In this, I reflect my own 'ancestry' of approach from Eldon Epp (my Ph.D. thesis supervisor) back through Colwell and on back to Hort. For discussion of the issues, see, e.g., G.D. Fee, 'Rigorous or Reasoned Eclecticism – Which?' in Epp & Fee, *Studies*, 124-40; E.C. Colwell, 'Hort Redivivus: A Plea and a Program', in Colwell, *Studies*, 148-71.

[23] D.C. Parker, *Codex Bezae: An Early Christian Manuscript and its Text* (Cambridge: Cambridge University Press, 1992). See also Parker's discussion, 'The Majuscule Manuscripts of the New Testament', in Ehrman & Holmes, 22-42.

we are to move toward the more soundly based theory and history of the text of the New Testament that many of us would hope for, we must have the full measure of historical information manuscripts provide about themselves, especially the early and important ones. It would be a valuable move for prospective graduate students looking for thesis research to be encouraged to tackle historically important witnesses in the sort of 'codicological' approach Parker has demonstrated.

When it comes to patristic evidence as well, recent studies show how more sophisticated methods of analysis can yield a more thorough and secure understanding of important witnesses. Here the work of several scholars can be cited as instructive for the future. G.D. Fee's methodological essay cited earlier is crucial in demonstrating the need for careful *analysis* of patristic citations of New Testament texts and in warning about the dangers of simplistic use of citations without adequate analysis.[24] In particular, Fee emphasises the prior need of a genuinely critical edition of the writing(s) of any Church Father studied, and the necessity of noting the varying citation habits of the Fathers, which often involve very loose quotations that might not be directly useful (and, in fact, might be misleading) in identifying the type of New Testament text that a given Father read. Several other recent publications show the value of combining this more sophisticated approach to patristic citations together with more carefully considered quantitative methods for identifying the textual affiliations of a given Father's citations. I would particularly mention Bart Ehrman's study of Didymus the Blind, the volume on Origen by Ehrman, Fee and Holmes, and other studies in the SBLNTGF series such as Mullen's new analysis of Cyril of Jerusalem.[25] As is commonly recognised, the patristic evidence is in principle uniquely valuable in that a Father can be dated and geographically placed, providing essential information for

---

[24] Fee, 'The Use of Greek Patristic Citations in New Testament Textual Criticism'.

[25] B.D. Ehrman, *Didymus the Blind and the Text of the Gospels* (see n.8 above), esp. 223-8 on the use of profiles; B.D. Ehrman, G.D. Fee, M.W. Holmes, *The Text of the Fourth Gospel in the Writings of Origen*, Vol. 1 (SBLNTGF 3; Atlanta: Scholars Press, 1992); R.L. Mullen, *The New Testament Text of Cyril of Jerusalem* (see n.8 above), correcting significantly the earlier study by J.H. Greenlee.

constructing a history of the New Testament text. But in fact the proper use of patristic evidence is more complicated than has sometimes been reflected in earlier studies.

As another example of the more thorough sort of studies that we must pursue if we are to make real progress, there is William Petersen's very recent (and impressively thorough) volume on the *Diatessaron*.[26] Both in breadth of treatment and control of the evidence, Petersen sets a new benchmark in studies of the *Diatessaron*, and at the same time models the rigorous scholarship we need to cultivate.

2. *Better Knowledge of Scribal Habits*

In any approach to text-critical decisions, arguments about transcriptional probability will continue to figure prominently. It is only in relatively recent decades, however, that we have had much movement toward a more well founded view of the actual habits and practices of ancient scribes in copying the New Testament writings. With Colwell's 1965 paper on scribal habits in New Testament papyri, we were given an advance on all previous work with an approach that focuses systematically on the scribal characteristics of individual textual witnesses.[27] In subsequent decades there appeared the studies of 𝔓66 and 𝔓75 by Fee,[28] and analysis of scribal characteristics of other particular witnesses such as Codex W[29] and very recently Parker's volume on Codex Bezae cited earlier.[30] The effect of these studies was broadly to show that scribal tendencies

---

[26] W.L. Petersen, *Tatian's Diatessaron: Its Creation, Dissemination, Use, and History in Scholarship* (VC Suppl 25; Leiden: Brill, 1994).

[27] E.C. Colwell, 'Method in Evaluating Scribal Habits', in Colwell, *Studies*, 106-24.

[28] G.D. Fee, *Papyrus Bodmer II (P66): Its Textual Relationships and Scribal Characteristics* (SD 34; Salt Lake City: University of Utah Press, 1968); *id.*, 'P75, P66, and Origen: The Myth of Early Textual Recension in Alexandria', in *New Dimensions in New Testament Study*, ed. R.N. Longenecker, M.C. Tenney (Grand Rapids: Zondervan, 1974), 19-45 (reprinted in Epp & Fee, *Studies*, 247-73).

[29] L.W. Hurtado, *Text-Critical Methodology and the Pre-Caesarean Text: Codex W in the Gospel of Mark* (SD 43; Grand Rapids: Eerdmans, 1981), 67-84.

[30] See J.R. Royse, 'Scribal Tendencies in the Transmission of the Text of the New Testament', in Ehrman & Holmes, 239-52, esp. 247 for references to other studies.

vary, sometimes significantly, and that we must attempt to establish the particular habits and preferences evident in particular witnesses, instead of invoking generalisations blindly. Also, the demonstration of coincidental harmonisations and other coincidental 'improvements' in such matters as Greek style warn us to be careful in making much of individual agreements of these kinds between manuscripts apart from overall agreement that is quantitatively significant. Moreover, the varying scribal practices may help us to get a better, more dynamic view of the processes that produced what we call 'text-types', which may in some sense represent the textual traditions resulting from different scribal practices, mentalities and purposes.

It is also important to note very recent studies of the early papyri that attempt to move toward a more programmatic view of scribal practices. Peter Head studied a number of fragmentary papyri of the Gospels with a view to categorising scribal tendencies in them.[31] But the most thorough such study is Royse's (unfortunately unpublished) thesis which dealt with six more extensive early papyri ($\mathfrak{P}^{45}$, $\mathfrak{P}^{46}$, $\mathfrak{P}^{47}$, $\mathfrak{P}^{66}$, $\mathfrak{P}^{72}$, $\mathfrak{P}^{75}$).[32] The clear effect of these studies of the papyri is to show how much more nuanced and careful we need to be in invoking traditional principles such as preferring the shorter reading, for Head and Royse agree in showing that omission is much more common than addition, at least in unintentional scribal tendencies.

3. *The Crucial Second Century*

The great text-critical work of the nineteenth century depended most heavily upon majuscule manuscripts of the fourth century and later, and the results could be taken cautiously as a reconstruction of the New Testament text of the fourth century. To be sure, based on the evidence available to him, Hort offered a theoretical view of the state of the New Testament text in the second century. But with the twentieth-century discovery and study of papyri from the third

---

[31] P.M. Head, 'Observations on Early Papyri of the Synoptic Gospels, especially on the "Scribal Habits"', *Bib* 71 (1990) 240-7.

[32] J.R. Royse, 'Scribal Habits in Early Greek New Testament Papyri', (Th.D. dissertation, Graduate Theological Union, 1981). See also *id.*, 'Scribal Habits in the Transmission of New Testament Texts', in *The Critical Study of Sacred Texts*, ed. W.D. O'Flaherty (Berkeley: Graduate Theological Union, 1979), 139-61; and *id.*, 'Scribal Tendencies'.

century (and perhaps a bit earlier), it is now possible to address the earliest stages of textual transmission with a much earlier and more extensive body of evidence to use in formulating and testing theories. The early New Testament papyri come from the pre-Constantinian period, before State and Church combined to work toward more programmatic standardisation in liturgy, belief and biblical text. A few of these papyri (esp. $\mathfrak{P}^{45}$, $\mathfrak{P}^{46}$, $\mathfrak{P}^{66}$, $\mathfrak{P}^{75}$) are early enough and perhaps just extensive enough to permit us to probe back into the second century, increasingly thought of as the crucial period of textual transmission.

Various and conflicting claims and approaches require testing. It is often enough claimed that the second century was the period in which most if not virtually all significant textual variation took place. It seems altogether likely that a great deal of textual variation took place then, but can we in fact confidently think that the second century was so overwhelmingly the time of the emergence of textual variation and later centuries so insignificant? Given the continued spread of Christianity in the third century and the continued diversification in belief and practice, for example, it would seem to me reasonable to think that this period also was very fruitful for the emergence of textual variants, both unintentional and intentional ones.

Moreover, the view that the second century was wholly a time of uncontrolled and loose transmission of the New Testament writings reflects, to some degree, earlier convictions that the type of text we find in Vaticanus was the product of a fourth-century recension and that the early New Testament papyri exhibit a free and inexact transmission of the text in the pre-Constantinian period. But more recent studies have clearly shown that the earliest extensive papyri exhibit at least *two* kinds of copying and types of text. One type, as exhibited in the Gospels in $\mathfrak{P}^{45}$ and $\mathfrak{P}^{66}$, is a comparatively free and fluid kind of text, confirming that the second and early third centuries did see the production of a good many variants and a corresponding mentality that cared more for copying what scribes saw as the sense of the text, with less concern for exact wording. But equally early evidence, $\mathfrak{P}^{75}$, shows another kind of text, in fact one strikingly in agreement with the fourth-century majuscule Vaticanus and its witness to a 'Neutral' or 'Alexandrian' text-type, and a corresponding scribal mentality clearly concerned with careful copying of the exemplar operative at least by the late second century.[33] In short, we are thereby warned against over-generalising and stereotyping the second-century period of textual transmission.

But important questions remain about the proper use of this and other relevant evidence in reconstructing the earliest period of the New Testament texts. The papyri so crucial as evidence all appear to have been produced in Egypt, so how representative are these manuscripts of the state of the New Testament text and the nature of its transmission more broadly outside of Egypt? Eldon Epp has been among those who have most candidly posed this question, and in intriguing studies has now offered an encouraging answer.[34] Based on indications of the surprisingly rapid and developed pattern of travel and written communication in the Graeco-Roman period and early Christian travel and communication more specifically, Epp affirms the likelihood that the early papyri, though of Egyptian provenance, may well be more widely representative of the transmission of the New Testament writings in the second and third centuries. Based on this early papyrus evidence, Epp sketches the characteristics of three major types of New Testament text in the second century or shortly thereafter: (1) a text-type characterised by a high degree of accuracy in copying ($\mathfrak{P}^{75}$, with $\mathfrak{P}^{66}$ a weaker witness), (2) another text-type with a textual complexion involving greater frequency of harmonisations among Gospels and a rather

[33] See now especially G.D. Fee, 'P75, P66, and Origen: The Myth of Early Textual Recension in Alexandria', in Epp & Fee, *Studies*, 247-73, building upon the earlier studies by C.L. Porter, 'Papyrus Bodmer XV (P75) and the Text of Codex Vaticanus', *JBL* 81 (1962) 363-76, and C.M. Martini, *Il problema della recensionalità del codice B alla luca del papiro Bodmer XIV* (AnBib 26; Rome: Biblical Institute Press, 1966).

[34] Epp posed the question about how representative the Egyptian papyri may be in 'A Continuing Interlude in New Testament Textual Criticism', *HTR* 73 (1980) 131-51 (reprinted as Chap. 6 in Epp & Fee, *Studies*, esp. 119); and also in Epp & Fee, *Studies*, 42-3. He offers reasons for taking the papyri as more than merely witnesses to Egyptian local textual traditions in two important essays: 'The Significance of the Papyri for Determining the Nature of the New Testament Text in the Second Century: A Dynamic View of Textual Transmission', in *Gospel Traditions*, 71-104 (reprinted in Epp & Fee, *Studies*, 274-98), and 'New Testament Papyrus Manuscripts and Letter Carrying in Greco-Roman Times', in *The Future of Early Christianity*, ed. B.A. Pearson (Minneapolis: Fortress Press, 1991), 35-56.

freer approach toward small stylistic and edifying 'improvements' (𝔓45), and (3) a text-type connected to or resembling strongly the text of Codex Bezae and characterised by a still freer treatment of the text involving such things as interpolations (𝔓29, 𝔓48, 𝔓38 and a few others).[35]

On a matter as important as this, it is necessary for other scholars to make further analysis of the relevant evidence and to probe the rationale Epp offers. But this means that one of the questions that ought to occupy New Testament textual critics is the proper interpretation and use of the papyri for understanding the transmission of the New Testament in the second century.[36]

That this is an important, indeed, somewhat urgent question is demonstrated by Helmut Koester, who claims that the second century was completely a period of instability that involved both minor and major revisions of the New Testament writings, making of very dubious value as approximations of the original texts all critical editions based on surviving manuscripts.[37] Koester makes a number of claims that cannot receive due attention here, asserting that there is no second-century manuscript evidence for the New Testament Gospels (thus ignoring the good possibility that 𝔓75 may be dated anywhere from 175-200 C.E.),[38] that 'in the period before 200 C.E. the Gospels were usually transmitted separately' (thus disregarding the implications of early codices of more than one Gospel such as 𝔓45 and 𝔓75 as well as the implications of the testimony of early Fathers such as Irenaeus),[39] and that the New Testament writings

---

[35] Epp, 'The Significance of the Papyri', in Epp & Fee, *Studies*, 286-95.

[36] Epp (*ibid.*, 283) cites J.N. Birdsall's call that 'the task of present-day criticism is to inaugurate an era in which we begin from the earliest evidence and on the basis of its interpretation discuss the later' (*The Bodmer Papyrus of the Gospel of John* [London: Tyndale, 1958], 7).

[37] Helmut Koester, 'The Text of the Synoptic Gospels in the Second Century', in *Gospel Traditions*, 19-37.

[38] Victor Martin, Rudolphe Kasser, *Papyrus Bodmer XIV: Evangile de Luc chap. 3-24* (Geneva: Bibliotheca Bodmeriana, 1961), 13-14.

[39] In addition, 𝔓64 and 𝔓67 (fragments of Matthew) and 𝔓4 (fragments of Luke), commonly dated from c. 200 C.E. or thereafter, have been shown to come from the same codex, and this codex has now been calculated as having probably contained all four canonical Gospels. Likewise, 𝔓75 (portions of Luke and John) has now been shown likely to have been a four-fold Gospel codex as well, which gives us at least two additional codices of

were not regarded as 'sacred scripture' at all in the second century (thus anachronistically collapsing together final decisions about canonical limits with earlier reverential practices with regard to New Testament writings, especially the four Gospels and epistles of Paul).[40] For our present purposes, I shall restrict the discussion to Koester's comments about text-critical matters.

Koester accuses New Testament textual critics of being 'surprisingly naïve' about the extent of second-century corruption of the New Testament text,[41] and as being 'deluded' in thinking that the state of the New Testament text evidenced c. 200 C.E. is '(almost) identical with the autographs'.[42] Instead, Koester asserts, the papyri are evidence only of 'archetypes of the textual tradition which were fixed ca. 200 C.E.' and which incorporated 'substantial revisions of the original texts' that were made 'during the first hundred years of transmission'.[43] Moreover, in Koester's view the only relevant evidence about the transmission of the New Testament in the second century is the use made of the New Testament writings as reflected in the Christian writers of that period. Thus, the rather periphrastic and harmonising citations we find in Justin Martyr are to be taken as direct evidence that the New Testament writings were copied in the same way, with free re-phrasing, harmonising and interpolation being standard scribal practice.[44]

---

approximately the same date as $\mathfrak{P}^{45}$ attesting the circulation of the four Gospels as a collection. See C.H. Roberts, *Manuscript, Society and Belief in Early Christian Egypt* (London: Oxford University Press, 1979), 13; and now T.C. Skeat, 'The Origin of the Christian Codex', *ZPE* 102 (1994) 263-8; and the discussion in G. Stanton, *Gospel Truth? New Light on Jesus and the Gospels* (London/Valley Forge, VA: Harper Collins/Trinity Press International, 1995), 16-19. Cf. Koester, *Ancient Christian Gospels* (Philadelphia/ London: Trinity Press International/SCM, 1990), 241-5. On Irenaeus' testimony see T.C. Skeat, 'Irenaeus and the Four Gospel Canon', *NovT* 34 (1992) 194-9.

[40] Koester, 'The Text of the Synoptic Gospels in the Second Century', 19.

[41] *Ibid.*, 19.

[42] *Ibid.*, 37.

[43] *Ibid.*, 37.

[44] *Ibid.*, 28-33. Koester also cites the 'Secret Gospel of Mark' as evidence of early and major revisions of New Testament writings, in this case, canonical Mark being (in Koester's view) a major re-writing of the original Mark, which is witnessed to by 'Secret Mark' (*ibid.*, 34-6).

Aside from his dubious assertion that the citation practices of early Christian writers are indicative of the copying practices of early Christian scribes, Koester ignores or misrepresents important matters. Precisely what new developments, what figures, what centres might have produced the radically new recensional 'archetypes' Koester attributes to c. 200 C.E.? Theories about recensions of the New Testament (e.g. Lucian) from later centuries when ecclesiastical structures and the political situation might more readily have facilitated them have not fared very well in the face of detailed studies of the historical evidence of manuscripts and Fathers of the relevant periods. Yet Koester alleges a recensional effort at a much more primitive period and so completely successful as to have thoroughly reformulated the New Testament writings and deceived virtually all modern textual critics! The very diversity in textual complexion and scribal approaches reflected in the papyri from the period in question (175-250 C.E.) points against the likelihood of the sort of successful recensional activity Koester posits.[45]

That such a radical challenge to New Testament textual critics and such a very different sketch of second-century transmission of the New Testament text can be offered by a major New Testament scholar indicates the importance of further, more careful analysis of and reflections on the evidence bearing on the second century. Here the papyri obviously are central, and have probably not yet been fully mined for all the information and implications they have to offer.[46]

---

[45] See also F.W. Wisse, 'The Nature and Purpose of Redactional Changes in Early Christian Texts: The Canonical Gospels', in *Gospel Traditions*, 39-54, whose arguments further work against Koester's claims. Additionally worth noting is the essay by J.N. Birdsall in the same volume ('The Western Text in the Second Century', 3-17), who offers indications of greater care being taken in the transmission of the New Testament writings in some Christian centres in the second century alongside other evidence of a comparatively more free textual tradition that may be the predecessor of the 'Western text'.

[46] On 𝔓[45], for example, see now T.C. Skeat, 'A Codicological Analysis of the Chester Beatty Papyrus Codex of the Gospels and Acts (P45)', *Hermathena* 155 (1993) 27-43, who re-checks and builds somewhat upon Kenyon's analysis in the printed edition. Skeat refers to Gunther Zuntz, 'Reconstruction of one leaf of the Chester Beatty Papyrus of the Gospels and Acts (P45)', *Chronique d'Egypte* 26 (1951) 191-211 (which I have not seen) as 'the only detailed description of the script and the scribal habits of the writer' (Skeat, 'Codicological Analysis', 42 n.1).

But, also, Koester's challenge points to the importance of New Testament textual critics taking account of all relevant evidence, manuscripts, writings of the Fathers, evidence about the transmission of early non-canonical Christian writings, and all relevant information about the development of Christianity (institutional and doctrinal) in the period in question. In all likelihood, the second century was crucial, as the period in which the New Testament writings circulate widely, begin to be collected, and, perhaps, begin to be translated. Though the materials for the task are still frustratingly limited and later than we would wish, we must make it a future desideratum to derive all that we can from them about the earliest century of textual transmission.

4. *Wider Historical Inquiry*

As the immediately preceding discussion shows, textual criticism cannot be pursued fully and cannot yield its best results without connecting with wider historical investigations of the early church. I recognise that in saying this I am only repeating the urgings of earlier scholars.[47] But my appeal has very recent examples to draw upon in which textual critics make the attempt to relate the study of textual variants to the history of early Christianity, and these examples point us in one potentially productive line of future investigation.

Bart Ehrman's recent volume on the relationship between textual variants and doctrinal controversies in early Christianity is a particularly timely example of one important line of inquiry.[48]

---

[47] This emphasis upon the study of the text in connection with the wider history of the early church appears, for example, in the magisterial discussion by J.N. Birdsall, 'The New Testament Text', *The Cambridge History of the Bible, Volume 1, From the Beginnings to Jerome*, eds P.R. Ackroyd, C.F. Evans (Cambridge: Cambridge University Press, 1970), esp. 374-7.

[48] Ehrman, *Orthodox Corruption*. See also P.M. Head, 'Christology and Textual Transmission: Reverential Alterations in the Synoptic Gospels', *NovT* 35 (1993) 105-29. An earlier study somewhat comparable to Ehrman's (but not apparently known to him) is the thesis of M.R. Pelt, 'Textual Variation in Relation to Theological Interpretation in the New Testament' (Ph.D. diss., Duke University, 1966). Ehrman cites G.E. Rice, 'The Alteration of Luke's Tradition by the Textual Variants in Codex Bezae' (Ph.D. diss., Case Western Reserve University, 1974), but does not note Howard Eshbaugh, 'Theological Variants in the Western Text of the Pauline Corpus'

Ehrman grants that there is no evidence of a programmatic christological revision of any New Testament writing in any textual witness, and that the total number of textual variants that can be shown to have a clearly doctrinal motive is quite limited, a small percentage of the total number of intentional variants reflected in the manuscript tradition.[49] Moreover, Ehrman is not always persuasive in his proposals as to the doctrinal motivations for this or that variant. But, with all such allowances, it is clear that there were deliberate changes made in passages of the New Testament writings here and there, that these variants can be more fully understood in the light of early Christian doctrinal controversies, and that these doctrinal controversies in turn are more fully appreciated when one notes that they affected the transmission of the New Testament.[50]

I suspect that few New Testament textual critics will find Ehrman's general claim about the influence of doctrine upon at least some textual variation surprising news.[51] We have all encountered examples in the course of examining the textual history of the New Testament. But Ehrman's discussions of specific variants are worth studying in assessing the claims of these readings with regard to establishing an original text of the documents in question. Moreover, Ehrman may succeed in alerting wider circles of students and scholars in New Testament and early Christianity to the relevance of text-critical inquiry beyond the specialised aims of textual criticism, and may even encourage a broader appreciation of this demanding discipline and of the expertise of those who practice it. In this too Ehrman is an instructive example, for in addition to interacting with and contributing to the wider historical inquiry into Christian origins, textual critics should be seeking to raise the profile and

(Ph.D. diss., Case Western Reserve University, 1975), and *id.*, 'Textual Variants and Theology: A Study of the Galatians Text of Papyrus 46', *JSNT* 3 (1979) 60-72.

[49] Ehrman, *Orthodox Corruption*, e.g. 46 n.124, 98-9.

[50] E.J. Epp argued that Codex Bezae showed an anti-Judaic tendency in a number of readings, which would approach a more pervasive effect of a religious tendency upon the text of a particular witness; *The Theological Tendency of Codex Bezae Cantabrigiensis in Acts* (SNTSMS 3; Cambridge: Cambridge University Press, 1966).

[51] See, e.g., the discussion of theological variants in Birdsall, 'The New Testament Text', esp. 328-9, 332-45.

estimate of the discipline among scholars generally, not only because of the political wisdom of doing so but also because of the scholarly benefits to all concerned.

In another recent volume, Harry Gamble argues persuasively that text-critical study should interact with all cognate matters involved in the writing, copying, circulation, collection and use of books in ancient Christianity and the wider Greek and Roman periods.[52] As Gamble shows, the textual history of the New Testament (or any document) is evidenced in physical objects, manuscripts of the texts themselves and other manuscripts reflecting the use of the writings (e.g., lectionary manuscripts, manuscripts of the Fathers), and these objects are social artefacts related to and reflecting groups interested in the writings and the needs and purposes of these groups. Thus, in Gamble's words, 'From this perspective a clean distinction between textual history and the history of literature is neither possible nor desirable'.[53] Gamble discusses the extent and limits of literacy, the physical characteristics of early Christian books (especially the Christian preference for the codex), the means of publication and circulation of writings, the emergence and development of Christian libraries, and the liturgical use of books in early Christian communities. It should take very little reflection to see how these matters are of direct relevance to the concerns of New Testament textual critics, and in turn how the questions and data of the history of the New Testament text are directly germane to the phenomena Gamble portrays.

For example, he shows that early in the second century Christian groups were involved in publishing Christian books, which would have required significant resources and efforts for what were still relatively small groups, as well as some concern and care in producing copies. Thus, we have another reason to see it as a bit dubious to over-generalise about an allegedly chaotic process of textual transmission among second-century Christian groups.[54] Though it is frequently assumed (and asserted) that there could have been no Christian scriptoria before 200 C.E., Gamble offers cogent reasons to think that a number of larger Christian communities (e.g.,

---

[52] Harry Y. Gamble, *Books and Readers in the Early Church: A History of Early Christian Texts* (New Haven/London: Yale University Press, 1995).
[53] *Ibid.*, 43.
[54] *Ibid.*, esp. 93-132, on the earliest centuries.

Antioch or Rome) may have had scriptoria in the early second century.[55] In addition to the widespread Christian preference for the codex, scribal practices such as the *nomina sacra* evident in the earliest surviving materials suggest elements of emerging textual conventions surprisingly early and impressively widespread.

In fact Gamble provides so much information and so many very promising lines of further inquiry that I cannot do justice to it all here. The point I wish to make is that his study gathers together and highlights a variety of matters that draw upon cognate specialisations such as palaeography, codicology, Greek and Roman studies, and others, that New Testament textual criticism must interact with regularly as we move into the future of the discipline.[56]

5. *Computerisation*

The final matter I wish to mention is the developing benefits to New Testament textual criticism from the appropriation of computer technology. Of course, for several decades now various scholars with an interest in textual criticism have worked at experiments in using computers, especially with a view to expediting the drudgery of manuscript collation and the counting of agreements in variants.[57] To date, major obstacles remain in the way of these aims, especially the necessity to transcribe the witnesses into machine-readable form (a highly labour-intensive process and fraught with the danger of introducing additional variants inherent in any copying process!) and the need for fully adequate software able to collate and in some level classify variants. Neither the transcription work nor the necessary collation/analysis software is commercially attractive for any firm involved in marketing computer material, and so it is difficult to say how fast any significant progress can be made.

There are, however, a few encouraging developments that might be harbingers of further good things to come. Recent software

---

[55] *Ibid.*, 121.

[56] The recent volume of essays on Codex Bezae (Parker & Amphoux) arising from a colloquium of textual critics, palaeographers and codicologists also illustrates the sort of collaborative and cross-specialisation work that we need to see more of in the future.

[57] For a helpful review of relatively current developments, see now R.A. Kraft, 'The Use of Computers in New Testament Textual Criticism', in Ehrman & Holmes, 268-82.

developments are aimed at facilitating the entry of textual data and the organisation and presentation of the data for text-critical analysis.[58] In addition, there is a very ambitious project based in Australia that is intended to provide wide computerised access to Greek manuscripts: the Electronic New Testament Manuscript Project. Though still at the pilot stage, the aims of the project are (1) to scan photographs of New Testament manuscripts to produce a computerised image 'archive' (permitting visual examination at the project's World Wide Web site by anyone with Internet access and appropriate software), (2) to transcribe the text of New Testament manuscripts into machine-readable form (so that one could consult the full text of manuscripts through the Internet, and could also collate and analyse readings by means of computer software), and (3) to catalogue the New Testament manuscripts available at the site, this catalogue being accessible and searchable via the Internet.[59] In order for these aims to be achieved, however, those who hold photographic rights for New Testament manuscripts will have to agree to the production of scanned images, and there will have to be a great deal of human labour made available (probably donated, but by all means well trained!) to transcribe the text of manuscripts carefully and check the transcriptions properly to assure full accuracy.

Any significant uses of computer technology for the work of textual criticism of the New Testament, uses that would materially simplify, expedite and improve upon more traditional measures, are still unfortunately the stuff of dreams. But such dreams occasionally become reality, and it is undeniable that such dreams fulfilled would be a major boon to the field.

---

[58] Two programs mentioned by Kraft which show some promise are COLLATE (for use on the Apple Macintosh system) and MANUSCRIPT (developed in connection with the International Greek New Testament Project); see Kraft, 271-3.

[59] The directors of the project are James K. Tauber and Tim Finney (the latter at Baptist Theological College of Western Australia), and the board of advisors include recognised textual critics and cognate specialists such as E.J. Epp, J.K. Elliott, Dieter Hagedorn, Alan Humm, L.W. Hurtado, R.A. Kraft, D.L. Mealand, and S.R. Pickering, as well as other scholars and interested experts in scholarly publishing. The URL for the project is as follows: http://www.entmp.org/

Conclusion

As one very interested observer (and occasional contributor) to the field, I have attempted to provide at least some indications that New Testament textual criticism may be a bit healthier (particularly in the English-speaking countries) as we near the end of this century, than it was in the 1970s. And I have described recent studies and developments that represent worthy contributions and that point toward issues, questions and sophistication that should be embraced. These developments in fact suggest that it is not too much to hope that New Testament textual criticism may again be recognised by wider circles of scholars as directly germane and broadly relevant to exegetical, literary, historical and theological study of the New Testament and early Christianity, and that textual critics may be able to proceed toward mapping more thoroughly the history of the New Testament text and toward developing a soundly based and widely received theory of the early transmission of the text.

It may seem daunting to imagine New Testament textual criticism following up the demanding leads given in the studies and developments described here. It may well be an impossible dream unless New Testament textual critics make a programmatic effort to collaborate even more fully than in the past, perhaps adapting the team-based and heavily collaborative research strategies regularly followed in the sciences.

I shall perhaps be regarded by some as naïvely optimistic, but I sincerely hope that New Testament textual criticism will rise to these challenges and, perhaps in light of the instructive contributions such as I have surveyed here, it is even reasonable to think that such hope is not merely sentiment but may be entertained with some modest confidence.

THE SYRIAC EVIDENCE FOR THE 'PRE-JOHANNINE TEXT' OF THE GOSPEL: A STUDY IN METHOD[1]

J.W. CHILDERS

I. *Introduction*

Preaching to his congregation in Antioch, St. John Chrysostom says:

> I think today must be a great festival, on account of the presence of our brothers, who have adorned our city today and embellished our church. In language, they are to us a backwards people, but in faith we harmonize. They lead quiet lives, having a temperate and reverend existence. For amongst these people are no disorderly theatres, nor horse races, nor immoral women, nor other urban chaos; instead, every indication of licentiousness is driven out and great temperance blossoms everywhere.[2]

Chrysostom is refering to the Syriac-speaking rural folk living around Antioch. His sermons occasionally draw attention to their high character and exemplary morality. Unsurprisingly, many of his works were translated from Greek into Syriac at an early time – amongst them the exegetical Homilies on the Gospel of John (HJn).

We are fortunate to have very ancient manuscripts of West Syrian origin[3] preserving this Syriac version. The British Library

---

[1] The subject matter of this article was briefly touched upon in part of my more general communication to the last Patristics Conference in Oxford (1995), entitled 'Chrysostom's Exegetical Homilies on the New Testament in Syriac Translation', and published in E.A. Livingstone, ed., *Studia Patristica* 33 (Leuven, 1997), 510-16.

[2] *De statuis ad populum Antiochenum,* 19 (PG 49.188).

[3] Yet the influence of the Syriac version on the East Syrian tradition is also apparent from the commentaries of Isho'dad of Merv, from *Gannat Bussame,* and the notices in the fourteenth-century catalogue of 'Abdisho', *Scriptorum ecclesiasticorum catalogus* (in Joseph S. Assemani, *Bibliotheca orientalis*

manuscript B.L. Add. 14,561 (Homilies 1-43) was copied in the sixth or seventh century.[4] Also from the same period is the volume B.L. Add. 12,161 (Homilies 60-88). Later are B.L. Add. 14,562 (seventh-eighth century) and Sin. Syr. 59[5] (ninth century), each originally having Homilies 60-88 but now somewhat fragmentary. In addition to these four excellent commentary manuscripts are numerous Syriac collections – some of them just as ancient – having extracts of the homilies according to specific purposes, e.g. anthologies, homiliaries, and catenae.

These texts are of interest for many reasons, not least because of their value for the textual criticism of the Greek homily texts, and in turn that of the New Testament, Greek and Syriac. With the current interest in Patristic citations, a full analysis of Chrysostom's citations in Greek is one of the most pressing *desiderata*.[6] Yet the textual critic is frustrated by two serious problems: 1) the quality of existing Greek editions (often poor), and 2) the state of the Greek manuscript tradition. As for the Greek text of HJn, the manuscript tradition is quite late, effectively beginning in the ninth or tenth century.[7]

The quality of existing editions is also discouraging, since they use only a small fraction of extant Greek manuscripts. We are left to rely mainly on the editions of Hieronymus Commelin, Henry S.

Clementino-Vaticanae, vol. 3, *de scriptoribus syris nestorianis* [Rome, 1725], 24, 26) and in *Chronicle of Seert* 1.67 (in Addai Scher, *Histoire Nestorienne (Chronique de Séert),* PO 5.2 [1910], 319); see also Anton Baumstark, *Geschichte der syrischen Literatur* (Bonn, 1922), 80.

[4] See William Wright, *Catalogue of Syriac Manuscripts in the British Museum Acquired since the Year 1838* (London, 1872), 2.469-71. The dating of these manuscripts is based on the learned paleographical estimates of the cataloguers.

[5] See Agnes Smith Lewis, *Catalogue of the Syriac MSS. in the Convent of S. Catharine on Mount Sinai* (*Studia Sinaitica* 1; London, 1894), 52; Murad Kamil, *Catalogue of all Manuscripts in the Monastery of St. Catharine on Mount Sinai* (Wiesbaden, 1970), 153.

[6] Bart D. Ehrman, 'The Use and Significance of Patristic Evidence for New Testament Textual Criticism', *New Testament Textual Criticism, Exegesis and Church History. A Discussion of Methods* (eds B. Aland & J. Delobel; Contributions to Biblical Exegesis and Theology 7 [Kampen, 1994]), 124.

[7] For a good overview of the Greek tradition, see the five volumes of *Codices Chrysostomici Graeci,* eds. Michel Aubineau, Robert E. Carter, and Wolfgang Lackner (Paris, 1968-83).

Savile and J.-P. Migne.[8] The combination of their testimony is more helpful than reliance on any one of them, but nevertheless between them they present only a small portion of the manuscript evidence.

II. *Boismard's Contribution to Our Knowledge of HJn*

Over forty years ago, P.W. Harkins recognized that existing editions did not provide an accurate portrayal of the state of the Greek text of HJn.[9] But with so many manuscripts to collate, re-editing the homilies seemed a colossal task – one which Harkins bravely undertook, but which he was unable to see through to completion. Now M.-E. Boismard is in the process of presenting new textual data on the Greek HJn.[10] His edition is useful because it presents a more diverse textual picture than any of its predecessors, and is therefore more representative of the Greek tradition. Also, recognizing that on external grounds the Syriac evidence is centuries older than existing Greek evidence, Boismard has utilized the Syriac of B.L. 14,561.

Unfortunately, Boismard does not aim to present the Greek text for its own sake, hence limiting the usefulness of his work. First, he uses only a handful of manuscripts. In 1967, Harkins claimed to have examined 80 out of some 140 available Greek witnesses.[11] Boismard has consulted only nine Greek manuscripts, augmenting them with Migne's text and using J.A. Cramer's edition of the catenae as a

---

[8] Commelin, *Expositio perpetua in Nouum Jesu Christi Testamentum,* 4 vols. (Heidelberg, 1603); Savile, *Sancti Johannis Chrysostomi Opera Omnia,* 8 vols. (Eton, 1612-13); Migne, PG 59.

[9] P.W. Harkins, 'The Text Tradition of Chrysostom's Commentary on John', Ph.D. dissertation (Michigan State University [Ann Arbor], 1948); see also *idem.*, 'The Text Tradition of Chrysostom's Commentary on John', *TS* 19 (1958) 404-12.

[10] This takes the form of the volumes in progress of *Un évangile pré-johannique,* of which volumes 1 and 2 have appeared, in two parts each: M.-É. Boismard & A. Lamouille, *Un évangile pré-johannique,* vol. 1: *Jean 1,1-2,12* (ÉBib 17-18; Paris, 1993); and under the editorship of Boismard alone: vol. 2 (ÉBib 24-25; Paris, 1994).

[11] Harkins, 'The Text Tradition of Chrysostom's Commentary on John', in StPatr 8.1, ed. F.L. Cross (TU 92; Berlin, 1966), 210-20.

control.[12] This small group of witnesses is notable for its textual diversity, and it may be that it portrays in broad outline the overall shape of the extant Greek text, but these few bits of evidence cannot fill the void left by the vast quantity of textual data remaining unedited. Also, in volume 2 Boismard drops seven of the nine manuscripts, presenting his text on the basis of only two similar ones, giving variants from Migne and Cramer for comparison. Second, Boismard is very selective about which homilies he edits and which parts of these homilies he presents: in volume 1, parts of Homilies 6 and 16-23, according to seven Greek manuscripts; and according to two manuscripts, parts of Homilies 8 and 11-13 in volume 1, parts of Homilies 23-35 in volume 2.[13]

Obviously, Boismard's volumes are not critical editions of the Greek homily texts. This is because for him the homily texts are only a means to another end, the identification and extraction of a 'pre-Johannine' text of the Gospel of John.[14] Boismard believes that the homilies cite a form of the Gospel text which was current at Antioch before the canonical form had gained universal prominence. It is the presence of this hypothetical text-form that determines which homilies are to be edited, and which portions of even these homilies are to be ignored; it is his estimate that two extant Greek manuscripts best preserve this presumably primitive text-form which causes Boismard to disregard the other witnesses. Amongst other strands of evidence, a critical role in this reconstruction is played by the Syriac manuscript B.L. Add. 14,561.

It is my own study of this Syriac text which has led me to analyze Boismard's hypothesis, particularly as it involves the Syriac. I focus on three issues: 1) the role Boismard assigns the Syriac in confirming his views about a 'pre-johannine' Greek text; 2) the methods Boismard uses to relate the Syriac to the Greek; and 3) his manner of presenting the Syriac evidence in the apparatus to his Greek edition. The first part of this study critiques Boismard's methods of correlating the Syriac to the Greek text and of presenting the Syriac evidence, which are evident mainly in volume 1.1 of *Un évangile pré-johannique*. These issues are of general importance, since it is crucial

---

[12] John Anthony Cramer, ed., *Catenae Graecorum Patrum in Novum Testamentum*, Vol. 2 (Oxford, 1844).

[13] Vol. 2 continues in the middle of Homily 23 where vol. 1 leaves off.

[14] Boismard, *Évangile pré-johannique*, 1.1.10.

for editors to employ responsible methods when attempting to relate a version to its hypothetical source text. Moreover, scholars using the versions and editions need to be more aware of the limitations and pitfalls. The second part of this study will evaluate Boismard's theories about the development of the Syriac tradition, which he presents in the introduction to the *critique* and *reconstitution* volume 1.2.

The second aforementioned issue – methods of relating the Syriac to its source text – is at the core. Determining the exact form of the Greek source text of Syriac translations can be a complex business, often capable of only imprecise results. Editors must take into account three limiting factors: 1) the linguistic limitations of Syriac in representing Greek; 2) the features of the translation technique(s) used to render the Greek; and 3) the forces at work within the transmission process. In my view, Boismard recognizes the importance of the first factor, the second he gives no special attention, and the third has been commandeered to serve the interests of his theory about the recensional history of the Syriac.

III. *Critique of Boismard's Use of the Syriac*

A. *Errors in the Presentation*

Unfortunately the presentation is marred by blatant errors. In volume 1.1, note 4 on page 76 cites the Syriac for two conflicting variants, and is obviously contradictory. A reading of the apparatus for Homilies 6, 20, 22, and 23 yields other instances, of which the following occur in Homily 22 alone (volume 1.1):

Location	*Boismard's Note*	*Actual Syriac Text*
p.136, n.18	om. σκόπει(τε) δέ Syr	includes ܐܬܒܩܘ ܓܝܪ ('for consider')
p.138, n.16	om. τοῦτο Syr	includes ܗܕܐ ('this')
p.140, n.9	βαλεῖν Syr	ܕܢܣܒ ('to take')[15]
p.134, n.5	δεικνύημεν Syr	ܬܚܣܡ (?)

[15] In this case, it appears that the error occurred because the note reference (i.e. the superscript 9) was misplaced. The variation is between δοῦναι and βαλεῖν, not λαβεῖν and βαλεῖν as the apparatus reference indicates.

The last instance deserves some comment. Most of the Greek manuscripts have δεικνύητε; manuscript M has δείκνυται, which Boismard adopts for his text. He reads the Syriac as if it reflects δεικνύημεν. Yet the commentary manuscript B.L. Add. 14,561 clearly has ܬܚܣܢܘܢ, which, if correct, must be a second-person verb. It is difficult to see how the sense of the root ܚܣܢ ('to have difficulty' or 'to prevail over') can fit in this context. One would expect the root ܚܘܐ ('to show'), which is in fact what an extract in the sixth- or seventh-century Syriac anthology B.L. Add. 14,612 has here: ܬܚܘܘܢ ('you will show').[16] The form in B.L. Add. 14,561 is the result of an understandable mistake; in any case, it could not be taken as a first-person verb as Boismard has done.

Beyond errors in the apparatus, there are also errors in Boismard's discussions. On page 31 of volume 1.2, we find the following presentation of texts:

ChrSyr	ܡܫܝܚ ܡܕܡ ܕܐܬܒ ܠܗܘܐ
Syr^P	ܡܫܝܚ ܡܕܡ ܕܐܬܒ ܢܗܘܐ
Syr^S	ܡܫܝܚ ܡܕܡ ܕܐܬܒ ܠܗܘܢ
B.L. Add. 14,561	ܕܡܕܡ ܕܐܬܒ ܢܗܘܢ

The most obvious mistake is ܬܒ for ܠܒ, four times. The second involves ܢܗܘܢ, since the manuscript actually has ܢܗܘܘܢ. These errors are small, possibly typographical, but they do not inspire confidence in the accuracy of a presentation such as this, for which minute precision is necessary.

B. *Problems with the Method of Relating the Syriac to the Greek*

In many instances, it would appear that Boismard has misread the Syriac, but it is actually his manner of presenting the evidence which is the problem. Of course it is understood that the edition is of the

[16] On this Syriac manuscript, see Wright, *Catalogue*, 2.696-701. Amongst other Chrysostomic extracts, the miscellaneous anthology includes the complete texts of Homilies 22 and 23 (ff. 59v-68v) and portions of Homilies 62 (f. 166r) and 85 (ff. 78r-80r). The translation is the same as that in the commentary manuscripts.

Greek text and is not meant to present the Syriac evidence systematically. Yet the Syriac is clearly important to his work; it takes its place amongst the other (Greek) witnesses[17] and its *siglum* 'Syr' appears regularly in the apparatus. But Boismard never clarifies his method of interpreting and presenting the evidence of the Syriac. The reader is easily misled. This usually happens where the Syriac is not explicitly mentioned, which implies either that it agrees with the reading of the main text or that it is subsumed under the category of *reliqui*. Typically one may trust the implication, but too many times the notes are misleading, producing errors by implication. Some examples:

Location	*Implied Syriac Reading*	*Actual Syriac Reading*
p.32, n.5	om. φησίν	include ܠܡ (≈ φησίν)
p.32, n.6	δὲ μή (against γάρ)	ܓܝܪ (≈ γάρ)
p.114, n.21	om. καί	include -ܘ (≈ καί)
p.138, n.8	om. ἤδη	include ܟܒܪ ('already')
p.140, n.19	include καὶ προσέθηκεν	om. same
p.148, n.4	om. ἀλλ'	include ܐܠܐ (≈ ἀλλά)

When employing versional evidence, an editor must be absolutely clear about the methods of presentation and follow the method consistently. These examples show that Boismard's edition is not always a reliable guide to the Syriac as a textual witness.

The seriousness of this state of affairs is magnified when one makes closer inquiry into the criteria used to determine when and where the edition will explicitly denote the Syriac (by means of the *siglum* 'Syr'). Instances of Greek variation appear to be the primary control; that is, since the edition is of a Greek text, it makes mention of the Syriac when Greek variants occur, to indicate which reading the Syriac supports. Often, of course, it does not mention the Syriac explicitly in such cases; hence the 'errors by implication' noted above. Otherwise, the method appears sensible – except for the fact that the Syriac evidence is so relatively primitive that it ought to be considered as a full and independent witness. Elsewhere I have shown that the Syriac version regularly features distinctive readings

[17] *Évangile pré-johannique*, 1.1.24.

and is capable of preserving very old readings which have vanished from the Greek texts currently known.[18] This is unsurprising, in view of the age of the translation and its manuscript witnesses; it happens for Biblical citations as well as the homily text proper. Boismard recognizes this, and in a few places advances the Syriac text as original. In other places, he notes some distinctive readings of the Syriac only in the apparatus. However, most of the distinctive readings are ignored altogether, and one wonders how Boismard has decided which are significant for comparing to the Greek.

This problem raises another question, involving those cases where he does explicitly give the Syriac evidence: How has Boismard taken account of the special features of the translator's technique, which are particularly apparent in the distinctive readings typically ignored by the edition, and how does he expect the reader using the edition to do so? It is misleading to give the Syriac evidence only where it agrees with certain variants, unless the editor explains the problems associated with the three factors mentioned above[19] as they bear upon the particular texts he is using – and then makes some effort to keep them in mind. This is especially true for translations which are not highly literal.

These are matters of method, relating both to the use of the Syriac as a witness and to the presentation and explanation of the data. Regarding Boismard's method, he indicates some respect for the limitations of Syriac in representing Greek; this is apparent in those apparatus notes where a question mark (?) accompanies the *siglum* 'Syr', few though they be.[20] However, in practice the edition is inconsistent, and no notice has been given of the limitations imposed by the translator's methods. Comparing the Greek to the Syriac, I have seen that the Syriac can responsibly be associated with Greek variants and is potentially a useful witness to the pre-medieval text – but only when handled carefully.[21] On numerous occasions in Boismard's edition, the Syriac evidence is supposed to be more clear

[18] See my D.Phil. thesis, 'Studies in the Syriac Versions of St. John Chrysostom's Homilies on the New Testament' (Oxford, 1996), 1.256-7 (also 268, 270, 274-5, 283-6).
[19] See p.53 above.
[20] He ostensibly relates the Syriac to particular Greek variants only 'quand elle peut rendre la différence' (*Évangile pré-johannique*, 1.2.23).
[21] See Childers, 'Studies in the Syriac Versions', 1.255-7, 292-3.

than it actually is. The following lists of examples refer to notes in the edition which give apparent agreements between the Syriac and some Greek witness(es) but which are potentially misleading because the Syriac translation is not capable of supporting the identifications without some qualification.[22]

Many of the instances involve particles or conjunctions, even ὅτι ≈ -ܕ:

Locations	*Greek Variant with which Syriac is Identified*
p.62, n.4	γάρ against οὖν
p.62, n.20	add οὖν
p.76, n.21	om. οὖν
p.66, n.4 and p.106, n.3	om. καί
p.74, n.6 and p.114, n.3	add ὅτι
p.78, n.18	add δέ
p.84, n.21 and p.88, n.7	add καί
p.106, n.14	δὲ against γάρ and οὖν

Some instances involve fine points of word order:

Locations	*Greek Variant with which Syriac is Identified*
p.56, n.5	φησὶ γεγενῆσθαι against γεγ. φησί
p.90, n.7	σπουδὴν τὴν πολλὴν against πολ. σπουδήν
p.136, n.1	μόνον τοῦτο against τοῦτο μόνον

Some instances reflect little appreciation for the difficulties associated with distinguishing certain forms of the Syriac perfect tense from the participle:[23]

Locations	*Greek Variant with which Syriac is Identified*
p.116, n.10	add καὶ λέγει (the Syriac has perfect-tense pointing)
p.142, n.22	ποιεῖ against ἐποίησεν (the Syriac has perfect-tense pointing)

---

[22] In each case, the apparatus mentions the Syriac explicitly, so there is no chance of 'error by implication'.

[23] See Childers, 'Studies in the Syriac Versions', 1.236, 257, and 325.

Other sorts of instances could be noted:

Locations	*Greek Variant with which Syriac is Identified*
p.74, n.7	add αὐτοῦ (abundant possessive suffixes are not very unusual)
p.62, n.15	οὐδὲ against οὐ (the translator is not totally consistent)

The last example is interesting because note 3 on page 146 (rightly) names the Syriac as an inconclusive witness ('Syr?') where the variants are οὐδέ and οὐκ, yet the note on page 62 is unqualified.

It must be acknowledged that, *prima facie*, most of the identifications are accurate. But what is their significance? If one consults a version only in instances of variation, inquiring, 'Which variant does the version support?', then one's results will be prejudiced and inaccurate. A broader reading of the version is required; often, the evidence one cannot get from an apparatus note is precisely what one needs in order to interpret the readings which are given. Regarding the above examples, issues of style are very important: I have found that the translator does not necessarily follow precise Greek word order within small phrases; Syriac idiom (and the translator's style) create seemingly superfluous possessive suffixes and relative pronouns (i.e. -ܕ ≈ ὅτι); I have also found the translator to be inconsistent in the way he handles Greek conjunctions and particles, as are other translators of the same period.[24] These (and other) stylistic features complicate things. In instances of Greek variation, it is perhaps worth noting the Syriac agreements, as Boismard does. Yet this should not be done without qualifying the occurrence of certain kinds of agreements, on the basis that the identifications do not necessarily indicate that the translator read the Greek text with which he apparently agrees; some agreements are coincidental. The reader must be made acquainted with these facts before the Syriac evidence becomes truly useful.

The deficiencies of *Un évangile pré-johannique* in this regard are perhaps best seen in the exploration of the distinctive Syriac readings noted in the apparatus. Note 3 on page 30 shows that the Syriac adds a phrase equivalent to καὶ διὰ τοῦτο (ܘܡܛܠ ܗܕܐ);

[24] *Ibid.*, 1.225-6.

similarly, note 9 on page 136 shows that the Syriac reflects διὰ τοῦτο (ܡܛܠ ܗܢܐ) rather than just τοῦτο. These things are true, but why does the apparatus ignore most of the many other places at which the Syriac has distinctive transitions and rhetorical or explanatory phrases? Even confining ourselves to this phrase only, we would expect to see similar notes elsewhere, since the Syriac 'adds' ܡܛܠ ܗܢܐ (≈ διὰ τοῦτο) twice more in Homily 20.[25]

The apparatus also mentions other sorts of distinctive Syriac readings, of which straightforward 'additions' and 'omissions' will be easiest to appreciate:

Location	*Greek Equivalent to Syriac Text*
p.26, n.16	om. ὃς κατασκεύασει τὴν ὁδόν σου
p.28, n.11	add ἄκουε παρ' ἡμῶν
p.104, n.15	add ἀλλά
p.110, n.11	om. καὶ οὕτως
p.112, n.3	om. ἀληθῶς

But again, one wonders why other comparable distinctive readings go unnoticed, such as the following:

Location	*Distinctive Syriac Readings*
p.28, line 34	add. ܒܕܘܟܬܐ ܐܚܪܬܐ ('in another place')
p. 32, line 74	om. τοῦ τε μαρτυρουμένου καὶ τοῦ μαρτυροῦντός ἐστιν
p.136, line 35	add. ܕܒܐܬܝܬܗ ܕܡܪܢ ܥܡܗ ('our Lord's coming with it')
p. 140, line 74 (n.22)	add ܠܨܒܘ̈ܬܐ ('to things'), against 1) τοῖς θαυματουργοῖς, 2) τῷ θαύματι, and 3) the omission of any indirect object

These examples could be multiplied. Other apparent expansions, double translations, amplifications, and distinctive alterations

[25] Lines 31 and 120 of the Greek edition (pp.106, 114).

warrant the same sort of notice given to the few which appear in the edition.[26]

In a few cases, Boismard puts forward the Syriac text as the only witness preserving the original text-form.[27] Generally, it is not difficult to see why he would assign such a value to most of the readings he selects; but it is difficult to see why many other interesting readings are given no notice at all. One category of such readings involves personal remarks on the part of the preacher[28] in the Syriac where the Greek is less personal:

Location	*Distinctive Syriac Readings*
p.28, line 21	add ܟܒܪ ܐܡܪ ܐܢܬ ('perhaps you will say')
p.28, line 29	add ܐܠܐ ܟܒܪ ܐܡܪ ܐܢܬ ('but perhaps you will say')
p.154, lines 43-4	ܐܡܪ ܐܢܐ ('I say'), against ἔμπροσθεν ἐδηλώσαμεν

The first two could be examples of the translator's clarifying rhetorical additions, but they could also be seen as primitive readings omitted for stylistic purposes at an early stage. In any case, Boismard's edition gives no indication of these readings.

In inter-textual analysis, there can be no substitute for direct reference to the Syriac text itself. Even when one has gained an appreciation for the general limitations of the Syriac in representing Greek, each translator's technique and every translation will contain fine and subtle features detectable only when one relies directly on the Syriac, features which supply crucial controls for the interpretation of the evidence. Yet not everyone will be able to consult the Syriac directly, and editions such as Boismard's are not intrinsically unhelpful. But it is all the more important that editions

---

[26] For examples of such readings, see Childers, 'Studies in the Syriac Versions', 1.249-53.

[27] See *Évangile pré-johannique*, p.40, n.5; p.42, n.16; p.76, n.8; p.150, n.6; p.152, n.17.

[28] Syriac idiom requires more personal elements (e.g. possessive suffixes) than the Greek, but the personal additions noted above are not required by grammar or idiom.

providing only indirect access to the Syriac do so according to a careful and consistent method which intentionally respects the three factors mentioned above.[29]

In the case of *Un évangile pré-johannique*, we have in essence a potentially helpful assortment of Syriac-Greek identifications (errors notwithstanding), but they have not been assembled according to consistent criteria and without more general information about the Syriac version, the reader is left without any means to use the data responsibly. Moreover, although a direct reading of the Syriac evidence presumably underlies Boismard's own use of the data, even his own interpretation is beset by the sorts of methodological difficulties one would expect a reader of his edition also to encounter. The implications of these misjudgements become clear in the following sections.

III. *The General Textual Affiliation of the Syriac HJn*

Boismard detects three main textual groups amongst the extant witnesses.[30] Without presuming anything about their interrelationships, it is possible to set them forth according to the witnesses he uses:[31]

1) B: Vat., Palatinus 32 (10th century), Homilies 9b-48
M: Athos, Koutloumousiou 32 (10th century)
Cr: Cramer, *Catenae graecorum patrum*

2) A: Paris, Bib. Nat., gr. 705 (9th century)
D: Jer., Gr. Pat., n. 82 (11th century)
Syr: B.L. Add. 14,561 (6th or 7th century)

3) B2: Vat., Palatinus 32 (11th century), Homilies 1-9a
C: Paris, Bib. Nat., gr. 707 (11th century)
J: Vat., Gr. 545 (11th century)
K: Moscow, Bib. Syn., gr. n. 94 (10th century)
N: Paris, Bib. Nat., gr. 713 (11th century)

[29] See Childers, 'Studies in the Syriac Versions', 1.299.
[30] See *Évangile pré-johannique*, 1.2.13-27.
[31] The designations, 'Group 1', etc., are my own.

R: Moscow, Bib. Syn., gr. n. 95 (11th century)
Migne

In Boismard's view, the two manuscripts in Group 1 have the so-called 'short text' of the Greek homilies, with which the catenae are supposed often to agree; for this reason, Boismard uses Cramer's edition in Group 1 as a control.[32] Groups 2 and 3 constitute the 'long text' but are separated from each other by sets of distinctive readings.

Boismard has used only a small fraction of the available Greek witnesses. Harkins read many more Greek manuscripts and also detected Groups 2 and 3, which he designates Families A and B, respectively. As for Group 1, he read only Vat. Palatinus 32 and decided that it was an idiosyncratic member of Family A (i.e. Group 2).[33] The work of both men makes it clear that these three groups exist, and Boismard's edition illustrates their differences.

Boismard rightly associates the Syriac with the 'long text' (i.e. Groups 2 and 3); the association is obvious and clear. But he also attempts a more precise identification of the quality of the Syriac text by putting it into Group 2 specifically,[34] the Greek part of which is in manuscripts A and D.[35] This is not unreasonable, since where A and D agree, the Syriac normally agrees with them, although the variants are usually small in significance. However, the picture is not simple. A survey of Boismard's apparatus shows that manuscripts A and D each have numerous distinctive readings and not infrequently one of them agrees with other witnesses against the other; in such cases, the Syriac shows no particular loyalty and may go in any direction. In many instances, the Syriac agrees with one or more other manuscripts against either A or D, though not against both when they speak in unison. Manuscript J agrees with A, D, and the Syriac in some sections; in others, manuscript D actually agrees with

[32] *Évangile pré-johannique*, 1.1.20-1.

[33] Harkins was primarily concerned with higher-numbered homilies than is Boismard initially; according to Boismard, this partially accounts for Harkins' different estimate of the quality of Vat. Palatinus 32 (*Évangile pré-johannique*, 1.2.11-2).

[34] See Boismard, *Évangile pré-johannique*, 1.2.22-3

[35] Harkins found other witnesses belonging to Family A (see 'Text Tradition of Chrysostom's Commentary on John' [1948] 73-4).

witnesses belonging to Group 1. Harkins found some manuscripts difficult to classify 'because of their confused condition',[36] and Boismard speculates about the presence of still another recension in certain Group 3 manuscripts with anomalous texts, but decides that they are the result of mixture.[37] The Greek tradition is complex and the Syriac does not agree overwhelmingly with any of the Greek textual groups or their edited manuscripts.

More important than its relationship to manuscripts A and D is the fact that the Syriac occasionally agrees with Group 1 witnesses, occasionally sharing readings with Greek manuscripts B and M against the other Greek witnesses. Some of the agreements are quite significant:

Location	*Greek Reading with which Syriac Agrees*
p.28, n.3	add ἴσως εἴποι τις ἄν M (B deest)
p.46, n.18	om. τὴν προφήτην M B
p.54, n.10	om. βαπτιστήν M B Cr
p.62, n.3	κηρῦξαι against δεῖξαι M B
p.76, n.18	om. ἀνθρώπων M B
p.84, n.11	om. ταῦτά εστι τὰ μαρτυροῦντα M B
p.86, n.18	om. ἐν πολλοῖς πολλάκις σπουδαῖον ὄντα M B
p.138, n.24	om. μὲν ὥστε καί M B

Other agreements are less significant, but worth noting:[38]

Location	*Greek Reading with which Syriac Agrees*
p.48, n.15	om. οὐκ ἄν M B
p.52, n.12	om. ὡς M
p.56, n.3	om. νῦν M
p.56, n.14	ἠπείγοντο against ἠπείγετο M B
p.56, n.18	om. πάλαι or πάλιν M B
p.60, n.9	om. τὰ from ἐδιδάσκοντο τὰ περὶ τοῦ Χρ. M B
p.74, n.17	om. τινά M
p.76, n.10	om. μοι M B
p.78, n.11	αὐτὸς against οὗτος M B
p.100, n.6	include μόνης M

[36] *Idem* (1966) 218, n.1.

[37] Boismard, *Évangile pré-johannique*, 1.2.24.

[38] The list is representative, not exhaustive.

p.108, n.16	om. περὶ αὐτοῦ M B
p.114, n.11	om. δὲ or δή B
p.138, n.13	αὐτῷ against αὐτοὶ and οὗτοι M
p.152, n.9	om. οὕτω M B

There are times when A and/or D agree with M and B, or where K agrees with M and B; in either case, the Syriac again is liable to be in agreement. Of course, B and M share many more distinctive readings which the Syriac does not have, but the Syriac has obviously been influenced by a form of the Greek text somehow related to one which was at least partially responsible for creating B and M.

Therefore, a preliminary study shows that the Syriac agrees mainly with the 'long text', perhaps Group 2 in particular, but that it also shares some readings peculiar to the 'short text' of Group 1. In view of the age of the Syriac translation and manuscript, its textual quality is very important. Far from disregarding the Syriac, Boismard utilizes the apparent mixture in it as one component in a comprehensive theory about the development of the Greek HJn – a theory which in turn requires a complex history of development for the Syriac.

IV. *Boismard's Theory about the Multi-Stage Development of the Syriac Text*

A. *Boismard's Position*

The broad patterns of textual grouping which Boismard and Harkins propose are quite reasonable, in view of the evidence. However, each also attempts to explain the relationships between the different groups. Harkins' position is easiest to summarize: Family A (Group 2) is the most primitive extant text-form; Family B (Group 3) represents a stylistically motivated revision.[39] The only Group 1 manuscript available to Harkins (Vat. Palatinus 32) did not commend itself to Harkins as a legitimate independent text-form.[40] Boismard's position is considerably more complex, and the following diagram summarizes its basic points:

---

[39] Harkins, 'Text Tradition of Chrysostom's Commentary on John' (1958), 411-12.
[40] Cf. *Évangile pré-johannique*, 1.2.12.

Diagram 1: *Development of the Greek Tradition of HJn (Boismard's Theory)*

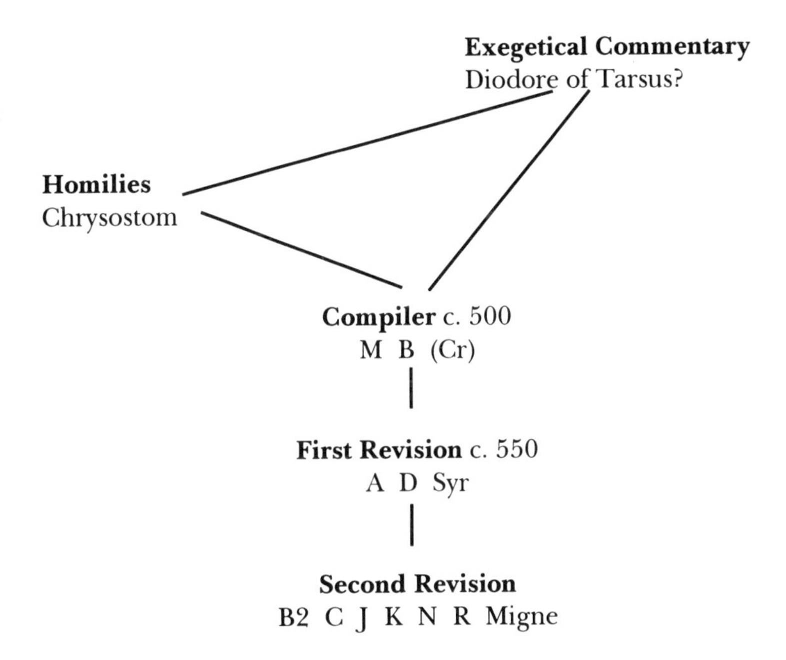

Boismard maintains that the Greek HJn underwent stages of compilation and revision. It is possible to summarize his conclusions as follows: 1) Someone other than Chrysostom prepared an exegetical commentary, probably Diodore of Tarsus.[41] 2) Chrysostom prepared some homilies on John's Gospel, using the commentary as a source. 3) A compiler, working at about the end of the fifth century, rescued the commentary from oblivion by uniting it with Chrysostom's homilies and added some of his own glosses. The 'short text' manuscripts (viz. B and M) are supposed to be witnesses

---

[41] Boismard insists that the exegetical commentary could not have been Chrysostom's work, pointing to alleged inner contradictions, discrepant themes, and diverse forms of Bible citations (*Évangile pré-johannique,* 1.2.191-6). He lists several reasons for suggesting Diodore, but ultimately appears to do so by default, perhaps on the grounds that no one else is as likely to have been in the right place at the right time to produce such a work and to influence Chrysostom (see *ibid.*, 1.2.196-205).

to this layer of the tradition. 4) A reviser added more material, some authentic Chrysostom and some of his own glosses, accommodating the Biblical citations to a Koine form and standardizing the style overall. The manuscripts of Group 2 are the best witnesses to this layer of the tradition. On the basis of the date of the Syriac manuscript, Boismard believes this work would have been done by 550 at the latest. 5) Finally, not content to let things alone, another editor modified things yet again, as editors will, thereby producing the text surviving essentially in Group 3 witnesses.

If Boismard is right, then we have possibly discovered the work of an important thinker of the early church and must extract it and place it within its proper context. However, before it is possible to evaluate Boismard's work, it must be put into context. Identifying and establishing a 'pre-Johannine' form of the Gospel text is Boismard's principal aim,[42] and it is his convictions concerning it which seem to supply the perspective from which Boismard interprets the Greek evidence. Yet it is possible to understand the situation differently, as Harkins shows; his views imply that the 'short text' would be a secondary development, perhaps the result of abbreviation. Either way, when relying solely on Greek witnesses, one can penetrate no further than the ninth century, and most witnesses are from the tenth to eleventh centuries.

This is why the early Syriac text is so important to Boismard. However, its textual quality turned out to be problematic: one must account for the apparent mixture of 'long' and 'short text' elements. Boismard hit upon an explanation which not only accounts for the mixture but actually strengthens his theory of the development of the Greek text – if the explanation is accurate. Assuming the priority of 'the short text', Boismard suggests that the extant Syriac witness to these homilies, viz. the text in B.L. Add. 14,561, is itself a composite entity. He posits a Syriac tradition of multiple layers: an early Syriac translation of 'the short text', later augmented by another translator on the basis of the 'long' Greek text.[43] The 'short text' elements reveal the hand of the first translator who translated a Greek text essentially like that of Group 1 witnesses. When the 'long' Greek text began to circulate (Group 2), a second translator revised the original

---

[42] See *ibid.*, 1.2.20-1 and especially 1.2.315-27.

[43] See *ibid.*, 1.2.26-34.

Syriac translation by augmenting and correcting it according to his 'long text' source. His revision was not completely perfect, leaving us with a somewhat mixed Syriac text-form.

If Boismard's conclusions about the Syriac are seen to be well-founded, then the Syriac text might support his theory and help it all hold together; if not, then we must account for this very early 'mixture' in some other way. In order to test Boismard's hypothesis, it will be necessary to evaluate any supporting evidence.

B. *External Syriac Evidence and the Date of the Translation*

Judging from the age of the commentary manuscripts, and the breadth and date of pertinent collection manuscripts, it is very likely that the Syriac HJn had been produced in their present form well before the seventh century. The translation style corroborates this;[44] its lack of stereotyping, its modest expansiveness, the length of translation unit, the lack of consistency in rendering compounds – all distinguish the Syriac HJn from the highly literal translations characteristic of the seventh century. Indeed, certain features suggest a pre-sixth-century date, such as the translator's inconsistent rendering of words related to σαρκωθέντα variously with ܠܒܫ ܦܓܪܐ, ܠܒܫ ܠܒܘܫܐ, ܗܘܐ ܦܓܪܐ, and ܐܬܓܫܡ,[45] and the dynamic characteristics of the translation (i.e. amplifications, double translations, filling out ellipses, etc.). Other lexical features fit this as well, such as the inconsistent ways of handling ἀρετή and σωτηρία, and the absence of many literal correspondences (e.g. μέν ≈ ܡܢ) which were becoming standard in the sixth century.[46] The

---

[44] See Childers, 'Studies in the Syriac Versions', 1.216-60.

[45] On the significance of this and other Christological terms, see André de Halleux, 'La philoxenienne du symbole', in *Symposium Syriacum 1976*, eds. François Graffin and Antoine Guillaumont (OCA 205; Rome, 1978), 295-315.

[46] On these and related issues, see especially the studies by Sebastian P. Brock, 'Aspects of Translation Technique in Antiquity', *GRBS* 20 (1979) 69-87; 'Towards a History of Syriac Translation Technique', in *III° Symposium Syriacum 1980*, ed. René Lavenant (OCA 221; Rome, 1983), 1-14; 'Some Aspects of Greek Words in Syriac', in *Synkretismus im syrisch-persischen Kulturgebiet,* ed. A. Dietrich (*AAWG.PH* 96; Göttingen, 1975), 80-108; 'Diachronic Aspects of Syriac Word Formation: an Aid for Dating Anonymous Texts', in *V Symposium Syriacum 1988*, ed. René Lavenant (OCA

occurrence of the adjectival form ܢܫܝܐ ('womanly') is ostensibly a feature of sixth-century translation, but the extreme rarity of such forms in the translation makes the evidence inconclusive – certainly the translation does not have the range and number of similar adjectival forms that one would expect from a translation made in the mid- to late-sixth century. In short, the external manuscript evidence and internal translational evidence suggest that the translation of HJn was made no earlier than the last part of the fifth century, but by the middle of the sixth. On the weight of the evidence, an earlier rather than later date within this range is preferable.

This puts some strain on Boismard's reconstruction; Philoxenus' citations from HJn in a florilegium dated 482(-4) suggest the existence of the same version in the late fifth century,[47] threatening Boismard's construct with virtual collapse. However, these citations are brief and differ textually from the text of the commentary manuscripts. The differences may be due to adaptation, but it is also possible that they were translated independently. Therefore, it is not possible confidently to use Philoxenus' florilegium for setting a more precise *terminus ante quem*. It can only be said that the extant Syriac version of HJn was in existence by c. 550 – though possibly between fifty and eighty years earlier – and that Boismard has less time for the evolution of 'short' to 'long text' than he prefers.

The broader Syriac tradition makes no mention of two or more distinct translations.[48] Nor do the extant manuscripts have any but the single Syriac version of the HJn; even slight revisions are rare.[49]

236; Rome, 1990), 321-30; 'The Christology of the Church of the East in the Synods of the Fifth to Early Seventh Centuries: Preliminary Considerations and Materials', in *Aksum Thyateira. A Festschrift for Archbishop Methodios of Thyateira and Great Britain,* ed. George Dragas (London, 1985), 125-42.

[47] The excerpts are in F. Graffin, ed., *Sancti Philoxeni Episcopi Mabbugensis Dissertationes Decem de Uno e sancta trinitate incorporato et passo,* vol. 5, *Appendices,* PO 41.1 (1982), 117. See also the studies, de Halleux, *Philoxène de Mabbog. Sa vie, ses écrits, sa théologie* (Louvain, 1963), 233-4, 238; F. Graffin, 'Le florilège patristique de Philoxène de Mabboug', in *Symposium Syriacum 1972,* ed. I. Ortiz de Urbina (Rome, 1974), 268.

[48] For instance, the notices of 'Abdisho' and *Chronicle of Seert* (see n.3 above).

[49] This is true of the commentary manuscripts (or the one, B.L. Add. 14,561, where the homilies edited by Boismard are involved) as well as the

If an earlier translation was made, it has left no independent impact on the surviving tradition. In the absence of corroborating external evidence, we must explore the internal evidence for double translation and distinct layers of recension.

C. *Internal Syriac Evidence*

As evidence for his hypothesis, Boismard draws attention to two features of the Syriac text itself: unevenness in the character of its Biblical citations; and a dislocation occurring in Homily 16. The latter subject involves a number of technicalities and will be considered in detail since it is so important to Boismard's views about the Syriac.

1. *The Dislocated Paragraph in Homily 16*

The dislocation which Boismard notices is important to his theory about the Syriac translation tradition,[50] but a textual and translation analysis of the pertinent texts involves such detail that it is necessary to present the texts here. The presentation of the Greek and Syriac texts will also illustrate comparative translation features mentioned elsewhere in this paper. Boismard's text and apparatus are given as they appear in the edition, except for line length:[51]

a) *The Greek and Syriac Texts*

Homily 16 on John[52]

1 καὶ οἱ ἀποσταλέντες*[1] ἦσαν ἐκ τῶν Φαρισαίων, φησί.*[2]
2 καὶ εἶπον αὐτῷ·*[3] τί οὖν βαπτίζεις;
3 *[4]⟦ εἰ σὺ οὐκ εἶ ὁ Χριστὸς οὔτε Ἠλίας οὔτε ὁ προφήτης;
4 ὁρᾷς ὡς οὐ μάτην ἔλεγον ὅτι εἰς τοῦτο αὐτὸν ἐναγαγεῖν ἠβούλοντο.
5 καὶ ἐξ ἀρχῆς μὲν αὐτὸ οὐκ ἔλεγον
6 ἵνα μὴ κατάφωροι γένωνται ἅπασιν.
7 εἶτα ἐπειδὴ εἶπεν· οὐκ εἰμὶ ὁ Χριστός,
8 πάλιν ἐκεῖνοι συσκιάσαι βουλόμενοι ἅπερ ἔνδον ἐτύρευον
9 ἐπὶ τὸν Ἠλίαν ἔρχονται καὶ τὸν προφήτην.

---

collections having parallel passages (see Childers, 'Studies in the Syriac Versions', 1.257-60).

[50] Boismard, *Évangile pré-johannique*, 1.2.32.

[51] The Greek witnesses are: B M K; and A D Syr; and C J N R Migne.

[52] The text is from Boismard, *Évangile pré-johannique*, 1.1.42, 44.

10 ὡς δὲ ἔφησε μηδὲ ἐκείνων τις εἶναι,
11 ἀπορούμενοι λοιπὸν καὶ τὸ προσωπεῖον ῥίψαντες,
12 γυμνῇ τῇ κεφαλῇ τὴν δολερὰν αὐτῶν ἐμφαίνουσιν γνώμην λέγοντες·
13 τί οὖν βαπτίζεις εἰ σὺ οὐκ εἶ ὁ Χριστός;
14 εἶτα πάλιν συσκιάσαι βουλόμενοι,
15 καὶ τοὺς ἄλλους προστιθέασι, τὸν Ἠλίαν [ ]*[5] καὶ τὸν προφήτην·
16 ἐπειδὴ γὰρ κολακείᾳ οὐκ ἴσχυσαν ὑποσκελίσαι,
17 ἐγκλήματι προσεδόκησαν αὐτὸν δύνασθαι ἀναγκάζειν
18 εἰπεῖν ὅπερ οὐκ ἦν.*[6] ἀλλ' οὐκ ἴσχυσαν.⟧
19 Ὢ τῆς ἀνοίας ! ὢ τῆς ἀλαζονείας καὶ τῆς ἀκαίρου περιεργίας !
20 ἀπεστάλητε μαθησόμενοι παρ' αὐτοῦ τίς εἴη καὶ πόθεν,
21 οὐχὶ καὶ νόμους αὐτῷ θήσοντες;*[7]
22 τοῦτο γὰρ πάλιν ἀναγκαζόντων ἦν ὁμολογῆσαι ἑαυτὸν Χριστόν.
23 ἀλλ' ὅμως οὐδὲ νῦν ἀγανακτεῖ
24 οὐδὲ λέγει τι τοιοῦτον [ ]*[8] οἷον εἰκός·
25 ὑμεῖς [ ]*[9] διατάττεσθε [ ].*[10]
26 ἀλλὰ πολλὴν πάλιν τὴν ἐπιείκειαν ἐπιδείκνυται.

*[1] sic B M K; ἀπεσταλμένοι reliqui
*[2] om. A D Syriac
*[3] sic Syriac; ἠρώτησαν αὐτὸν λέγοντες B M (ἐπηρώτησαν K D); ἐπηρώτησαν αὐτὸν καὶ εἶπον αὐτῷ reliqui.[53]
*[4] The text in double brackets (lines 3-18 in the Greek) is absent from B M K and given according to A D J R Syriac.[54]
*[5] sic A D J R Syriac; add. λέγω C N Migne
*[6] sic A D J R Syriac; 2 3 4 1 C N Migne
*[7] θήσετε Migne
*[8] sic B M K; add. πρὸς αὐτούς reliqui
[9] sic B; add. ἐμοί reliqui; ἐμοί ὑμεῖς A (Syriac?)
*[10] sic B M K; add. καὶ νομοτεθεῖτε reliqui

For purposes of discussion, the foregoing line numbering will be treated as standard.

[53] Boismard's reading of the Syriac here is incorrect; the Syriac represents (ἐπ)ηρώτησαν.
[54] Boismard's note is not accurate since the Syriac block of text does not include line 3.

B.L. Add. 14,561[55]

ܗܠܝܢ ܕܝܢ ܕܐܫܬܕܪܘ ܡܢ ܦܪ̈ܝܫܐ ܗܘܘ	1
ܘܫܐܠܘܗܝ ܘܐܡܪܘ ܠܗ. ܘܡܢܐ ܡܥܡܕ ܐܢܬ	2
ܐܢ ܐܢܬ ܠܐ ܐܝܬܝܟ ܗܘ ܡܫܝܚܐ ܘܠܐ ܐܠܝܐ ܘܠܐ ܗܘ̇ ܢܒܝܐ.	3
ܐܘ ܡܢ ܠܠܗܘܬܐ ܘܡܥܡܪܢܘܬܐ.*[1] ܘܥܠ ܣܪܒܘܬܐ ܦܘܪܫܘܬܐ	19
ܐܫܬܕܪܘ ܠܡܐܠܦ ܡܢܗ ܕܡܢܘ ܘܡܢ ܐܝܟܘ.	20
ܠܐ ܗܘܐ ܕܐܟܦ ܢܬܡܗܐ ܬܫܡܫܬܗܘܢ ܠܗ.	21
ܗܕܐ ܓܝܪ ܬܘܒ ܕܐܝܠܝܢ ܕܚܙܝܢ ܕܐܡܪܝܢ ܥܠ ܢܦܫܗ ܕܗܘܝܘ ܡܫܝܚܐ ܐܬܬܥܝܪ ܗܘܬ.	22
ܚܙܝܬ ܕܠܐ ܦܪܝܫܐܝܬ ܐܡܪ ܗܘܝܬ. ܕܒܗܕܐ ܒܥܝܢ ܗܘܘ ܕܢܪܡܘܢܝܗܝ.	4
ܘܡܢ ܦܘܡ ܗܝ ܗܕܐ ܠܐ ܐܡܪܘ.	5
ܕܠܐ ܠܚܠܝܨ ܢܛܠܒܐ ܕܐܦܘܗܝ.	6
ܡܢ ܒܬܪ ܕܝܢ ܕܐܡܪ ܕܠܐ ܐܢܐ ܐܢܐ ܡܫܝܚܐ.	7
ܬܘܒ ܗܢܘܢ ܗܠܝܢ ܒܪ ܡܬܫܟܚܝܢ ܕܡܕܡ ܕܒܡܫܡܫܬܗܘܢ ܣܟܠܝܢ ܗܘܘ ܢܫܐܠܘܢ	8
ܠܘܬ ܗܕܐ ܕܐܠܝܐ ܐܝܬܝܟ ܘܢܒܝܐ.	9
ܒܪ ܕܝܢ ܐܡܪ ܕܐܦ ܠܐ ܚܕ ܡܢ ܗܠܝܢ ܐܝܬܘܗܝ,	10
ܒܝܬ ܦܘܪܬܟܐ ܢܦܠ ܘܠܬܫܘܒܬܐ ܫܪܘ.	11
ܘܓܠܝܐܝܬ ܬܪܝܨܬܗܘܢ ܒܥܒܬܐ ܡܘܕܝܢ ܘܐܡܪܝܢ	12
ܡܢܐ ܗܟܝܠ ܡܥܡܕ ܐܢܬ. ܐܢ ܠܘ ܐܢܬ ܗܘ ܡܫܝܚܐ.	13
ܒܪ ܕܝܢ ܬܘܒ ܓܪܝܢ ܗܘܘ ܠܡܚܣܦܘ	14
ܐܦ ܗܠܝܢ ܐܚܪ̈ܢܐ ܡܗܝܡܢܝܢ ܠܐܠܝܐ ܘܠܢܒܝܐ.	15
ܡܛܠ ܓܝܪ ܕܡܫܟܚܐ ܠܐ ܐܫܟܚܘ ܕܢܬܠܘܢܝܗܝ.	16
ܒܪ ܪܥܝܢܐ ܡܟܝܠ ܡܗܡܝܢ ܗܘܘ ܕܡܓܪܝܢ ܠܡܓܪܝܘܗ	17
ܕܢܐܡܪ ܡܕܡ ܕܠܐ ܐܝܬܘܗܝ ܗܘܐ. ܐܠܐ ܠܐ ܐܫܟܚܘ.	18
ܗܘ̇ ܕܝܢ ܐܦ ܠܐ ܗܟܢܐ ܡܬܕܪܒ.	23
ܘܠܐ ܐܡܪ ܠܗܘܢ ܡܕܡ ܕܪܙܐ ܗܘܐ ܠܗ̇ ܕܡܬܐܪܒ ܠܡܐܡܪ.*[2]	24
ܕܐܝܬܘܗܝ ܠܗ ܦܘܡܐ ܐܝܬܘܗܝ. ܘܢܒܝܘܬܐ ܦܫܝܩ ܐܝܬܘܗܝ ܠܗ.	25
ܐܠܐ ܢܚܝܘܬܐ ܡܠܝܐܬܐ ܬܘܒ ܡܫܝܚܐ.	26

1 And these who were sent were from the Pharisees,
2 and they asked him and said to him, 'And why do you baptize,
3 if you are not the Christ, nor Elijah, nor the prophet?'

[55] The text is from ff.64va-65ra.

19 O the folly and the arrogance!*[1] And for the sake of[56] vain cunning
20 you were sent to learn from him who and whence he was;
21 was it not also to impose law upon him?
22 For again this (question) was of those compelling (him) to say about himself that he is the Christ.
4 You see that I was saying not vainly that by this they were wanting to make him fall.
5 And at first this is not what they said,
6 so that their wile would not be evident to everyone.
7 But after he said, 'I am not the Christ',
8 again these very ones, being diligent to conceal that which by their device they were plotting,
9 come to that about Elijah and the prophet.
10 And after he said that he also is not one of these,
11 they fell into a state of uncertainty and they dropped (their) mask,
12 and they openly expressed their evil mind and said,
13 'Why then do you baptize, if you are not the Christ?'
14 Wanting still to conceal (their intent),
15 they also add these others: Elijah and the prophet.
16 For since by flattery they were unable to ensnare him,
17 thence through accusation they were expecting to be able to force him
18 to say the thing that he was not; but they were unable.
23 But thus neither was that one indignant,
24 nor did he tell them what would have been appropriate for him who preaches to say:*[2]
25 'You command me, and you impose laws upon me',
26 but he again exhibits great calmness.

*[1] punctuation (strong break [!]) supplied by editor
*[2] ܠܡܐܡܪ ('to say') is written in the original hand over an erasure of about seven letters (at the beginning of the line)

[56] The Syriac text has a comparatively superfluous ܥܠ (≈ περί) before ܣܪܝܩܘܬܐ (≈ περιεργία), as if the translator read an additional περί, perhaps even by accident. The Syriac is legitimate but has quite a different sense.

b) *The Distinct Texts and their Interrelationships*
Three things are immediately noticeable about these texts. First, whereas most Greek texts have lines 3-18 in the position given, Greek manuscripts B, M, and K lack the material altogether.[57] Second, the Syriac contains the material, but in a slightly different position. In the Syriac, the block consists of lines 4-18 (line 3 remains in place after line 2, a discrepancy which Boismard neglects to point out), but it is placed between Greek lines 22 and 23. The line numbering which accompanies the Syriac text clarifies this. Hence there are three extant forms of text: the long Greek text (manuscripts A, C, D, J, N, R, and the printed editions), the short text (B, M, and K), and the Syriac text. Third, all three text-forms make sense as they are;[58] only with the assistance of pre-conceived notions could one form of text be defended as original on the basis of content.

We must entertain four possibilities: either one of the three extant text forms is essentially original, or the original form is presently unknown in extant witnesses; the preferred possibility should account for all three extant text forms. Boismard maintains that the shortness of the short text is not a result of deliberate abbreviation, but is in fact original.[59] In his view, instead of having suffered numerous intentional omissions, the short text was essentially the primitive textual base which an editor later expanded to produce the long text. But for the case in Homily 16 under consideration, we must ask: Which long text-form does the editor produce – that of the Greek, or that of the Syriac? Whether the former or the latter, it becomes very difficult to explain why a parallel dislocation would have occurred subsequently in the other long text, unless some of the expansions originally circulated as detached units or as a set of notes keyed to specific points in the existing early short recension, to be read alongside or copied into it. In this imaginative scenario, the dislocation would occur when scribes copied the expansion into different places, thereby producing the two similar long text-forms, Greek and Syriac.

---

[57] In the first part of Homily 16, manuscript K often agrees with B and M.

[58] If the displaced block in the Syriac were lines 3-18 instead of lines 4-18, then it would not make sense, because line 3 must follow line 2 (or perhaps be combined with line 13) in order to make sense.

[59] Boismard, *Évangile pré-johannique*, 1.2.32.

Boismard avoids this problem by moving from the realm of Greek transmission into that of the Syriac, suggesting that the extant Syriac text is the result of two translations. The first Syriac translation was of the short Greek text; when the long Greek text became available a later translator expanded the Syriac on the basis of it. Sewing these two elements together in the Syriac created the present dislocation when the second translator slightly misplaced the block of text. Yet despite Boismard's implication that the displacement would have been accidental,[60] the anomaly involving line 3 indicates that the Syriac form of text is at least partially the result of intentional activity. Perhaps the editor/translator decided that the block of text ([3]4-18) gave a better sense when inserted between lines 22 and 23 instead of between lines 2 and 19, but he had to detach line 3 from the block in order to keep that line connected to line 2, since line 3 is the second half of a Biblical citation (John 1:25) and makes sense only following line 2 directly. Alternatively, one could suppose that the entire block (lines 3-18) had been dislocated, but a later scribe (Greek or Syriac) noticed the disjunction involving line 3 and moved only it to its proper place, thereby producing the text presently reflected in the Syriac. Still, though the theory that the short text is original is troubled by complications and requires some imagination, it is plausible.

Yet two other possibilities must be considered: that either the long Greek form or the Syriac form best represents the original text. The notion that the Syriac form may be original is cast into serious doubt by the fact that both Greek forms are in agreement as to the scope of the block of text in question (lines 3-18), and the placement of line 3 in the Syriac, although problematic, is easier to explain if the Syriac form is secondary; in other words, it is very difficult plausibly to explain both the long and short Greek texts as derived somehow from the dislocated form of text underlying the Syriac. The Syriac text-form is not original. However, it is plausible to suppose that the long Greek text-form is primitive and the other two arise from it. In this scenario, the absence of the block of text from the short text, and its dislocation in the Syriac, would have occurred because of an accidental omission, perhaps a misplaced leaf.[61] This

[60] 'Le réviseur a inseré le texte ... à une mauvaise place' (*ibid.*).

[61] There are no other obvious causes of accidental omission (e.g. homoioteleuton). Such errors are known to have happened. Compare the

incident produced two streams in the tradition: one without the block (the short text), and another which had undergone a correction that replaced but slightly dislocated the block (the Syriac text-form), in connection with which line 3 was detached and re-joined to line 2.

According to this theory, the omission must be of a different sort than the numerous other 'omissions' of the 'short text', which are characteristically much shorter, consisting of words, brief phrases, sometimes a sentence,[62] and would presumably have been deliberate. Deliberate omission does not recommend itself highly in this case in Homily 16. On the one hand, many smaller 'omissions' occur throughout the short text of the homilies; this pattern characterizes the short text and cannot generally be considered accidental. On the other hand, in the homilies edited by Boismard, an 'omission' of comparable length occurs in only one other place, Homily 17.[63] In that passage, the Syriac agrees with the Greek long text form against the short text (B and M).[64] So these two 'omissions' occupy their own class, and the case in Homily 16 is actually unique, because dislocations in the Syriac like that in Homily 16 occur nowhere else amongst the edited homilies. If the short text is secondary, the two lengthy omissions could be accidental and need not be the result of an editorial policy of abbreviation which must otherwise have been at work to produce the short text as it now is.

---

famous transposition of Ecclesiasticus 30:25-33:13a and 33:13b-36:16a, large enough to involve an entire quire (see *Sapientia Iesu filii Sirach*, ed. Joseph Ziegler [*Septuaginta Vetus Testamentum Graecum* 12.2; Göttingen, 1965], 267-93, and the discussion in Sidney Jellicoe, *The Septuagint and Modern Study* [Oxford, 1968], 307). Even modern editors can make this sort of mistake: the discovery of some Syriac Sahdona fragments by Brock ('A Further Fragment of the Sinai Sahdona MS', *Muséon* 81 [1968] 139-54) revealed that de Halleux had (understandably) ordered the text inaccurately (see *Martyrius (Sahdona), Oeuvres spirituelles*, vol. 1, *Livre de Perfection*, ed. de Halleux [CSCO, *Scriptores Syri* 86-9; Leuven, 1960-65], 200, 201, 214-15, 252-5).

[62] The very largest are about 30% the length of our passage; two occur in Homily 16, another in Homily 17, and one in Homily 29 (see Boismard, *Évangile pré-johannique*, 1.1.40, n.12; 42, n.5; 56, n.22; 2.1.120, n.14).

[63] The text involved is actually about 30% longer than that in Homily 16 (see Boismard, *Évangile pré-johannique*, 1.1.66).

[64] K is defective.

Therefore, the present state of the text in this passage can *a priori* be explained on the basis of either an original short Greek text-form or an original long Greek text-form, the Syriac text-form being secondary in either case. Respecting the three extant text-forms and the nature of their interrelationships, it becomes obvious that the fourth option, the positing of a hypothetical (lost) Greek text underlying them all (a text which must in turn explain the origin of each of the three extant forms) would actually multiply the complications and should be avoided.

The issues surrounding the dislocation are bound up with issues concerning the transmission history of the Greek HJn, which is complex and cannot be resolved here. Adequately explaining the variant forms of the single passage will require a complete analysis of the Greek tradition and a theory which comprehensively interprets the relationships between the diverse forms of the extant Greek text. Boismard's explanation is plausible, but the opposite explanation is just as plausible – perhaps more so, since Boismard's theory requires an elaborate multi-recensional development in both Greek and Syriac traditions.

It remains to adduce other evidence for or against the notion that a late version of the 'long text' supplanted an early Syriac version of the 'short text', and that the two translations have been interwoven to create the Syriac HJn inhabiting existing manuscripts.

c) *The Translation Style of the Dislocated Paragraph*

Boismard adduces such evidence, having to do with a Biblical citation in the dislocated paragraph. Before discussing this particular aspect of translation style, it will be helpful to study other more general stylistic features. If the dislocated paragraph is definitely the work of a second translator working many years after the first translator of the 'short text', then one would hope to find stylistic differences.

However, the translation style of the dislocated paragraph is consistent with that seen throughout the Syriac HJn.[65] The translator takes as his translation unit the Greek phrase or clause. In most clauses, the Syriac word order is quite close to that of the Greek (e.g.

[65] See the thorough analysis in Childers, 'Studies in the Syriac Versions', 1.215-60.

line 17), but in others he departs from the Greek order unnecessarily (e.g. line 6). His representation of particles and conjunctions is imprecise: he does not attempt to translate μέν (line 5); he uses ܕܝܢ (≈ δέ) for εἶτα (line 7); he adds -ܘ (≈ καί) to render a participle (line 12); and he adds ܡܟܝܠ ('thence') as a linking element (line 17). The methods of rendering participles, finite verbs, and infinitival phrases do not set the text apart stylistically; certain inconsistencies exist, but even these are consistent with the method used elsewhere. Line 8 provides an example of the occasionally less literal renderings which crop up in the Syriac HJn.

Not only are these features consistent with the overall style of HJn, but they constitute a style no different from that occurring in the immediate context (viz. lines 1, 2, 19-26), which belongs to the 'short text' and is supposed to be that of an earlier translation. The translation in these lines is not more literal – compare the interpretive phrase in line 24 or the use of ܕܝܢ (≈ δέ) for ἀλλά in line 23; nor is it less literal – compare the remarkably faithful word order in line 20. There is no indication that the dislocated paragraph has been rendered by a different translator.

It is possible to question the significance of the foregoing conclusion: What if two translators, working not many years apart, have employed very similar methods, so that the works of distinctive hands would not be of such a distinctive character? Or, has the possibility been overlooked that the acknowledged inconsistencies of style in the Syriac HJn are due precisely to the work of multiple hands? In response, it must first be remembered that the stylistic inconsistencies in HJn are no greater than in other Syriac translations of the same period, so it is unnecessary on grounds of style to suggest anything other than a single translator. Second, supposedly definite representatives of the hypothetical first and second translators have been studied (viz. the dislocated paragraph and its immediate context) but without discovering any distinguishing features of style. Finally, if it is to be maintained that the two translators have very similar styles or that the distinctive qualities of each have been effectively erased or heavily obscured in the process of fusion and revision, we are left to wonder where is the evidence for two translations and multiple Syriac layers.

The only stylistic evidence Boismard offers involves a minor variation in the citations of John 1:25.[66] The occurrences are in lines 2-3 and 13 above, but it will be helpful to compare their texts here to the Syriac Biblical versions:

John 1:25 (Homily 16)
2 .... τί οὖν βαπτίζεις;[67]
3 ⟦ εἰ σὺ οὐκ εἶ ὁ Χριστὸς οὔτε Ἠλίας οὔτε ὁ προφήτης;

13 τί οὖν βαπτίζεις εἰ σὺ οὐκ εἶ ὁ Χριστὸς; .... ⟧

B.L. Add. 14,561

2 .... ܘܡܢܐ ܡܥܡܕ ܐܢܬ.
3 ܐܢ ܐܢܬ ܠܐ ܐܝܬܝܟ ܗܘ ܡܫܝܚܐ ܘܠܐ ܐܠܝܐ ܘܠܐ ܗ̇ܘ ܢܒܝܐ.

13 ܡܢܐ ܗܟܝܠ ܡܥܡܕ ܐܢܬ. ܐܢ ܠܘ ܐܢܬ ܗܘ ܡܫܝܚܐ.

2 .... 'And why do you baptize,
3 if you are not the Christ, nor Elijah, nor the prophet?'

13 'Why then do you baptize, if you are not the Christ?'

Peshitta[68]

1 ܡܢܐ ܗܟܝܠ ܡܥܡܕ ܐܢܬ.
2 ܐܢ ܐܢܬ ܠܐ ܐܝܬܝܟ ܗܘ ܡܫܝܚܐ ܘܠܐ ܐܠܝܐ ܘܠܐ ܗܘ ܢܒܝܐ.

1 'Why then do you baptize,
2 if you are not the Christ, nor Elijah, nor the prophet?'

---

[66] Boismard, *Évangile pré-johannique,* 1.2.32-3.
[67] The text in double brackets (lines 3-18 in the Greek) is absent from B M K and given according to A D J R Syriac.
[68] The Peshitta text is from Philip Edward Pusey and George Henry Gwilliam, eds, *Tetraeuangelium sanctum juxta simplicem syrorum versionem* (Oxford, 1901).

Old Syriac (Sinaitic and Curetonian)[69]

1 ܠܡܢܐ *[1]ܗܟܝܠ ܡܥܡܕ. ܐܢܬ

2 ܐܠܐ ܗܘܝܬ *[2] ܡܫܝܚܐ ܐܦܠܐ ܐܠܝܐ ܘܐܦܠܐ ܢܒܝܐ.

1 'Why *[1]then do you baptize,
2 if you*[2] were neither Christ nor Elijah and not the prophet.'

*[1]Sinaitic resumes here
*[2]+ܐܢܬ(explicit subject pronoun) Sinaitic

Boismard draws attention to the fact that in the supposed 'short text' material of line 2, the translator has rendered τί οὖν with ܘܡܢܐ ('and why'), whereas within the paragraph in question (line 13) the Syriac has ܠܡܢܐ ܗܟܝܠ ('why then') in agreement with the Greek homily text, the Peshitta, and the Old Syriac. This is taken to show that different translators are at work, the earlier giving a distinctive form of the citation and the later giving a form accommodated to the norm of the Syriac Bible. Yet this conclusion takes no notice of the fact that this sort of 'discrepancy' between the Syriac and Greek happens frequently in this translation, especially where conjunctions are concerned,[70] and transitions involving τί are particularly vulnerable to expansion and alteration.[71] Biblical citations are not immune to the shaping power of the translator's style. Furthermore, Boismard chooses to ignore the rest of the Syriac homily text in line 13, which has a very distinctive form of the citation reminiscent of the supposedly distinctive style which he claims belongs to the first translator, associated with line 2 and the 'short text'. So, according to the controls brought by the translation itself and according to the method implied by Boismard's own observation, this particular

---

[69] The Old Syriac text is from Agnes Smith Lewis, ed., *The Old Syriac Gospels* (London, 1910).

[70] See Childers, 'Studies in the Syriac Versions', 1.225-6.

[71] Boismard himself notices a similar occurrence elsewhere in Homily 16, where ܘܡܢܐ ('and what?') renders τί οὖν in connection with a Biblical citation (see *ibid.*, 1.1.40; 1.2.33). See Childers, 'Studies in the Syriac Versions', 1.231, 251 for other examples.

occurrence does not offer substantial evidence for the theory of two translations.

2. *Old Syriac Citations and the 'First' Translation*
Boismard observes that translators of the period handle Biblical citations in three different ways: they may translate the Greek directly; they may rely on the Biblical version with which they are familiar; or they may adopt an intermediate method, respecting the variants of their Greek source texts but using the phraseology of a familiar version.[72] He also provides examples of each method from the Syriac text of HJn, highlighting the fact that the translator sometimes exhibits signs of Peshitta influence. Yet he assumes that a translator will have been influenced by only one Biblical version and that echoes of the Old Syriac in HJn indicate 'que cette traduction provient en fait deux niveaux différents'.[73]

Out of a total of nine homilies, Boismard draws attention to nine instances of citation in four of the homilies – although the instances involve only three passages of Scripture. One instance involves John 1:29 and the addition of ܗܐ ('behold'). Boismard is perhaps over-confident in detecting certain Old Syriac influence here,[74] but the possibility cannot be disregarded.[75]

---

[72] Boismard, *Évangile pré-johannique*, 1.2.27-30.
[73] *Ibid.*, 1.2.31.
[74] *Ibid.* Both Old Syriac manuscripts have the reading, but the reading also occurs in a few other Biblical witnesses (see Constantine von Tischendorf, ed., *Novum Testamentum Graece. Editio octava critica maior* [Leipzig, 1869-72], 1.750-01), presumably because of the parallel statements in 1:29, 35; more significantly, the translator of HJn adds ܗܐ ('behold') no fewer than three times in Homily 23 where the extant Greek has nothing parallel to it (although none of these other instances involve a Biblical citation). The translator naturally uses ܗܐ ('behold') for words related to ἰδού, but also consistently for καίτοι and even for μὴν on occasion.
[75] The reading also occurs in the translations of Titus of Bostra, *Contra Manichaeos*, 4.59 (ed. Paul Antony de Lagarde, *Titi Bostreni contra Manichaeos libri quatuor syriace* [Berlin, 1859]), and Eusebius of Caesarea, *Theophania*, 109 (ed. S. Lee, *Eusebius, Bishop of Caesarea, on the Theophania* [London, 1842]). Cf. Ignatius Ortiz de Urbina, ed., *Vetus evangelium syrorum et exinda excerptum Diatessaron Tatiani* (*Biblia Polyglotta Matritensia* 6; Madrid, 1967), 21, 253-5.

Stronger indications of the influence of a 'pre-Peshitta' Bible text involve two out of three citations of John 1:31 (Homilies 17 and 21) and one out of five citations of John 1:46 (Homily 16).[76] The latter enjoys not only the support of the Sinaitic Old Syriac, but also strong support in Ephrem, *Commentary on the Diatessaron*, iv.19.[77] In these instances, it appears virtually certain that the translator has been influenced by a text like that of the Old Syriac and like that upon which Ephrem relies.

After studying the Syriac more broadly (Homilies 6, 22, 23, 37, 62, 83, 84), it is possible even to add a few more such instances to those which Boismard detects (e.g. the citation of John 2:5 in Homily 22 and of John 11:16 and 11:18 in Homily 62).[78] These Old Syriac contacts are striking. However, the homilies are replete with Biblical citations, nearly all of which show no such influence. Whether appearing in 'short' or 'long text' material, they tend to follow a pattern observed throughout the Syriac HJn:[79] the normal pattern of the Syriac citations is to follow the Greek quite closely. Hence the Syriac citations are of value to textual critics concerned with the pre-medieval Greek text. However, Peshitta influence is not unusual, particularly for citations of verses upon which the homily in question is especially focused exegetically (e.g. Homily 84 is especially concerned with John 18:35-19:15). Even where Peshitta influence is obvious, the Syriac HJn often preserves the original scope of the citation more accurately than the medieval Greek text. These remarks only summarize broadly the contours of a pattern observable throughout the Syriac HJn, but it is the pattern's

[76] Cf. *Évangile pré-johannique*, 1.2.30-1.

[77] Ephrem, *Commentaire de l'évangile concordant. Texte syriaque, folios additionnels*, ed. Louis Leloir (Louvain, 1990). The Armenian is also in agreement (*Commentaire de l'évangile concordant. Version arménienne*, ed. Louis Leloir [CSCO 137, 145; Louvain 1953-54]).

[78] For details, see Childers, 'Studies in the Syriac Versions', 1.278-81, 289-90.

[79] Also, citations in the higher-numbered homilies are more likely to exhibit Peshitta influence than those in the lower. This is probably because the higher-numbered homilies quote more scripture in relation to the quantity of homily text and because the quotations are more systematic, thereby facilitating ready reference to a Biblical version on the part of the translator (see the detailed analysis in Childers, 'Studies in the Syriac Versions', 1.261-97).

regularity which determines why Boismard was able only to detect a few echoes of the Old Syriac.

Such a relatively tiny handful of distant echoes do not necessitate the identification of two separate translations. The echoes are neither strong nor consistent enough to build a pattern allowing separation into distinct groups of text. As in the Syriac Homilies on Matthew[80] and elsewhere, the influence of the Old Syriac version crops up sporadically in early Syriac literature and need not delineate separate hands. The early period of the development of Syriac Biblical versions is shrouded in a tantalizing haze of mystery typically broken for a moment by just such enigmatic occurrences. Also, translators are never absolutely consistent – even when they try to be, which is rare enough. When comparing Syriac translation styles and practices, particularly prior to the seventh century, a few exceptions are not sufficient to support a theory requiring distinct translations. If we are to believe that a more definite pattern no longer exists, save in faint and inconsistent echoes, only because of the normalizing hands of a later translator, we are still bereft of solid evidence and must again wonder where is the basis for a theory of multi-layer translation.

V. *Conclusions*

Only one aspect of Boismard's position remains to be discussed before these evaluations are brought to a conclusion. In the Greek tradition, witnesses to the 'short text' (Group 1) and manuscript D – which is supposed to show 'short text' influence – refer to the homilies with the term λόγος instead of ὁμιλία like 'long text' manuscripts.[81] The Syriac uses the term ܡܐܡܪܐ (*memra*, i.e. 'discourse, homily') for individual homilies and ܦܘܫܩܐ ('commentary') for the volume, which Boismard associates with the sense of λόγος in the 'short text' that consists largely of exegetical commentary.[82] Yet the two Syriac terms are completely standard; they are generic and so common in the Syriac exegetical and

[80] See Childers, 'Studies in the Syriac Versions', 1.174-83.
[81] See Boismard, *Évangile pré-johannique*, 1.2.26.
[82] *Ibid.*, 1.2.33-4.

homiletical genres that nothing can be made of their occurrence in HJn.

Boismard's work is useful for the limited information it presents about the Greek tradition and as a first step towards understanding the Syriac version, but his treatment of the Syriac is troubled by several problems. Beyond the simple errors, inconsistencies in the manner of presentation make it very difficult to use the Syriac evidence or even to feel confident that the editorial policies underlying the presentation are trustworthy. The textual affiliation of the Syriac in broad terms is clear enough, but the Greek tradition is so complex that it is impossible yet to be precise. Two things must happen before precision will be possible: first, the full texts of all the Greek homilies must be edited according to a much broader spectrum of the manuscript evidence; second, the whole extant Syriac text must be made available to facilitate a complete comparison.

As for Boismard's suggestion that the Syriac HJn consist of two separate translations, his is an unnecessarily complex accounting for the evidence. The position that two translations of the Syriac were made, or that the Syriac text consists of multiple layers, is unsubstantiated. The dislocated paragraph presents some problems, but it is easier to explain as a Greek dislocation underlying the Syriac rather than a Syriac dislocation; it cannot sustain the weight of a theory of thoroughgoing revision. Also, Boismard's disregard for translation technique not only compromises the usefulness of his edition but further brings his theory into question. Before one can understand fully the significance of the text of a translation, one must take into account features of translation technique. This is true for Biblical versions as well as Patristic versions. It is true of homily material as well as Biblical citations, although the latter often warrant special treatment because of the more widely diverse forces acting upon them.

Those wishing to use versional evidence responsibly must do more than refer casually to apparatus notes indicating generic correspondences. Editors of versions and texts must give careful attention to issues of style and acquaint the user with the problems pertaining to the texts in question, perhaps with the help of specialist studies alert to these issues.[83] Those labouring to extract Biblical citations from Patristic works know well the problems which can arise if one does not take into account the context of the citation, including the immediate textual context and the broader context of the author's manner of quoting, and so forth. However, when working with translations of Patristic texts, they must also pay heed to another dimension of context – that consisting of the features of the receptor language and the translator's own style. The danger is to treat Biblical citations as separate entities and to rely on the Greek Biblical text and the texts of Biblical versions for criteria of interpretation, ignoring important controls offered by the translation itself, such as the translation technique. Measured according to translation style, the two supposedly distinct texts ('short' and 'long') within the Syriac HJn appear to be identical. The presence of some diverse forms of citations do not negate this fact. The version exhibits a certain unevenness in style, but no more than is usual for Syriac translations of the period; essentially, we find a single, coherent method of translation – hardly compatible with a theory of multi-layer translations.

A proper application of controls shows that the support for Boismard's theory about the Syriac is so slender that it cannot uphold the bulk of his elaborate reconstruction. The significance of this is not inconsiderable, since his understanding of the Syriac underpins his views on the Greek tradition. If Boismard is to be rejected it remains to explain how the Syriac can agree so frequently with the 'short' Greek text, while agreeing mainly with the 'long text', when the translation style in the two sets of material is the same. The answer depends on the future publication of complete Greek and Syriac texts according to as broad a representation of the manuscript evidence as possible. But perhaps the best answer will turn out to be the simplest: that the pre-medieval Greek text on which the Syriac is based was not precisely like either of the two main

[83] E.g. Jan Joosten, *The Syriac Language of the Peshitta and Old Syriac Versions of Matthew* (*Studies in Semitic Languages and Linguistics* 22; Leiden, 1996); or in a different but related vein, Y. Maori, 'Methodological Criteria for Distinguishing Between Variant *Vorlage* and Exegesis in the Peshitta Pentateuch', in *The Peshitta as a Translation. Papers Read at the II Peshitta Symposium,* eds P.B. Dirksen and A. van der Kooij (*Monographs of the Peshitta Institute Leiden* 8; Leiden, 1995), 103-20.

streams surviving in Greek manuscripts, but more like the longer than the shorter. In other words, the Syriac has the form it does simply because its Greek source text had such a form.

At present, it can only be said that Boismard's explanation of the Syriac is unfounded and lends no support to his hypothetical reconstruction of the development of the Greek HJn. Instead, the oldest extant evidence (viz. the Syriac version) witnesses to a 'mixed' text in the late fifth or early sixth century and provides no evidence for the early text-form which Boismard postulates. In any case, it is clear that before we can read the Greek HJn with confidence we must resolve the issues of the Greek tradition and that doing so demands reference to the Syriac.

THE CONSTRUCTION OF BIBLICAL CERTAINTY: TEXTUAL OPTIMISM AND THE UNITED BIBLE SOCIETIES' *GREEK NEW TESTAMENT*[1]

K.D. CLARKE & K. BALES

1. *A Brief History of the United Bible Societies' Greek New Testament*

In 1955 work began on the United Bible Societies' first edition of *The Greek New Testament* (UBS^1), which was finally published in May 1966.[2] In comparison with other Greek editions of its day, the United Bible Societies' edition had several distinct features, including, in similar fashion to J.A. Bengel's 1734 Greek edition,[3] a letter-rating system that indicated the editorial committee's judgement regarding the certainty of those readings selected to represent the earliest biblical texts. Since 1966 the United Bible Societies' *Greek New Testament* has gone through various printings including a second edition (UBS^2; 1968), a third edition (UBS^3;

---

[1] This paper briefly summarizes and extends a number of arguments found in the much more detailed monograph by Kent D. Clarke entitled *Textual Optimism: A Critique of the United Bible Societies' Greek New Testament* (JSNT Suppl 138; Sheffield: Sheffield Academic Press, 1997). A warm thank you is extended to Sheffield Academic Press for their permission to reuse portions of this work.

[2] For various reviews of UBS^1, see M. Black, 'The Greek New Testament', *SJT* 19 (1966) 486-8; R.P. Markham, 'The Bible Societies' Greek Testament: The End of a Decade or Beginning of an Era?', *BT* 17 (1966) 106-13; Anonymous, 'Notes of Recent Exposition', *ExpTim* 77 (1966) 353-4; I.A. Moir, 'The Bible Societies' Greek New Testament', *NTS* 14 (1967) 136-43; and W.B. Wallis, 'An Evaluation of the Bible Societies' Text of The Greek New Testament', *Bulletin of the Evangelical Theological Society* 10 (1967) 111-13.

[3] See J.A. Bengel, *Novum Testamentum Graecum* (Tübingen: George Cottae, 1734). For a further summary of Bengel's text-critical methodology, see his still valued New Testament commentary *Gnomon Novi Testamenti* (2 vols.; ed. J. Steudel; Tübingen/London: David Nutt, ^{3}1850), § VIII, xv-xx.

1975), a third-corrected edition (UBS$^{3corr.}$; 1983), and most recently a fourth edition (UBS^{4}; 1993).

Major changes to UBS^{2} included forty-five alterations in the letter-rating system and five modifications of the text or punctuation.[4]

UBS^{3} contained a thorough revision of the Greek text and a partial revision of the textual apparatus, but J.K. Elliott identified the modification of letter-ratings which indicate textual certainty as perhaps the most significant alteration made to UBS^{3}: 'UBS 3rd edn is presented as a less confident text. The editors have occasionally downgraded the printed text where variants are shown by reducing the rating'.[5]

UBS$^{3corr.}$ was intended to act as an interim between UBS^{3} and UBS^{4}, and it was modified in order to more closely conform to NA^{26}. The letter-ratings remained identical to UBS^{3}.[6]

UBS^{4} eliminated approximately 300 variant units cited in the earlier UBS editions, and included approximately 285 new variant units thought to be of greater importance to the reader's understanding of the text's history and exegetical considerations.[7] One final modification made to UBS^{4}, and the issue of primary concern in this paper, is the redefinition of the various *A*, *B*, *C*, and *D* letter-rating levels and the subsequent re-evaluation of all 1437 sets of variants cited in the textual apparatus.

---

[4] For various reviews of UBS^{2}, see K. Aland, 'The Greek New Testament: Its Present and Future Editions', *JBL* 87 (1968) 179-86; J.K. Elliott, 'The United Bible Societies' Greek New Testament: An Evaluation', *NovT* 15 (1973) 278-300; and J.M. Ross, 'The United Bible Societies' Greek New Testament', *JBL* 95 (1976) 112-21.

[5] J.K. Elliott, 'The United Bible Societies' Greek New Testament: A Short Examination of the Third Edition', *BT* 30 (1979) 137-38. For other reviews of UBS^{3}, see *idem*, 'The Third Edition of the United Bible Societies' Greek New Testament', *NovT* 20 (1978) 242-77; and M. Black, 'The United Bible Societies' Greek New Testament Evaluated – A Reply', *BT* 28 (1977) 116-20.

[6] See J.K. Elliott's review of UBS$^{3corr.}$ in *NovT* 26 (1984) 377-9.

[7] The minor discrepancy between these figures and those given on page 2* of UBS^{4} is the result of the editorial committee using the term 'passages' which may include more than one letter-rated variant. For full details see Chapter 2, Section B of Clarke, *Textual Optimism*.

2. *A Numerical Survey of the UBS Letter-Ratings*

By means of the letters *A*, *B*, *C*, and *D* (more technically called 'evaluation of evidence letter-ratings') the UBS^4 editorial committee has sought to indicate the relative degree of certainty for readings chosen to represent the biblical text: *A* indicates that the text is certain, *B* indicates that the text is almost certain, *C* indicates that the committee had difficulty in deciding which variant to place in the text, and *D* indicates that the committee had great difficulty in arriving at a decision.[8]

Whereas Elliott characterized the text of UBS^3 as 'less confident' in the light of occasional and moderate letter-rating downgradings, by contrast UBS^4 exhibits remarkable letter-rating inflation and upgrades. A comparison of the distribution of these 'evaluation of evidence letter-ratings' throughout each of the five UBS editions makes this particularly clear. Table 1 shows the pattern of upgradings.

The figures in this Table not only suggest that UBS^4 has introduced an extensive upgrading to the critical apparatus letter-ratings for many variants, but further reveal, when each UBS edition is compared, several emerging and broader trends. UBS^1 and UBS^2 closely resemble each other, which is understandable given that they are the first two editions produced by the United Bible Societies and are only separated by a two-year time span. UBS^3 and the interim UBS$^{3corr.}$ are essentially identical; however, both editions show some small degree of change from UBS^1 and UBS^2. Revealing of the UBS^4 letter-rating upgrades are the distributions shown in the Totals given in Table 1. So, for example, among each of the UBS^1, UBS^2, UBS^3, and UBS$^{3corr.}$ editions, there is an average of 130 *A* rated variants. These 130 *A* rated variants in each of the first four editions make up approximately 9% of all the letter-rated variants in total. UBS^4 increases this number to 514 *A* rated passages, thereby constituting 36% of all letter-rated variants in this edition. This is an increase of approximately 384 *A* rated variants in UBS^4. Finally, *D* rated passages abruptly descend from an average of 134 in each of the first four editions (making up about 9% of all letter-rated variants) to only

[8] See UBS^4, 3* for these letter-rating designations.

Table 1 – Analysis of Variant Letter-Ratings (A, B, C, D)

Biblical Book	1st Edition Variants (UBS¹)					2nd Edition Variant (UBS²)					3rd Edition Variants (UBS³)					3rd Corr. Edition Variants (UBS³corr.)					4th Edition Variants (UBS⁴)				
	A	B	C	D	*Tot.*	A	B	C	D	*Tot.*	A	B	C	D	*Tot.*	A	B	C	D	*Tot.*	A	B	C	D	*Tot.*
Matthew	8	76	93	8	***185***	9	75	91	10	***185***	9	69	94	13	***185***	9	69	94	13	***185***	34	73	53	1	***161***
Mark	49	54	59	8	***170***	43	59	60	8	***170***	40	59	57	14	***170***	40	59	57	14	***170***	46	50	45	1	***142***
Luke	7	47	97	26	***177***	7	47	97	26	***177***	7	45	100	25	***177***	7	45	100	25	***177***	45	78	44	0	***167***
John	30	57	76	9	***172***	27	58	78	9	***172***	27	55	78	12	***172***	27	55	78	12	***172***	46	65	42	1	***154***
Acts	10	76	87	19	***192***	11	77	84	20	***192***	11	76	84	21	***192***	11	76	83	21	***191***	74	81	42	1	***198***
Romans	12	35	42	2	***91***	12	34	42	3	***91***	11	32	42	6	***91***	11	32	42	6	***91***	41	21	22	1	***85***
1 Corinthians	7	16	30	6	***59***	8	14	31	6	***59***	8	14	30	7	***59***	8	14	30	7	***59***	23	22	14	1	***60***
2 Corinthians	0	9	19	6	***34***	0	6	23	5	***34***	0	6	22	6	***34***	0	6	22	6	***34***	12	18	10	0	***40***
Galatians	1	12	5	4	***22***	1	12	5	4	***22***	1	11	5	5	***22***	1	11	5	5	***22***	16	3	9	0	***28***
Ephesians	0	12	8	3	***23***	0	11	9	3	***23***	0	11	9	3	***23***	0	11	9	3	***23***	15	12	8	0	***35***
Philippians	0	8	7	1	***16***	0	8	7	1	***16***	0	9	6	1	***16***	0	9	6	1	***16***	10	7	4	0	***21***
Colossians	1	5	11	5	***22***	1	5	11	5	***22***	1	5	11	5	***22***	1	5	11	5	***22***	8	12	8	0	***28***
1 Thessalonians	2	5	4	0	***11***	2	5	4	0	***11***	2	4	5	0	***11***	2	4	5	0	***11***	9	3	3	0	***15***
2 Thessalonians	0	2	7	0	***9***	0	2	7	0	***9***	0	2	7	0	***9***	0	2	7	0	***9***	3	3	2	0	***8***
1 Timothy	2	5	4	0	***11***	2	5	4	0	***11***	2	5	4	0	***11***	2	5	4	0	***11***	15	2	2	0	***19***
2 Timothy	0	2	6	0	***8***	0	2	6	0	***8***	0	2	6	0	***8***	0	2	6	0	***8***	2	5	1	0	***8***
Titus	0	2	2	0	***4***	0	2	2	0	***4***	0	2	2	0	***4***	0	2	2	0	***4***	2	1	1	0	***4***
Philemon	0	2	2	0	***4***	0	2	2	0	***4***	0	2	2	0	***4***	0	2	2	0	***4***	2	3	0	0	***5***
Hebrews	2	11	20	5	***38***	2	12	19	5	***38***	2	12	19	5	***38***	2	12	19	5	***38***	20	12	12	0	***44***
James	1	6	7	4	***18***	1	7	6	4	***18***	1	7	7	3	***18***	1	7	7	3	***18***	7	12	4	0	***23***
1 Peter	1	9	16	2	***28***	1	10	15	2	***28***	1	10	14	2	***27***	1	10	14	2	***27***	20	9	8	0	***37***
2 Peter	0	4	10	6	***20***	0	4	10	6	***20***	0	4	10	6	***20***	0	4	10	6	***20***	8	8	7	1	***24***
1 John	2	11	10	2	***25***	2	12	9	2	***25***	2	12	8	3	***25***	2	12	8	3	***25***	19	8	5	0	***32***
2 John	0	3	3	0	***6***	0	4	2	0	***6***	0	4	2	0	***6***	0	4	2	0	***6***	4	2	0	0	***6***
3 John	0	1	2	0	***3***	0	1	2	0	***3***	0	1	2	0	***3***	0	1	2	0	***3***	1	1	0	0	***2***
Jude	0	2	3	1	***6***	0	2	3	1	***6***	0	2	3	1	***6***	0	2	3	1	***6***	9	0	3	1	***13***
Revelation	1	14	72	5	***92***	1	14	72	5	***92***	1	14	71	6	***92***	1	14	71	6	***92***	23	30	18	1	***72***
Overall Totals =	***13***	***486***	***702***	***122***	***1446***	***13***	***490***	***701***	***125***	***1446***	***12***	***475***	***700***	***144***	***1445***	***12***	***475***	***699***	***144***	***1444***	***51***	***541***	***367***	***9***	***1431***
Overall Percent=	***9***	***34***	***49***	***8***	***100***	***9***	***34***	***48***	***9***	***100***	***9***	***33***	***48***	***10***	***100***	***9***	***33***	***48***	***10***	***100***	***36***	***38***	***26***	***1***	***101***

9 in UBS4 (constituting 1% of all letter-rated variants).[9] With a decrease of 125 *D* rated variants in UBS4, one should perhaps question the relevance of this entire *D* category. In effect, the United Bible Societies' evaluation of evidence drops from a four-point scale as in previous UBS editions to a three-point scale in UBS4.

3. *Variants that have been Newly Added or Dropped Out of UBS4*

Whereas UBS1 to UBS3corr. utilize a majority of the same variants, UBS4 eliminates a substantial number of these and replaces them with totally new variants (see Table 2). Some may assert that it is the addition of these new variants in UBS4 that gives rise to the escalating number of *A* or *B* rated passages, and to some extent this may hold true.[10] However, even taking this into consideration one cannot dismiss the fact that the newly added variants placed within UBS4 constitute only a small percentage of the actual fluctuations occurring in this edition.

Table 2 – Old and New Variants in UBS4

Variant Letter-Ratings	Total Variants in UBS4	Total Old Variants in UBS4	Total New Variants in UBS4
A	514 (36%)	346 (30%)	168 (59%)
B	541 (38%)	479 (42%)	62 (22%)
C	367 (26%)	312 (27%)	55 (19%)
D	9 (1%)	9 (1%)	0 (0%)
Totals =	1431	1146	285

It is also interesting to note the changes made to the letter-ratings of variants in UBS4 with a prior history in earlier UBS editions.

[9] These nine *D* rated passages are Mt 23:26; Mk 7:9; Jn 10:29; Acts 16:12; Rom 14:19; 1 Cor 7:34; 2 Pt 3:10; Jude 5; and Rev 18:3.

[10] There are several biblical books that may indicate this type of conclusion. Ephesians, 1 Timothy, 1 Peter, 1 John, and Jude are perhaps the more obvious ones.

Table 3 – Comparison of Variants in UBS3 / 3corr. and UBS4

Variant Letter-Ratings	Total Variants in UBS3 / 3corr.	Total Old Variants in UBS4	Change of Figure in UBS4
A	126 (9%)	346 (30%)	+220
B	475 (33%)	479 (42%)	+4
C	699 (48%)	312 (27%)	-387
D	144 (10%)	9 (1%)	-135
Totals =	1444	1146	N/A

Although the figures for 'newly added variants' have been eliminated from the UBS4 totals, the number of *A* rated variants or *A* letter-ratings still experiences a very large increase. The number of *B* rated variants or *B* letter-ratings remains similar between the editions, while the *C* and *D* rated variants or letter-ratings are significantly reduced.

A second category to be examined is the letter-rated variants that, although included in earlier UBS editions, have now been removed from UBS4. In spite of the fact that these variants are not included in UBS4, their exclusion provides us with an important insight into UBS4 as a whole. (See Table 4.)

Table 4 – Variants Dropped and Added in UBS4

Variant Letter-Ratings	Number of Variants Dropped in UBS4	Number of New Variants in UBS4
A	23 (8%)	168 (59%)
B	99 (33%)	62 (22%)
C	162 (54%)	55 (19%)
D	16 (5%)	0 (0%)
Totals =	300	285

4. *The United Bible Societies' Explanation for the Letter-Rating Upgrades*

What clarification, if any, is given by the United Bible Society to vindicate the comprehensive revisions of variant letter-ratings? On page v of the preface to UBS4, the following statement is made: 'The Committee also redefined the various levels in the evaluation of evidence on the basis of their relative degrees of certainty. Thus the evaluation of all the 1437 sets of variants cited in the apparatus have been completely reconsidered.' A closer look at these newly fashioned demarcations reveals the extent of variation that occurs between the first four UBS editions and UBS^4. The definitions for the *A*, *B*, *C*, and *D* letter-ratings are identical in UBS^1 to UBS$^{3corr.}$.[11] The letter *A* signifies that the text is virtually certain; the letter *B* indicates that there is some degree of doubt; the letter *C* means that there is a considerable degree of doubt whether the text or the apparatus contains the superior reading; and the letter *D* shows that there is a very high degree of doubt concerning the reading selected for the text. Turning to UBS^4, we have already seen that the letter *A* indicates the text is certain; the letter *B* indicates that the text is almost certain; the letter *C*, however, indicates that the committee had difficulty in deciding which variant to place in the text; and the letter *D*, which occurs only rarely, indicates that the committee had great difficulty in arriving at a decision.[12] The original ratings, defined on the basis of their 'relative degrees of certainty', have been redefined on the basis of their 'degree of doubt'.

Despite the vague terminology used by the UBS editorial committee, it should likely be conceded that the various levels in the evaluation of evidence have actually been redefined one step higher. Thus, *A* ratings have increased in their level of confidence from 'almost (virtually) certain' to 'certain', while *B* ratings have increased from a less confident 'some degree of doubt' to a more confident 'almost certain' etc. It should, then, be harder for variants to maintain their letter-rating as prescribed in the earlier UBS editions, but not only do many of these variants maintain their old letter-rating, a very large number of them actually move upward to a new letter grade. Nor is this process consistent. There is an increase in the number of *A* and *B* rated passages, but also a decrease in the number of *C* and *D* rated passages.

5. *Conclusion*

Given UBS^4's radical departure from all previous editions in respect to its ascription of *A*, *B*, *C*, and *D* letter-ratings, and subsequently the

---

[11] See pp. x-xi of UBS^1 and UBS^2, and pp. xii-xiii of UBS^3 and UBS$^{3corr.}$.
[12] See p. 3* of UBS^4.

edition's new and superior degree of textual certainty, the explanation provided by the editorial committee not only fails to adequately justify the UBS4 letter-rating upgrades but also appears to be logically fallacious. One would think that a revision of this nature and extent would be clearly outlined and founded upon strong theoretical support. To be simply told by the committee that the letter-rating upgrades, and consequently a much more certain Greek text, are the result of a redefinition of the various levels in the evaluation of evidence hardly satisfies the requirements of a critical edition which, according to A.E. Housman, is an inappropriate name if an editor 'is allowed to fling his opinions in the reader's face without being called to account and asked for his reasons'.[13] As it now stands, an unfounded letter-rating upgrade appears to have taken place and may instil in users of UBS4 a false sense of textual optimism.

[13] A.E. Housman, *M. Manilii Astronomicon* (5 vols.; London: Richards Press, 1903-30), 5.xxxiii.

USING PROBABILITY THEORY AS A KEY TO UNLOCK TEXTUAL HISTORY

G.P. FARTHING

Orientation

I wish to find out what can be known about the history of small parts of the New Testament tradition. I leave an understanding of the whole to later generations. I believe much can be learnt from 'manuscript combinations'.

A 'manuscript combination' is a multiple list showing which manuscript(s) support each of the variations in the wording found at some point in the text being examined.

Take the following piece of text (Luke 1.17):

και αυτος προελευσεται ενωπιον αυτου / ℵ A B^2 D W Θ Ψ 053 $f^{1.13}$ 𝔐 co
και αυτος προσελευσεται ενωπιον αυτου / B* C L al
και αυτος προπορευσεται ενωπιον αυτου / 945 pc

The variation in the third word produces the following manuscript combination:

Luke 1.17 / προελευσεται :: προσελευσεται :: προπορευσεται /
ℵ A B^2 D W Θ Ψ 053 $f^{1.13}$ 𝔐 co :: B* C L al :: 945 pc

In the theoretical examples that I give below I will not offer any representation of the text of these manuscripts, nor of the position of variations in the theoretical text, but confine comments to the manuscript combinations which arise. Shorn of content and position information, important in real examples, the manuscript combination becomes simply a multiple set of sigla as follows:

ℵ A B^2 D W Θ Ψ 053 $f^{1.13}$ 𝔐 co :: B* C L al :: 945 pc

The example above has three different forms of the text; in my theoretical examples I will restrict the discussion to texts which show only two different forms. This is done only to simplify and shorten the explanations as the theory can deal equally well with multiple text forms.

I next ask: 'What manuscript combinations can arise from various patterns of textual copying?' The first pattern of textual copying arises from the creation of unique irreversible changes.

Unique Irreversible Changes

Each unique irreversible change, by definition, occurs only once in the whole tradition and is never spontaneously corrected.

What manuscript combinations arise from unique irreversible changes? This depends on the history of the manuscripts involved. I will examine the effect of unique irreversible changes in two simple histories or stemmata.

Diagram 1

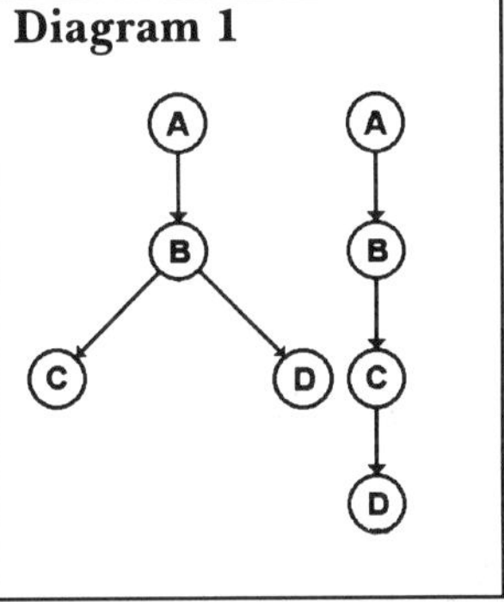

In the star form stemma, Diagram 1, left, C and D are separate copies of B which is a copy of the original A.

In the linear stemma, Diagram 1, right, D is a copy of C which is a copy of B which is a copy of the original A.

i) (Diagram 2) If a unique irreversible change is made in copying the text of A to produce B, this changed text will also appear in C and D. Since the changes we are considering are irreversible, the reading of A cannot spontaneously reappear in C or D. The resulting manuscript combination has to be A :: B C D. This applies to both stemma forms. The manuscript combination can be seen from the diagram by placing the manuscripts connected by solid lines on one side of the double colon divider and A (in this diagram on its own) on the other.

ii) (Diagram 3) If a unique irreversible change occurs in the copying of C from B the manuscript combination will be different in each stemma. In the star form stemma only C will have the new form as D will have to follow B; a unique irreversible change cannot be repeated in two copying events (e.g. B-C and B-D). In the linear stemma D will follow C as the reading of A and B cannot spontaneously reappear in D. Thus in the star form stemma a unique irreversible change in B-C must produce A B D :: C and in the linear form stemma it must produce A B :: C D.

iii) (Diagram 4) If a unique irreversible change is made in the copying of D from its parent the manuscript combination will be the same in both stemma. D will appear in opposition to the other three manuscripts as it has no children to pass its new reading to: A B C :: D.

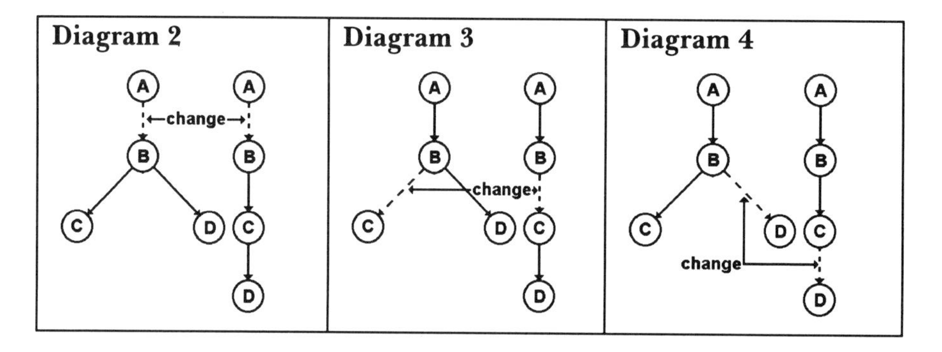

Having looked at all the possible copying events we may summarise the possible manuscript combinations for each stemma arising from unique irreversible changes:

Table 1			
Star Form Stemma		**Linear Form Stemma**	
A :: B C D	**possible (i above)**	A :: B C D	**possible (i above)**
A B :: C D	impossible	A B :: C D	**possible (ii above)**
A B C :: D	**possible (iii above)**	A B C :: D	**possible (iii above)**
A B D :: C	**possible (ii above)**	A B D :: C	impossible
A C :: B D	impossible	A C :: B D	impossible
A C D :: B	impossible	A C D :: B	impossible
A D :: B C	impossible	A D :: B C	impossible

The result here is that where changes are unique and irreversible the form of the underlying stemma is betrayed by the resulting manuscript combinations. Two restrictions apply. First, if very few manuscript combinations are considered many details of the stemma will be invisible. Second, if our manuscripts are a small selection of what was once a much larger group we can, at best, only recover how the extant manuscripts relate to one another (with just a few intermediaries inferred to have existed where the data justifies such conclusions). We can know nothing about most lost manuscripts. This second restriction will apply in all work with New Testament manuscripts.

Unique irreversible changes support the observation that 'community of error implies community of origin'. Where the textual critic can identify changes in the text which are likely to have occurred just once and are unlikely to have allowed simple correction to the original text he/she may use such changes to produce a stemma or history of the texts involved. However the identification of such changes is not a simple matter.

Any change in the text which seems a clear improvement in style or 'clarification' of theology can appear so to several scribes on several occasions and may not be unique.

Any simple error, say of homoioteleuton, may be committed by several scribes, especially from the same manuscript.

'Strange' or 'silly' errors may be more readily identifiable as unique irreversible changes, such as reading the genealogy in Luke across the columns it was written in instead of down them, thus giving nearly everyone the wrong parent. While such errors may not occur more than once they are easily detectable and reversible.

In practice I suspect that it is very difficult to find what are probably unique irreversible changes. It has to be an art rather than a science as one needs to enter, as far as possible, into the mind of the scribes of the time. I find I cannot proceed along this path with any confidence myself. Rich blessings on those who are able to do so.

Non-Unique Reversible Changes

Each non-unique reversible change, by definition, may occur more than once in the tradition and occasionally may be spontaneously corrected.

If a non-unique reversible change occurs in the copying event A-B of the star form stemma we cannot be sure of the resulting manuscript combination until the behaviour of the text in the copying events B-C and B-D is determined.

i) (Diagram 5) In the star form stemma, if the new text form in B is copied unchanged to C and D the resulting manuscript combination is A :: B C D.

ii) (Diagram 6) In the star form stemma, if in copying C from B the text of A is restored in C while D follows B the manuscript combination A C :: B D results.

iii) (Diagram 7) In the star form stemma, if the text of A reappears in D but C follows B the manuscript combination A D :: B C results.

iv) (Diagram 8) In the star form stemma, if the text of A reappears in both C and D the manuscript combination A C D :: B results.

Each of these last three manuscript combinations can arise only if a change can be reversed at one or more subsequent copying events.

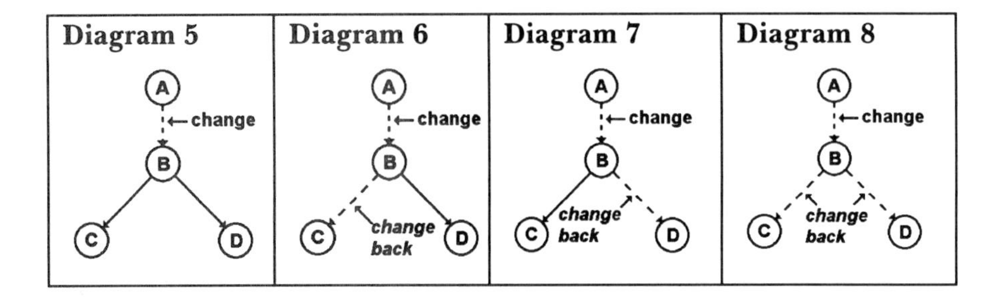

Next I consider the possibilities if A and B share the original reading. Again the resulting manuscript combinations depend on subsequent changes in copying C and D.

v) (Diagram 9) In the star form stemma, if the text of A and B is faithfully transmitted to C but changed in copying D, the result is a manuscript combination A B C :: D.

vi) (Diagram 10) In the star form stemma, if the text of A and B is faithfully transmitted to D but changed in copying C, the result is a manuscript combination A B D :: C.

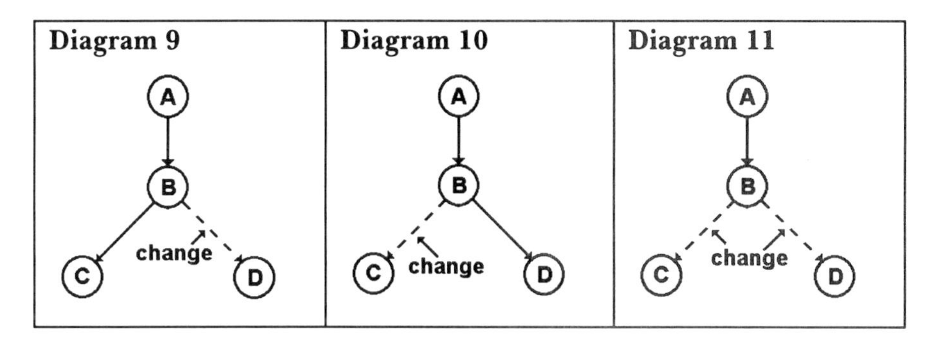

vii) (Diagram 11) In the star form stemma, if the text of A and B is changed in copying both C and D (allowed because this form of change is non-unique), the result is a manuscript combination A B :: C D.

viii) (Diagram 12) In the linear form stemma, if the text of A is changed in copying B but this new text is then copied unchanged to C and D, the resulting manuscript combination is A :: B C D.

ix) (Diagram 13) In the linear form stemma, if the text of A is changed in copying B and then restored in copying C, with D following C, the manuscript combination A C D :: B results.

x) (Diagram 14) In the linear form stemma, if the text of A is changed in copying B, this new text is then copied unchanged to C but the text of A is restored in copying D, the resulting manuscript combination is A D :: B C.

xi) (Diagram 15) In the linear form stemma, if the text of A is changed in copying B and then restored in copying C and again changed in copying D (so that it agrees with B), the manuscript combination A C :: B D results.

Each of these last three manuscript combinations can arise only if a change can be reversed at one or more subsequent copying events.

xii) (Diagram 16) In the linear form stemma if the text of A is faithfully transmitted to B and C but changed in copying D, the result is a manuscript combination A B C :: D.

xiii) (Diagram 17) In the linear form stemma if the text of A is faithfully transmitted to B but is changed in copying C and this reading faithfully transmitted to D, the result is a manuscript combination A B :: C D.

xiv) (Diagram 18) In the linear form stemma if the text of A is faithfully transmitted to B but is changed in copying C and then reverts to that of A and B in copying D, the result is a manuscript combination A B D :: C.

Diagram 12	Diagram 13	Diagram 14	Diagram 15	Diagram 16	Diagram 17	Diagram 18
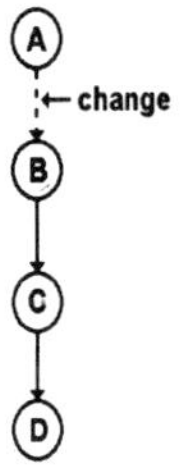 A ←change B C D	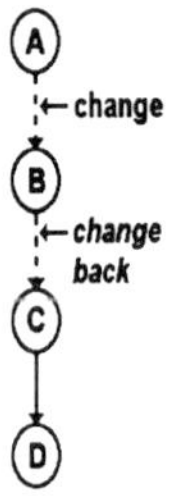 A ←change B ←change back C D	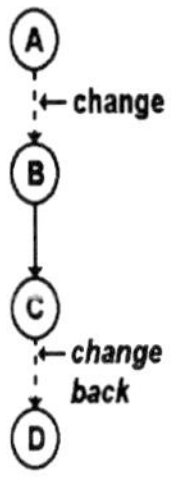 A ←change B C ←change back D	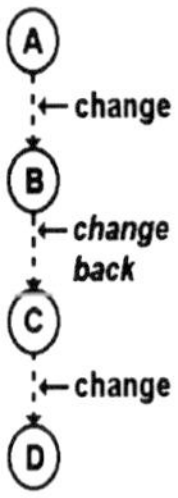 A ←change B ←change back C ←change D	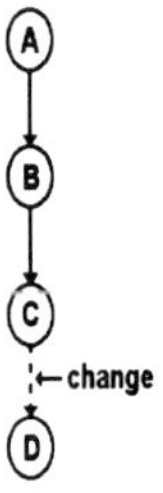 A B C ←change D	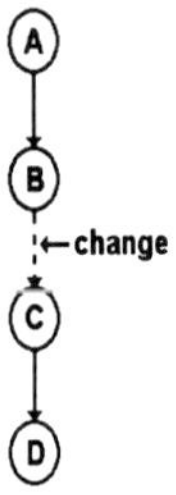 A B ←change C D	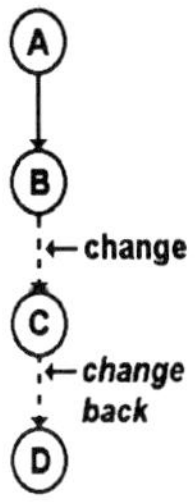 A B ←change C ←change back D

Having looked at all the possible copying events with non-unique reversible changes we may summarise the possible manuscript combinations for each stemma.

Table 2			
Star Form Stemma		**Linear Form Stemma**	
A :: B C D	**possible (i above)**	A :: B C D	**possible (viii above)**
A B :: C D	**possible (vii above)**	A B :: C D	**possible (xiii above)**
A B C :: D	**possible (v above)**	A B C :: D	**possible (xii above)**
A B D :: C	**possible (vi above)**	A B D :: C	**possible (xiv above)**
A C :: B D	**possible (ii above)**	A C :: B D	**possible (xi above)**
A C D :: B	**possible (iv above)**	A C D :: B	**possible (ix above)**
A D :: B C	**possible (iii above)**	A D :: B C	**possible (x above)**

The result is that where changes are non-unique and reversible all the manuscript combinations are possible for both underlying stemmata.

The problem, as I see it, is that I believe that nearly all, if not all, changes to the New Testament text are essentially non-unique and reversible. If I am correct the presence or absence of particular manuscript combinations is of no help in finding the stemma underlying the relationships of a group of manuscripts.

It is, of course, still open to workers to seek instances of unique irreversible changes but my mind has gone in another direction.

Possibility and Probability

Consider the manuscript combination A B D :: C, which is possible for both the star form and linear form stemmata above if changes are non-unique and reversible. In the star form stemma this manuscript combination is formed by the reading of A being faithfully transmitted to B and then to D while a change occurs in copying C; one change in text is needed to achieve this manuscript combination. However in the linear stemma a different sequence is involved; the reading of A is transmitted faithfully to B but a change now occurs in copying C with a change back to the original text in copying D so that D's text now matches that of A and B. In the linear form of stemma two independent changes are needed to achieve this manuscript combination.

Both stemmata have the *possibility* of forming the manuscript combination A B D :: C but consideration will suggest that the events in the star form stemma are more *probable* than those in the linear stemma. My reasoning is simply that the most probable result of copying any portion of the text is that the text will be copied without change; most of our text is copied without change, only a small part is changed at each copying. Thus it seems to me sensible to suggest that a scenario which involves only one change will be much more *probable* than a scenario involving two independent changes.

Such a distinction will not apply to all manuscript combinations, such as A :: B C D which requires only one change in both stemmata, but it will apply to some.

Since an event being less probable means it will happen less often (and if it is much less probable it should happen much less often), might it be possible to distinguish the underlying stemma of a set of manuscripts by the relative frequency of manuscript combinations rather than the presence or absence of particular combinations, even if the changes are non-unique reversible changes? I believe it is possible to some extent and will now attempt to show this.

A Reminder of Simple Probability Theory
The probability of an event happening is represented algebraically by a letter 'p' and must have a value between 0 and 1. A probability of 0 means that the event cannot happen, a probability of 1 that it will happen in all instances. A probability of less than 1 but more than 0 means that the event will sometimes happen and sometimes not. If one attempts to make an event, of probability p, happen N times it will happen approximately p x N times and not happen approximately (1 - p) x N times. The probability of an event not happening, which is 1 - p, is often signified by the letter q; thus q = 1 - p and p = 1 - q.

Since a dice has six faces the probability of throwing a dice and getting any particular number is 1/6 or $0.16666\dot{6}$. A six is no more difficult than any other number. If you throw a dice 100 times it will show five approximately $0.16666\dot{6}$ of 100 times, that is 17 times (real events must happen a whole number of times!).

The probability of a sequence of events is the product of the probabilities of the events separately. The probability of throwing a six (or any other specific number) is $0.16666\dot{6}$. The probability of not throwing a six (or any other specific number) is 5/6 or $0.83333\dot{3}$. Thus the probability of throwing a six followed by 'not a six' is $0.16666\dot{6} \times 0.83333\dot{3}$ or $0.13888\dot{8}$.

When one says that the number of times something happens is approximately so and so, the degree of approximation is not arbitrary. The amount by which the frequency of the event can wander from the normal is usually fixed at one or two, sometimes as much as three 'standard deviations'. If the probability of an individual event is p, the probability of it not happening is q and the number of times it is attempted is N then one standard deviation is $\sqrt{(p \times q \times N)}$. Thus throwing a six 100 times ($p = 0.16666\dot{6}$; $q = 0.83333\dot{3}$; $N = 100$) has a spread of two or three times a standard deviation of $\sqrt{(0.16666\dot{6} \times 0.83333\dot{3} \times 100)} = 3.72678$. I normally use two standard deviations so the number of sixes in 100 throws is $16.66666 \pm (2 \times 3.72678)$ which is between 23.45 and 8.55, or between 23 and 9 in whole numbers. Thus if one threw a dice 100 times and six came up 10 times there would be no reason to suppose there was anything wrong with the dice, even if a friend threw the same dice 100 times and six came up 22 times. But if the six came up once for you and 90 times for your 'friend' you would have sure grounds for complaint.

Copying Described as a System of Probabilities

It is quite straightforward to use probabilities to describe a scribe at work. The work being copied is considered as a known number of changeable elements.

There are considerable theoretical issues involved in a fuller description of just what these changeable elements are and how many there would be in a given work. A discussion of these issues would be a considerable distraction from the present argument and so I ask the reader to allow that there will be a definite number of elements considered and copied by the scribe, whether these be whole or part words, phrases, clauses or sentences – or more likely a complex combination of them all.

During the copying of a new manuscript (one particular copying event) the scribe reads (or hears) and writes each element in order. Mostly what is written is what was read, occasionally it is different to what was read. If there are N elements and a probability of p of each element being changed (and thus a probability of 1 - p of each element not being changed) then:

N x p elements will be changed in copying the new manuscript and

N x (1 - p) elements will not be changed.

It is useful to anchor these figures in visible facts by noting that the number of elements changed in copying the new manuscript is simply the number of differences between the new manuscript and its original. This figure can be found directly by careful comparison of the two manuscripts.

One objection that might be raised at this point is that the scribe does not produce a new manuscript by randomly selecting things to change. Changes occur through many complex causes such as defects of sight, carelessness, stylistic opinions and so on. Such an objection would arise from a misunderstanding of what is being claimed. The use of a probability describes only *how many* changes are likely, it makes no statement about *why* changes occur. The *results* of throwing a dice can be described using a probability equation as I did above, but the *reason* for the dice coming up with a particular number on each occasion is to do with the exact pressure on it when it was thrown, the exact direction of that pressure, the air currents present, the distance to the table top and no doubt much more. The probability equation knows nothing about these practicalities, nor does it need to. Equally the probability equation describing a copying event does not need to know about *why* changes occur (they are important in the whole work of textual criticism, but simply not pertinent to this approach) but rather asks *how many* changes occur. It is exactly because my method looks at frequencies of combinations, rather than reasons for changes, that it may have value in offering independent insight into the copying process.

The observation that the number of changes in a copying event (which equals the number of differences between the original and copy manuscripts) is given by p x N is of no help if just two manuscripts are considered. If only two manuscripts are in view then neither p nor N can be found because there is not enough information.

I now consider what happens if our copy is itself copied by a scribe with no knowledge of the original. For ease of description I call the original manuscript A, the first direct copy of it B, and the direct copy of B I call C. The number of elements being copied is N for all manuscripts. This would appear to be untrue where an element in, for instance, A is omitted in, for instance, B. But this element is potentially present in all, simply actually present in one and actually absent in another. There is no difference, I believe, between allowing an element of form 'x' in some manuscripts to have form 'y' in others, and allowing an element whose form is the presence of a word or words in some manuscripts and whose form is the absence of that word or those words in others.

The probability of each element in A changing when B is copied is p[AB] and the probability of each element in B changing when C is copied is p[BC]. There is no reason to suppose that p[AB] and p[BC] will be the same. If different scribes are involved these probabilities might be very different.

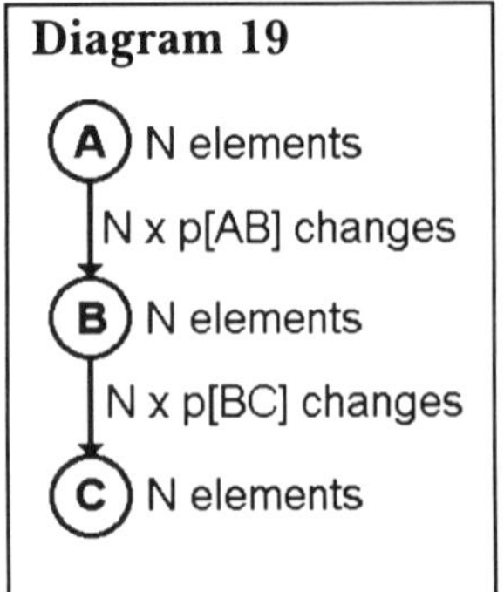

The number of changes in copying B from A will be the number of elements in the work (N) multiplied by the probability of change (p[AB]) which is represented as N x p[AB]. Similarly for copying C from B the changes will be N x p[BC] in number. (See Diagram 19.)

This copying process can be shown in a more detailed diagram as changes in text elements where the original form is represented by the capital letter ‘O’ and the alternate, or error, form represented by the lower case ‘e’.

Diagram 20

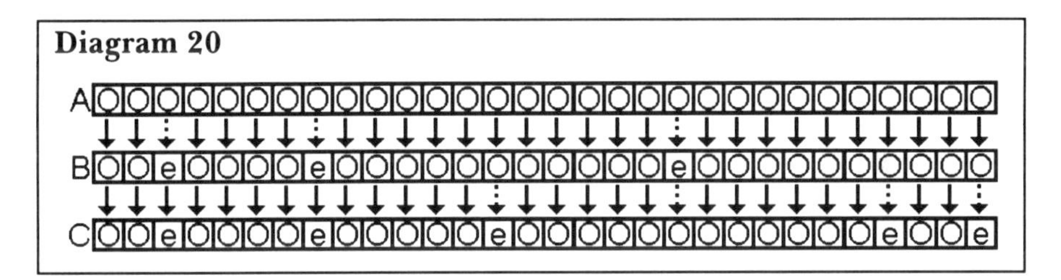

Sometimes a change occurs in copying B from A (there are three such changes in Diagram 20) and sometimes in copying C from B (there are four such changes in Diagram 20). In one case, about two thirds of the way along, one element changes in both copyings so that C agrees with A against an error in B. Thus A differs from B in three places, B differs from C in four places but A differs from C in only five places because of the element which changes on both copyings.

With these definitions it is straightforward to calculate the frequency of each manuscript combination that is possible for these three manuscripts. I choose to look at manuscript combinations because I find them the most informative aspect of the data which describes manuscript relationships.

The manuscript combination A :: B C is formed by a change in an element of the text during the copying of B from A and then no change in that same element when C is copied from B (see Diagram 21).

The probability of a change in copying B from A is p[AB]. The probability of no change in copying C from B is (1 - p[BC]). The number of elements is N. Thus among N elements the total number of times elements will change when B is copied but not when C is copied is the product of these three numbers:

Frequency of A :: B C = N x p[AB] x (1 - p[BC])

Please note that the resulting figure, and those given below, are subject to some latitude as described above.

The manuscript combination A B :: C is formed by no change in elements of the text during the copying of B from A but then a change when C is copied from B (see Diagram 22).

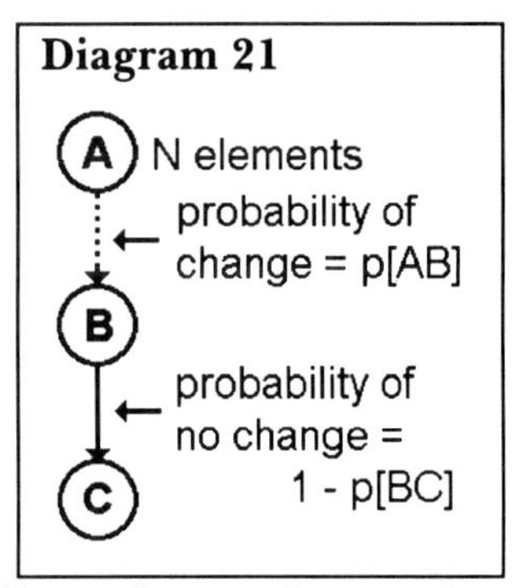

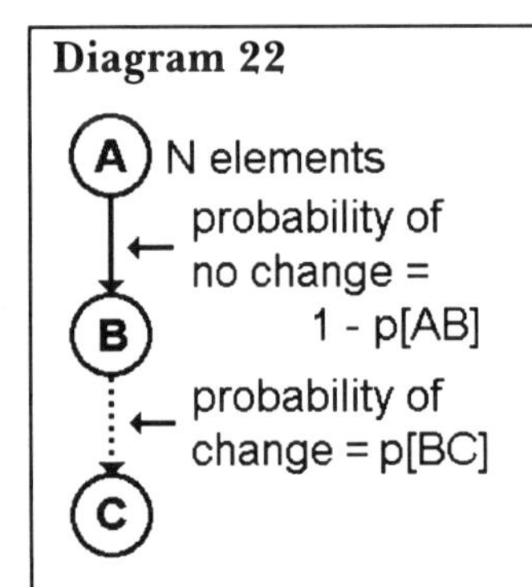

The probability of no change in copying B from A is (1 - p[AB]). The probability of a change in copying C from B is p[BC]. The number of elements is N. Thus among N elements the total number of times elements will not change when B is copied but change when C is copied is the product of these three numbers:
Frequency of A B :: C = N x (1 - p[AB]) x p[BC]

The manuscript combination A C :: B is formed by a change in an element of the text during the copying of B from A and then a change back to the original form when C is copied from B (see Diagram 23). The probability of a change in copying B from A is p[AB]. The probability of a change in copying C from B is p[BC]. The number of elements is N. Thus among N elements the total number of times elements will change when B is copied and when C is copied is the product of these three numbers:

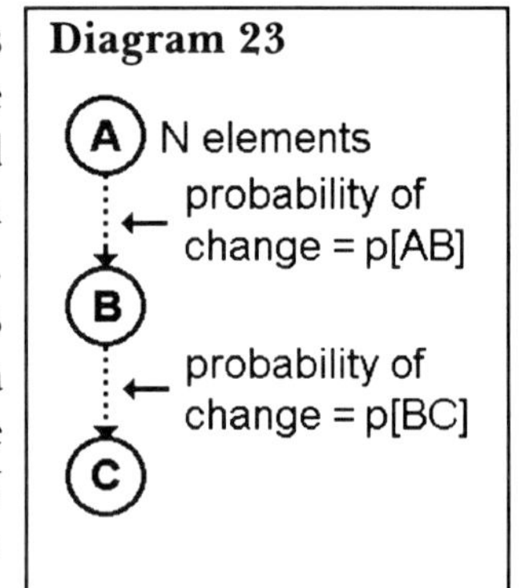

Frequency of A C :: B = N x p[AB] x p[BC]

This last combination A C :: B is formed by one or more elements of the text being changed and this change then being reversed. Since I believe real changes of the New Testament text to be non-unique and reversible I allow this behaviour in my model. Since, in order to simplify the argument presented, I have allowed each element of the text to have only two forms there is no examination of the situation where the second change (in copying C from B) produces a third form of the element. Having restricted my argument to two forms the second change must return the element to its original form.

I do not attempt to show the frequency of the manuscript combination where all three manuscripts agree because, while it can be calculated from the theoretical model, it cannot in reality be counted. The number of times two or more similar texts agree is very high indeed, if one considers every way in which even two words might differ as indicating the number of ways in which two identical words do in fact agree.

It might make matters clearer if I put real and possible figures to these formulae. I suggest that in copying B from A the scribe makes 75 errors or changes. I suggest that in copying C from B the next scribe makes 120 changes. I suggest that the number of elements in the text might be 3000. Thus the probability of a change in copying B (p[AB]) is 75 ÷ 3000 or 0.025. The probability of a change in copying C (p[BC]) is 120 ÷ 3000 or 0.04. Then:

Frequency of

A :: B C	= N x p[AB] x (1 - p[BC])	= 3000 x 0.025 x 0.96	= 72 ± 16.76
A B :: C	= N x (1 - p[AB]) x p[BC])	= 3000 x 0.975 x 0.04	= 117 ± 21.21
A C :: B	= N x p[AB] x p[BC]	= 3000 x 0.025 x 0.04	= 3 ± 3.46

In one respect these combination figures reflect the information we started with. The number of differences between A and B (which are shown in the manuscript combinations A :: B C and A C :: B) is probably 72 plus 3 which equals 75 as stated. Equally the number of differences between B and C (which are shown in the manuscript combinations A C :: B and A B :: C) is probably 3 plus 117 which equals 120 as stated.

In another respect we have learnt that approximately three elements in the text will change in the copying of B from A and then change back in the copying of C from B. The characterisation of the changes as non-unique and reversible allows the manuscript combination A C :: B; the characterisation of the text as N elements with a probability of change p allows control of the frequency of this combination. Inspection of a real group of manuscripts would show whether any form of this model accurately describes the relationships of those manuscripts.

The degree of latitude in the frequency of the manuscript combination A C :: B is interesting in that it means that this combination could occur as little as zero times or as many as six times (seven is not entirely improbable).

Distinguishing Possible Stemmata by Frequency of Manuscript Combinations

My earlier discussion was in terms of manuscript combinations occurring in two simple, but different, stemmata – one linear and the other a star form. I will now show how the differences in form between these stemmata show up in manuscript combinations.

Diagram 24

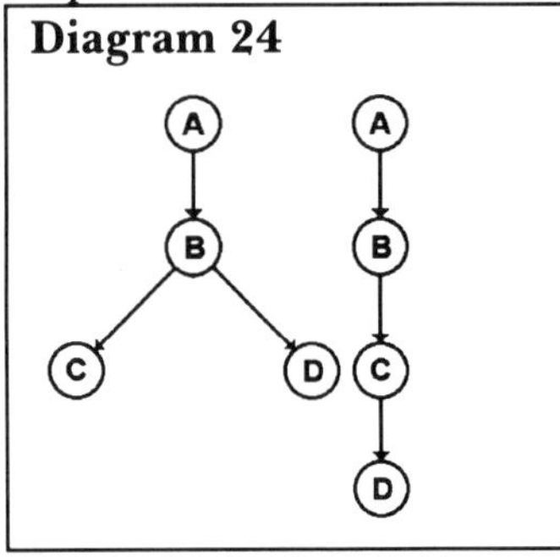

I begin with the two stemmata in Diagram 24. I assume there to be 3000 elements in each manuscript (N = 3000). I assume that in copying B, 75 changes are made (therefore p[AB] = 75/3000 = 0.025). I assume that in copying C, 120 changes are made (therefore p[BC] = 120/3000 = 0.04). I assume that in copying D, 30 changes are made (therefore p[BD] in the star form stemma and p[CD] in the linear form stemma = 30/3000 = 0.01).

The working for each manuscript combination is shown below with a table to summarise the results.

Table 3

Star Form Stemma manuscript combination frequencies:	
A :: B C D = N x p[AB] x (1 - p[BC]) x (1 - p[BD])	= 3000 x 0.025 x 0.96 x 0.99 = 71.28 ± 16.68
A B :: C D = N x (1 - p[AB]) x p[BC] x p[BD]	= 3000 x 0.975 x 0.04 x 0.01 = 1.17 ± 2.16
A B C :: D = N x (1 - p[AB]) x (1 - p[BC]) x p[BD]	= 3000 x 0.975 x 0.96 x 0.01 = 28.08 ± 10.55
A B D :: C = N x (1 - p[AB]) x p[BC] x (1 - p[BD])	= 3000 x 0.975 x 0.04 x 0.99 = 115.83 ± 21.11
A C :: B D = N x p[AB] x p[BC] x (1 - p[BD])	= 3000 x 0.025 x 0.04 x 0.99 = 2.97 ± 3.45

A C D :: B = N x p[AB] x p[BC] x p[BD]	= 3000 x 0.025 x 0.04 x 0.01 = 0.03 ± 0.35
A D :: B C = N x p[AB] x (1 - p[BC]) x p[BD]	= 3000 x 0.025 x 0.96 x 0.01 = 0.72 ± 1.70
Linear Form Stemma manuscript combination frequencies:	
A :: B C D = N x p[AB] x (1 - p[BC]) x (1 - p[CD])	= 3000 x 0.025 x 0.96 x 0.99 = 71.28 ± 16.68
A B :: C D = N x (1 - p[AB]) x p[BC] x (1 - p[CD])	= 3000 x 0.975 x 0.04 x 0.99 = 115.83 ± 21.11
A B C :: D = N x (1 - p[AB]) x (1 - p[BC]) x p[CD]	= 3000 x 0.975 x 0.96 x 0.01 = 28.08 ± 10.55
A B D :: C = N x (1 - p[AB]) x p[BC] x p[CD]	= 3000 x 0.975 x 0.04 x 0.01 = 1.17 ± 2.16
A C :: B D = N x p[AB] x p[BC] x p[CD]	= 3000 x 0.025 x 0.04 x 0.01 = 0.03 ± 0.35
A C D :: B = N x p[AB] x p[BC] x (1 - p[CD])	= 3000 x 0.025 x 0.04 x 0.99 = 2.97 ± 3.45
A D :: B C = N x p[AB] x (1 - p[BC]) x p[CD]	= 3000 x 0.025 x 0.96 x 0.01 = 0.72 ± 1.70

The following table compares the frequencies of each manuscript combination rounded to the nearest whole number and without the figure indicating how much each could vary from the mean figure given:

Table 4

Manuscript Combination	Star Form Stemma	Linear Form Stemma
A :: B C D	72	72
A B :: C D	1	116
A B C :: D	28	28
A B D :: C	116	1
A C :: B D	3	0
A C D :: B	0	3
A D :: B C	1	1

Two things are notablc about these figures. First the same figures appear in both sets of data, but second that they differ in order.

I claim that given the frequencies of manuscript combinations from real manuscripts it should be possible to deduce a great deal about the underlying stemma and so the history of copying of those manuscripts.

The chief proviso is that a good number of combinations are needed. The reader will have noticed that when figures of uncertainty or possible spread are given above they become proportionately greater as the frequency of the combination decreases. So for a frequency of 115.83 a spread of plus or minus 21.11 is given, that is plus or minus 18%; whereas for a frequency of 0.72 the spread possible is plus or minus 1.70, or 236%. This is one of the reasons I have begun my work on the Gospel of Luke, one of the longest texts in the New Testament.

An Example Using Real Data

The following data refers to the Gospel of Luke and the manuscripts 69, 124 and 230 collated against the Textus Receptus in those places where the whole of Family 13 exists and where variation shows only two forms.[1]

Table 5

Manuscript Group	**Frequency of the MS Combination**
69 :: 124, 230, TR	627
69, 124 :: 230, TR	198
69, 124, 230 :: TR	118
69, 230 :: 124, TR	42
124 :: 69, 230, TR	198
124, 230 :: 69, TR	30
230 :: 69, 124, TR	149

Inspecting these figures it is quite clear what the main outline of the underlying stemma must be.

Each manuscript (The Textus Receptus is not, of course, a 'manuscript' but will be treated here as a single entity) has many 'singular' readings and must stand away from the centre stemma along its own arm. (See Diagram 25.)

[1] Data from J. Geerlings, *Family 13 (The Ferrar Group): The Text According to Luke* (SD 20; Salt Lake City, 1961).

The high number of agreements between 69 and 124 and between 230 and TR suggest a common tradition with 69 and 124 at one end and 230 and TR at the other. (See Diagram 26.)

This stemma explains perfectly the four singular figures and the agreements of 69 and 124 and of 230 and TR.

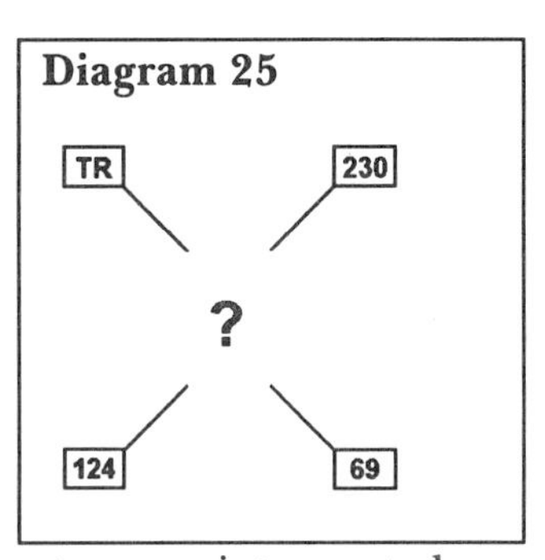

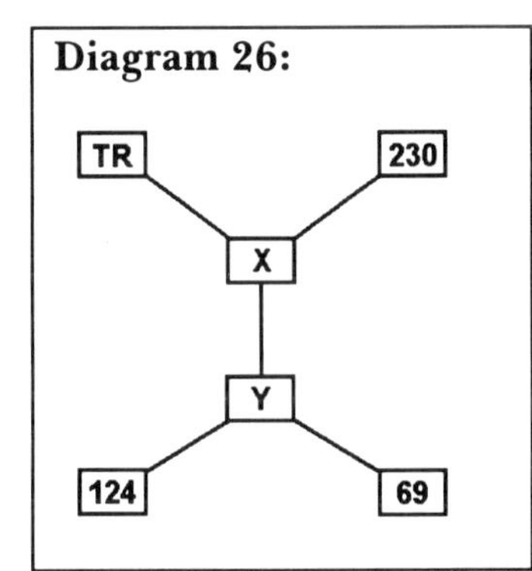

However this stemma, interpreted as relating to unique irreversible changes, does not explain the 42 agreements between 69 and 230 against 124 and TR, nor the 30 agreements between 124 and 230 against 69 and TR.

My approach, assuming non-unique reversible changes, is to tell my computer what the underlying stemma might be and ask it to calculate the numbers of changes on each stem of the stemma that best explain the frequencies of the various manuscript combinations. Tables 6 and 7 and Diagram 27 show the computed result.

Table 6

Manuscript Combination	Actual Frequency	Calculated Frequency	Allowable Error	Actual Error
69 :: 124, 230, TR	627	627.29	± 46.206	+0.29
69, 124 :: 230, TR	198	198.10	± 27.479	+0.10
69, 124, 230 :: TR	118	116.12	± 21.252	-1.88
69, 230 :: 124, TR	42	39.008	± 12.433	-2.992
124 :: 69, 230, TR	198	197.62	± 27.447	-0.38
124, 230 :: 69, TR	30	33.369	± 11.507	+3.369
230 :: 69, 124, TR	149	150.85	± 24.120	+1.85

Table 7	
Changes on stem X - TR	151.68
Changes on stem X - 230	202.25
Changes on stem X - Y	220.83
Changes on stem Y - 69	751.29
Changes on stem Y - 124	227.12
Notional Number of elements in text	4207
Degrees of Freedom	1
Chi squared error	0. 62378
(P(1.323) = 0.25 and P(0.4549) = 0.50)	

Diagram 27

4207 elements each:

TR
151.68
X
202.25
220.83
230
Y
227.12
124
751.29
69

I have drawn the stemma with TR as the origin partly because I believe this to be the case and partly to make reading the diagram easier.

Clearly the frequencies calculated for this form of stemma, assuming non-unique reversible changes, correspond very well to the real figures. I thus claim that this stemma, with the computed number of changes on each stem and the notional number of elements in the text offer, collectively, a credible explanation of the history of this group of manuscripts. My answer cannot be claimed as the only one, it is simply one which deserves consideration because of the accurate correspondence between theory and reality.

There is in fact another credible explanation. The basic stemma, as already admitted, explains the four 'singular' readings and the agreements 69, 124 :: 230, TR. The remaining two combinations could be explained as the result of contamination from the Textus Receptus.

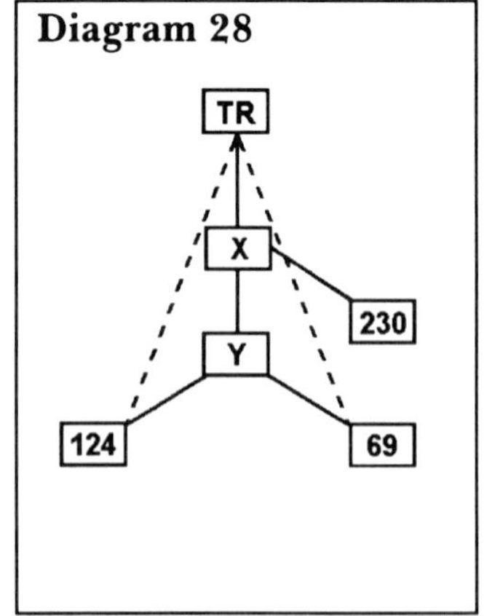

Diagram 28

The explanation would run like this: In forty-two places where the group text differs from TR this group text has been replaced by that of the TR in copying 124 so that 69 and 230 appear to have forty-two agreements not explained by the stemma.

A similar argument of supposed contamination of 69 would produce thirty agreements between 124 and 230 which are not explained by the simple stemma.

Thus the true stemma, according to this approach, requires two dotted lines to put the full picture. (See Diagram 28.)

Interestingly this explanation, in respect of this stemma, relies on a form of reversible change. If the group text, differing from that of TR, is later obscured by a scribe substituting some elements of the TR in a later manuscript the text has, in this manuscript and these places, reverted to its original form from a later form. This is only true, of course, if TR is seen as the origin of the group. However if another manuscript is seen as the origin then the contamination from the TR brings about the same effect as multiple occurrence of errors by the 'secondary text' of the TR (if it is not the origin of the group) being spread to other parts of the stemma as contamination.

Thus I claim that the choice is not between accepting that a significant number of changes in our text do become reversed or that they do not, but that the choice is between whether they happen sometimes by spontaneous change (my theory) and sometimes by contamination or always by contamination. Equally I take it as indisputable that forms of text do crop up in apparently unrelated traditions – the choice is whether they do so sometimes by chance and sometimes by conflation or contamination (my theory) or always by some means of spread through contamination or conflation.

How are we to distinguish between these explanations? I cannot offer a proof that my theories are correct but simply indicate reasons for accepting them which I find compelling.

My first argument is that in my theories only one process explains the relationships of the four manuscripts quoted above. The theory of contamination requires two processes: copying and contamination. The second process, contamination, is parasitic on the first and so contamination cannot exist without copying but copying should exist at times without contamination. But I have yet to find any groups of manuscripts which do not offer the sort of anomalous or awkward manuscript combinations which contamination is used here to explain. I suggest if it is to stand as an explanation of such awkward manuscript combinations then contamination must be seen as an all pervading process from which virtually no manuscript is free. If this is thought to be true then I suspect that we must all but abandon attempts to derive stemmata. While I believe accidental contamination and deliberate conflation did occur I equally believe it was not the rule but the exception and explain the awkward manuscript combinations as mostly chance occurrences.

I reinforce my doubts here by reference to the example above. The manuscript combination 69, 230 :: 124, TR is explained by forty-two readings from TR contaminating the copying process which formed 124 from its indicated ancestor Y. This copying process shows 198 differences between 124 and Y from combination 124 :: 69, 230, TR to which we must add the forty-two differences introduced by the contamination making 240. Thus forty-two of the 240 differences between Y and 124 (or 17.5%) are readings from TR contaminating the process of copying. The manuscript combination 124, 230 :: 69, TR is explained by thirty readings from TR contaminating the copying process which formed 69 from Y. The differences between Y and 69 from the combination 69 :: 124, 230, TR number 627. Thus thirty out of 657 (627 + 30) changes are contamination in this case, being 4.6%.

If the contamination process is as ubiquitous as is necessary to explain the general occurrence in all traditions of awkward and non-stemmatic manuscript combinations, why is it here so unevenly demonstrated, with one copying process contaminated to 17.5% whilst another is contaminated only to 4.6%? If the unevenness is accepted as indicative of an uneven process, where are the New Testament examples, even one example, of manuscripts whose relationships are totally explained by unique irreversible changes, without contamination?

My second area of doubt about the 'contamination' explanation of awkward manuscript combinations is that, while it seems eminently reasonable in the case of the four manuscripts cited above, such explanations become rapidly convoluted for more complex stemmata. I illustrate this, in Table 8, with an example of a five manuscript stemma.

Table 8 – Data of manuscripts 13, 230, 826, 828, TR

Manuscript Group	**Frequency of the MS Combination**
13 :: 230,826,828,TR	238
13,230 :: 826,828,TR	11
13,230,826 :: 828,TR	5
13,230,828 :: 826,TR	1
13,230,826,828 :: TR	157
13,826 :: 230,828,TR	18
13,826,828 :: 230,TR	477

13,828 :: 230,826,TR	27
230 :: 13,826,828,TR	143
230,826 :: 13,828,TR	2
230,826,828 :: 13,TR	6
230,828 :: 13,826,TR	14
826 :: 13,230,828,TR	13
826,828 :: 13,230,TR	29
828 :: 13,230,826,TR	187

In this data, from the same text extent as my first example, again all possible manuscript combinations actually occur. Thus unique irreversible changes alone cannot be used to map their relationships. Either the changes involved are non-unique and reversible or there is considerable contamination from TR or some other source.

My analysis follows in Tables 9 and 10 and Diagram 29.

Table 9

Manuscript Combination	Actual Frequency	Calculated Frequency	Allowable Error	Actual Error
13 :: 230,826,828,TR	238	236.01	± 29.97	-1.99
13,230 :: 826,828,TR	11	10.135	± 6.36	-0.865
13,230,826 :: 828,TR	5	8.0462	± 5.67	+3.0462
13,230,828 :: 826,TR	1	1.5045	± 2.45	+0.5045
13,230,826,828 :: TR	157	152.73	± 24.33	-4.27
13,826 :: 230,828,TR	18	25.210	± 10.02	+7.210
13,826,828 :: 230,TR	477	468.40	± 41.16	-8.60
13,828 :: 230,826,TR	27	26.981	± 10.36	-0.019
230 :: 13,826,828,TR	143	152.27	± 24.29	+9.27
230,826 :: 13,828,TR	2	1.5066	± 2.45	-0.4934
230,826,828 :: 13,TR	6	10.166	± 6.37	+4.166
230,828 :: 13,826,TR	14	8.0218	± 5.66	-5.9782[2]
826 :: 13,230,828,TR	13	12.711	± 7.12	-0.289
826,828 :: 13,230,TR	29	31.597	± 11.21	+2.597
828 :: 13,230,826,TR	187	186.60	± 26.79	-0.40

[2] This figure is just outside the 'allowable error' set at two standard deviations but well within three so is acceptable as the overall error figure is acceptable.

Table 10	
Changes on stem X - TR	179.07
Changes on stem X - 230	178.39
Changes on stem X - Y	565.51
Changes on stem Y - 826	12.76
Changes on stem Y - Z	18.44
Changes on stem Z - 13	303.36
Changes on stem Z - 828	242.55
Notional No. of elements in text	4884
Degrees of Freedom	3
Chi squared error	7.6509
(P(7.815) = 0.050)	

Diagram 29

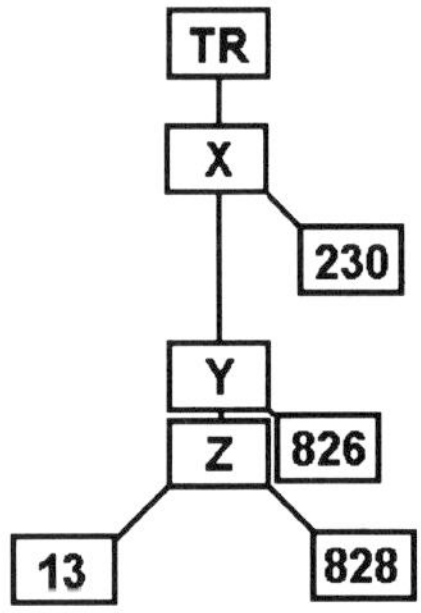

TR
X
230
Y
Z
826
13
828

Thus my theory explains the relationships of these manuscripts very well as a simple stemma.

If the same data is explained by a simple stemma with contamination of TR the process becomes more complex.

The simple stemma has the same basic shape as my result though the number of differences along each stem will be different. (See Diagram 30.) This stemma accounts directly for seven of the manuscript combinations (printed in Table 11 in bold type), leaving a further eight to be explained by contamination.

Table 11

MS Combination	Frequency
13 :: 230,826,828,TR	**238 (stem Z - 13)**
13,230 :: 826,828,TR	11
13,230,826 :: 828,TR	5
13,230,828 :: 826,TR	1
13,230,826,828 :: TR	**157 (stem X - TR)**
13,826 :: 230,828,TR	18
13,826,828 :: 230,TR	**477 (stem X - Y)**
13,828 :: 230,826,TR	**27 (stem Y - Z)**
230 :: 13,826,828,TR	**143 (stem X - 230)**
230,826 :: 13,828,TR	2
230,826,828 :: 13,TR	6
230,828 :: 13,826,TR	14
826 :: 13,230,828,TR	**13 (stem Y - 826)**
826,828 :: 13,230,TR	29
828 :: 13,230,826,TR	**187 (stem Z - 828)**

Diagram 30

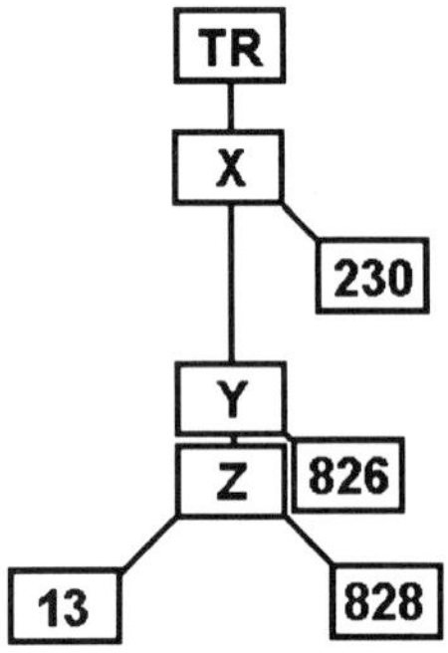

TR
X
230
Y
Z
826
13
828

Some manuscript combinations are easy to deal with as in our previous example. For instance the twenty-nine occurrences of 826, 828 :: 13, 230, TR can be explained by contamination of thirteen masking changes occurring in the stem X - Y which only then appear in 826 and 828. Similarly the eighteen occurrences of 13, 826 :: 230, 828, TR can be accounted for by contamination of 828 masking changes occurring in the stem X - Y. But the fourteen occurrences of 230, 828 :: 13, 826, TR need identical but independent contamination of 13 and 826. Similarly the eleven occurrences of 13, 230 :: 826, 828, TR need identical independent contamination of 826 and 828. Such coincidence I find less than satisfactory.

When I look at the figures, as with the example earlier, I find the stem Y - 826 to have thirty-nine differences of which 66.7% are contamination from TR (Table 12). However on stem Z - 828 only 15.4% of the changes are contamination (Table 13).

Table 12

MS Combination	Freq.
826 :: 13,230,828,TR	**13**
13,230 :: 826,828,TR	11
13,230,828 :: 826,TR	1
230,828 :: 13,826,TR	14

Table 13

MS Combination	Freq.
828 :: 13,230,826,TR	**187**
13,230 :: 826,828,TR	11
13,230,826 :: 828,TR	5
13,826 :: 230,828,TR	18

I find this sort of discrepancy unsatisfactory in itself and the more unsatisfactory since my theory offers a complete explanation under the single concept of non-unique reversible changes as opposed to the double concept of unique irreversible changes with varying levels of contamination.[3]

[3] For more information see my article, 'Desk & Discipline: the impact of computers on Bible Studies', in *Proceedings of the Fourth International Colloquium; Bible & Computer*, Association Internationale Bible et Informatique (AIBI) en collaboration avec le Werkgroep Informatica, Vrije Universiteit Amsterdam (Paris: Honore Champion Editeur, 1995) 214-22.

PART TWO

TEXTS

THE SIGNIFICANCE OF NON-CONTINUOUS NEW TESTAMENT TEXTUAL MATERIALS IN PAPYRI

S.R. PICKERING

In broad terms, three forms of evidence are available for reconstructing the Greek text of the New Testament:

(1) Greek manuscripts;
(2) the versions (translations into languages other than Greek);
(3) quotations and allusions.

Until late in the nineteenth century, the surviving evidence in these three categories was known from texts preserved by the medieval library tradition. Then papyri from the sands of Egypt (and elsewhere) began to come to light, mainly in Greek but also in Latin, Coptic and other languages. These finds include texts on papyrus, parchment, ostraca, wooden tablets and other writing materials. Among the finds are the remains of copies of New Testament books written in Greek.

Classification According to Writing Material

When standard lists of these fragmentary New Testament copies were produced, distinctions were made according to the writing materials on which the texts were preserved. Those on parchment were listed with the parchments of the medieval library tradition, while those on papyrus were given their own list, the 𝔓 list.

This distinction according to writing material is arbitrary, since in principle the same text could be copied out on any writing material. But what was an arbitrary distinction came to have a profound effect on the way in which New Testament scholars view the finds. The term 'New Testament papyri' came to be applied especially to texts in the 𝔓 list. This is a tendency which still persists.

In the New Testament text-critical field, 'papyri' which are actually on parchment have been caught up under the heading of the uncials (or majuscules), while the finds on ostraca, wooden tablets and other writing materials are not systematically catalogued and discussed at all.

Provision was made in the numbering of uncials for the inclusion of talismans (0152) and ostraca (0153); but this arrangement is clearly inadequate even for these two categories (using only one number for whole categories, and subsuming them in a list designed for parchments), and in any case has not been actively applied.[1]

Problems of partial or complete exclusion from the standard lists are not limited to papyri but apply to various other forms of text, both literary and documentary, including liturgical materials and inscriptions.[2] The problems also go beyond the Greek materials to materials in other languages, for example Coptic. The Coptic papyri as a category are not considered here.

Classification According to Content

Added to this problem of differentiation according to writing material is a second problem of differentiation according to content.

Those papyri catalogued with the uncials or in the 𝔓 list are, in the main, continuous texts, that is texts which were originally written out as continuous and complete copies of whole books.[3] There are

---

[1] Cf. K. Aland (ed.), *Kurzgefaßte Liste der griechischen Handschriften des Neuen Testaments*, I: *Gesamtübersicht* (ANTF 1; Berlin, 1963) 50; (2nd ed., 1994) 33.

[2] On the absence of various kinds of material from the standard lists cf. D.C. Parker, 'The Majuscule Manuscripts of the New Testament', in Ehrman & Holmes (22-42), 27-28: 'I may note in passing that, with their removal from the list [of majuscules], certain kinds of evidence have dropped out of sight. I have referred to the marginalia of the Paris MS of the Octateuch, and to the talismans and ostraca. In addition, a number of inscriptions, epigraphic and painted, have never been part of any list of the evidence available to us.' The Paris manuscript has quotations in the margins from the Gospels, Acts and Pauline Epistles (*ibid.*, p.26).

[3] In some cases a large part of a book but not the whole book may have been copied. For example, the Coptic codex G^{67} (New York, Pierpont Morgan Library, Glazier Collection) begins with Acts 1:1 and closes at Acts 15:3. Evidently in this case Acts was copied in two volumes.

also the lectionaries, which have their own list. Some independent extracts have crept into the lists,[4] but not in an organised way,[5] and papyri which contain New Testament quotations and allusions are left out of the standard New Testament catalogues altogether.

The Catalogue *of van Haelst; the* Repertorium *of the Münster Institut*

The situation has been partly rectified by the catalogue of Jewish and Christian literary papyri of J. van Haelst.[6] This covers texts on any writing material, and has a section for New Testament papyri, which includes both continuous texts and extracts. The section also has cross-references to texts elsewhere in the catalogue which contain New Testament quotations and allusions. But the *Catalogue* does not aim at completeness in its recording of New Testament quotations and allusions, and the cross-references within the New Testament section are therefore only a sample of what the papyri contain.

In contrast to the comprehensive approach of van Haelst's *Catalogue*, the *Repertorium* of the Münster Institut für Neutestamentliche Textforschung is limited to texts on papyrus writing material specifically.[7] The first volume has a category of 'Varia' which could perhaps in principle be extended to include a wide range of extracts, quotations and allusions (cf. e.g. Var. 29 = P.Ant. II 54, a

---

[4] Cf e.g. 𝔓10 = P.Oxy. II 209 (Romans 1:1-7); 𝔓12 = P.Amh. I 3 (b) (Hebrews 1:1). See below for extracts of the Gospel of John in the 𝔓 list.

[5] The following statement with regard to the list of lectionaries is revealing: 'The lectionaries included in the list of New Testament manuscripts present a most varied assortment of types, even apart from about two hundred entries which actually should not have been included at all because they are only broadly of a liturgical nature, containing only scattered New Testament texts (this heritage from the past will not easily be shed)' (K. Aland and B. Aland, *The Text of the New Testament* [2nd ed.; Grand Rapids/Leiden: Eerdmans/Brill, 1989] 163).

[6] J. van Haelst, *Catalogue des papyrus littéraires juifs et chrétiens* (Paris: Publications de la Sorbonne, 1976).

[7] K. Aland (ed.), *Repertorium der griechischen christlichen Papyri*, I: *Biblische Papyri. Altes Testament, Neues Testament, Varia, Apokryphen* (Patristische Texte und Studien 18; Berlin/New York, 1976). The series of the Institut in which the readings of New Testament papyri are presented, *Das Neue Testament auf Papyrus*, is for texts in the 𝔓 list.

miniature bifolium with part of the Lord's Prayer). The second volume of the *Repertorium* covers patristic materials, but again it is limited to texts on papyrus, and the volume is not designed to catalogue systematically all the New Testament quotations and allusions which these texts include.[8]

A Neglected Body of Evidence

There is therefore a whole body of New Testament textual evidence which awaits the concentrated attention of specialists. The quotations and allusions in papyri have been almost entirely overlooked by New Testament scholarship, even though quotations and allusions are a recognised form of New Testament textual evidence.

Papyri preserving works of known authors, such as Didymus the Blind, are likely to be caught up as patristic literature, and considered for their quotations and allusions. But there are many more papyri containing New Testament quotations and allusions which have never been drawn into the mainstream of New Testament text-critical scholarship.

Hence, the extracts, quotations and allusions in papyri are largely neglected evidence for reconstructing the New Testament text and tracing its transmission.

The Value of the Evidence

It appears that there has been a tendency to regard this evidence as second-rate, on the grounds that a text such as a school exercise or a

[8] K. Aland (†) and H.-U. Rosenbaum, *Repertorium der griechischen christlichen Papyri*, II: *Kirchenväter-Papyri*, Teil I: *Beschreibungen* (Patristische Texte und Studien 42; Berlin/New York, 1995). See the introduction, lxv-lxvi, on future volumes of the *Repertorium*: II.2 (in preparation) is an index volume, and will include addenda and corrigenda to Band I; Band III will be for published literary texts not identified with a known author (although it is hoped that some will be identified in the volume); plans for future volumes on letters, hagiographica and liturgica, and documents before 400, remain to be clarified. The Varia category of Band I now runs to Var. 65 (an additional 31 texts) (lxv). See xliv-xlvi for discussion of the decision to limit the volumes to texts on papyrus.

magical text is a less reliable transmitter of textual information than continuous texts.

There is some justification for this view if one assumes that the writer of a school exercise, for example, is less interested in careful copying than a scribe trained to copy continuous texts, or if one assumes that the writer of a private letter is more likely to quote from memory than a scribe working from an exemplar.

But such arguments have limited value. It is well known that scribal errors and alterations have introduced a multitude of discrepancies into the transmission of continuous texts – so much so that just as much caution is needed in evaluating a continuous text as would be needed in evaluating a text reproduced as a school exercise.

Even if one were to assume that in general school exercises or magical texts are less reliable transmitters, it would clearly be fallacious to argue that they can *never* transmit a passage according to the wording which one would expect from a continuous text. Taken word by word, a non-continuous text may be every bit as reliable a transmitter as a continuous text.

The question of textual value goes beyond the merely verbal level. A manuscript is of text-critical value not only in the individual words which it contains, but in the evidence it provides for the scribal approaches which influenced the wording.

In this respect, an alleged weakness of non-continuous texts – the likely extent of scribal interference – turns out to be one of their great strengths for New Testament text-critical purposes.

Even on the assumption that a New Testament text in a school exercise or magical text could be heavily influenced by the context in which the text is being reproduced, one is at least in a position to evaluate the kinds of influences likely to have affected the text.

On the other hand, in the case of a continuous text, there is less information on the immediate copying context – and yet the same kinds of influences may have been at work as in the case of a school exercise or other type of non-continuous text.

It emerges, therefore, that the neglect of non-continuous texts not only has meant leaving a large body of textual material in obscurity, but also has meant a failure to bring the evidence of these texts to bear on the better known continuous texts.

P.Vindob. G 2312

Let me propose as an example a papyrus in Vienna which has been available for consultation since late last century, when it was described, with a photograph, in a guide to the Vienna collection of papyri.[9] The papyrus, from the Fayum, is on display in the permanent exhibition of the papyrus collection of the Austrian National Library,[10] where it is dated to the sixth century.[11]

The papyrus is rectangular in shape, about 6 cm high by 15 cm broad. These are the original dimensions. The text is preserved complete except for some minor lacunae, with margins preserved on all four sides. The back is blank. Seven asterisk-shaped signs across the top of the text link the papyrus to the genre of magical texts. There are horizontal and vertical fold marks, indicating that the papyrus was folded into a small packet about 2.5 by 2 cm, as typically

---

[9] P.Vindob. G 2312 = Stud.Pal. XX 294 (van Haelst, *Catalogue*, no.195; the Psalm text is Rahlfs 2031). The papyrus, no. 528, was described by C. Wessely in *Führer durch die Ausstellung der Papyrus Erzherzog Rainer* (Vienna, 1894) 124-5, fig. on p.125, including comments by E. Bormann. It was edited by C.F.G. Heinrici, *Die Leipziger Papyrusfragmente der Psalmen* (Beiträge zur Geschichte und Erklärung des Neuen Testaments 4; Leipzig, 1903) 31-2; and re-edited by C. Wessely, *Studien zur Paläographie und Papyruskunde*, vol. XX (Leipzig, 1921) no. 294. The text is reproduced (from Stud. Pal. XX) in Wessely, *Les plus anciens monuments du christianisme écrits sur papyrus*, II (PO 18.3; Paris, 1924) 411 [187]; also in H. Leclercq, 'Papyrus', *Dictionnaire d'archéologie chrétienne et de liturgie* XIII (1937: coll. 1370-1520) coll. 1386-87, fig. 9690 (across coll. 1387-8) 'X. Amulettes chrétiennes, no. 8'. The papyrus is described in A. Rahlfs, *Psalmi cum Odis* (Septuaginta Societatis Scientiarum Gottingensis 11; Göttingen, 1931) 15; also in the following exhibition catalogues: E.M. Ruprechtsberger, (ed.), *Syrien. Von den Aposteln zu den Kalifen* (Linzer Archäologische Forschungen 21; Linz, Stadtmuseum Nordico, 1993) Pap. 14 (472 and fig.); M. Ernst (ed.), *Die Wüste spricht. Papyri beleuchten Literatur und Alltagsleben der Antike. Katalog zur gleichnamigen Ausstellung in der Bibliotheksaula der Universitätsbibliothek Salzburg, 16. April bis 5. Juli 1996. Exponate der Papyrussammlung der Österreichischen Nationalbibliothek* (Salzburg: Institut für Neutestamentliche Bibelwissenschaft, 1996) 52-3.

[10] I am grateful to Mag. Andrea Donau of the Austrian National Library for generously clarifying various details and assisting with the bibliography.

[11] Heinrici (p.31) assigned the papyrus to perhaps the fourth century. The date given in Stud. Pal. XX, *AMC* and *DACL* is VI-VII. Van Haelst reported IV (Heinrici) and VI-VII (Wessely).

done with texts carried about as amulets. Beneath the asterisks are nine lines of text, the last of which contains Coptic material such as one expects in magical invocations. Otherwise the text is entirely taken up with biblical quotations in Greek (see the Appendix at the end of this chapter for a transcription):

Lines	*Biblical Text*
2-4	Psalm 90:1-2
5-7	Romans 12:1-2
8-9	John 2:1-2.

In the text of John, the wording from καὶ to Γαλιλαίας corresponds exactly to a known form of wording for John 2:1a. The papyrus agrees with witnesses which have τῇ τρίτῃ ἡμέρᾳ instead of τῇ ἡμέρᾳ τρίτῃ. The former phrasing is read by B Θ f^{13} *pc* and the papyrus adds to the evidence for this wording. The latter phrasing is read by the majority of witnesses and is followed by the Nestle-Aland edition. Before Κανά, $\mathfrak{P}^{75}$ has the article τῇ, but this papyrus does not.

After Γαλιλαίας, the scribe skips to verse 2, where the papyrus supports omission of καί before ὁ Ἰησοῦς. καί is omitted by a few Greek manuscripts, including the first scribe of $\mathfrak{P}^{66}$, and by some versional witnesses. However, in this papyrus the omission of καί could be a deliberate innovation, since by skipping over the end of verse 1 the papyrus has not yet mentioned that the mother of Jesus was invited to the wedding. This fact is supplied by an adaptation in verse 2, where the papyrus reads καὶ ἡ μήτηρ αὐτοῦ instead of καὶ οἱ μαθηταὶ αὐτοῦ.[12]

We might explain this re-phrasing as a result of quotation from memory, or as resulting from paraphrase and compression. But that does not change the fact that up to a point the papyrus represents a standard piece of New Testament transmission.

We might even suggest that the papyrus version represents the way some people thought of the incident, with the emphasis on Jesus being invited rather than on his mother as the first-named invited guest. This could in turn suggest a reason for the omission of καί in some manuscripts: the word could have been dropped to avoid the impression that Jesus was merely an accompanying guest. An

[12] The papyrus has the spelling μήρτηρ.

increased emphasis on Jesus and the relative de-emphasising of his mother are precisely what the papyrus conveys.

Such an alteration could be expected, for example, in a sermon which was telling the story in a way that partly kept to the wording of the text and partly re-told the story in a free way. Hence, for example, we find Athanasius saying that, 'on the third day the Lord reclined together (with others) at Cana in Galilee at the marriage'.[13]

The methodologies needed for text-critical evaluation of such a reference in patristic material can be applied to the papyrus to clarify the various levels at which the papyrus contributes useful information for reconstructing the text and placing it in its transmissional context.

We can also compare the character of the papyrus text with the character of liturgical materials. The combination of Psalm, Epistle and Gospel in the papyrus would encourage this comparison. The extracts in the papyrus could stand for longer texts. The variations noted in the John passage could reflect liturgical reformulation.[14]

The passage from Romans 12:1-2 presents some variant readings of greater or lesser interest, and also introduces a new element for consideration. At the end of line 6, the scribe has begun the word συ(ν)σχηματίζεσθε (or -αι) but stopped in the middle of the word. This suggests the possibility that the scribe was copying out a text mechanically, perhaps without full understanding of the context, and was willing to cut a word short to fit the space available even though the result did not make complete sense. On the other hand, the scribe may have understood the content perfectly well, but was nevertheless willing to cut the word short, perhaps on the assumption that the rest of the text represented by the written portion – say the rest of a liturgical pericope – could be safely assumed.[15]

Although this feature points to arbitrary interference in the textual transmission, it also suggests that the scribe may have been

---

[13] τῇ τρίτῃ ἡμέρᾳ συνανεκλίθη Κύριος ἐν Κανᾶ τῆς Γαλιλαίας εἰς τὸν γάμον (*Sermo contra omnes haereses*, vol. 28, p.516) [TLG]. Note that Athanasius has the reading τῇ τρίτῃ ἡμέρᾳ.

[14] Heinrici, p.31, discusses the papyrus in relation to the liturgical use of the Psalms in combination with New Testament pericopes.

[15] Note that where alpha falls at the end of a line (as in the case of συνσχημα) the scribe finished off the line by lengthening the final stroke of alpha.

working from a written copy, which will have served to act as a control on the scribe's activity. In this light some of the transmissional peculiarities could be attributed to an exemplar and so put back at least one copying stage.

We can conclude that the scribe (or the scribe's text) moves in and out of exact correspondence to a standard form of the New Testament passages, shifting in a flexible way between word-for-word transmission and free forms of transmission.

This flexibility raises the question of what scribes considered textual transmission to be. Did they consider that they were transmitting the text (a) if they conveyed what they regarded as the essential meaning or (b) when they reproduced an exemplar verbatim, or almost verbatim? The question has great significance for the evaluation of New Testament textual transmission generally.

Text-critical aspects of the Psalm text should also be considered, in the expectation that they may throw light on the scribe's approach to copying more generally, and therefore possibly on the scribe's approach to the New Testament texts as well as the Psalm text.[16]

Collecting, Presenting and Evaluating the Non-Continuous Evidence

The challenge lies ahead of how to draw the textual information of this papyrus and others like it into the mainstream of New Testament text-critical study.

It is clear that the papyrus contributes relevant information of many different kinds, and only a complete re-edition of the text, with extensive commentary, could do justice to the varied data to be derived from it.

Quite possibly the ideal approach would be to produce editions of all such papyri, including commentaries done with an eye to their New Testament text-critical contributions. This may be a task for the next few decades, perhaps to be carried out in a flexible way by sensitising New Testament scholarship to the need for progressively improving its stock of papyrus editions and commentaries. A trend of this type has been occurring in the case of the Egerton gospel.[17] The fact that commentaries are still appearing on that text is a

---

[16] See Heinrici, p.32.

[17] P.Egerton 1 (= Egerton Pap. inv. 2), also referred to as P.Lond.Christ. 1.

warning of the magnitude of the task involved in widening the net to cover all the papyri containing New Testament quotations and allusions.[18]

The transmissional questions which arise are numerous and often subtle, and evaluation of them is influenced by advances in other areas of New Testament textual criticism. It is unsafe to assume that the problems can be solved quickly and completely. Even an extensive re-edition of a text is unlikely to remain permanently definitive.

In this situation, it is perhaps necessary to determine what is the irreducible minimum for satisfactory progress. An essential reference point must be a catalogue listing every relevant papyrus and noting the New Testament extracts, quotations and allusions which each papyrus contains. The catalogue will have to be kept up to date by additions and corrections as published material is better understood and as new texts are published. In view of current technological advances, a version of the catalogue on the Internet would make it readily and inexpensively accessible. A hard-copy version would be needed as well, given the fixity and convenience which printed books provide.

The next step is possibly suggested by several factors connected with the transcription of the texts. The transcriptions are nowhere collected in one place, and access to the full range of them depends on having an extensive papyrological library on hand.[19] There is also the fundamental need to ensure that transcriptions are as accurate as possible, and amended from time to time in the light of improved readings. Accurate transcriptions are an essential basis for accurate commentaries.

These considerations suggest that it may be advisable to build up a collection of transcriptions, with marginal notes indicating the New Testament materials within the texts. Such a collection would form a basis and reference point, designed to stimulate and respond to international scholarship in this area.

---

[18] For a recent discussion of the Egerton papyrus cf. K. Erlemann, 'Papyrus Egerton 2: 'Missing Link' zwischen synoptischer und johannischer Tradition', *NTS* 42 (1996) 12-34.

[19] The prospects for future availability on the Internet of the full range of texts (including textual apparatus) need to be evaluated.

The collection of transcriptions would function in a way similar to a hand edition of the New Testament: an *editio minor*, in preparation for an *editio maior* and associated commentaries.

There is some duplication built into this proposal, since editions of the texts will already exist, and re-editions of some or all of them can be expected in other places, for example in the Thesaurus Linguae Graecae or the Duke Data Bank of Documentary Papyri. But the duplication is perhaps unavoidable if the transcriptions are to be specially useful to New Testament text-critical scholars.

The scale of the task should not be underestimated; but a solution to the problem of scale must be found if it is accepted that the evidence of these materials is crucial for New Testament text-critical work.

The approach of revised transcriptions is that adopted in the recent International Greek New Testament Project volume for texts in the 𝔓 list of papyri of the Gospel of John.[20] A complementary work could collect transcriptions of papyrus extracts, quotations and allusions for the Gospel of John. A project is currently in progress at Macquarie University to produce at least a sample collection of such materials for the Gospel of John, but the exact form which the finished product should take is under consideration.

The papyri in the IGNTP volume illustrate the fact that texts admitted to the 𝔓 list are quite diverse in their format and purpose. The volume contains twenty-three papyri, assigned to dates between the second and the seventh centuries. Twenty-one of the texts are from codices. These include some well-known texts, including the Bodmer codices of John ($\mathfrak{P}^{66}$) and Luke and John ($\mathfrak{P}^{75}$); the text of John in the Chester Beatty codex of the Gospels and Acts ($\mathfrak{P}^{45}$); and the fragment of John at Manchester ($\mathfrak{P}^{52}$). Eighteen or nineteen of the texts are continuous texts,[21] including in this number six or seven texts which were written out in segments of a few verses at the top of each page with *hermeneiai* beneath. Four of the texts contain

[20] *The New Testament in Greek*, IV: *The Gospel According to St. John*, edited by the American and British Committees of the International Greek New Testament Project, Volume One: *The Papyri*, ed. W.J. Elliott and D.C. Parker (NTTS 20; Leiden, 1995). The IGNTP also has in preparation a volume of transcriptions of fragmentary texts of the Gospel of John catalogued in the standard list of uncials.

[21] Including a text possibly in roll form, $\mathfrak{P}^{22}$.

extracts: 𝔓2 (Luke and John, Coptic and Greek); 𝔓44A (Matthew and John); 𝔓44B (John); and 𝔓93 (John; individual sheet?). These four are very fragmentary and the purposes for which they were produced are not entirely obvious. Some of them may be linked with the lectionary tradition. One (𝔓93) has unprofessional features which suggest private use. In any case, the four texts, although included in the 𝔓 list, are not straightforward examples of continuous texts. So far as they are preserved, however, they contain only New Testament materials,[22] either extracts from John alone or extracts from John and another Gospel (Matthew or Luke).

There are other texts on papyrus containing verses of John which have not been catalogued in the 𝔓 list but which surely have strong claims to consideration for New Testament text-critical purposes (see Table 1 for a list of examples).

In addition to the Vienna amulet already mentioned, there are other amulets which use verses selected from John, especially verses from the beginning of the Gospel. John 2:1, found in the Vienna amulet, was also evidently popular.[23]

Works containing Johannine quotations and allusions draw on a range of chapters. Some of the works involved have been ascribed to known authors; some are unidentified theological works or apocryphal texts; one is the harmony fragment from Dura-Europos.

To such evidence in literary and sub-literary works must be added the evidence of non-literary texts, in particular private letters.

From the full range of non-continuous evidence certain sub-groups emerge. Gospel incipits have already been noticed. Another important sub-group are papyri containing part or all of the Lord's Prayer (from Matthew 6). Some of these contain the Lord's Prayer, or an extract from it, alone. Others have the Lord's Prayer combined with other material, including Gospel incipits.

The emergence of sub-groupings and other patterns shows that the non-continuous material is capable of throwing light not only on questions of textual reconstruction but on broader questions relating to the circulation and use of New Testament materials.

---

[22] Except that some contain *hermeneiai*.

[23] Cf. P.Mich. inv. 3718; Wadi Sarga 5, p.31.

Table 1
Examples of papyri containing non-continuous texts of the Gospel of John[24]

No.	*H no.*	*Reference*	*Contents*	*Date*	*Format*	*Provenance*
1	H586	P.Egerton 1 (inv. 2)	The 'Unknown Gospel' or Egerton Gospel. OT and NT quotations and allusions	c. 150? c. 200?	P cod	Unknown (Oxyrhyn-chus?)
2	H691 KV69	P.Egerton 2 (inv.3) [+PSI inv. 2101 (KV68)]	Origen (?), Gospel commentary (?). Old and New Testament quotations, including Jn 1:14, 29; 6:55	Early III	P cod	Unknown
3	H699	P.Dura 10	Gospel harmony (Tatian, *Diatessaron*?). Cf. Mt 27, Mk 15, Lk 3,23; Jn 19	Early III	D roll	Dura-Europos
4	H1159 KV53a	P.Lit. Palau Rib. 13 (P.Palau Rib. inv. 68 + 207)	Unidentified theological text. Quotes Eph 4:13, Col 2:9, Jn 14:8, 5:16	IV	P cod	Unknown

[24] The examples are mainly from van Haelst, *Catalogue* (whose numbering appears in the column labelled *H no.*; KV numbers are also shown there for texts catalogued in Aland / Rosenbaum, *Repertorium*, II: *Kirchenväter-Papyri*, Teil I). Various identifications, datings and other details may need revision. The texts are shown in approximate date order, but the dates are not exact, and in many cases other datings have been proposed. Under *Format*, the abbreviations indicate P(apyrus), D = parchment (*derma*), O(stracon), cod(ex), (individual) s(heet).

5	H731	BKT VI 7 1	Amulet. Cross. Trinitarian formula. Ps 90:1. Incipits of the Four Gospels. Ps 117:6-7. Ps 17:2. Mt 4:23. Liturgical formula	IV (?)	D s	Fayum
6	H689 KV62	MPER, N.S. IV 51	Origen (?), *Commentary on Genesis.* OT and NT quotations, including Heb 12:2, Phil 2:7-8, Jn 14:30, Heb 4:15	IV-V	P cod	Unknown
7	H423	PSI VI 719	Amulet with a cross; Χ[ριστὲ σῶτε]ρ; Jn 1:1, Mt 1:1, Jn 1:23, Mk 1:1, Lk 1:1, Ps 90:1, Mt 6:9 (beginning of Lord's Prayer); doxology; Amen; Χριστός; crosses	IV-V	P s	Oxyrhyn-chus?
8	H693	P.Bour. 3 + P.Achm. 1 etc.	Origen (?), Homily on John 3:5 or 1 Corinthians 2:13ff. (?). OT and NT quotations and allusions, including John 4:6ff., 13, 14, 9:39	V	P cod	Panopolis
9	H959	P.Oxy.VIII 1151	Amulet. Prayer of Joannia against the devil and every evil. Allusion to Jn 5:2. Quotation of Jn 1:1-3. Prayer against fever, to the patrons of Oxyrhynchus	V?	P s	Oxyrhyn-chus

10	H897	P.Cair. 10696	Ps 21:20-23 (selected words). Prayer with mention of martyrs. Incipits of Lk, Mt and Jn. Invocation to Phocas and Mercurius	V-VI	P s	Unknown
11	H684	Cairo, Egyptian Museum, JE 88746	Origen, *On the Pasch,* I-II. OT and NT quotations and allusions, especially Ex and Jn	VI	P cod	Toura
12	H720	BGU III 954 = Pap.Graec. Mag. 9	Prayer of Silvanus to God and Serenus for healing and protection, Lord's Prayer (Mt 6:9-13), doxology, Jn 1:1, Mt 1:1, allusion to the Nicene Creed, invocation to Serenus	VI	P s	Heracleo-polis Magna
13	H632 KV50	MPER, N.S. IV 54	Chrysostom, *Homily 29 On John,* cap. 2 (excerpts?). Includes Jn 3:27	VI	P s	Fayum
14	H1135	P.Harr. I 127	Homily? Perhaps a quotation of Jn 6:54 or 6:86	VI	P s	Unknown
15	H195	Stud.Pal. XX 294 (P.Vindob. G 2312)	Ps 90:1-2. Rom 12:1-2. Jn 2:1-2. A line of Coptic (including *nomina barbara)*	VI	P s	Fayum

16	H628a (olim 633) KV7	P. Ant. III 111	Basil of Caesarea, *Regulae brevius tractatae (erotapokriseis).* NT quotations including Jn 8:23, 15:13	VI-VII	P cod	Antinoopolis
17	H+	MPER, N.S. XVII 10	Amulet with Jn 1:5-6	VI/VII	D cod	Unknown
18	H1150	P.Mich. inv. 3718	OT and NT quotations (including Jn 2:1) followed by allegorical interpretations	VII	P cod	Unknown (prob. Oxyrhynchus)
19	H621 KV78	BKT VI 5	Alexander II (bishop of Alexandria), *Paschal Letter*. OT, NT and literary quotations, including Jn 1:14, 18	713/719/ 724	P roll	White Monastery
20	H386	Chicago, Univ. of Chicago, MS 125 (Hendecourt roll)	Mk l:1-8. Lk l:l-7. Jn 1:1-17. Mt 6:9-13 (Lord's Prayer). Nicene Creed. Ps 68	XII or XIII?	D roll	Egypt?
21	H434	Wadi Sarga 5, p.31	Jn 2:1	Date?	O	Wadi Sarga (Monastery of St. Thomas)

P.Abinn. 19

The overlapping of text-critical enquiry in the narrow sense with broader historical questions can be illustrated by reference to a papyrus in the fourth-century archive of Abinnaeus, a cavalry commander in the Fayum. P.Abinn. 19, a letter to Abinnaeus, contains a New Testament quotation or allusion referring to a cup of water. The writer is seeking special treatment for a soldier, asking Abinnaeus to release him from active service, or at least see to his welfare, so that he can return to his widowed mother. The request is prefaced by pious sentiments, including the words, '... a cup of water to one of these little ones, he will not lose his reward':

8 [πο]τ̣[η]ρ̣ι̣ο̣ν̣ υδα-
9 ⟦δα⟧τος ε̣ν̣ι των̣ [μικ]ρων [τ]ουτων
10 ουκ απολλι τον [μ]ι̣σθον εαυτου. ...

The editors suggested that this is a conflation of Mk 9:41 and 9:42:[25]

41 ὃς γὰρ ἂν ποτίσῃ ὑμᾶς ποτήριον ὕδατος ἐν ὀνόματι ὅτι Χριστοῦ ἐστε, ἀμὴν λέγω ὑμῖν ὅτι οὐ μὴ ἀπολέσῃ τὸν μισθὸν αὐτοῦ. 42 καὶ ὃς ἂν σκανδαλίσῃ ἕνα τῶν μικρῶν τούτων κτλ.	For whoever gives you a cup of water to drink because you bear the name of Christ, truly I say to you that he will not lose his reward. And whoever causes one of these little ones to stumble ...

Certainly these verses contain the key phrases ποτήριον ὕδατος and οὐ μὴ ἀπολέσῃ τὸν μισθὸν αὐτοῦ (41), and ἕνα τῶν μικρῶν τούτων (42). But the verses differ between themselves as to context, and a conflation would involve taking one or more of the phrases out of context.

The hypothesis of conflation, and the removal of phrases from their context, can be avoided by connecting the papyrus text with Matthew 10:42. All three key phrases occur in that verse if an attested variant reading is allowed.

The wording of the verse in the Nestle-Aland edition is:

καὶ ὃς ἂν ποτίσῃ ἕνα τῶν μικρῶν τούτων ποτήριον ψυχροῦ μόνον εἰς ὄνομα μαθητοῦ, ἀμὴν λέγω ὑμῖν, οὐ μὴ ἀπολέσῃ τὸν μισθὸν αὐτοῦ.	And whoever gives one of these little ones just a cup of cold (water) to drink (as having) the name of a disciple, truly I say to you, he will not lose his reward.

[25] H.I. Bell, V. Martin, E.G. Turner, D. van Berchem, eds, *The Abinnaeus Archive. Papers of a Roman officer in the Reign of Constantius II* (Oxford, 1962), 8ff. They also noted Matthew 10:42 and 18:6 for comparison.

This form of the text lacks the word ὕδατος (which the papyrus has), but some witnesses for the verse read ποτήριον ὕδατος ψυχροῦ instead of ποτήριον ψυχροῦ, viz. D lat sy$^{s.c}$ co Origen Cyprian (so NA^{27}). These are witnesses with 'Western' or potentially 'Western' affiliation.[26]

The papyrus text may therefore be a further witness for this variant reading and possibly for circulation of the verse in a text with 'Western' affinities. Re-assigning the words of the papyrus to Matthew instead of Mark means that the papyrus becomes evidence for (1) use of the verse concerned; (2) use of the variant reading; (3) use of a quotation rather than an allusion; and (4) use and circulation of the Gospel of Matthew.[27]

At present, evidence such as this letter provides is outside the mainstream of New Testament textual scholarship. But New Testament text-critics clearly have an exceptionally important part to play in bringing their text-critical skills to bear in the analysis of such evidence. At first sight a letter to a cavalry commander may seem an out-of-the-way source for textual specialists, but the textual evidence is lying there to be used, and the use of it will inevitably throw light on transmissional and historical questions of importance to New Testament textual studies and to other fields of research as well.

Textual and Historical Contributions of the Non-Continuous Materials on Papyrus

Some of the major questions to be considered in relation to the non-continuous evidence are, in the first instance at least, primarily textual or transmissional, while other major questions are of broad historical importance. The following are some considerations which have to do primarily with textual matters, and some considerations of a more general historical nature.

(a) *Textual*

The non-continuous materials on papyrus:

---

[26] NA^{26} also listed (Cl), i.e. Clement of Alexandria, with some variation, but this does not appear in NA^{27}.

[27] The writer of the letter could have been aware of the passages in Mark as well.

(i) extend the range of textual evidence. They provide evidence for verses for which no continuous evidence may survive at all, and for books and verses for which no continuous evidence may survive from particular times or places. They provide evidence for the nature and distribution of text-types;

(ii) have not passed through the filter of scribal copying and re-copying since the time that they were written, in contrast to many of the patristic quotations and allusions preserved via the medieval library tradition;

(iii) can be used to test the influence of the context of copying on the readings of a text, including the influence of (1) general social and cultural milieux, (2) specific milieux such as the ascetic or monastic, (3) circumstances of theological controversy (e.g. in the Egyptian context, the Melitian schism, Christological controversies), (4) multilingual environments;

(iv) can throw light on issues of textual distribution and control (e.g. the influence of a major ecclesiastical centre such as Alexandria);

(v) can be used to test and refine methodological approaches, including those developed for patristic texts.

(b) *More Broadly Historical*

The non-continuous materials on papyrus link New Testament texts with:

(i) particular provenances;
(ii) particular dates;
(iii) the historical conditions of textual transmission.

Conclusion

An outstanding feature of the non-continuous papyrus materials is the way in which they are set within a rich textual and historical matrix. Whether as extracts, quotations or allusions, they occur in conjunction with other textual materials and as part of an array of evidence reflective of the settings in which the papyri were produced.

These papyri provide invaluable evidence for studying the interaction of the New Testament texts and the circumstances of the transmission and use of the texts. It is of paramount importance to place clearly in view this combination of evidence, and to analyse the New Testament materials from both the text-critical and the more generally historical points of view.

APPENDIX

Revised transcription of P.Vindob. G 2312

This transcription is based on published photographs.[28]

→	(Seven asterisk-shaped signs)	
	ο κατοικων εν βοηθια του υψ[ισ]του εν σκεπη το[υ θ(εο)]υ̣	*Ps. 90:1-2*
	του ου(ρα)νου αυλισθεσεται ερι τω̣ κ̣(υρι)ω αντιλημπτωρ μου	
	ει και καταφυγη μου ο θ(εο)ς β[ο]η̣θος μου και ελπιω επ αυ	
5	παρακαλω υμας αδελφοι δια των εκτηρμων του θ(εο)υ	*Rom. 12:1-2*
	π[α]ραστησαι τα σωματα υμων ψυχην σωξαν ευα-	
	ρεστον την λογικην λατριαν και μη συνσχημα	
	και τη τριτη ημερα γαμος εγενετο εγ Κανα της Γα-	*Jn 2:1-2*
	λιλαιας εκληθη δε̣ ο Ι(ησου)ς και η μηρτηρ αυτου μετ αυ	
10 (*m.2*)	(not fully deciphered)	

2. l. βοηθεια : θ̅]υ̅ pap. θεο]υ̣ Heinrici, but the space suits the abbreviated form. **3**. ουν̅ο̅υ̅ pap. : l. αυλισθησεται : l. ερει : τ[ω] Heinrici, Stud. Pal., *AMC* : κ̣̅ω̅ pap. κυριω Heinrici; θω̅ Stud. Pal.; θ̅ω̅ *AMC* : **4**. θ̅ς̅ : β[ο]ηθος Heinrici; β[οη]θος Stud. Pal., *AMC* : αυ[τον] Heinrici; αυ[τ(ον)] Stud. Pal.; but αυ is at the extreme right of the papyrus and there is no room to finish the word : **5**. υ of υμας may have a sign somewhat like a circumflex above it (cf υμων in 6) : l. οικτιρμων : [τ]ου Stud. Pal., *AMC;* but the τ is clear : θ̅υ̅ pap. : **6-8.** The tails of α at the ends of these lines are drawn out : **6**. υ of υμων has a sign somewhat like a circumflex (or inverted circumflex?) above it : l. ζωσαν. ζωσαν Heinrici; σωξαν Stud. Pal.; σωζαν *AMC* : **8**. l. εν; εν Heinrici : **9**. ι̅ς̅ pap. : l. μητηρ : αυ at end: α is written small. αυ[του] Heinrici, *AMC*, but there is no room for the supplement. αν Stud. Pal. : **10**. According to Heinrici the line contains Coptic magical names. The line includes αδωναι κ̅ς̅ and at the end σαβαωθ.

[28] See the plates in *Führer* and *DACL* (n.9 above). The lines are numbered here to include the asterisks. The lines were left unnumbered by Heinrici. In *AMC* the numbering includes the line of asterisks, but in Stud. Pal. XX the numbering applies to the text only (hence lines 1-9 there correspond to lines 2-10 in the numbering used here). Accents are added in Stud. Pal.

THE RELEVANCE OF LITERARY CRITICISM FOR THE TEXT OF THE NEW TESTAMENT. A STUDY OF MARK'S TRADITIONS ON JOHN THE BAPTIST

E. GÜTING

Textual criticism looks back upon a long tradition of painstaking work.[1] Wherever variation became apparent, manuscripts have been studied, ancient translations have been compared, the testimony of the Fathers has been gathered. The apparatuses of our editions are improving,[2] but let us admit that they are still far from satisfactory.

---

[1] I wish to thank Professor Christopher M. Tuckett for valuable remarks on a draft of this essay.

[2] The presentation of evidence in editions needs careful consideration. As units of variation are defined and witnesses are listed, by implication the text-critical evaluation of the material presented is regularly imposed on this material. In a recent article ('Der editorische Bericht als Kommentar zur Textkonstitution und zum Apparat in Editionen des Neuen Testaments', in *Editio* 7 (1993) 94-108), I have stated some standards an editor ought to meet when listing the data that support or fail to support his text-critical decisions. Other authors, too, are discussing methodological issues involved in selecting or ignoring variants and witnesses: T. Baarda, 'What Kind of Critical Apparatus for the New Testament Do We need? The Case of Luke 23:48', in B. Aland & J. Delobel (eds), *New Testament Textual Criticism, Exegesis and Church History. A Discussion of Methods*, (Kampen: Kok Pharos, 1994), 37-97; E.C. Colwell, 'Method in Classifying and Evaluating Variant-Readings (with E.W. Tune)', in Colwell, *Studies*, 96-105; J.K. Elliott, 'The International Project to Establish a Critical Apparatus to Luke's Gospel', *NTS* 29 (1983) 531-8; *idem*, 'The Purpose and Construction of a Critical Apparatus to a Greek New Testament', in W. Schrage (ed.), *Studien zum Text und zur Ethik des Neuen Testaments. Festschrift zum 80. Geburtstag von Heinrich Greeven* (Berlin/New York: de Gruyter, 1986), 125-43; *idem*, *A Survey of Manuscripts Used in Editions of the Greek New Testament* (Leiden: Brill, 1987); W.J. Elliott, 'The Need for an Accurate and Comprehensive Collation of All Known Greek NT Manuscripts with their Individual Variants noted *in pleno*', in Elliott, *Studies*, 137-43; E.J. Epp, 'Toward the Clarification of the Term "Textual Variant"', in Elliott, *Studies*, 153-73 (reprinted in Epp & Fee, *Studies*, 47-61); M. Silva, 'Modern Critical Editions and Apparatuses of the

With satisfaction, however, we notice that energetic work on the testimony of the Church fathers and also on some of the heretics is being taken up. Our methodology in using this testimony is being refined.[3]

New Testament exegesis has been aware for a long time that New Testament texts are not absolutely devoid of secondary accretions, of glosses, of additions. Some of our exegetes have been reluctant to admit the facts whenever manuscript testimony to corruption in our Greek texts is lacking. Let us be clear about this: I regard it as a deficiency of an edition, if *cruces interpretum* are not marked within its edited text. A user of such an edition would have to conclude either that the editor considers his edited text to be free from corruption or, else, that he was failing in one of his responsibilities, the task of *recensio*.

Today I wish to open discussion on two apparent glosses in the gospel of Mark, namely 1:2-3 and 9:12b. Manuscript evidence to support my view is not at hand in the case of 9:12b. It is not unequivocal in the case of 1:2-3. Hence the author who set out to write his book is our decisive witness.[4]

Greek New Testament', in Ehrman & Holmes, 283-96; M.L. West, *Textual Criticism and Editorial Technique* (Stuttgart: Teubner, 1973).

[3] See my review of U. Schmid, *Marcion und sein Apostolos. Rekonstruktion und historische Einordnung der marcionitischen Paulusbriefausgabe* (Berlin/New York: de Gruyter, 1995) in *NovT* 42 (1997) 396-405, and B.D. Ehrman, 'Heracleon and the "Western" Textual Tradition', *NTS* 40 (1994) 161-79. Cf. also the surveys of G.D. Fee, J.L. North, and S.P. Brock, in Ehrman & Holmes, 196-236.

[4] There is evidence that the present text of Mark is marred by further glosses not generally recognized as secondary texts. One of these is to be found in Mk 10:32. Nigel Turner called attention to an irregular δέ in this verse: 'οἱ δέ does not mark a change of subject' (Turner, *Syntax*, 37). His suggestion that καί be read here is not acceptable, though. There is a wide selection of variant readings which indicate a disturbed text. It is preferable to follow the testimony of D K fam[13] 28 700 1010 a b. Mark's καὶ ἐθαμβοῦντο was glossed in various ways. Several textual critics have recognized corruption here and have made suggestions to heal it. G. Zuntz proposed omitting καὶ ἐθαμβοῦντο of which our gloss is a fuller and simpler version. C.H. Turner suggested the conjecture ἐθαμβεῖτο. Cp. G. Zuntz, 'Ein Heide las das Markusevangelium', in H. Cancik (ed.), *Markus-Philologie. Historische, literargeschichtliche und stilistische Untersuchungen zum zweiten Evangelium* (Tübingen: Mohr, 1984), 205-22, see 215; C.H. Turner, *The Study of the New*

1. *A Gloss in Mark 9:12b:*

καὶ πῶς γέγραπται ἐπὶ τὸν υἱὸν τοῦ ἀνθρώπου, ἵνα πολλὰ πάθῃ καὶ ἐξουδενηθῇ;

The passage Mk 9:11-13 is considered a redactional text. It was not merely inherited by Mark, he wrote it. R. Bultmann argued that verse 11 refers to 9:1. Lightfoot agreed.[5] In this passage Jesus gives privileged instruction to his disciples. The question about the teaching of the Scribes takes up a theme vital for a Jewish-Christian community. If Elijah needs to appear before the consummation of the age, how can Christian claims be upheld? Jesus supplies the answer. But the meaning of this saying does not lie at its surface: 'But I say unto you Elijah has come. And they did to him as they wished, as it is written with regard to him.' The thoughtful reader is meant to gather that John is the Elijah *redivivus* alluded to. Matthew who copies this text enlarges. Under such circumstances the view is absolutely intolerable that Mark should have inserted the gloss himself. I refer to Johannes Weiß, Rudolf Bultmann, Alexander Pallis, Ernst Lohmeyer, Norman Perrin, Gerd Theißen.[6]

Or is there a convincing interpretation of the text? Taken as a gloss its meaning would be: How is it possible to find a Scriptural reference stating that the Son of man must suffer much and be put to nothing? An answer cannot well refer to the central passage which

---

Testament 1883 and 1920 (Oxford: Clarendon Press, ³1926), 62. The paper presented here discusses readings which lack the specific evidence used in the traditional text-critical procedures.

[5] R. Bultmann, *Geschichte der synoptischen Tradition* (Göttingen: Vandenhoeck & Ruprecht, ²1931), 132 and note 1; R. Bultmann, *Geschichte der synoptischen Tradition. Ergänzungsheft*, ed. G. Theißen & P. Vielhauer (Göttingen: Vandenhoeck & Ruprecht, ⁵1979), 51. R.H. Lightfoot, *History and Interpretation in the Gospels* (London: Hodder & Stoughton, 1935), 92.

[6] As quoted in note 5. Cf. also J. Weiß, *Das älteste Evangelium. Ein Beitrag zum Verständnis des Markus-Evangeliums und der ältesten evangelischen Überlieferung* (Göttingen: Vandenhoeck & Ruprecht, 1903), 233; A. Pallis, *Notes on St. Mark and St. Matthew* (London: Milford, ²1932), 31; E. Lohmeyer, *Das Evangelium des Markus* (Göttingen: Vandenhoeck & Ruprecht, ¹⁰1937), 183 note 1; N. Perrin, 'The Christology of Mark: A Study in Methodology', in *JR* 51 (1971) 173-87 (reprinted in W.R. Telford (ed.), *The Interpretation of Mark* [Edinburgh: T&T Clark, ²1995], 125-40, especially 135).

Mark has in mind. For this quotation is carefully prepared by the text of the first announcement of the passion (8:31). Its ἀπεδοκίμασαν (12:10f) is forceful and well placed at the climax of a parable with fatal momentum.

Does the context of 9:12b give clues to a commentator? Pesch considers this passage as part of a pre-Markan passion narrative.

Motives are merged.[7] The question 9:12b according to Pesch has the function of associating both men in their common destiny.[8] The verb ἐξουδενηθῇ refers to the text Ps 89:39 (LXX 88:38f) καὶ ἐξουδένωσας ... τὸν χριστόν σου. By taking up the imagery of the suffering righteous one the destiny of both men is brought into focus.

Since, however, the question 9:12b remains unanswered, we demand who asked it.

Werner H. Kelber approaches our passage from a less traditional point of view. In describing the narrative design of Mark he focuses his interest upon the hermeneutical and theological consequences recognizable in a stage of conscious literary transformation of received oral materials.[9]

Kelber calls attention to the function of Scripture references within the specific context of Mark's passion narrative. Reporting on an article of Howard C. Kee[10] he states: 'The author proceeded from

---

[7] R. Pesch, *Das Markusevangelium. II. Teil, Kommentar zu Kap. 8,27 – 16,20* (Freiburg: Herder, [4]1991), 71. The view that Mark is merely a redactor of a pre-Markan *Grundschrift* has been criticized. There seems to be wide agreement on Mark's use of pre-Markan material, but also a growing recognition of a distinct measure of creativity directed by the theological aims of this author. 'Mark is a composite text which displays considerable awkwardness at pericope level but considerable sophistication when viewed holistically.' See W.R. Telford, 'The Pre-Markan Tradition in Recent Research (1980-1990)', in F. van Segbroeck, C.M. Tuckett, G. Van Belle & J. Verheyden (eds), *The Four Gospels. Festschrift Frans Neirynck*, vol. 2 (Leuven: University Press and Peeters, 1992), 693-723, here 711.

[8] R. Pesch, *ibid.*, 79.

[9] W.H. Kelber, *The Oral and the Written Gospel. The Hermeneutics of Speaking and Writing in the Synoptic Tradition, Mark, Paul, and Q* (Philadelphia: Fortress Press, 1983).

[10] H.C. Kee, 'The Function of Scriptural Quotations and Allusions in Mark 11-16', in E.E. Ellis & E. Gräßer (eds), *Jesus und Paulus. Festschrift für Werner*

the observation that "the number of quotations from and allusions to scripture increases sharply" at the point where the narrative moves toward death. In Mark 11-16 Kee tabulated 57 scriptural quotations, approximately 160 allusions to scripture and 60 scriptural influences'.[11] This reliance on the authority of Scripture to give his passion narrative the desired emphasis is paralleled, as Kelber says, by the use of Scriptural allusions in some Markan Son of man sayings. 'In Mark 9:11-13 the passion of the Son of man is linked by divine necessity (*dei elthein prooton*) with that of Elijah, and both deaths are in accord with Scripture (9:12 *poos gegraptai*; 9:13 *kathoos gegraptai*).'[12] Accordingly the text of 9:12b is meaningful within Mark's design, if we follow this author here. We do not, and perhaps I will be permitted to repeat the statement that Mark does not give his Scripture reference at this early juncture of his narrative. In fact, there is no Scripture reference required, as far as Mark is concerned.

2. *Glosses in Mark 1:2-3:*

καθὼς γέγραπται ἐν τῷ Ἠσαΐᾳ τῷ προφήτῃ· ἰδοὺ ἀποστέλλω τὸν ἄγγελόν μου πρὸ προσώπου σου ὃς κατασκευάσει τὴν ὁδόν σου. φωνὴ βοῶντος ἐν τῇ ἐρήμῳ· ἑτοιμάσατε τὴν ὁδὸν κυρίου, εὐθείας ποιεῖτε τὰς τρίβους αὐτοῦ.

2.1 *Textual Evidence*

The beginning of the gospel of Mark is by no means void of textual alterations. A carefully phrased proem like the one written by the author of the gospel of Luke apparently commands some respect on the part of scribes. They desist from improving. As a consequence alterations in Luke 1:1-4 are less numerous and less momentous than the ones to be studied in Mark. The apparatus of NA^{27} lists one variant only involving Luke 1:3.[13]

Greek manuscripts, ancient versions and early Fathers are divided upon the originality of the phrase υἱοῦ θεοῦ in Mark 1:1.

Georg Kümmel zum 70. Geburtstag (Göttingen: Vandenhoeck & Ruprecht, 1975), 165-88.

[11] W.H. Kelber (see note 9), 196f.

[12] *Ibid.*, 196.

[13] A fuller apparatus is supplied by IGNT, *Luke*, I.1-2.

Many Church fathers are listed among the witnesses for the omission, among them Irenaeus and Origen.[14]

Some authors, indeed, were reluctant to consider υἱοῦ θεοῦ or as some witnesses have it υἱοῦ τοῦ θεοῦ as a gloss. The editors of UBS4 enclosed one form of the addition within square brackets. Their hesitation was explained by the strong testimony for the addition, among them B D and W, and also by the consideration that υἱοῦ θεοῦ could have been omitted by oversight.[15] There are strong arguments, however, to support the view that we meet an ancient gloss here.

One of them is based on the observation that this unit of variation is transmitted in three forms. Rather than assuming that some scribes replaced υἱοῦ θεοῦ by υἱοῦ τοῦ θεοῦ we may take the differing form of the apposition together with an early and widespread testimony for the omission as an indication that an addition was inserted at more than one occasion or place of origin.

A second argument is based on the observation that this verse is not the only one in Mark to transmit such an addition. As is well known, two similar additions to the text of Mark are found in Mk

---

[14] Origen, *Commentarii in Iohannem* I.13.81 (E. Preuschen, *Der Johannes-kommentar* [GCS 10; Leipzig, 1903], 18); I.24.128 and 129 (Preuschen, 134); Origen, *Contra Celsum* II.4 (P. Koetschau, *Schriften vom Martyrium: Buch I-IV gegen Celsus* [GCS 1; Leipzig, 1899], 131); Basil, *Contra Eunomium* II.15.15 (B. Sesboüé, G-M. de Durand, & L. Doutreleau, *Contre Eunome suivi de Eunome Apologie* [SC 299, 305; Paris, 1982, 1983], 58). The late character of the insertion is underscored by the observation that in Irenaeus it is transmitted together with the obviously corrected reading '*in prophetis*', see III.16.3 and III.10.6. Already in 1905 A. Merx called attention to this text-critical observation: A. Merx, *Die vier kanonischen Evangelien nach ihrem ältesten bekannten Texte. Übersetzung und Erläuterung der syrischen im Sinaikloster gefundenen Palimpsesthandschrift*, II.2. *Die Evangelien des Markus und Lukas* (Berlin: Reimer, 1905), 3, note 1. In the Greek text of Irenaeus, *Adv. haer.* III.11.8 (F. Sagnard, *Contre les hérésies, Livre III* [SC 34; Paris, 1952], 198]), we find 'Ἀρχὴ τοῦ εὐαγγελίου [...] ὡς γέγραπται ἐν Ἠσαΐᾳ τῷ προφήτῃ. In a note Sagnard adds: ''Ιησοῦ Χριστοῦ add. edd., quae uoces desunt in Barocciani 206 ut in lat.' (*loc. cit.*). J.M. Alexanian, 'The Armenian version of the New Testament', in Ehrman & Holmes, (157-72) 159, calls attention to the fact that the evidence of the Armenian version in support of the omission is not correctly rendered in the UBS3 (118). It is correctly given, however, in UBS4 (117).

[15] Metzger, *Textual Commentary II*, 62.

8:29, namely ὁ υἱὸς τοῦ θεοῦ or ὁ υἱὸς τοῦ θεοῦ τοῦ ζῶντος. Scribes, then, were eager to insert such phrases at appropriate places.

There is a third argument for this text-critical decision based on a consideration proper to this paper. The admission of this gloss into the text of Mark implies a modern disregard for the care with which this author introduces concepts and referential matter into the contexts of his book. A heavenly voice, unheard by onlookers, imparts this item of information in the context of a narrative unit, often referred to as prologue. As Frank J. Matera and others pointed out, this voice imparts privileged information to the reader, information which is withheld from the *dramatis personae*, save the person addressed.[16]

Not a few authors defended the originality of υἱοῦ θεοῦ by stating that an omission by oversight is easily explained where a series of *nomina sacra* is involved.[17] In a recent text-critical study Bart D. Ehrman appealed to a fresh observation to meet the fallacy of such an argument within this debate. 'In further support of this view is a practical consideration that until quite recently has been entirely overlooked. It should strike us as somewhat odd that the kind of careless mistake alleged to have occurred here, the omission of two rather important words, should have happened precisely where it does – within the first six words of the beginning of a book ... I should note that recent manuscript analyses have indeed demonstrated that scribes were more conscientious transcribers at the beginning of a document.'[18] Υἱοῦ θεοῦ, of course, is a secondary

---

[16] F.J. Matera, 'The Prologue as the Interpretative Key to Mark's Gospel', *JSNT* 34 (1988) 3-20 (reprinted in W.R. Telford (ed.), *The Interpretation of Mark* [Edinburgh: T&T Clark, ²1995], 289-306). The value of this fascinating interpretation is not impaired by the circumstance that this author fails to realize that υἱοῦ θεοῦ is not part of Mark's text, cf. pp. 4 and 6 (290 and 292).

[17] R. Pesch, *Das Markusevangelium, I. Teil. Einleitung und Kommentar zu Kap. 1,1 – 8,26* (Freiburg: Herder, ⁵1989), 74 note a.

[18] Ehrman, *Orthodox Corruption*, 73; *idem*, 'The Text of Mark in the Hands of the Orthodox', *LQ* 5 (1991) [143-56] 150f; P.M. Head, 'A Text-Critical Study of Mark 1:1. The Beginning of the Gospel of Jesus Christ', *NTS* 37 (1991) [621-9] 629.

addition to complete the list of references to this important concept of Mark (cp. 1:11, 3:11, 5:7, 9:7, 12:6, 13:32, 14:61, 15:39).[19]

Critical editions inform us that the series of verses inserted between Verses 1 and 4 show three forms. Some witnesses have verse three and omit the text of the quotation blended from two sources, Ex 23:20 and Mal 3:1.

Other witnesses merge the text of this blend of quotations to the text of verse 3, a slightly adapted quotation from Isa 40:3.

Two witnesses add further verses taken from Luke. Both add to the quotation from Isa 40:3, but they do not exactly follow either the text of their Lucan source, as far as we can gather, or the text of Isa 40:4-8. The text of Old Latin c and of W may be taken from the apparatuses of Tischendorf and von Soden, or from the respective editions of Sanders and of Matzkow-Aland.[20] Since the texts of both manuscripts differ from each other and do not find the support of any other known manuscript tradition, it is obvious that these additions were added much later than the ones we have to consider.

For our purpose it is not necessary to discuss the text of the Washington Gospels and Colbertinus in detail. These manuscripts bear witness to a desire of early scribes to augment the scriptural base of Mark's references to John the Baptist. If verse 2b of chapter 1 could be proven to be secondary, this would lengthen the list of such insertions.

---

[19] 'In no other passage in the Gospels is there any evidence that "Son of God" was ever omitted from the text', P.M. Head, 'Christology and Textual Transmission: Reverential Alterations in the Synoptic Gospels', *NovT* 35 (1993) [105-29] 115; *idem*, 'A Text-Critical Study of Mark 1.1', 627. Among the authors who defended the shorter text are the following exegetes: Merx, *Die vier kanonischen Evangelien*, II.2, p.3; J. Wellhausen, *Das Evangelium Marci* (Berlin: Reimer, ²1909), 3; G. Wohlenberg, *Das Evangelium des Markus* (Leipzig: Deichert, ³1930), 36; J. Sickenberger, *Die Geschichte des Neuen Testamentes* (Bonn: Hanstein, ⁴1934), 32; J. Slomp, 'Are the Words "Son of God" in Mark 1.1 Original?', *BT* 28 (1977) [143-50] 146, 150; A.Y. Collins, 'Establishing the Text: Mark 1:1', in Fornberg & Hellholm, 111-27.

[20] H.A. Sanders (ed.), *Facsimile of the Washington Manuscript of the Four Gospels in the Freer Collection* (Ann Arbor: The University of Michigan, 1912); A. Jülicher (ed.), *Itala. Das Neue Testament in altlateinischer Überlieferung, nach den Handschriften herausgegeben von Adolf Jülicher, durchgesehen und zum Druck besorgt von Walter Matzkow †, und Kurt Aland.* II. *Marcusevangelium* (Berlin: de Gruyter, ²1970).

In addition to the disorders listed, according to Tischendorf, there is indication of Patristic testimony to the effect that 1:2b is not uniformly supported by this branch of our tradition. In his *Octava* Tischendorf lists three Fathers who according to him did not read 1:2b in the context of a quotation. These are Basil the Great, Epiphanius, and Victorinus.[21]

It is doubtful, however, whether this conclusion bears scrutiny. It is true, two of these references may be taken to support Tischendorf's conclusion. Basil writes: Ἀρχὴ τοῦ εὐαγγελίου Ἰησοῦ Χριστοῦ καθὼς γέγραπται ἐν τῷ Ἠσαΐᾳ τῷ προφήτῃ· φωνὴ βοῶντος.[22] Comparing the beginnings of the four gospels Basil praises the theological approach of the gospel of John as a climax of this genre. The *incipit* of John is quoted verbatim, the *incipit* of Matthew and Mark, likewise. The beginning of Luke is not quoted, but is characterized briefly, instead.

Basil's text of Mark as quoted above is augmented by C V and numerous later (or inferior) witnesses with the insertion of ἐν τῇ ἐρήμῳ. If this is the younger text, as the editor seems to assume, we find here an inclination to enlarge similar to the one observed in the gospel manuscripts c and W mentioned above. But Basil's quotation of Mark does not prove beyond doubt that Basil read exactly what he quotes. Basil may well have shortened his text in order to improve the structure of his argument. At least, we cannot wholly exclude this possibility.

The reference of Epiphanius to Mark may be seen in a similar way. Μᾶρκος ... ἀλλὰ ἀπὸ τῆς ἐν τῷ Ἰορδάνῃ πραγματείας ποιεῖται τὴν εἰσαγωγὴν τοῦ εὐαγγελίου καί φησιν, ἀρχὴ τοῦ εὐαγγελίου ὡς γέγραπται ἐν Ἠσαΐᾳ τῷ προφήτῃ, φωνὴ βοῶντος ἐν τῇ ἐρήμῳ, κτλ.[23] The characterization of the narrative design of Mark's *incipit* in another passage of this author asserts that Mark quoted the Law and the prophets. We read: πῶς τε ὁ Μᾶρκος περὶ τῶν ἐν τῷ κόσμῳ πεπραγματευμένων ‹διηγήσατο› καὶ φωνῆς βοώσης ἐν τῇ ἐρήμῳ περί ‹τε›

[21] C. Tischendorf, *Novum Testamentum Graece*, vol. I (Leipzig: Giesecke & Devrient, ³1869), 217.

[22] *Contra Eunomium*, II.15.15 (Sesboüé, de Durand, Doutreleau, 58).

[23] *Panarion*, LI.6.4 (K. Holl, *Epiphanius: Panarion, Haer. 34-64* [GCS 31; Leipzig, 1922], 255).

τοῦ κυρίου τοῦ διὰ προφητῶν πεπροφητευμένου καὶ νόμου.[24] But it is not evident which quotation he found in his manuscript. If this τοῦ διὰ προφητῶν πεπροφητευμένου καὶ νόμου refers to a transmitted reading ἐν τοῖς προφήταις (1:2a), this would be an indication of a late form of Mark's *incipit* as found by Epiphanius. In quoting he drops at least Ἰησοῦ Χριστοῦ. The text of the manuscript he quoted is not clear.

The text of Victorinus in his *Commentarii in Apocalypsin* is too short to support the view of Tischendorf. He writes: 'Marcus incipit sic: initium evangelii Iesu Christi sicut scriptum est in Esaia'.[25] What follows is attributed to Hieronymus by Haussleiter.[26]

On the other hand, there is no doubt that Origen found both quotations in his gospel of Mark. His testimony to this effect is impressive. Not only does he quote *in extenso*, he adds that the author altered the wording of both quotations in a characteristic way. For he replaces τὰς τρίβους τοῦ θεοῦ ἡμῶν of Mal 3.1 by τὰς τρίβους αὐτοῦ, and he omits ἔμπροσθέν μου from the text of Isa 40.3: οὐ παρέθετο τὸ προσκείμενον τὸ »Ἔμπροσθέν μου«.[27]

---

[24] *Panarion*, LXIX.22.4 (J. Dummer, *Epiphanius: Panarion, Haer. 65-80* [GCS 37; Berlin, ²1985], 173). Insertions into the reconstructed text are emendations of Karl Holl.

[25] *Comm. in Apocalypsin*, IV.4 (J. Haussleiter, *Victorini episcopi Petavionensis Opera* [CSEL 49; Vienna, 1916], 52).

[26] Alexander Globe stated that Irenaeus is one of the authors who testify to the omission of 1:2b from the text of Mark. This statement is not justified, as A.Y. Collins pointed out: 'He is correct in stating that Irenaeus cited only vss. 1 and 3 from John 1 and only vss 1 and 18 from Matthew 1. The paraphrase of Luke 1, however, must include at least vs 8, as well as vs 5, because only vs 8 mentions Zachary's offering sacrifice to God. Globe's statement that Irenaeus omits the quotation from Malachi in Mark 1:2 is misleading, because it implies that the following quotation from Isaiah is cited. It is not. In fact, the quotations of Irenaeus are selections, not "contractions".' (A.Y. Collins, 'Establishing the Text: Mark 1:1', 113.) See A. Globe, 'The Caesarean Omission of the Phrase "Son of God" in Mark 1:1', *HTR* 75 (1982) 209-18.

[27] *Comm. in Iohannem*, I.24.131 and I.26.137 (Preuschen 135, 136).

2.2 *Lachmann's Critique of the Traditional Insertion of vv. 2 and 3 into the Text of Mark*

As early as 1830 Lachmann voiced the opinion that the verses Mark 1:2-3 are no part of the original text of this author. This opinion falls into line with the observation that the state of preservation of the gospel of Mark is far from excellent. 'Often where our traditions fluctuate considerably this may contribute to reaching a decision. The abundance of fluctuating readings in the Gospel of Mark leads everyone to the conviction that its transmission was hardly careful and that certainly in a number of passages it is corrupted.'[28]

In passing Lachmann gives his position on the Synoptic question. He has not found evidence to support the view that Mark knows the text of either of the other Synoptic gospels[29] or, to be more specific, that he abstracts Old Testament quotations from one of the Synoptic gospels in order to use them in a different function and context.[30]

Already here we find an argument which we read also in the second edition of his Greek New Testament. Mark 'never uses a passage of the Old Testament except in direct speech'.[31]

In addition to this argument which appeals to a literary reading of Mark's narrative, Lachmann takes exception to two specific shortcomings of the Received Text.

a. A quotation to give legitimation to the forerunner quoted in the name of the evangelist himself is out of harmony with the evident purpose of his introduction. 'If indeed the author designed to do something extraordinary in the beginning of the book, something he did not do again, certainly a testimony of Holy Scripture on behalf of Christ was needed rather than one on behalf of the forerunner.'[32]

b. The quotation disrupts the easy flow of the narrative and obstructs the understanding of an important point the author wishes to make. 'What is more, these words interrupt the progression of speech, make it totally incomprehensible, speech which is – without them – simple and smooth: ἀρχὴ τοῦ εὐαγγελίου Ἰησοῦ Χριστοῦ υἱοῦ

[28] C. Lachmann, 'Rechenschaft über seine Ausgabe des Neuen Testaments', *TSK* 3 (1830) [817-45] 841 [my translation].
[29] *Idem*, p. 843.
[30] *Idem*, p. 844.
[31] *Idem*, p. 843.
[32] *Idem*, p. 844.

θεοῦ ἐγένετο Ἰωάννης, βαπτίζων ἐν τῇ ἐρήμῳ καὶ κηρύσσων βάπτισμα μετανοίας εἰς ἄφεσιν ἁμαρτιῶν.[33]

Lachmann summarized his critique of these glosses in the *Praefatio* to the second volume of his Greek New Testament of 1850.

> Mark 1:1.4 Ἀρχὴ τοῦ εὐαγγελίου Ἰησοῦ Χριστοῦ υἱοῦ θεοῦ ἐγένετο Ἰωάννης βαπτίζων ἐν τῇ ἐρήμῳ. These words were singled out by Origen 4.15e: 'For how can John be a beginning of the gospel?' Nor can these words, ἐγένετο Ἰωάννης βαπτίζων ἐν τῇ ἐρήμῳ, be understood in any reasonable way if separated from the preceding words, unless you allow the matter to have been told unexpectedly and without plan, this 'John made his appearance baptizing in the desert...' But in the beginning of Mark the interjection subverts the true interpretation. It is an annotation by pious readers, if I am not mistaken, in contrast to the practice of this evangelist who does not use the words of Old Testament authors unless they come from the lips of those whom he causes to speak. Therefore, when one of these readers had added what usually was placed here, ὡς γέγραπται ἐν τῷ Ἠσαΐᾳ τῷ προφήτῃ φωνὴ βοῶντος ἐν τῇ ἐρήμῳ, ἑτοιμάσατε τὴν ὁδὸν κυρίου, εὐθείας ποιεῖτε τὰς τρίβους αὐτοῦ, another reader succeeded him who decided that what Luke and Matthew had put somewhere else ought to be inserted here, ἰδοὺ ἀποστέλλω τὸν ἄγγελόν μου πρὸ προσώπου σου, ὃς κατασκευάσει τὴν ὁδόν σου. Because the name Isaias did not suit these words, they had to write what others have, namely ἐν τοῖς προφήταις. In conflict with the same practice of Mark, which I have stated to have been observed by him in quoting testimonies of sacred Scripture, is what we read in 15:28 and what is omitted by many and the best manuscripts καὶ ἐπληρώθη ἡ γραφὴ ἡ λέγουσα καὶ μετὰ ἀνόμων ἐλογίσθη, a text Luke gives at a far distant passage in a speech of Christ 22:37.[34]

---

[33] *Idem*, p. 844.
[34] C. Lachmann, *Novum Testamentum Graece et Latine*, vol. II (Berlin: Reimer, [2]1850), p.VIf.

Lachmann argued that none of the passages quoted in Mk 1:1-3 were supplied by the author, but were inserted by certain readers, pious men, as he surmised. I wish to underscore a few points in this argument. Lachmann refers his readers to a literary reading of Mark's text. He expects them to observe that Mark as the author of a gospel disclaims any argument from Scripture in his own name. Lachmann, too, is convinced that the approach of this author to his narrative was not rash, but that he proceeded with care. Clouds may overshadow the figures of a scene, but to surprise the reader by an ill-assorted series of quotes is not to be expected of an accomplished narrator. Lachmann, the distinguished editor of *Der Nibelunge Not mit der Klage*, of the *Iwein*, of *Lucretius*, refers to the argument from context adding only necessary detail. He asks Origen to state what he himself wishes to say. In concluding, Lachmann quotes another example of an inappropriate interjection. Both force the author to forgo his role as a narrator and make him a teacher. Lachmann's example parallels two closely related arguments, an argument from style as supported by excellent witnesses and an argument from style supported by no witness at all. Both lead to the recommendation of a shorter text on the authority and experience of a literary critic and editor, one of the finest in the history of our discipline.[35]

2.3 *The Syntax of the First Sentence of Mark's Gospel*

Lachmann's arguments force us to consider whether the beginning of Mark's gospel has been handed down to us in its original wording. There are evident insertions, namely the appositions υἱοῦ θεοῦ and υἱοῦ τοῦ θεοῦ, and also in some traditions additional verses. There is

[35] Lachmann's view was endorsed by Ch.H. Weiße, *Die evangelische Geschichte kritisch und philosophisch bearbeitet*, vol. I (Leipzig: Breitkopf, 1838), 258; J. Wellhausen, *Das Evangelium Marci*, 3f.; *idem*, *Einleitung in die ersten drei Evangelien* (Berlin: Reimer, ²1911), 44, note 1; A.F. Loisy, *L'Evangile selon Marc* (Paris: Nourry, 1912), 55f.: 'Celle-ci est d'ailleurs un cas unique dans le second Evangile, ou le narrateur n'allègue jamais de l'Ancien Testament; elle vient en surcharge et ne se lie pas au récit, qu'elle glose par anticipation.' W. Marxsen called attention to the fact that the passage quoted presents the only 'Reflexionszitat' used by this author. He did not discuss the critical position developed by Carl Lachmann: W. Marxsen, *Der Evangelist Markus. Studien zur Redaktionsgeschichte des Evangeliums* (Göttingen: Vandenhoeck & Ruprecht, ²1959), 18, note 4.

at least one scribal correction, namely the variant ἐν τοῖς προφήταις, A W fam^{13} vg^{ms} sy^{h} Irenaeus lat.[36] Textual criticism enables us to gain from the transmitted variants the evidently more original form.

Is this evidently more original form of the text Mark's text? If stylistic anomalies are visible against the background of Mark's Greek, this may cast doubt on the transmitted text and may give additional support to Lachmann's observation of an ancient corruption. If there are no anomalies in the first verses of Mark, it ought to be possible to reconstruct its syntax in a convincing way.[37]

A number of exegetes argued that the prologue proper of Mark began with the conjunction καθώς. This implies that Mark placed a subordinate clause at the beginning of his prologue and, also, that the words ἀρχὴ τοῦ εὐαγγελίου Ἰησοῦ Χριστοῦ are meant to be a superscription.[38] It is widely conceded that Mark, when using εὐαγγέλιον, refers to some oral proclamation of his time and not to a written gospel in its later technical sense.[39] The view that ἀρχὴ τοῦ εὐαγγελίου Ἰησοῦ Χριστοῦ refers to the first part of Mark's text, or is meant to introduce the whole gospel in a solemn manner would tend to lead to the assumption that this part of Mark's gospel was added at a time when its text needed to be edited. This conclusion, however, is rarely ever suggested.[40]

---

[36] See above, 150-1.

[37] In his analysis of Mark 1:1-15 M. Eugene Boring presents a concise review of the options discussed in the exegetical literature: M.E. Boring, 'Mark 1:1-15 and the Beginning of the Gospel', *Semeia* 52 (1990) 43-81.

[38] F.J.A. Hort championed this view and defended the 'separateness of v.1': F.J.A. Hort, 'Notes on Select Readings', in Westcott & Hort, vol. 2, Appendix, 23. This view was taken up, among others, by J. Wellhausen, *Das Evangelium Marci* (Berlin: Reimer, ^{2}1909), 3; M.-J. Lagrange, *Evangile selon Saint Marc* (Paris: Gabalda, ^{4}1929), 1; V. Taylor, *The Gospel according to St. Mark* (London: Macmillan, ^{2}1966), 152; R. Pesch, *Das Markusevangelium* I. Teil, 74; and by M.E. Boring, *op. cit.*, 47f.

[39] 'Im NT ist εὐαγγέλιον die mündliche Predigt, nie werden die Briefe oder die Evangelien εὐαγγέλιον genannt', G. Friedrich, 'εὐαγγέλιον', *TWNT* II.733. In the context of the Sayings gospel Q the term εὐαγγελίζεσθαι is discussed by James M. Robinson: J.M. Robinson, 'The Sayings Gospel Q', in F. Van Segbroeck, C.M. Tuckett, G. Van Belle & J. Verheyden (eds), *The Four Gospels 1992. Festschrift Frans Neirynck*, vol. I [361-88] 370-2.

[40] This suggestion is proposed by G. Friedrich, *op. cit.*, 724, note 52, with a reference to Tatian and the Evangeliarium Hierosolymitanum. I will seek to

There are authors who do not not accept this view. Gerhard Arnold, for instance, argued that a quotation introduced by καθὼς γέγραπται is never, in all the instances listed by him, construed with what follows. 'All quotations introduced in this way refer to an immediately preceding context.'[41] Similarly J. Keith Elliott stated: 'In Mark (8 instances) and Matthew (21:6, 26:24, 27:10 *v.l.*, 28:6) the καθὼς clause follows the main clause. The only instance where this rule is in question is at Mark 1:2.'[42] Arnold's conclusion, therefore, is that 1:2f must be construed with what precedes and that 1:4 is the beginning of a second sentence. Arnold compared opening remarks in numerous hellenistic and classical writings and considered 1:1-3 as an example of such opening remarks. While this view is hardly convincing here,[43] what Arnold writes about καθὼς cannot easily be brushed aside. Parallels for this καθὼς in Mark as presented by Vincent Taylor[44] are not quite to the point.[45]

If ἀρχὴ is not an element of a traditional *topos* of an opening paragraph, it may not refer to the beginning of the book which Mark is about to write. On the other hand I agree with the view of Arnold that alleged parallels for a superscription ἀρχὴ τοῦ εὐαγγελίου Ἰησοῦ Χριστοῦ do not really support this interpretation. In particular the introduction in Hos 1:2f ἀρχὴ λόγου κυρίου πρὸς Ωσηε is not a superscription.[46]

---

show that this proposition is based on a misunderstanding of Mark's narrative design, see below.

[41] G. Arnold, 'Mk 1,1 und Eröffnungswendungen in griechischen und lateinischen Schriften', *ZNW* 68 (1977) [123-7] 123 [my translation].

[42] J.K. Elliott, 'καθως and ωσπερ in the New Testament', *Fil Neotest* 4 (1991) [55-8] 55. Similarly R.A. Guelich, '"The Beginning of the Gospel". Mark 1:1-15', *BR* 27 (1982) [5-15] 6.

[43] The prologue of Mark shows little contact with the conventions of ancient προοίμια, πρόλογοι, or the less formal *incipits*; see D.E. Smith, 'Narrative Beginnings in Ancient Literature and Theory', *Semeia* 52 (1990) 1-9, and R.C. Tannehill, 'Beginning to Study "How Gospels Begin"', *Semeia* 52 (1990) 185-91.

[44] V. Taylor, *The Gospel according to St. Mark*, 153.

[45] Mark lacks the sequence καθὼς ... οὕτως in our passage. In 1 Cor. 2:9 ἀλλά refers to matter already discussed; see G. Arnold, *op. cit.*, 124.

[46] The superscription of Hosea is found in verse 1:1 of the book; cf. G. Arnold, *op. cit.*, 123.

Several authors gave attention to the specific ways in which Mark introduces explanatory and referential matter in the form of a parenthesis.[47] The manner in which this material is embedded into narrative units occasionally engenders misunderstanding. C.H. Turner recommended an interpretation of Mk 1:1-4 in which 1:2-3 appears as a parenthesis. And H.J. Holtzmann argued that a text comprising only 2a.3 could be accepted as a parenthesis more easily than the traditional text could.[48] We ought to notice, however, that the stylistic anomaly of Mark's καθὼς γέγραπται is not dealt with in a convincing way on the basis of such an interpretation. Nor is it admissible to use an *argumentum ad hominem* here, as Boring does.[49] The view that an author ending on Mark 16:8 could have done anything is not acceptable.

Another anomaly is noticeable in the series of quotations allegedly assembled by the author of this gospel. On comparing ἐν τοῖς προφήταις with the reading ἐν τῷ Ἠσαΐᾳ τῷ προφήτῃ we decided that the former looks like a scribal correction of the latter text. And the list of witnesses representing both readings seemed to support our decision. There is yet a third variant to be considered at this point of the transmitted text, namely the reading of D Θ fam1 700 ℓ844 ℓ2211 Irenaeus Origen *partim* Epiphanius: ἐν Ἠσαΐᾳ τῷ προφήτῃ.

If we compare this text with the preferred reading of ℵ B L Δ 33 565 892 1241 2427 syp.hmg copt Origen *partim* ἐν τῷ Ἠσαΐᾳ τῷ προφήτῃ, we are inclined to regard it as another scribal correction dependent upon the preferred text. The article certainly is awkward.

---

[47] C.H. Turner, 'Notes on Marcan Usage, IV. Parenthetical clauses in Mark', *JTS* 26 (1924/25) 145-56 (reprinted in Elliott, *Language*, 23-35); M. Zerwick, *Untersuchungen zum Markus-Stil. Ein Beitrag zur stilistischen Durcharbeitung des Neuen Testaments* (Rome: Pontificio Instituto Biblico, 1937), 130-8.

[48] H.J. Holtzmann, *Das Evangelium nach Marcus*, in *idem*, *Die Synoptiker: Hand-Commentar zum Neuen Testament* II (Tübingen/Leipzig: J.C.B. Mohr [Paul Siebeck], 31901), 111f. The view that 1:2b is a secondary gloss added to Mark's text is defended by, among others, M.-J. Lagrange, *Evangile selon Saint Marc*, 4; J. Sickenberger, *Die Geschichte des Neuen Testamentes* (Bonn: Hanstein, 41934), 33; A.E.J. Rawlinson, *The Gospel according to St. Mark* (London: Methuen, 71949), 6; V. Taylor, *The Gospel according to St. Mark*, 153.

[49] M.E. Boring, 'Mark 1:1-15 and the Beginning of the Gospel', *Semeia* 52 (1990) 50. Boring criticizes M.A. Tolbert, *Sowing the Gospel. Mark's World in Literary-Historical Perspective* (Minneapolis: Fortress, 1989), 241-6.

For we know that Mark is particular about his articles when introducing characters for the first time. Is it safe to assume that the article here goes back to the author? Among the quotations in the Fathers which I have noted I have only once seen a text which took up this article. All other quotations had ἐν Ἠσαΐᾳ τῷ προφήτῃ.[50]

This text, which apparently is considered acceptable by the authors quoting it, may in part lead back to manuscripts which had this corrected reading. In other cases obviously the Fathers put down what they considered correct: ἐν Ἠσαΐᾳ τῷ προφήτῃ. If so many of them are positive about this stylistic feature, how can we assume that the author himself was inattentive in this respect right at the beginning of a gospel? When introducing John, when introducing Jesus, Mark is careful to use the anarthrous form of the names.[51] Evidently the assumption is to be preferred that καθὼς γέγραπται ἐν τῷ Ἠσαΐᾳ τῷ προφήτῃ κτλ. was supplied by some later hand, not by the author.

C.H. Turner acted as a spokesman of ancient exegetes, of Origen, of Basil, of Victor of Antioch. He considered 1:2f as one of the characteristic parentheses of this author and argued that the syntax of 1:1 must be seen as connected with 1:4. 'The beginning of the proclamation of good news about Jesus as Messiah and Son of God, was John the Baptizer's preaching in the wilderness of a baptism of repentance for remission of sins.'[52]

---

[50] Irenaeus, *Adv. haereses* III.11.8 (Sagnard 198); Origen, *Comm. in Iohannem* I.13.81 (Preuschen 18); Origen, *Contra Celsum* II.4 (Koetschau 131); Basil, *Contra Eunomium* II.15.15 (Sesboüé, de Durand, & Doutreleau 58); Epiphanius, *Panarion* LI.5.4 (Holl 255); Victorinus IV.4 (Haussleiter 52). It is true that there is one passage in Origen which has Ἀρχὴ τοῦ εὐαγγελίου Ἰησοῦ Χριστοῦ καθὼς γέγραπται ἐν [τῷ] Ἠσαΐᾳ τῷ προφήτῃ· Ἰδοὺ ἐγὼ ἀποστέλλω τὸν ἄγγελόν μου πρὸ προσώπου σου, namely Origen, *Commentarii in Iohannem* I.24.128 and 129 (Preuschen 134) and the manuscripts seem to support the article. But the editor of Origen, Preuschen, prefers the form of text quoted in *Contra Celsum* and remarks: 'τω fehlt S. 17,32 u[nd] C. Cels. II 4 [I.131.14 Koetschau] u. ist wohl mit D. 1. 22 alii Iren zu str[eichen]' (134).

[51] C.H. Turner in dealing with Markan usage apparently does not notice the reason for his omission of the article in 1:9. His respect for the evidence, however, leads him in both the cases he discusses to decisions which are, at least in my opinion, correct. Cf. C.H. Turner, in Elliott, *Language*, 137.

[52] C.H. Turner, 'Marcan Usage: Notes, Critical and Exegetical, on the Second Gospel', *JTS* 28 (1926/27) 146 (Elliott, *Language*, 24).

I prefer to accept the arguments of Carl Lachmann and consider it possible that in some passages of our gospels corruption took place, even if manuscript evidence for the original text is missing. Corruption normally leaves traces and I have dealt with some of these. I am not willing to consider the admission of this possibility as a serious deficiency in a literary analysis of our sources.[53]

I summarize the result of these considerations regarding Mark's text: ἀρχὴ τοῦ εὐαγγελίου Ἰησοῦ Χριστοῦ ἐγένετο Ἰωάννης ὁ βαπτίζων ἐν τῇ ἐρήμῳ κηρύσσων βάπτισμα μετανοίας εἰς ἄφεσιν ἁμαρτιῶν.

1. This sentence states the close association of the public appearance of John with what was later styled the gospel of Jesus Christ.

2. The form of this sentence can be characterized as a summary such as Mark usually places at the beginning of a major section of his narrative.

3. This sentence is pregnant in its conciseness; it avoids unnecessary articles to give the beginning of the book dignity: ἐν τῇ ἐρήμῳ κηρύσσων βάπτισμα μετανοίας εἰς ἄφεσιν ἁμαρτιῶν.

4. The first word of this sentence is predicative. For this reason the anarthrous ἀρχὴ is correct, it conforms to Colwell's rule.

5. The decision to place a predicate at the beginning of a book is perfectly admissible. An author who speaks an Aramaic dialect, as we assume Mark to have done, will normally tend to use such word order for various purposes. Here we see the author aiming at dignified speech. His keynote requires further comment in a section which will follow.[54]

---

[53] Recently Christopher M. Tuckett argued for a balanced consideration of source-critical and text-critical data with special reference to the much discussed problem of the minor agreements in triple-tradition material. Some decades ago Frederick C. Grant argued that there is necessarily a certain degree of overlap involving form-critical and text-critical considerations. Cf. C.M. Tuckett, 'The Minor Agreements and Textual Criticism', in G. Strecker (ed.), *Minor Agreements. Symposium Göttingen 1991* (Göttingen: Vandenhoeck & Ruprecht, 1993) [119-42] 138, 142; F.C. Grant, 'Where Form Criticism and Textual Criticism Overlap', *JBL* 59 (1940) 11-21.

[54] See below.

2.4 *The Source of the Secondary Quotations in Mark 1:2f*
A number of authors have endeavoured to explain the purpose and function of Scriptural quotations in Mark's gospel.[55] They have analysed these texts in the context of Mark's redactional work or, more recently, they have analysed this evidence in an effort to understand Mark's literary and narrative techniques. These authors did not consider the alternative that Mark 1:2f was added to meet some later need.

Recent studies on the text of Q stress that the use of Scripture references is not a common element in Q. Sections incorporating Scripture quotations are ascribed to later editorial stages in the production of this written source.[56] We find explicit references in the temptation narrative and in Q 7:27.

James M. Robinson, in an analysis of 'conscious organizing intentions' in Q,[57] found traces of a formative stage in the theology of the Q community in which reasons for the ascription of the Son of God title were still discussed, and in which also the title ὁ ἐρχόμενος in its specific context within Q had not yet become a formally fixed element. A cento of clauses from Isaiah in Q 7:22 'serves to define Jesus' Inaugural Sermon and his healing of the Centurion's Boy as validating the ascription to him of the title ὁ ἐρχόμενος.'[58] The *inclusio* Q 7:18-35 does not yet presuppose the text of Luke 4:1-10 which apparently was formed at a later stage to give substance to some of

[55] D.S. New, *Old Testament Quotations in the Synoptic Gospels, and the Two Document Hypothesis*, SBLSCS 37 (Atlanta: Scholars Press, 1993); W.S. Vorster, 'The Function of the Use of the Old Testament in Mark', *Neot* 14 (1981) 62-72; H.C. Kee, 'The Function of Scriptural Quotations and Allusions in Mark 11-16', in E.E. Ellis & E. Gräßer (eds), *Jesus und Paulus*, 165-88; A. Suhl, *Die Funktion der alttestamentlichen Zitate und Anspielungen im Markusevangelium* (Gütersloh: Gütersloher Verlagshaus Gerd Mohn 1965).
[56] Arland D. Jacobson states, *The First Gospel. An introduction to Q* (Sonoma, Ca: Polebridge, 1992), 90f.: 'There are several signs of lateness in the temptation pericope: The use of the title, "Son of God", the use of the LXX and, indeed, of the only explicit quotations in the whole of Q; the apparently late literary form; and the use of the name for the Evil One, which is attested nowhere else in Q.'
[57] J.M. Robinson, 'The Sayings Gospel Q', in F. Van Segbroeck (ed.), *The Four Gospels 1992. Festschrift Frans Neirynck*, vol. I (Leuven: University Press and Peeters 1992), 361-88.
[58] *Ibid.*, 365.

the positions of the Q community in confrontation with their opponents.

> However, the distinctiveness of the role of the Son of God title in the Temptation must be seen more sharply: Christological titles are almost never derived or justified in the canonical texts themselves, but are rather presupposed and used as commonly known and accepted. But here the Temptation is built primarily (in two of the three tempations) around defining and defending that title. Jesus rejects the devil's inferences from that title, and validates himself as conforming to the true meaning of the title, in that he knows and observes Torah faithfully (he quotes Deut. 8,3; 6,16; 6,13 with the quotation formula, γέγραπται, found elsewhere in Q only at 7.27).[59]

Robinson concludes that the baptism of Jesus was included in the 'narrative preface of Q'.

> If the Baptism of Jesus, with the heavenly voice identifying him as ὁ υἱός μου ὁ ἀγαπητός is to be included in Q, then the temptation (Q 4.1-13) would be the authoritative Christian interpretation, similar to the role of Q 7.19-22 in Christianizing the title John had used, ὁ ἐρχόμενος (Q 3.16). These two instances of the formation of christology are rather unique in the New Testament, perhaps indicative of the archaic traditions preserved in Q.[60]

We have to bear in mind that the gospel of Mark is an early literary venture and that its presentation of Scriptural evidence necessarily exposes early phases of a process of research which sought to augment this evidence in the course of a number of years. Christian scribes who were engaged in this type of research had to overcome various difficulties. Not the least of these difficulties was the problem of gaining access to handwritten copies of prophetic and other Scriptures.

---

[59] *Ibid.*, 384.
[60] *Ibid.*, 385.

Insight into this problem of early Christian authors may be gained from a later source, from the gospel of Matthew. While the evangelist was able to consult the text of Isaiah, there are data which lead to the inference that Matthew did not have accesss to a copy of the Dodekapropheton, or to a scroll of Jeremiah, an author who for other reasons is only rarely used in early Christian texts.[61] Matthew uses Scriptural quotations from Q and also texts quoted by Mark. To these he adds further traditions to shape his formula quotations.

In comparing this approach of Q to address a current problem of its time with the design of Mark's narrative gospel we observe characteristic differences. While Q uses Scripture to introduce claims concerning Christological titles such as ὁ ἐρχόμενος and Son of God, Mark with a similar aim designs narrative. Mark relies on authoritative voices. One of them is the answer of Christ in Mk 9:13. Another voice is reported in 1:7, ἔρχεται ὁ ἰσχυρότερός μου.

Similarly the first use of the Son of God title in Mark is ascribed to the Divine voice in 1:11. This settles it for Mark, while for Luke in a later phase of gospel production a Scriptural quotation is considered suited to such an occasion.[62]

---

[61] U. Luz, *Das Evangelium nach Matthäus, 1.Teilband Mt 1-7*, EKKNT I/1, (Zürich/Einsiedeln/Köln: Benziger and Neukirchen: Neukirchener Verlag, 1985), 135 with notes 6 and 7. I refer here to results of a study of Dietrich-Alex Koch, *Die Schrift als Zeuge des Evangeliums. Untersuchungen zur Verwendung und zum Verständnis der Schrift bei Paulus*, Beiträge zur historischen Theologie 69 (Tübingen: J.C.B. Mohr [Paul Siebeck], 1986), 45f.

[62] Several authors consider the quotation of Psalm 2:7 in Luke 3:22 as the original text. Bart D. Ehrman defended this reading; Ehrman, *Orthodox Corruption*, 62-7; *idem*, 'The Text of the Gospels at the End of the Second Century', in Parker & Amphoux, 106. Greeven and Boismard/Lamouille in their synopses printed it: see A. Huck & H. Greeven, *Synopse der drei ersten Evangelien mit Beigabe der johanneischen Parallelstellen – Synopsis of the First Three Gospels with the Addition of the Johannine Parallels* (Tübingen: J.C.B. Mohr [Paul Siebeck], 1981), 18, and M.-E. Boismard & A. Lamouille, *Synopsis Graeca Quattuor Evangeliorum* (Leuven & Paris: Peeters, 1986), 20. I am not quite convinced that Robinson's suggestion of a 'narrative-preface of Q' is warranted. The form of the introduction, which must have included elements like Ναζαρα, πασα η περιχωρος του Ιορδανου, and at least the fact of Jesus' baptism, is a problem not yet solved. I refer my listeners to an analysis of Robinson's argument by R. Uro, 'John the Baptist and the Jesus Movement: What Does Q Tell us?', in R.A. Piper (ed.), *The Gospel Behind the*

Whether scribes who copied Mark relied on the tradition of Q for the insertion of 1:2b, or whether they cited either Mt 11:10 or Lk 7:27, cannot be ascertained. But the form of the quoted text makes it unlikely that there is an independent origin for the quotation in Q. The Markan text omits ἔμπροσθέν σου and is, therefore, secondary to a form which exhibits a full parallelism as found in Q.

If Mark 1:2a.3 is not Markan, it could have been taken from Q, which we reconstruct on the evidence of minor agreements.[63] Occasionally the view has been taken that the quotation of Isa 40:3 in Mt 3:3 and Lk 3:4 in these authors could be traced to Q.[64] This view would find some support in the realization that the quotation from the book of Isaiah is no original portion of Mark's text. But we know little about the beginning of the Sayings gospel Q. If Mark 1:2-3 is not Markan, this insertion would reflect a desire of its readers and scribes to possess whatever evidence had been assembled in an early period.

2.5 *Final Control: A Gloss Impairs Mark's Narrative Design*

The beginning of this essay presented evidence of secondary influences bearing upon the transmission of Mark's opening sentence. An anomaly visible against the background of Mark's role as author of a narrative gospel was forcefully argued by Carl Lachmann. I considered his argument *in extenso*. Exegetical work

---

Gospels: Current Studies on Q (Leiden/New York/Köln: Brill, 1995), 231-57, here 237-9.

[63] Recent endeavours to prove the acquaintance of Mark with a written text of the Sayings gospel Q, as argued by Harry T. Fleddermann, and also by David C. Catchpole and J. Lambrecht, have been questioned on methodological grounds by Frans Neirynck and Ismo Dunderberg. See F. Neirynck, 'Assessment', in H.T. Fleddermann, *Mark and Q. A Study of the Overlap Texts* (Leuven: University Press and Peeters, 1995), 263-307; I. Dunderberg, 'Q and the Beginning of Mark', *NTS* 41 (1995) 501-11.

[64] 'Again, in all three Gospels John's preaching is introduced by the quotation from Isaiah φωνὴ βοῶντος κτλ. Seeing that in no other case does the editor of Mark himself introduce a quotation or reference to the Old Testament it is probable that this also occurred in Q'; B.H. Streeter, 'St. Mark's Knowledge and Use of Q', in W. Sanday (ed.), *Studies in the Synoptic Problem, by Members of the University of Oxford* (Oxford: Clarendon Press, 1911), 165-83, see 168.

concentrated upon the interpretation of Mark's first sentence reveals obvious difficulties. The position of καθὼς within the transmitted text raises objections which support the view that this portion was grafted upon the original text. Finally, the division of witnesses over an article in the enlarged text-form was considered as an indication of its secondary origin: ἐν τῷ Ἠσαΐᾳ does not conform to Mark's style (cf. 7:6; 12:36).

Mark introduces his narrative without introducing himself. Even his prologue is a narrative text. I suggest a final control: an effort to interpret 1:1-13 as an original entity designed to enlighten the reader for what he has to expect.

Mark shares privileged information, as Frank J. Matera stated. He introduces characters. At the same time he is careful to raise expectations and to spread elements of indistinctiveness likely to raise questions. Let us consider his design.

Almost everywhere in his gospel in speaking of persons Mark uses arthrous forms. This is not in conflict with standards of Koine Greek. He never does this, however, when introducing persons. Here the anarthrous form is in sole use: ... ἐγένετο Ἰωάννης, ...ἦλθεν Ἰησοῦς. All this proves that the author is fully aware of what is involved in his task of introducing persons, preparing scenes, selecting his terms. Mark does not introduce John with the obvious term of his contemporary Flavius Josephus (*Ant.* XVIII 116-119). Instead of ὁ βαπτιστής, a term he knows, he writes ὁ βαπτίζων.

Mark introduces two persons. For our investigation it is important to see how he accentuates the difference. Several of his passages throw light upon this theme. To begin with, the work of both figures is placed within a common local frame (1:5; 3:7ff.), but it involves temporal difference (1:14). At an important juncture the author implies that a common task joins both men. Yet it is not Mark, as a narrator, who takes responsibility for this statement, but one of his figures: 'The baptism of John, was heaven its origin or were men?' (11:30).

No attention is given to the home town of John nor to his parents. The desert as place of his activities is set in relief. Since the arid area called desert borders the Jordan river, we find no contradiction in this concept.

When introducing the second figure, Jesus, the narrative unity of location is guarded. This also serves to unite the figures. But there is no co-operation. Jesus is baptized in the Jordan as it is said. It is understood that the recipients of John's baptism immersed themselves. The account is short. There is no explicit mention of a meeting of the two men. The reader may even gain the impression that the baptized Galilean remains unknown to the Baptist. The heavenly sign is revealed to Jesus, the heavenly voice remains unknown to all, except to the readers of this account.

It is possible to read the privilege of a heavenly voice as a commission, the victorious encounter with Satan as an initiation. All this is not told with reference to John, but refers to Jesus.

John is depicted in the midst of streams of visitors. The whole of Jerusalem and all of Judea crowd together. They confess their sins.

In comparison Jesus appears to be alone. His place of origin, Nazareth in Galilee, is mentioned. No word is spoken about other Galileans. His work is not yet begun. Yet his activity is depicted as being guided by the Spirit. Mark does not use an adjective. This word is introduced not at this point of Mark's narrative, but earlier in a saying of John. The stronger one baptizes with Holy Spirit.

Jesus overcomes Satan, angels serve him where beasts of the desert roam. Him, of whom great things are said, no description describes.

It is telling, I think, how sparingly abstract terms appear in this account. The first sentence mentions τὸ εὐαγγέλιον, but there is no explanation. The first sentence speaks of Jesus Christ, but no further remark is added in clarification. The 'Vorgeschichte' explicitly states the origin of the ἐξουσία of Jesus, but this word is not yet used. Never in the whole text of his gospel does the narrator call him the 'Son'. Never does he make use of the title 'Son of man'. It is reserved. And the word κύριος, used in several scenes, conveys the impression that the author is wholly unfamiliar with this aspect of Christian terminology, which he is not.

If we are asked which 'Textsorte' we read here, the answer must be unequivocal. Mark enters as a narrator, he does not come as a teacher, nor as an author. Whenever he speaks himself, he is telling a tale – unless he explains or establishes contact with a listener.

The whole prologue is replete with elements of narrative climax. The first verb makes a statement as 1:14f. does, after which the narrative has begun: καὶ ἐξεπορεύετο ... καὶ ἐβαπτίζοντο ... καὶ ἦν ... καὶ ἐκήρυσσεν.

After this the narrative continues with aorists: καὶ ἐγένετο ἐν ἐκείναις ταῖς ἡμέραις ἦλθεν ... καὶ ἐβαπτίσθη ... καὶ ... εἶδεν ... καὶ φωνή. Twice in this second part of the 'Vorgeschichte' the familiar dramatic εὐθύς of our author makes its appearance. We know that he does not use ἰδού in narrative.

Finally, another dramatic expedient appears, Mark's historic present.

Fittingly, as we expected in this accomplished narrative, tension is relaxed. Three imperfects linger on our minds. So, we are led inexorably to the conclusion that Mark is telling a 'Vorgeschichte'.

To discover a series of Scripture verses in this text amounts to discovering disorder.

Summary

For a long time literary criticism has been an established procedure for the student of the New Testament. Its present discussion is integrating new aspects, but its value and function within the continuing interplay of methods have not been challenged. Insights into the meaning of literary genres, into the communicative structures operating in the relation of an audience and its author, especially as studied within the frame of reference of Greco-Roman antiquity, insights into literary devices and their contributions to form gained from modern and from classical literatures have all led to a refinement in its approaches. Yet still it is the task of literary criticism to clarify purpose and occasion in the production of a literary work, to delimit the date and circumstances of its publication, to define its genre, to ascertain its integrity and state of transmission, and to analyse, if at all possible, stages of its genesis.

In contemporary contributions to the textual criticism of the New Testament it is not always perceived to what degree the perspectives and results of literary criticism are a basic element of editorial procedure.

For textual criticism itself as well as for all other areas of New Testament studies it is essential, however, that unity and coherence of all procedures are discussed and consciously maintained.

In the course of a study of Mark's traditions on John the Baptist evidence is adduced to show that textual criticism is methodologically dependent upon the results and perspectives of literary criticism. The scope and experience of literary analysis are apt to lead textual criticism into new strategies of analysis and argumentation.

With regard to the text of Mark it is argued that the transmitted text received glosses in 1:2-3 and 9:12b.

THE BEATITUDES OF 'THE MOURNING' AND 'THE WEEPING': MATTHEW 5:4 AND LUKE 6:21B

T. BAARDA

1. *Introduction*

The Sermon on the Mount and the Sermon on the Plain present us with two macarisms which look like 'twins':

Mt 5:4	μακάριοι οἱ πενθοῦντες,	ὅτι αὐτοὶ παρακληθήσονται.
Lk 6:21b	μακάριοι οἱ κλαίοντες νῦν,	ὅτι γελάσετε.

There is an inversion found in the 'Woe' in Lk 6:25:

οὐαί, οἱ γελῶντες νῦν, ὅτι πενθήσετε καὶ κλαύσετε.

If the expression πενθεῖν καὶ κλαίειν were not a common expression, one would be inclined to suggest that Luke betrays here his knowledge of the saying concerning the mourning as found in Matthew. In that case the form in Matthew would be original, the more so because it fits in the prophetical promises.[1] This, in its turn, would suggest that the verb κλαίω was substituted for πενθέω by Luke, the more so because the verb γελάω is a specific Lukan verb (6:21 and 25). On the other hand, several commentators have pleaded that the Lukan form is original, and that of Matthew secondary.[2] A third

---

[1] Cf. R. Bultmann, Πένθος, πενθέω, *TWNT* VI (1959) 40-3, esp. 42.9-11, 43.21-29.

[2] Cf. A. Resch, *Aussercanonische Paralleltexte zu den Evangelien* II (TU 10; Leipzig: Hinrichs, 1895), 65f. Resch refers to the LXX translation of בכה in Gen. 23.2 (πενθῆσαι); he could also have referred to Gen. 50:3. So he posits the reading בכה as source for the Hebrew Gospel, and claims that παρακληθήσονται is redactional in Matthew. See also A. Harnack, *The Sayings of Jesus*, tr. J.R. Wilkerson (London: Williams & Norgate, 1908), 48; R.

view is that both beatitudes are independent traditions.[3] This contribution does not enter into that debate, but poses the question how a harmonist like Tatian would treat them. Would Tatian see here two different sayings or would he be tempted to harmonize them?

I. *Luke 6:21b,* Μακάριοι οἱ κλαίοντες*: Its Place and Form in Tatian's Harmony*

A. *The Eastern Diatessaron*

2. *The last reconstruction*

In the most recent reconstruction of the Diatessaron, the beatitudes are given in the order of Matthew (5:3, 4, 5, 6, 7, 8, 9, 10, 11).[4] One may wonder why Ignaz Ortiz de Urbina chose this order and left out any reference to the Lukan parallels. His neglect of the Lukan material is the cause of the omission of Luke 6:21b. In the first part of his reconstruction, however, that is in the large and useful collection of the Syriac patristic quotations, he presents the following 'quotations' of the Matthaean 'parallel':

[393]	Mt 5:4	ܛܘܒܐ ܠܐܒܝ̈ܠܐ ܕܗܢܘܢ ܢܬܒܝܐܘܢ 'blessing to the mourners, for they will be comforted'.[5]
[394]	Mt 5:4 / Lk 6:21	Beatum sit (illis) qui flebunt, quia ipsi ridebunt. 'blessing for those who will weep, for they will laugh'.[6]

Bultmann, *Die Geschichte der synoptischen Tradition* (Göttingen: Vandenhoeck & Ruprecht, ^{8}1970), 114 (except for the 2nd p. plur.).

[3] E.g. H.-Th. Wrege, *Die Überlieferungsgeschichte der Bergpredigt* (WUNT 9; Tübingen: Mohr [Siebeck], 1968), 16-17.

[4] I. Ortiz de Urbina, *Vetus Evangelium Syrorum et exinde excerptum Diatessaron Tatiani* (Biblia Polyglotta Matritensia Ser. VI; Madrid, 1967), 219. Unfortunately, the Arabic Diatessaron is of no use, since it does not include Lk 6:21b. Cf. N.P.G. Joosse, *The Sermon on the Mount in the Arabic Diatessaron* (Diss. Vrije Universiteit; Amsterdam, 1997), 71f.

[5] Ortiz de Urbina, *Vetus Evangelium,* 31: E? Ass. 3, 473.

This is the only reference to Luke 6:21b which he mentions in his extensive list of quotations of the beatitudes.[7] When we turn over to his reconstruction of the Diatessaron any reference to Luke disappears. He only gives as a reconstruction of Mt 5:4 in the following form:[8]

[ܛܘܒܝܗܘܢ ܠܐܒܝ̈ܠܐ. ܕܗܢܘܢ ܢܬܒܝܐܘܢ]

This text, 'blessed are the mourning, for they will be comforted', was based on no concrete text found in any witness. Apparently he corrected the text of the Pseudo-Ephraemic quotation (see above, 393), but due to the fact that this quotation is not a genuine quotation of Ephraem he adduces it in square brackets to denote the measure of uncertainty of his reconstruction. His neglect of the text of Aphrahat in the case of Mt 5:4 is striking, since we know from his second *Demonstration* that Aphrahat knew the blessing of the ܐܒܝ̈ܠܐ.[9] The newly found part of the Syriac text of Ephraem confirms the fact that this verse was included in the Syriac Diatessaron (ch. VI.1a) in the form ܛܘܒܝܗܘܢ ܠܐܒܝ̈ܠܐ, 'blessed are the mourning'.[10] The fact that the ܐܒܝ̈ܠܐ, 'the mourners', are mentioned is proof that the Diatessaron contained Mt 5:4, μακάριοι οἱ πενθοῦντες .... But what about the text of Luke 6:21b, to which Ortiz de Urbina refers as a quotation of Ephraem, preserved in the Armenian translation of the Diatessaron Commentary? Why did he leave this text out in his reconstruction of the Diatessaron?

---

[6] Ortiz de Urbina, *Vetus Evangelium,* 31: Armenian Commentary of Ephraem, on the basis of the Latin translation of L. Leloir, *Saint Éphrem, Commentaire de l'Évangile concordant, Version arménienne* (CSCO 145, Arm. 2; Louvain: Durbecq, 1954), 54.

[7] Ortiz de Urbina, *Vetus Evangelium,* 31-33 (nrs. 389-413).

[8] Ortiz de Urbina, *Vetus Evangelium,* 219.

[9] Cf. W. Wright, *The Homilies of Aphraates, the Persian Sage (...)* I, *The Syriac Text* (London: Williams & Norgate, 1869), 41.11 [II.17]; J. Parisot, *Aphraatis Sapientis Persae Demonstrationes* (Patrologia Syriaca I.1; Paris: Firmin-Didot, 1894), 89.10 [II.19].

[10] L. Leloir, *Saint Éphrem, Commentaire de l'Évangile Concordant, Texte Syriaque (Manuscrit Chester Beatty 709), Folios additionnels* (Paris: Peeters, 1990), 56.10; cf. also ch. VI.1b ...ܠܗܘ ܕܐܒܝܠ, 'to him who (is) mourning'.

3. *The earliest reconstruction*

Th. Zahn was the first to reconstruct the Diatessaron.[11] His sources were, first of all, the Armenian commentary of Ephraem on the Diatessaron, which he knew through the Latin translation of Aucher and Moesinger.[12] His reconstruction of the verse (Mt 5:4), which he inserts between Mt 5:5 and 5:6, reads as follows:

> 'Beati qui flent [lugent], quoniam ipsi consolabuntur [*angefleht werden*]',

to which he observes: '...*flent* scheint eine Mischung mit Lc 21 zu sein...;[13] *lugent* gebe ich nach A (= Aphrahat)...: *Er verhiess den Trauernden....*'. In his source, that is the translation of Moesinger, he found *after* references to Mt 5:3, Mt 5:5, Mt 5:6, Mt 5:8, and *before* Mt 5:9 the following beatitude:

> 'Beati, qui flent, quoniam ipsi consolabuntur'.

This was somewhat confusing for Zahn. As a matter of fact, he found here the verb 'consolabuntur' which reminded him of Mt 5:4 (παρακληθήσονται), but 'qui flent' suggested that Lk 6:21b (κλαίοντες) was meant. That is why Zahn concluded that the Diatessaron contained a mixture of these sayings. Unfortunately for Zahn he was misled by the translation of Moesinger. The Armenian text of the commentary actually reads:[14]

> Երանի իցէ որ լայցեն, զի նոքա ծիծաղեսցին:

There is no doubt that this should be translated as 'Blessed are they that weep; for they shall laugh', that is, exactly the text of Luke 6:21b. This was the translation of Robinson in the reconstruction of the Ephraemic text of Hill.[15] Hill and Robinson inserted this beatitude between Mt 5:3 and Mt 5:5, as if it contained the wording

---

[11] Th. Zahn, *Tatian's Diatessaron* (FGNK I; Erlangen: Deichert, 1881); our text is treated in *op. cit.*, 131 (cf. annotation *ibid.*, 132, n.3).

[12] G. Moesinger, *Evangelii concordantis Expositio facta a Sancto Ephraemo Doctore Syro, in Latinum translata a R.P. Ioanne Baptista Aucher (...)* (Venice: Library of the Mechitarists, 1876), 63.

[13] Zahn, *Diatessaron,* 132, n.7, repeats the observation that vs. 4 (Zahn incorrectly vs. 3) and Lk 6:21b were combined.

[14] L. Leloir, *Saint Éphrem, Commentaire de l'Évangile concordant, Version arménienne* (CSCO 137, Arm. 1; Louvain: Durbecq, 1953), 72.5f.

[15] J. Hamlyn Hill, *A Dissertation on the Gospel Commentary of S. Ephraem the Syrian* (Edinburgh: T&T Clark, 1896), 83, with a reference to Lk 6:21; *idem, The Earliest Life of Christ (...) being the Diatessaron of Tatian* (Edinburgh: T&T Clark, 1894), 341, with a reference to both Mt 5:5 and Luke 6:21.

of Mt 5:4. This was due to Hill's procedure. In his reconstruction of Ephraem's Diatessaron text the order of Ephraem's quotations was determined by the order in the Arabic Diatessaron. In Hill's translation of the Arabic Diatessaron it was actually Mt 5:4 ('Blessed are the mournful: for they shall be comforted'), not Lk 6:21b, that took this place.[16] He does not give, however, a reference to Ephraem's text in his translation of the Arabic text.

4. *The hypothesis of Plooij, 1923*

In 1923, D. Plooij published his famous booklet on the Liège manuscript of the Dutch Diatessaron.[17] His thesis was that this mediaeval Dutch text was derived from an early Latin Diatessaron, which in its turn was translated from Syriac. This Dutch text presented the following text of Mt 5:4 (between Mt 5:5 and Mt 5:6):

'Salech syn die weenen want si selen werden ghetroest',

which may suggest a Latin original with the wording 'Beati qui flent quia consolabuntur'. Plooij interpreted this as the 'Lukan form' which is also attested in the Diatessaron of Ephraem: 'beati qui flent quoniam ipsi consolabuntur'.[18] At first sight his case seems strong, but the weakness is that he quoted the text of Ephraem from the Latin translation of Aucher-Moesinger, which, as we have seen, incorrectly rendered the Armenian text in the latter part of the quotation. In his splendid edition of the Liège Diatessaron Plooij amply discusses the text in his apparatus. His assumption is that the Diatessaron contained the text of Mt 5:4 in a Lukan form: '*weenen, flent* (Lk vi.21) is the reading of the Diatessaron; Ta^{ephr63}: beati qui flent'. He finds support now in Aphrahat: 'Aphr. I, 89^{11}: ܒܟܝܢ *flentes*'. But he saw a difficulty, for Aphrahat also had the reading ܐܒܝ̈ܠܐ, *lugentes* (89^{10})'. He considers the possibility that Aphrahat, in his Diatessaron, may have read 'a combined text', which would find a parallel in Tertullian's *De Patientia* 11: 'flentes atque lugentes'.[19] Was

---

[16] Hill (*Dissertation,* 83, n.4) shows, however, his awareness that Ephraem had a different order.

[17] D. Plooij, *A Primitive Text of the Diatessaron, The Liège Manuscript of a Mediaeval Dutch Translation* (Leyden: Sijthoff, 1923).

[18] Plooij, *Primitive Text,* 37, cf. 68.

[19] One may also mention here Clement, *Strom.* IV.vi.26.1 (O. Stählin & L. Früchtel, *Clemens Alexandrinus* II [Berlin: Akademie-Verlag, 1960], 259.18f.): ὁ κλαίων καὶ ὁ πενθῶν διὰ δικαιοσύνην, as an example of conflation.

Plooij, in his booklet of 1923, misled by the wrong translation of Aucher and Moesinger, 'beati qui flent quoniam ipsi consolabuntur'? In his edition of the Liège mansucript, he had to admit that *consolabuntur* had to be changed into *ridebunt,* due to an observation made by Schäfers.[20] This should have warned him that the reference of Ephraem was not to Mt 5:4 but to Lk 6:21b. If he had taken notice of the fact that Ephraem quoted the beatitude of the weeping *after* the blessing of the hungry and thirsty after justice (Mt 5:6) and the pure of heart (Mt 5:8) and *before* the blessing of the peacemakers (Mt 5:9) he would have been obliged to reconsider his evaluation of the Liège text. Instead, he maintained his position that the Diatessaron read the text of Mt 5:4 in the form of Luke.

5. *The contribution of Aphrahat*

In his Homily on Love, Aphrahat refers to the beatitudes of Jesus in the following way:[21]

> In his great love He gave blessing (ܛܘܒܐ) to *the poor in their spirit* (Mt 5:3), and He promised *the peacemakers* that they would be his brothers and would be called sons of God (Mt 5:9),[22] and He promised to *the meek ones* that they would inherit the Land of Life (Mt 5:5), and He promised *the mourners*, that they will be entreated (Mt 5:4), and He promised *the hungry* abundance in his kingdom (Mt 5:6), and *those who (are) weeping* He gladdens them by his promise (Lk 6:21b), and He promised *the merciful* that they will receive mercy (Mt 5:7), and to *those who (are) pure in their heart* He said that they will see God (Mt 5:8), and again He promised *those who (are) persecuted on account of righteousness,* that they will enter the kingdom of heaven (Mt 5:10), and *those who (are) persecuted because of his name* he promised to them blessing and rest in his kingdom (Mt 5:11).

---

[20] J. Schäfers, *Eine altsyrische antimarkionitische Erklärung (...)* (Münster, 1917), 234.

[21] Wright, *Homilies*, 41.8-17 (Hom. II.17); Parisot, *Demonstrationes,* 89.6-18 (Dem. II.19).

[22] This strange place for the beatitude is also attested in the text of Faustus of Mileve, who may have used the Diatessaron. Cf. L. Leloir, *Le témoignage d'Éphrem sur le Diatessaron* (CSCO 227, Subs. 19; Louvain, 1962), 122, for the three quotations from Augustine's *Contra Faustum,* 5.1, 3 and 7.

From this survey it is obvious that Aphrahat knew two beatitudes, one concerning the mourners (Mt 5:4) between Mt 5:5 and 5:6, one concerning the weeping (Lk 6:21b) between Mt 5:6 and Mt 5:7. The suggestion of Plooij that Aphrahat knew from his Diatessaron text a mixture of Mt 5:4 and Lk 6:21b at the position of Mt 5:4 is not corroborated by the facts.

6. *The reconstruction of Leloir 1962*

The reconstruction of Leloir published in 1962 was based upon his own translation of the Armenian text. It presents the following order of the beatitudes:

Mt 5:3	Beatum sit pauperibus in spiritu suo...
Mt 5:5	Beatum (sit) mitibus...
Mt 5:6	Beatum (sit) (ei) qui esuriens et sitiens erit iustitiam...
Mt 5:8	Beatum sit (eis) qui mundi sunt corde, quoniam ipsi Deum videbunt.
Lk 6:21/Mt 5:4	Beatum sit (eis) qui flebunt, quoniam ipsi ridebunt...
Mt 5:9	Beatum sit pacificis, quoniam ipsi filii Dei vocabuntur.
Mt 5:10	Beatum sit (eis) qui persecutionem patientur propter iustitiam...

Leloir observes that Ephraem follows not only the Lukan form but also the Lukan order in the case of Lk 6:21/Mt 5:4. He concludes that this commentator does not offer this blessing in its proper place, that is in the second place as in the Eastern texts[23] or the third place as in the Western texts[24] of the Diatessaron. But he refers to the fact that Faustus of Mileve seems to have found it in his (Diatessaron?) text at the fifth place between the blessing of the pure of heart (Mt 5:8) and the blessing of the hungry for justice (Mt 5:6). But the problem is that this order neither agrees with that of Ephraem nor with that of Aphrahat. So he speculates that these authors may have known a Diatessaron text with 'une double citation de la béatitude des affligés', the first time with ܐܒ̈ܝܠܐ, the mourners, i.e. Mt 5:4, early in the series, possibly after the blessing of the meek ones (Mt

[23] Leloir mentions the Arabic Diatessaron and the Persian Harmony (*op. cit.*, 122).

[24] Leloir mentions the Latin, Dutch, Italian harmonies, and the Pepysian Harmony (*op. cit.*, 122).

5:5), the second time after the blessing of the hungry and thirsty.[25] The problem is that the Armenian Ephraem has preserved only the second of these blessings (Lk 6:21b) in his commentary text.[26]

7. *The newly found Syriac text*

The new Chester Beatty fragment, published in 1990, is most interesting for our discussion of the Ephraemic text of the beatitudes, for we find here the following order in Leloir's translation:[27]

Mt 5:3	Beatitudo pauperibus in-spiritu-eorum...
Mt 5:5	Beatitudo mitibus...
Mt 5:4/Lk 6:21	Beatitudo lugentibus...[28]
Mt 5:6	Beatitudo iis qui-esuriunt et-sitiunt iustitiam...
Mt 5:4/Lk 6:21	Beatitudo iis qui-flent...
Mt 5:7	Beatitudo misericordibus...
Mt 5:8	Beatitudo iis qui-mundi... in-corde eorum, quoniam illi videbunt Deum
Mt 5:9	Beatitudo facientibus pacem, quoniam-filii Dei vocabuntur.
Mt 5:10	Beatitudo iis qui-persecutionem-patiuntur propter iustitiam...

If we compare the two lists of blessings in the Armenian translation (see section 6) with that in the Syriac manuscript, it turns out that the latter offers nine blessings against seven in the Armenian text. But even the order is different. The Armenian has the order: Mt 5:3–Mt 5:5–Mt 5:6–Mt 5:8–Lk 6:21–Mt 5:9–Mt 5:10, the Syriac offers this order: Mt 5:3–Mt 5:5–**Mt 5:4**–Mt 5:6–Lk 6:21–**Mt 5:7**–Mt 5:8–Mt 5:9–Mt 5:10 (the additional blessings printed in bold letters). The place of Lk 6:21 is in the Armenian between Mt 5:8 and 5:9, whereas in the Syriac it is found between Mt 5:6 and 5:7. Leloir has kept to the older attribution of the blessing of the weeping to both Matthew

[25] Leloir, *Témoignage*, 122f.

[26] Another problem is that the lists of Ephraem and Aphrahat are divergent in some details, but this problem deserves a separate inquiry.

[27] Leloir, *Saint Éphrem, Commentaire* (Syr. 1990), 56, 58. I reproduce here his translation of the blessings to enable a comparison with the Latin translation of the Armenian in section 6.

[28] Leloir attributes this verse (lugentibus) and the other verse (qui flent) to Mt 5:5.

(5:4) and Luke (6:21), and consequently he also attributes the blessing of the mourning to both Matthew and Luke. There is no reason to maintain that attribution: the *mourning* refers to Matthew, the *weeping* to Luke. In his 'Critical Remarks' to the newly found manuscript, Leloir concludes that the Gospel of Tatian seems to have contained 'une double citation de la béatitude des affligés'.[29] If we may trust the Syriac text this is obvious, but still there is the puzzling problem where the Lukan text (6:21b) should be located.

8. *A riddle in the Syriac text of Ephraem*

The new Chester Beatty text of Ephraem's comments on the Sermon on the Mount is longer than the Armenian translation. After the exegesis of the beatitudes in the Armenian translation (ch. VI.1 = Syr. ch.VI.1a) the Syriac text presents another paragraph (ch. VI.1b). This begins with the blessing of those who are reviled and persecuted (= Mt 5:11). The author of this passage – Ephraem or an interpolator? – lays emphasis on the expression 'on account of me' (ܡܛܠܬܝ = ἕνεκεν ἐμοῦ), and concludes that this is valid for all the blessings: the poor in spirit (Mt 5:3), the mourning (Mt 5:4), the meek one (Mt 5:5), the one who is hungry and thirsty for justice (Mt 5:6), the one who is pure in heart (Mt 5:8), all of them were in that position 'on account of me'. The commentator concludes this paragraph with a reference to Mt 5:16. It is intriguing that the commentator summarizes the beatitudes in the order of the Greek text, Mt 5:3–5:4–5:5–5:6, and then 5:8. If it is Ephraem who wrote this passage he deviates from the order in the preceding paragraph, especially with regard to the place of Mt 5:4. It is, of course, possible that Ephraem loosely refers to the beatitudes that he dealt with in ch. VI.1a, so that his choice of the blessings was more or less at random. But still it strikes the reader that the order of the verses 3–4–5 in the second paragraph is in agreement with the ordinary text (= Sy$^{s.p.h}$) against that of his first paragraph (3–5–4). This latter order is in agreement with the Curetonian Old Syriac. The reading is attested by other textual witnesses:[30] Greek D 33, the Old Latin (a aur c d ff^{1}

[29] Leloir, *Saint Éphrem, Commentaire* (Syr. 1990), xvi-xvii.

[30] Cf. the apparatus of C. Tischendorf, *Novum Testamentum Graece* I (Leipzig: Hinrichs, 1872), H. von Soden, *Die Schriften des Neuen Testaments* II (Göttingen: Vandenhoeck & Ruprecht, 1913), 10; S.C.E. Legg, *Nouum Testamentum Graece* (Oxford: Clarendon, 1940), *ad loc.*; NA^{27}, 9; UBS^{4}, 11.

$g^{1.2}$ h l m and k),[31] manuscripts of the Vulgate, and one Bohairic manuscript (Δ).[32] If we take into account that both Aphrahat and Ephraem (VI.1a) have this order, it may be assumed that this order was found in the Greek manuscript that Tatian used for his harmony in Rome around 170 A.D.

9. *The place of Mt 5:4 and Lk 6:21b*

In the preceding pages we have found several solutions as to the location of Mt 5:4 and Lk 6:21b. For the sake of clarity we will list them here:

Zahn:	Mt 5:4/Lk 6:21b	between Mt 5:5 and Mt 5:6
$Hill^{rec}$:	(Mt 5:4) Lk 6:21b	between Mt 5:3 and Mt 5:5
$Hill^{note}$:	(Mt 5:4) Lk 6:21b	between Mt 5:5 and Mt 5:6
Plooij:	Mt 5:4/Lk 6:21b	between Mt 5:5 and Mt 5:6
Leloir:	(?) Mt 5:4	between Mt 5:5 and Mt 5:6
Leloir:	(?) Lk 6:21b	between Mt 5:6 and Mt 5:7
Ortiz:	Mt 5:4 [Lk 6:21b]	between Mt 5:3 and Mt 5:5

If we compare the texts of the Syriac and Armenian witnesses we find the following order:

Aphrahat:	Mt 5:4	between Mt 5:5 and Mt 5:6
	Lk 6:21b	between Mt 5:6 and Mt 5:7
Ephraem (A):	Mt 5:4	————————
	Lk 6:21b	between Mt 5:6 and Mt 5:7

Von Soden and Merk also listed other Greek manuscripts: Δ 543 544 565 700 (von Soden & Merk), 21 28 399 (von Soden), but since these do not appear in other critical editions this may have been due to error.

[31] k reads 'plangentis' (= plangentes) instead of 'qui lugent'.

[32] Besides Aphrahat and Ephraem (Legg) we find several other Church Fathers in the apparatuses, e.g. Origen (Tischendorf, von Soden, UBS^4, NA^{27}), Ammonius (Tischendorf), Eusebius (Tischendorf, UBS^4, NA^{27}), Clement (Tischendorf, von Soden), $Chrysostom^{pt}$ (UBS^4), Basilius (Tischendorf, von Soden), Gregory of Nyssa (Tischendorf, von Soden), $Theodoret^{vid}$ (UBS^4), Hilary (Tischendorf), Ambrose (UBS^4), Jerome (Tischendorf, UBS^4) and Augustine (UBS^4). It would be worthwhile to study the contribution of these authors closely; cf. the criticism of M. Barnard, *The Biblical Text of Clement of Alexandria in the Four Gospels and the Acts of the Apostles* (TSt V.5; Cambridge: Cambridge University Press, 1899), 4 (contra Tischendorf).

Ephraem (S):	Mt 5:4	between Mt 5:5 and Mt 5:6
	Lk 6:21b	between Mt 5:6 and Mt 5:7
Ephraem (S?):	Mt 5:4	between Mt 5:3 and Mt 5:5

There is ample reason to assume that Aphrahat and the genuine text of Ephraem have preserved the correct places of the beatitudes of Mt 5:4 (between Mt 5:5 and Mt 5:6) and Lk 6:21b (between Mt 5:6 and Mt 5:7).

10. *The form of Lk 6:21b in the Syriac Diatessaron*

(a) The Greek text of Luke 6:21b reads in our editions as follows:

μακάριοι οἱ κλαίοντες νῦν, ὅτι γελάσετε.

It is the counterpart of the 'woe' in Lk 6:25b:

οὐαί, οἱ γελῶντες νῦν, ὅτι πενθήσετε καὶ κλαύσετε.

Ephraem quotes only the beginning of verse 21b: ܛܘܒܝܗܘܢ ܠܐܝܠܝܢ ܕܒܟܝܢ, 'Blessed are those that (are) weeping...'. He omits the word νῦν, but we cannot be certain of the fact that he actually read the phrase without this particle in his text, because, as so often, he may have abbreviated his text here. In the Armenian translation (see section 3) we find a complete text, namely 'blessed are they that weep, for they shall laugh'. Did the Armenian translator find this already in his Syriac text? Or did he himself add the second phrase? If he found it in his Syriac text, one may ask whether this was the original Syriac text (in that case the copyist of the Chester Beatty manuscript has abbreviated the verse) or a text that was supplied by the copyist of his Syriac model? There is no answer possible in view of the witnesses. Did Ephraem omit the particle νῦν?[33] In other words, was it in the Diatessaron or not? The other witness, Aphrahat, does not help us either (see above under section 5), for he speaks only of the weeping (ܠܕܒܟܝܢ) in a loose allusion. The νῦν is omitted in only a few witnesses,[34] but we find it in all extant Syriac witnesses:[35]

[33] This is the assumption of the collaters for the IGNT, *Luke*, 122, who added Ephraem among the witnesses for the omission.

[34] In cursive 2145 (von Soden), Marcion (NA^{27}).

[35] Cf. G.A. Kiraz, *Comparative Edition of the Syriac Gospels*, III, *Luke* (Leiden: Brill, 1996), 101.

Sy^s: ܛܘܒܝܗܘܢ ܠܕܒܟܝܢ ܗܫܐ ܕܢܓܚܟܘܢ
'blessed are those who weep now, for they will laugh'.

Sy^p: ܛܘܒܝܟܘܢ ܠܕܒܟܝܢ ܗܫܐ ܕܬܓܚܟܘܢ
'blessed are you who weep now, for you will laugh'.

As usual the Harklean text follows the Greek in its pedantic way:

Sy^h: ܛܘܒܬܐ ܠܟܘܢ ܕܒܟܝܢ ܐܢܬܘܢ ܗܫܐ ܡܛܠ ܕܬܓܚܟܘܢ
'blessed are you who weep now, because you will laugh'.

This strong attestation of ܗܫܐ (=νῦν) in Syriac tradition seems to plead in favour of its presence in the Diatessaron as well, but certainty cannot be achieved. The quotation in Tatian's Oration, ch. 32, γελᾶτε δὲ ὑμεῖς, ὡς καὶ κλαύσοντες,[36] is too loose to draw any firm conclusion from it with respect to the text that Tatian knew.

(b) Ephraem's Syriac text agrees with that of Sy^s in that it has ܛܘܒܝܗܘܢ, not ܛܘܒܝܟܘܢ (= Sy^p, cf. Sy^h). This might imply that Ephraem's Diatessaron text also read ܕܢܓܚܟܘܢ, 'for *they* will laugh', instead of 'for *you* will laugh' (= γελάσετε). The 3rd p. plur. γελάσονται[37] or γελάσουσιν[38] is also attested in Greek Ms. W (γελάσουσιν), in Old Latin e ('beati qui nunc plor*ant*, quoniam ride*bunt*'),[39] in Sahidic manuscripts (**ΝΑΙΑΤΟΥ ΝΕΤΡΙΜΕ ΤΕΝΟΥ. ϪΕ ϹΕΝΑϹⲰΒΕ**),[40] and in the Armenian version (երանի որ լան այժմ,

---

[36] E. Schwartz, *Tatiani Oratio ad Graecos* (Leipzig: Hinrichs, 1888), 33.14.

[37] According to Tischendorf (484) -σονται in Old Latin e g^1, in Armenian, in Marcion (acc. to Tertullian), in Origen (three out of four times), in Eusebius (three times). Von Soden (266) lists this wording for Old Latin e, Marcion, Origen and Eusebius.

[38] Cf. NA^27, 172 -σουσιν W e sy^s sa^mss; Mcion^t; IGNT, *Luke*, 122, finds γελάσουσιν in W Old Latin e, Old Syriac S, Armenian, Ethiopic, and Augustine.

[39] A. Jülicher (W. Matzkow-K. Aland), *Itala* III, *Lucas-Evangelium* (Berlin-New York: De Gruyter, ^2 1976), 63. One may see also Vulgate Ms. G (Tischendorf: g^1), which has in the first stichos 'lugunt' instead of 'fletis', but it has not the 3rd p. plur. in the second stichos. The wording 'lugunt' is introduced from Mt 5:4.

[40] Cf. G. Horner, *The Coptic Version of the New Testament in the Southern Dialect*, II (Oxford: Clarendon, 1911), 105: Ms. 111, 86, cf. 114 (only the first verb).

զի ծիծաղեսցին).[41] The Ethiopic text has the same reading.[42] Marcion's text[43] also seems to have known the reading γελάσουσιν, and some other early Christian authors apparently use this or a similar form.[44] This may have been a rather early, Western reading, if it was in the Diatessaron of Tatian as well.

B. *The Western Diatessaron*

11. *Introduction*

In our discussion of the Syriac Diatessaron we came across the theory of D. Plooij that the mediaeval Dutch Diatessaron had its provenance in an early pre-Victor Latin Diatessaron which in its turn was derived from a Syriac Diatessaron. The form of the text of Mt 5:4/Lk 6:21b was one of his test cases: 'Salech syn die weenen want si selen werden ghetroest', which presupposes a text like 'Beati qui flent, quia consolabuntur'. This was actually the text that Plooij found in Ephraem's commentary on the Diatessaron ('Beati qui flent quoniam ipsi consolabuntur'). We have already mentioned the fact that this was a wrong translation of the Armenian (given by Aucher & Moesinger). What Ephraem wrote down in his comments was actually the text of Luke 6:21b: 'Beati qui flent (Syr-Arm), quoniam ipsi ridebunt (Arm)'. This has nothing to do with Mt 5:4. The newly found Chester Beatty manuscript offers besides the allusion to Lk 6:21b also an allusion to Mt 5:4: ܛܘܒܝܗܘܢ ܠܐܒܝܠܐ, 'Beatitudo lugentibus'. There is no mixture of these texts, but each one of them

[41] J. Zohrab, *Astowacašownc' Matean Hin ew Nor Ktakaranac*, IV (Venice: San Lazzaro, 1805), 129; Zohrab notes that there are also manuscripts with the reading in the 2nd p. plur.; B.O. Künzle, *Das altarmenische Evangelium* I (Bern: Lang, 1984), 183, who annotates that Edshmiadzin 229 has a marginal note with the 2nd. p. plur.

[42] IGNT, *Luke*, 122, mentions **Et** (PP, Par 32, Bodl. 40); I had no access to the Lukan text of this version.

[43] Cf. A. Harnack, *Marcion: Das Evangelium vom fremden Gott* (Leipzig: Hinrichs, ^{2}1924; Repr. Darmstadt: Wissenschaftliche Buchgesellschaft, 1960), 101*; Harnack reconstructs Marcion's text as μακάριοι οἱ κλαίοντες, ὅτι γελάσουσιν, on the basis of Tertullian, Adv. Marc. IV.14, 'beati plorantes (qui plorant), quia (quoniam) ridebunt'.

[44] See the notes above with the attestations of Tischendorf, Von Soden, NA^{27}, and IGNT, *Luke*.

is found in its own location in the series of beatitudes. So there is no direct connection between the Eastern witnesses of the Diatessaron and the Liège manuscript of the Western Diatessaron traditions.

12. *The Latin and Italian Diatessaron*

Even if one may be tempted to assume that there was an early, unrevised Latin Diatessaron prior to the Codex Fuldensis, it is still this latter manuscript of Victor of Capua that has to be the starting-point for an inquiry into the Western Diatessaron tradition. We find here[45] the following order of the beatitudes: Mt 5:3 (pauperes spiritu) – 5:5 (mites) – 5:4 (qui lugent) – 5:6 (qui esuriunt et sitiunt iustitiam) – 5:7 (misericordes) – 5:8 (mundo corde) – 5:9 (pacifici) – 5:10 (qui persecutionem patiuntur propter iustitiam). The same order is found in the Codex Sangallensis,[46] the Codex Casselanus,[47] the Codex used by Zachary of Besançon,[48] and in the two Munich manuscripts collated by Vogels.[49] The Tuscan Diatessaron is in agreement with this order,[50] as is also the Venetian Diatessaron.[51] There is no trace of Lk 6:21b in any of these harmonies.

13. *The Middle Dutch and Middle German Harmonies*

(a) The theory of Plooij (see above §3) was based upon a reading in the most famous of these harmonies, the Liège Diatessaron. All the

---

[45] E. Ranke, *Codex Fuldensis (...) ex manuscripto Victoris Capuani* (Marburg-Leipzig: Elwert, 1868), 45 (ch. XXIII).

[46] E. Sievers, *Tatian, Lateinisch und altdeutsch* (Repr. Paderborn: Schöningh, 1960: = ²1892), 47f. (ch. XXII).

[47] C.W.M. Grein, *Die Quellen des Heliand, nebst einem Anhang: Tatians Evangelienharmonie herausgegeben nach dem Codex Casselanus* (Kassel: Kay, 1869), 146 (ch. XXIII).

[48] Zachariae Chrysopolitani, *In Unum ex Quatuor sive de Concordia Evangelistarum libri quatuor,* I (PL 186; Paris, 1854), 119-122.

[49] H.J. Vogels, *Beiträge zur Geschichte des Diatessaron im Abendland* (Münster i. W.: Aschendorf, 1919), 94.

[50] M. Vatasso, A. Vaccari, *Diatessaron Toscano,* Part II of V. Todesco, A. Vaccari, & M. Vatasso, *Il Diatessaron in volgare Italiano* (Città del Vaticano: Biblioteca Apostolica, 1938), 222 (§ 23).

[51] V. Todesco, *Il Diatessaron Veneto,* in Todesco, Vaccari, & Vatasso, *op. cit.* Part I, 39-40.

Dutch or Flemish harmonies[52] have the same *order* of the beatitudes as found in the Latin and Italian harmonies,[53] which is also true for the Middle German harmonies.[54] We may add here the testimony of the Pepysian Harmony[55] which reproduces the Matthaean beatitudes of Mt 5:3-11, again in this order.

(b) It is, however, quite interesting that all these Diatessaron texts have 'who weep' in Mt 5:4.[56] Is this a rendering of 'qui lugunt'?[57] Or did the Latin Diatessaron which was the model of this harmony tradition contain a different verb ('flere'). One might think of a reminiscence of the Lukan text 'beati qui nunc fletis'[58] or 'Beati qui nunc plorant'.[59] One might, however, also consider the possibility that this hypothetical Old Latin Diatessaron read 'Beati plangentes' or 'Beati qui plangunt'.[60] It is at least noteworthy that both the Venetian harmony ('beati qelli che pianççeno') and the Tuscan harmony ('beati coloro che piangano') seem to suggest a Latin model that contained the reading 'beati qui plangunt'.

(c) It is difficult or at least speculative to decide this matter. One finds the reading 'who weep' also in the Rhyme Bible of Jacob of

---

[52] Cf. C.C. de Bruin, *Diatessaron Leodiense* (Leiden: Brill, 1970), 40.15-22 (§35); *idem, Diatessaron Cantabrigiense* (Leiden: Brill, 1970), 15.2-10 (§37); *idem, Diatessaron Haarense* (Leiden: Brill, 1970), 15.23-31 (§37); the Stuttgart ms. in: J. Bergsma, *De Levens van Jezus in het Middelnederlandsch* (Leiden: Sijthoff, 1895-1898), 40.15-32 (§37).

[53] The Stuttgart manuscript omits Mt 5:6 due to parablepsis; it is found in the Hague manuscript, cf. Bergsma, *Levens*, 40 app.

[54] Chr. Gerhardt, *Diatessaron Theodiscum* (Leiden: Brill, 1970), 23.2-10.

[55] M. Goates, *The Pepysian Gospel Harmony* (London: Early English Text Society, 1922), 26-7 (§24).

[56] S, C, Hr: 'die wenen', L: 'die weenen'; Theod. 'die da weinent'. Cf. *Pepysian Harmony*, 26.31: 'Yblissed ben [hij] that wepen'.

[57] A. Jülicher (W. Matzkow, K. Aland), Itala, I, *Matthäusevangelium* (Berlin-New York: De Gruyter, [2]1972), 20; 'lugunt' in aur, d, f, h, q, 'lugent' in [a] [b] c ff[1] g[1] l (the addition 'nunc' in aur Vg, is derived from Luke, cf. add. νῦν in ℵ[c] 33 399 713 892 Sah Boh[ms]).

[58] Cf. Jülicher (a.o.), *Itala* III, *Lucasevangelium,* 63; this is the reading of aur, b, ff[2], l ('modo' instead of 'nunc'), q and r[1]; an inversion 'fletis nunc' is found in c.

[59] So Ms. e, cf. [a] 'beati qui ploratis nunc'.

[60] Cf. Old Latin k, 'beati plangentis'.

Maerlant,[61] but the same expression occurs also in other mediaeval Dutch texts which seem to be derived from the Vulgate text of Matthew ('qui lugunt/lugent),[62] unless they are influenced by the Dutch harmony tradition.

(d) The conclusion must be somewhat ambivalent. It is possible that the the verb 'wenen' (to weep) in Mt 5:4 was influenced by the Lukan diction (6:21b), but at the same time one cannot wholly exclude the alternative, namely that Latin 'lugere' was rendered with 'wenen'.

14. *Further proof in the Old High German?*

An identification of 'lugere' and 'to weep' is possible, as one may conclude from the Old High German translation in the Gallen manuscript, where we read 'Salige sint thie thar vvuofent,...'.[63] This looks like an immediate rendering of 'beati qui lugent' in the Latin parallel text. The verb 'vvuofan' is used as translation of various verbs, such as 'flere',[64] 'plorare',[65] 'lamentare',[66] 'lacrimare',[67] 'se plangere'[68] and finally 'lugere'.[69] In cases in which 'lugere' and 'flere' are connected the Old High German renders 'lugere' with 'vvuofan'. So we read in Lk 6:25 for 'lugebitis et flebitis': 'ir vvuofet inti riozet',

[61] J. David, *Rymbybel van Jacob van Maerlant,* II (Brussel: Hayez, 1859), 467 (lines 22691-4): 'Salech sijn si/die gone die weenen/ (Ja om haer sonden/wilmen weenen/ Jof omme ander liede mesdaet)/Want haer troost te comene staet' ('Blessed are they, those who weep (yes, for their sins one wants to weep, or for the trespasses of others), for their comfort is about to come'). Maerlant is usually indebted to Petrus Comestor, but in the latter's *Scholastic History* the beatitudes are not found, so that Maerlant must have followed another source. Experts have sometimes suggested a close connection between Maerlant and the Liège harmony of the Dutch Diatessaron.

[62] See for example C.C. de Bruin, *Novum Testamentum Devotionis Modernae* (Leiden: Brill, 1979), 4 ('Salich zijn die weynen...'); C.C. de Bruin, *Lectionarium Amstelodamense* (Leiden: Brill, 1970), 300 ('Salech siin die weenen...').

[63] Sievers, *Tatian,* 47.29-31.

[64] Mk 5:38; Lk 7:13; 19:41; 22:62; 23:28; Jn 20:11 (*bis*).

[65] Mt 2:18; Jn 11:31, 33; 16:20; 20:13.

[66] Mt 12:17; Lk 23:27.

[67] Jn 11:35.

[68] Mt 24:29.

[69] Mt 5:4(5); Lk 6:25; Mk 16:10.

and again in Mk 16:10 for 'lugentibus et flentibus': 'vvuofenten inti riozenten'. The verb 'flere' is rendered in these cases with the verb 'riozan',[70] which also is found as a rendering of 'plangere'.[71] This may be an indication that 'lugere' could have been rendered in the vernacular texts with the verb 'to weep'.

15. *Conclusion*
The Western Diatessaron text of the Diatessaron tradition has the inversion of Mt 5:4 and Mt 5:5 in agreement with the Eastern witnesses. This inversion seems to have had a highly 'Western' character, since it is found in D, in the Old Latin tradition and the Vulgate, and in the Old Syriac Curetonian text. One cannot exclude the possibility that both the Old Syriac and the Old Latin were influenced by the Diatessaron. On the other hand, since the inversion is also attested in some Greek manuscripts (such as D 33), it is quite plausible that the original (Greek) Diatessaron itself was influenced by a Greek text that Tatian knew from his Roman residence. In that case the Diatessaron of Tatian would become the oldest witness to the inversion. The Western and Eastern Diatessaron traditions are, however, with respect to the order of the beatitudes, different in that the Western texts have not preserved the text of Luke 6:21b.

II. *Matthew 5:4* μακάριοι οἱ πενθοῦντες*: Its Form in the Diatessaron*

16. *The allusion of Aphrahat*
In the list of beatitudes of the second treatise of Aphrahat we find a most intriguing paraphrase of the text of Mt 5:4:[72]

ܘܡܠܟ ܠܐܒܝ̈ܠܐ ܕܠܗܘܢ ܢܬܒܝܐܘܢ

This is the text of Ms. B; the text of Ms. A is different, for both editors tell us that it reads: ܢܗܘܘܢ ܡܬܒܝܐܝܢ, but they do not tell us

[70] See also Jn 16:20 ('riozet').
[71] Cf. Mt 11:17 ('ruzut'); Lk 23:27 ('ruzzun').
[72] Wright, *Homilies*, 41.11 [II.17], Parisot, *Demonstrationes*, 89.10 [II.19]. The text is neglected in Ortiz de Urbina's collection of quotations.

clearly which words this variant stands for. It is most likely however, that this manuscript read:[73]

ܘܡܣܒܪ ܠܐܒܝܠܐ ܕܠܗܘܢ ܢܗܘܘܢ ܡܬܒܝܐܝܢ

It is difficult to say what the meaning of this sentence is. The first words are clear enough: 'And he promises the mourning'. This is, in this section of Aphrahat's allusions to the macarisms, the usual paraphrase for the blessing. So we must assume that Aphrahat read in his copy of the Diatessaron ܛܘܒܝܗܘܢ ܠܐܒܝܠܐ, 'blessed are the mourning', the same text as is found in the Syriac versions (Sy^s.c.p^, Ephraem). Before we enter into an examination of the following words we may offer here the common text of Syriac tradition.

17. *The text in the Evangelion da-Mepharreshe*

The text which we find in the Syriac texts (Sy^s.c.p^) reads as follows:

ܛܘܒܝܗܘܢ ܠܐܒܝܠܐ ܕܗܢܘܢ ܢܬܒܝܐܘܢ

'Blessed are the mourning, for they will be comforted'.[74]

This is the text which Ortiz de Urbina presents as that of the Diatessaron,[75] though with some reservation. His source text was, in fact, a spurious work of Ephraem,[76] which has a deviation from the usual pattern of the beatitudes. The Greek verb παρακληθήσονται is rendered with the Ethpa'el of the verb ܒܝܐ, which, in the Pa'el, means 'to console, to comfort'.[77] The same passive form of the verb is used elsewhere to render the passive of παρακαλέω, for example in Mt 2:18 (inf., Sy^s.c.p.h^) and Lk 16:25 (ptc., Sy^h^).[78] In Lk 16:25

[73] Wright, *op. cit.*, 41 app.; Parisot, *op. cit.*, 89 app.; cf. Zahn, *Diatessaron*, 78f., 132, n.3, 177, n.7.

[74] Cf. G.A. Kiraz, *Comparative Edition of the Syriac Gospels*, I, *Matthew* (Leiden: Brill, 1996), 48.

[75] Ortiz de Urbina, *Vetus Evangelium*, 219.

[76] Ortiz de Urbina, *Vetus Evangelium*, 31, nr. 393 (= E? Ass. 3, 473).

[77] The Pa'el renders the active form of παρακαλέω, cf. Acts 16:40, 20:1,2; 2 Cor 1:4, 2:7, 7:6; Eph 6:22; Col 4:8; 1 Thess 4:18, 5:11; 2 Thess 2:17; Tit 1:9; once παραθυμέομαι, Jn 11:31. Παρακαλέω in the sense of 'to request, call for help' is rendered sometimes with (ܡܢ) ܒܥܐ, cf. Mt 14:36 (Sy^s.c.p^); Mt 26:53 (Sy^s.p^); Mk 1:40 (Sy^s.p^); Mk 5:10,17,23 (Sy^s.p^); Mk 6:56 (Sy^s.p^); Mk 8:22 (Sy^s.p^).

[78] Cf. also 1 Cor 14:31; 2 Cor 1:4, 1:6; Col 2:2; 1 Thess 3:7. Cf. Rm 1:12.

(παρακαλεῖται), however, another verb is used in the earlier Syriac tradition cf. Sys.c: ܡܬܢܝܚ and Syp: ܡܬܬܢܝܚ, 'he (is) being at rest'.[79]

18. *Reappraisal of the allusion of Aphrahat*

(a) In the light of this it is quite unexpected that Aphrahat offers here a reading with the verb ܟܫܦ, which occurs only in the Ethpa'el in the sense of 'to pray (in a low voice), make supplication, supplicate' (δέομαι, ἱκετεύω, etc.).[80] In Mt 8:5, παρακαλῶν αὐτόν, the Syriac texts have rendered the text as follows, ܘܒܥܐ ܗܘܐ ܡܢܗ, 'and he was asking from Him' (Sys.c.p, Ephraem).[81] Syc adds here the words ܘܡܬܟܫܦ ܠܗ, 'and supplicating him'. It looks as if the translator of this text combines two translations of the Greek wording.

(b) What is the meaning of the text of Mt 5:4 in Aphrahat? The first person to interpret the words was the Armenian translator,[82] who renders the second half of the verse with [զի][83] զնոսա[84] աղաչեսցեն,[85] '[for] to them they will pray'.[86] This seems to be the

[79] Cf. 2 Cor 7:7; one may be tempted to believe that in Lk 16:25 the translator read παρακλινεῖται instead of παρακαλεῖται. The usual equivalent of the passive verb (Ethpe'el, or Ettaph'al?) is (ἐπ-) ἀναπαύομαι. That is the reason why von Soden, *Schriften*, II, 338, notes that the Arabic Diatessaron and Sys, Sypal (Ms. C) read ἀναπαύσεται.

[80] Cf. Syh Mt 9:38 (Sys.p: ܒܥܐ ܡܢ), Syh Lk 22:32 (Sys.c.p: ܒܥܐ) for δέομαι.

[81] Cf. Leloir, *Commentaire* (Syr. 1990), 80.30 (VI.22a); Syh has here the verb ܐܦܝܣ, lit. '(to try) to convince, persuade', which is the usual rendering of παρακαλέω in the Harclean text, except for Mt 2:18 and Lk 16:25.

[82] G. Lafontaine, *La version arménienne des oeuvres d'Aphraate le Syrien* (CSCO 382, Arm. 7; Louvain: CSCO, 1977), 41.7.

[83] Lafontaine omits this particle (= Syriac ܕ), but it is found in the manuscripts N S T U V W X Y.

[84] զնա in Mss. U V, նոքա (nominative: 'these' or 'they') in N S T W X Y.

[85] աղաչեսցին in Ms. U, մխիթարեսցին in Mss. N S T W X Y. The latter verb means 'will be comforted' and is the reading in the Armenian Vulgate, which is in agreement with the Greek text.

[86] Lafontaine, '(quod) precabuntur illos'; idem, *La version arménienne* (...), I (CSCO 383, Arm. 8: Louvain: CSCO, 1977) 22.31f.

correct rendering of the Syriac phrase,[87] despite the difficulty that most translators had with this peculiar wording.[88] The ܐܒ̈ܝܠܐ, the mourning or mourners,[89] are apparently the saintly ascetes whom the believers may ask for intercession or help.

19. *Comparable renderings in Lk 6:25, 2:25 and 16:25.*
(a) The interpretation of παρακληθήσονται in Mt 5:4 as 'to them they will pray', seems remarkable, but there is reason to think that this was not exceptional. For in Lk 6:25, the Woe on the Rich, Aphrahat[90] presents the following translation ܕܢܣܒܬܘܢ ܒܥܘܬܟܘܢ, 'you have received your prayer'[91] for the Greek ὅτι ἀπέχετε τὴν παράκλησιν ὑμῶν, 'for you have got your consolation'. In the Peshitta we find the rendering ܒܘܝܐܟܘܢ, 'your consolation', but the Syro-Sinaitic text agrees with Aphrahat. From the newly found Syriac text of Ephraem's Commentary on the Diatessaron it appears that Ephraem read the same word as we found in Aphrahat and Sys. Ephraem writes (ch. VI.2):[92]

ܘܝ ܠܟܘܢ ܥܬܝ̈ܪܐ. ܗܘ ܕܝܢ ܠܐܝܠܝܢ ܕܗܕܐ ܗܝ ܒܠܚܘܕ ܒܥܘܬܗܘܢ

'Woe to you rich ones – this however concerns those for whom this is only their prayer', i.e., those whose only interest, the only object of their prayers, is to become rich. It is obvious now that this wording

[87] Cf. G. Bert, *Aphrahat's des persischen Weisen Homilien* (TU III.3-4: Leipzig: Hinrichs, 1888), 37, '...dass man sie anflehen werde'; so also already Zahn, *Diatessaron,* 78.
[88] Burkitt, *Evangelion,* II, 196: '...that they should be entreated for'; A. Hjelt, *Die altsyrische Evangelienübersetzung und Tatians Diatessaron besonders in ihrem gegenseitigen Verhältnis,* (FGNK VII.1; Leipzig: Deichert, 1903), 138: '...sie werden gebeten werden'; P. Bruns, *Aphrahat, Unterweisungen,* I (Fontes Christianae 5.1; Freiburg: Herder, 1991), 115: '...dass sie angerufen werden'; these scholars have phrased it as if a passive verb was given here. The translation of M.-J. Pierre, *Aphraate le sage Persan: Les exposés,* I (SC 349; Paris: Cerf, 1988), 262: 'que l'on intercédera pour eux', is certainly wrong.
[89] The word denotes in Syriac especially the anachoretes or monks, who withdraw themselves from the world for the sake of their own sins and the sins of society, and thus become saints.
[90] Parisot, *Demonstrationes,* 921.15-16 (XX.17); cf. Bert, *Aphrahat's Homilien,* 319, n.6; 37, n.2.
[91] That is, you have received the things which you had prayed for.
[92] Leloir, *Commentaire* (Syr. 1990), 58. 24-25.

('their prayer') was present in his copy of the Diatessaron, and it is clear that the same is true for Aphrahat; the conclusion must be that this was the earliest rendering of the word in Syriac that also influenced the Vetus Syra. This means that παράκλησις was understood as 'request', 'prayer'.[93] This may explain the rendering of Aphrahat's text in Mt 5:4.

(b) There is another verse in Luke, 2:25, where προσδεχόμενος παράκλησιν τοῦ Ἰσραήλ causes a different translation in Syriac. In Sy^{p} we find the adequate rendering ܘܡܣܟܐ ܗܘܐ ܠܒܘܝܐܗ ܕܐܝܣܪܝܠ, 'and expecting the consolation of Israel' (cf. Sy^{h}). In Sy^{s}, however, we read ܘܡܩܒܠ ܗܘܐ ܒܥܘܬܐ ܕܐܝܣܪܝܠ, 'and receiving the prayer of Israel', which partly agrees with Old Latin e, 'expectans *praecem* Isdrahel'.[94] For this text we miss the testimonies of Aphrahat and Ephraem, but one cannot exclude the possibility that the Old Syriac text was influenced by the Syriac text of the Diatessaron. Unfortunately, Ephraem's commentary in ch. II.16, on Simeon, is not preserved in Syriac. The Armenian text reads զմխիթարութիւն ժողովրդեանն ընդունէր նա, 'consolation of the people he received'.[95] The verb agrees with that of Sy^{s} (ܡܩܒܠ ܗܘܐ), not with the Armenian Vulgate (ակն ունէր, 'expected, hoped), the Peshitta (ܡܣܟܐ ܗܘܐ, 'was expecting'), or the Greek text (προσδεχόμενος). One may wonder whether the 'consolation' was introduced by the Armenian translator, so that he rendered instead of խնդրուածք, 'prayer', the usual text of the Armenian Vulgate.[96]

(c) It may be useful to compare also the text of Lk 16:25 here, where, as we have already mentioned, παρακαλεῖται has been rendered with ܡܬ[ܬ]ܢܝܚ, 'is at rest'. In Aphrahat's paraphrasing of this verse (XX.9) we find a quite different interpretation: ܘܝܘܡܢܐ ܕܝܢ ܒܥܝܬ ܡܢܗ ܘܠܐ ܡܥܒܪ ܠܟ, '*Today you are asking (praying) from him*

---

[93] This meaning is found in Greek, cf. 2 Cor 8.4, 17, where Sy^{p} also has ܒܥܘܬܐ, whereas the same word is rendered with ܒܘܝܐܐ, 'consolation', in 2 Cor 1:3, 4, 5, 6, 7; 7:4, 13.

[94] Cf. Merx, *Die vier kanonischen Evangelien nach ihrem ältesten bekannten Texte,* II.2, *Markus und Lukas,* (Berlin: Reimer, 1905), 206.

[95] Leloir, *Commentaire* (Arm.), 31.9.

[96] This means that the translator was aware of the fact that Ephraem referred to Lk 2:25; Leloir and McCarthy have not seen the reference.

and he does not help you',[97] where the Greek reads νῦν δὲ ὧδε [*v.l.* ὅδε] παρακαλεῖται. The last words of the sentence seem at first sight merely an addition to the text by Aphrahat, but we should keep in mind that the same idea is found in Ephraem's commentary on the Diatessaron: 'And Abraham called him "my son" and (still) he was not able to help him (ܘܠܡܥܕܪܗ ܠܐ ܐܫܟܚ)'.[98] In this connection it is highly interesting that in extracts from a Letter to Publius ascribed to Ephraem[99] a remarkably analogous reading is found: ܡܛܠ ܗܢܐ ܒܥܐ ܐܢܬ ܡܢܗ ܕܢܥܕܪܟ, 'therefore you (are) asking from him to help you'.[100] For our purpose it is sufficient to see that Aphrahat may have read in his Diatessaron a text which differed from the common Syriac tradition in three respects:

i) it was based upon a Greek text with ὅδε instead of ὧδε (Sy$^{s.c}$: ܗܪܟܐ),[101] a variant which Tatian may have read in a Roman copy of Luke (it is also found in the text of Marcion!);[102]

ii) it reads ܝܘܡܢܐ, 'today', instead of ܗܫܐ, 'now' (Sy$^{s.c.p.h}$). One may compare Sy^{s} ܠܝܘܡܢܐ, instead of ܠܗܫܐ Sy$^{p.h}$, for ἕως τοῦ νῦν in Mt 24:21.

iii) the verb παρακαλεῖται was understood as meaning 'he was prayed', or: 'he was asked for'.[103] This agrees with the understanding of the verb παρακαλέω and the noun παράκλησις mentioned in Lk 6:24 and Lk 6:21b in the texts mentioned above.

---

[97] Wright, *Homilies,* 383.16-17; Parisot, *Demonstrationes*, 908.14-15; cf. Bert, *Aphrahat's Homilien,* 37, n. 6; 319, n.6. Cf. also Ortiz de Urbina, *Vetus Evangelium,* 118, nr. 1499, cf. 257.

[98] Leloir, *Commentaire* (Syr. 1963), 152.10-11.

[99] F.C. Burkitt, *S. Ephraim's Quotations from the Gospel* (TSt VII.2; Cambridge: Cambridge University Press, 1901), 70-72, esp. 71f.; cf. *idem*, *Evangelion* II, 135-6; Leloir, *Évangile,* 89; Ortiz de Urbina, *Vetus Evangelium,* 119, nr. 1506, ascribes this incorrectly to Ephraem's commentary (E. cD 148).

[100] The text continues with 'just as he was asking from you to help him, and you did not wish (to do so)'.

[101] The Peshitta reads ܗܐ, ἰδού or ἴδε.

[102] Harnack, *Marcion,* 221-2.

[103] Burkitt, *Quotations,* 71, mentions also the reading 'nunc hic rogatur' instead of '... consolatur' in Cyprian, *Testimonia,* iii.61. Leloir, *Évangile,* 89, n.37, notes that there are also manuscripts which have 'consolatur' in this passage.

20. *Conclusions*
One may ask whether this rendering of the verb is an idiosyncrasy of Aphrahat. But this is hardly the case, for we find similar interpretations in other sources, cf. Mt 8:5 in Sy^{c}, Lk 2:25 in Sy^{s}, Lk 6:24 in Sy^{s} and Ephraem. In the latter case there is reason to believe that it was the Diatessaron reading. It is hardly imaginable, therefore, that the variants of Aphrahat were the author's own translations from the Greek text to emend the readings that he found in his Gospel text.[104] One might then consider that the author borrowed these readings from a different branch of the Vetus Syra tradition. Or did these readings come from Aphrahat's copy of the Diatessaron? The latter position is taken by scholars like Zahn, Baethgen[105] and Bewer.[106] Hjelt, however, pleads for the idea that Aphrahat was dependent in these cases on the Old Syriac 'Separate' Gospels.[107] His arguments are: first, that the translator of the Old Syriac version was not so well equiped for his task, and secondly, that Tatian had a great command of the Greek language so that he was the last person from whom one would expect such unlucky translations of παρακαλέω and παράκλησις. But this latter argument is not valid. It is based upon the idea that Tatian himself was responsible for the Syriac text of the Diatessaron. This view, however, is only a mere guess. In my view – which is, indeed, also a mere guess – Tatian was the author of a Greek text of the Diatessaron, which afterwards was translated into Syriac. Who the translator was is not known, but even if it was Tatian himself, one cannot deny the possibility that he could have interpreted παρακαλέω / παράκλησις in the sense of 'to pray', 'to beg' and 'request' in these passages and so introduced the verbs ܐܬܒܥܝ, or ܒܥܐ, and the noun ܒܥܘܬܐ, where we would have expected the meanings 'to comfort'

[104] The question whether Aphrahat himself might have translated the Greek verb and noun in a different way is difficult to answer. Bert's verdict (*Aphrahat's Homilien*, 37, n.2), 'da Aphr. sicherlich des Griechischen nicht mächtig gewesen ist', was prompted by Zahn's remark (in the same words) in his treatment of the problematic texts (*Diatessaron*, 78). But are we sure about it?
[105] F. Baethgen, *Evangelienfragmente der Griechischen Text des Cureton'schen Syrers* (Leipzig: Hinrichs, 1885), 69.
[106] Bewer is mentioned by Hjelt, *Evangelienübersetzung*, 139, n.1.
[107] Hjelt, *Evangelienübersetzung*, 139, cf. 131, n.1.

and 'consolation'. Of course, one cannot wholly exclude the possibility that Aphrahat knew a version of the Old Syriac Separated Gospels besides the Diatessaron, and could have used it in these instances. But since in one of these instances there is absolute proof that his wording was found also in the Diatessaron, one cannot deny that what some think to be a wrong translation of the Greek wording was already present in the Syriac harmony. This may imply that the translator responsible for the Syriac translation of the harmony could made such 'mistakes'. This in its turn may plead in favour of the view that Aphrahat may, indeed, have quoted the Syriac Diatessaron in Mt 5:4, with the text 'Blessed are the mourning, for to them they will pray' or '... they will be praying'. It was only later, in the early Syriac Separate Gospels, that this interpretation of the text was replaced by the reading '... for they will be comforted'. This latter reading is also the form of Mt 5:4 in the Western Diatessaron tradition: 'beati qui lugent, quoniam ipsi consolabuntur', although it has preserved its place between Mt 5:5 and Mt 5:6.[108] This research into the text of the original Diatessaron has led me to the following conclusions with respect to the procedure of the harmonist:

1. He found Mt 5:4 and Lk 6:21b in his Gospel texts and judged them to be two separate sayings.
2. He did not yield to the temptation to combine or harmonize them, as some have suggested.
3. He placed the verse Mt 5:4 between Mt 5:5 and 5:6, and the verse Lk 6:21b between Mt 5:6 and 5:7.
4. He gave a rather peculiar translation of Mt 5:4, in that he understood παρακαλέω as 'to pray, to beg'.
5. He changed the 2nd p. plur. in Lk 6:21b into a 3rd. p. plur., so that he followed in this respect the pattern of Matthew's beatitudes.

This conclusion is valid, if the Eastern witnesses of the Diatessaron are taken into account. As to the Western testimony, it has to be observed that the original pattern of the Diatessaron has been neglected in that no longer were two verses included, but only one. The more likely view is that Lk 6:21b lost its place in the harmony. But we cannot exclude the possibility that Mt 5:4 and Lk 6:21b were combined by the editor of the early Latin Diatessaron.

[108] Cf. above, §§ 4, 11, 12, 13, 14, 15, for a broader discussion of the Western witnesses of the harmony.

THE DURA-EUROPOS GOSPEL HARMONY

D.C. Parker, D.G.K. Taylor, M.S. Goodacre

1. *Introduction*

The discovery of Dura during the First World War was followed by excavations between 1928 and 1937. The high points of discovery for the team included the Christian chapel, the Synagogue, the Mithraeum and the small fragment of text with which we are concerned. Its discovery was described by the Director of the expedition, Clark Hopkins:[1]

> In early March, during the sixth season, the work was slackening off as the trenches began to be blocked out for closing .... Not much, therefore, was expected from the dig when in one of the baskets of finds from the embankment a piece of parchment three inches square appeared... It was one of those chance finds, a fragment of parchment found two blocks away and on the other side of the Great Gate from the Christian building. How it got into the debris at that point remains a mystery, and how it happened to be preserved and then discovered is another. Since it was impossible to sift the great mass of the embankment, we depended on the sharp eyes of workmen. A small piece of parchment, dirt brown, appearing in the shovelled dirt and dust required good fortune as well as sharp eyes.

---

[1] C. Hopkins (ed. B. Goldman), *The Discovery of Dura-Europos* (New Haven/ London, 1979), 106f. The *editio princeps* of the fragment was produced by C.H. Kraeling, *A Greek Fragment of Tatian's Diatessaron from Dura* (StD 3; London, 1935). The text was re-edited for the Final Report, with minimal variations, by C.B. Welles in C.B. Welles, R.O. Fink, & J.F. Gilliam, *The Parchments and Papyri*, = *The Excavations at Dura-Europos conducted by Yale University and the French Academy of Inscriptions and Letters, Final Report* V.1, ed. A. Perkins (New Haven, 1959), 73-4 & Plate IV.1.

Description

The fragment is of a column of a parchment roll, with writing only on the recto.[2] It is approximately rectangular in shape with almost straight edges, which suggests that it may have been cut down with a knife. It now measures 9.5 x 10.5 cm. Portions of fifteen lines survive, of which one cannot be read. The original column width was approximately 10 cm. Lines 1-5 have between thirty and thirty-nine letters in the *editio princeps*,[3] 6-14 have between twenty-five and twenty-six.

The text preserves an account of certain female disciples who witnessed Jesus' crucifixion, and an introduction to the story about Joseph of Arimathea. The wording does not correspond to that of any one of the canonical gospels, but appears to be a conflated text.

The present location is Yale University Library (New Haven, Connecticut), and its shelf mark is Pg. Dura 10.[4] It is included in the

---

[2] That it is a roll is not taken as certain by E. Crisci, 'Scritture greche palestinesi e mesopotamiche (III secolo A.C. – III D.C.)', *Scrittura e Civiltà* 15 (1991) 125-83 and Plates I-XXVII, 176 n.245. He refers to it as a codex in the text, 176. Against this one must make the obvious observation that there is no sign of there ever having been any writing on the verso, which strongly suggests that this fragment formed part of a scroll. It is possible to argue that the fragment came from an unfinished codex or represents a scribal exercise, but neither strike us as being particularly likely given the passage chosen and the cost of parchment. We also note that in addition to the large, interconnected, holes near the centre of the fragment which are apparently due to abrasion, and those along the bottom margin due to abrasion and/or worm damage, there are a series of small, isolated, holes along the right-hand margin. These are most clearly visible in a photograph which accompanies an article by M.-J. Lagrange, 'Deux nouveaux textes relatifs à l'Évangile', *RB* 44 (1935) 321-7, Plate XIV. (This is the only photograph of the fragment known to us which is photographed against a black, as opposed to a white, background.) These too might well be no more than worm damage, but it is worth considering the possibility that they are in fact the remains of holes produced when two sheets of parchment were sewn together into a scroll. That rolls were used at Dura can be seen from Pg. Dura 17 (*Final Report*, 93 & Pl. XIII), a legal text, in which two joining pieces of leather have been preserved. and the holes for the sewing or lacing are approximately 1 cm apart.

[3] Cf. n.1 above.

[4] Formerly Dura Parchment 24.

Münster catalogue of New Testament Greek manuscripts, with the number 0212.

The History of Investigation

It has generally been assumed without much investigation that our fragment, 0212, is of Tatian's Diatessaron. The identification was made by Kraeling, the first editor. It was accepted by most contemporary writers.[5] Plooij suggested that 0212 was a translation of just the section of Tatian dealing with the Passion of Christ, and his doubts have since been echoed and amplified by Petersen.[6] After the initial interest, little thorough attention has been given to the fragment in recent years.[7] The present study seeks to fill this gap with a full survey.

Date, Palaeographical Comments, and Context

The Christian chapel had been found in January, 1932. The parchment came to light two blocks north of the chapel, on the other side of the Great Gate whence the road led west to Palmyra.[8] The parchment was in the embankment thrown up against the inner side of the city wall, built as part of its last defence. This embankment was

---

[5] A. Baumstark, 'Das griechische "Diatessaron"-Fragment von Dura-Europos', *OrChr* 32 [III.10] (1935) 244-52; F.C. Burkitt, 'The Dura Fragment of Tatian', *JTS* 36 (1935) 255-9; M.-J. Lagrange, 'Deux nouveaux textes relatifs à l'Évangile', *RB* 44 (1935) 321-7; *idem*, *Critique textuelle II, La Critique rationelle* (Paris, 1935) 627-33; H. Lietzmann, 'Neue Evangelienpapyri', *ZNW* 34 (1935) 291-3; A. Merk, 'Ein griechisches Bruchstück des Diatessaron Tatians', *Bib* 17 (1936) 234-41; K. Peters, *Das Diatessaron Tatians* (OCA 123; Rome, 1939); D. Plooij, 'A Fragment of Tatian's Diatessaron in Greek', *ExpTim* 46 (1934-35) 471-6.

[6] W.L. Petersen, *Tatian's Diatessaron. Its Creation, Dissemination, Significance, and History in Scholarship* (VC Suppl 25; Leiden, 1994), 225 (where he appears sceptical). See further his contribution in H. Koester, *Early Christian Gospels. Their History and Development* (London/Philadelphia, 1990), 403-30, esp. 412f.

[7] G.D. Kilpatrick, 'Dura-Europos: The Parchments and the Papyri', *GRBS* 5 (1964) 215-25; B.M. Metzger, *The Early Versions of the New Testament: Their Origin, Transmission, and Limitations* (New York/Oxford, 1977), 11-12; W. Petersen, *Tatian's Diatessaron*, 196-203 & *passim*. M.-É. Boismard, *Le Diatessaron: De Tatien à Justin* (ÉBib 15; Paris, 1992), 83-91.

[8] I.e. on Wall Street, west of Block L8, near Tower 18.

constructed after 254,[9] because a parchment of that date was also found in it. Dura fell to the Sassanians for the last time in 256-7 (no coin later than that date was found). Thus, the *terminus ante quem* is certain. The *terminus post quem* must be determined palaeographically.

C.H. Roberts observed that the hand 'stands midway between the earlier rounded hands and the later "Biblical style"'.[10] Unfortunately, he assumed an association with the chapel (known on archaeological evidence to have been created at a point between 222 and 235), and did not offer any palaeographical support. Of course, since he accepted the identification of the fragment as Tatianic, he also assumed that it had to be dated after about 172. The view that it is on the way to biblical majuscule is criticised by Cavallo (who does not discuss the date).[11] Perhaps in support of this criticism is the character of the hand's bilinearity, with its strong upper line. Crisci accepts the Tatianic identification, but ignores the question of a relationship to the chapel. His conclusion that 0212 belongs to the first half of the third century therefore appears to be independent testimony, but we shall withhold judgement for the present.

Study of the hand may be advanced beyond the accounts offered by Roberts in 1956 and by Cavallo in 1966. Most hands available for comparison thirty years ago, let alone those available to Kraeling twenty years before that, represent the findings of Egyptian explorations. But now we have materials from other areas.[12] The papyri and parchments from Palestine and Mesopotamia have been carefully studied by Crisci. His study, which includes a thorough analysis of 0212, deserves recapitulation. His study of Greek manuscripts from Qumran, Murabba'at, Nahal Hever and Dura Europos leads him to the conclusion that, while there is a great variety of scripts in Palestine, demonstrating the degree and variety of Hellenistic influence, 'la scrittura dei manoscritti greco-giudaici,

---

[9] Perhaps on the occasion of the city's reconquest and refortification by the Romans after a short period of Sassanian rule in 252/253. Cf. F. Millar, *The Roman Near East, 31 BC – AD 337* (Cambridge, Mass./London, 1993), 162.

[10] C.H. Roberts, *Greek Literary Hands 350 B.C. – A.D. 400* (Oxford, 1956), 21.

[11] G. Cavallo, *Ricerche sulla maiuscola biblica* (Studi e testi di papirologia 2; Florence, 1966), I.47-8, n.7.

[12] There is a useful list in H.M. Cotton, W.E.H. Cockle, & F.G.B. Millar, 'The Papyrology of the Roman Near East: A Survey', *JRS* 85 (1995) 214-35.

soprattutto tra il I secolo a.C. e il II d.C., mostra innumerevoli e cospicue analogie con le scritture greche mesopotamiche, esemplificate dai materiali di Dura Europos'.[13] His analysis of 0212 furnishes examples of the links between this Dura manuscript and those from Palestine:

> La tendenza ad esguire *alpha* con l'occhiello triangolare e sporgente sotto il rigo di base si riscontra in altri esempi d'area greco-orientale, sopratturo, come s'è visto, provenienti dalla regione del Mar Morto; più in generale, l'aspetto d'insieme della scrittura, la tendenza ad allagare le lettere e a spaziegiarle embrerebbero ascriversi tra le caratteristiche delle grafie greco-orientali; a PgDurae 10 accosterei, per esemplificare la ricorrenza di analoghi stilemi, il rotolo dei *Piccoli Profeti* ritrovato nella regione del Nahal Hever, sul Mar Morto, e PMur. 108.[14]

While it remains true that our knowledge of the hands is far from complete, and even that the materials are inadequate for us to reach any assured conclusions, Crisci has succeeded in making a good case that the manuscripts which he examines have distinctive characteristics over against, in particular, Egyptian styles.

We return to the problem of dating. Here the Minor Prophets roll can be of no direct use to us, since it has been placed by P.J. Parsons in the end of the first century B.C.[15] However, the comparable material listed by him does help. It includes P.Oxy. 27.2471 (B.L. Pap. 3054), a cancellation of a loan dated to about the year 50 A.D. Turner describes this hand as 'upright rounded decorated capitals'.[16] The prime example of this hand which he illustrates is a manuscript of Plato dated to the 'later' second century. Both these manuscripts show some of the features of 0212 – some fluctuation in the formation of *alpha* (certainly more evident in

---

[13] Crisci, 158.

[14] *Ibid.*, 176.

[15] E. Tov, with the collaboration of R.A. Kraft and a contribution by P.J. Parsons, *The Greek Minor Prophets Scroll from Nahal Hever (8HevXIIgr): The Seiyâl Collection I* (DJD VIII; Oxford, 1990), 19-26.

[16] E.G. Turner, *Greek Manuscripts of the Ancient World* (Oxford, 1971), 106-9 and plates 62-4.

0212), wide *mu*, rather shallow *beta*. Not paralleled is the long flat upper part of *sigma*, executed of course as a separate stroke. This comparison may, however, be of little help, since there is no way of providing a comparative chronology between Egyptian and Mesopotamian hands. It must, moreover, be conceded that we have no way of knowing where 0212 was copied; we only know where it ended up. There is, it is true, a 'Dura style', but it is composed largely of hands producing non-literary texts, and so is of little use for present purposes. Welles in the *Final Report* suggests that the hand may be modelled on a Herodotus papyrus (Pg. Dura 1) dated to the first half of the second century.[17] But the points of comparison are not compelling: breadth and wide spacing of letters (in fact some letters in Pg. Dura 1 are somewhat compressed), and similarity of *alpha*, *rho* and *upsilon*.[18]

As has already been indicated, it is the association with the chapel that has encouraged scholars to believe in a third century date. This was argued by Kraeling and Hopkins. The chapel was made out of part of an existing house at some time between 222 and 235 (a coin of Alexander Severus, who reigned between these dates, is our evidence). A date at the later end of this period seems to be preferred by the archaeologists. The hypothesis presumably requires that the parchment was produced for the new place of worship, and such a date is palaeographically possible. The other piece of evidence is that the chapel was destroyed for the building of the embankment. It is thus not impossible that the parchment found its way into the embankment at the same time.

There is some circumstantial evidence to support such a provenance. The style of paintings in the Christian chapel is, by contrast with those in the synagogue, in the Mithraeum and in other temples, that of the westernised Near East, with Graeco-Roman influence. In Hopkins' words, 'Durene Christianity came from the West and remained in the Western tradition, not quite that of the

[17] C.B. Welles *et al.*, *op. cit.*, 52.

[18] Welles also claims that there are similarities with a Latin manuscript, the *Feriale Duranum* (PDura 54). But this is written in *capitalis*, and it is hard to see how one could effect a comparison between the two hands. Thus another reason for dating 0212 in the third century (the *Feriale* was copied after 225, so Welles, 191) is without foundation.

catacombs, but rather that of Westernised Syria'.[19] There is nothing in the appearance of this Greek fragment to render it incompatible with such a culture and, if Crisci is to be followed, something to support it.[20] However, while both chapel and text bear witness to Christian presence in the city, this does not necessarily link the two in either space or time.

Indeed, the present rectangular shape of 0212 and its neatly trimmed edges suggest that the original complete document was not simply caught up in the destruction of the chapel (which would presumably have produced a less regular appearance). Two alternative explanations suggest themselves. First, it is possible that by the time of the chapel's destruction the original roll had already ended its useful life there and had then been cut up for patches or padding, or so that the verso could be used for writing rough notes. But is it really likely that a leather roll would have worn out in the nineteen to thirty-two years between the chapel's construction and the building of the embankment? Second, it may have been carried to the embankment in this cut-down form from elsewhere. In either case the proposed link with the chapel begins to seem rather tenuous.

Most of what has been argued above is negative. But there is still a conclusion to be drawn, based on the following evidence. First, the connection between the parchment and the chapel is unproven, and indeed seems somewhat suspect to us, and therefore must not be used as evidence for the dating of the parchment. Second, none of the analogous manuscripts encourage us to argue for a third century date rather than for one in the second century. It may therefore be concluded that the parchment was produced at some point between

---

[19] Hopkins, 117. Kilpatrick argued for an even more thoroughly Greek Christian community, from the evidence of the inscriptions in the chapel ('Dura-Europos: The Parchments and the Papyri', 220-2). Notice should also be taken, however, of the presence of at least one Syriac graffito within the chapel (C.B. Welles, 'Graffiti and Dipinti', in C.H. Kraeling, *The Christian Building* [*Final Report* VIII.2; New Haven, 1967], 91).

[20] The suggestion, made by Hopkins, that the paintings in the chapel draw on the Harmony, because scenes from various Gospels are depicted, carries no weight. The surprise would be to find a collection of paintings depicting the life of Jesus which did not draw on all the Gospels.

the second part of the second century and the building of the embankment, and we would prefer a late second century date.

Method of Analysis

The following matters require our attention:

(1) The reconstruction of the text of 0212.

(2) The original language of the text preserved in 0212. Is it a translation from Syriac? Two kinds of evidence need to be scrutinised:

(a) Are there Syriacisms? It is necessary to be particularly aware of the need to attempt to distinguish between translation and bilingualism. It should be noted that Dura contained a significant Aramaic-speaking population.[21]

(b) Does 0212 contain gospel readings that make it probable that it is derived from a Syriac *Vorlage*?

(3) Is 0212 a fragment of Tatian's Diatessaron? As we have seen, Kraeling had no doubt that it was. But Diatessaronic study has changed in sixty years. The fragment could be from Tatian, Justin, or could be something else – for example, a Passion Harmony. The methodology chosen for assessing the possibility that 0212 is a fragment of Tatian's Diatessaron is the reconstruction of Tatian's original text from other sources, and a subsequent comparison with the text of the Dura fragment. It should be noted that Kraeling only compared the fragment with the Arabic Diatessaron, Codex Fuldensis and the Liège Harmony. This is an inadequate basis for such a comparison.

If the fragment is Tatianic, and the text proves to be a translation out of Syriac, then we will also have evidence concerning the original language of the Diatessaron.

(4) Finally, we should not lose sight of the significance of the fragment for the recovery of the text of the separated Gospels of the New Testament. It remains one of the oldest parchment manuscripts containing the Gospels, and is the only surviving Gospel scroll on parchment.[22] In enquiring whether we can recover readings of the

[21] See, for example, parchments 28 (although, of course, this Syriac deed of sale was actually written in Edessa), 151, and 152, on pp.142, 413, 414 of the *Final Report*.

[22] D.C. Parker, 'The Majuscule Manuscripts of the New Testament', Ehrman & Holmes, 22-42, esp. 28-30.

Gospel manuscripts from which it was compiled we need, once we have set aside readings caused by compositional needs, to look for distinctive agreements and disagreements with extant manuscripts.

2. *Reconstruction of the Text*

Kraeling and the *Final Report* differ (apart from the use of dots under letters[23]) only in lines 10 and 11 (for which see below).[24] We wish to suggest several small corrections, and so to facilitate our discussion of these readings we will first give our reconstruction of the text of 0212, and a translation.

Reconstruction of 0212:

[ζεβεδ]αι̣ο̣υ και ϲαλωμη κ[αι] α̣ι̣ γυ̣ν̣α̣ικεϲ
[εκ τω]ν̣ ακολουθηϲαντων α̣[υ]τω *υ* απο τηϲ
3 [γαλιλαι]α̣ϲ ορωϲαι τον ϲ̅τ̅α̅· *υυυυ* ην δε
[η ημερ]α παραϲκευη *υ* ϲαββατον επεφω̣
[ϲκεν ο]ψ̣ιαϲ δε γενομενηϲ επι̣ τ̣[η π]α̣ρ̣[α
6 [ϲκευη] *υ* ο εϲτιν προϲαββατον προϲ
[ηλθεν] ανθρωποϲ βουλευτη̣[ϲ υ]π̣α̣ρ
[χων α]π̣ο̣ εριν̣μαθαια[ϲ] π̣[ο]λ̣ε̣ω̣ϲ τηϲ
9 [ιουδαι]αϲ ονομα ιω[ϲηφ] α[γ]αθοϲ δι
[καιοϲ] ων μαθητηϲ τ̣[ο]υ̣ ι̅η̅· κ̣ε̣[
[κρυμ]μ̣ενοϲ δε δια τ̣ο̣ν̣ φο̣βον τ̣ων

[23] Used to indicate partially legible letters. It might be noted here that we have employed the usual Leiden system for transcribing the text, a convenient summary of which can be found in A.G. Woodhead, *The Study of Greek Inscriptions* (Cambridge, 1959), Ch. 1. The italic *υ* in the transcription represents a single blank letter space.

[24] All other transcriptions of 0212 known to us simply reproduce that of Kraeling or Welles. I. Ortiz de Urbina, *Vetus Evangelium Syrorum et exinde excerptum Diatessaron Tatiani* (Biblia Polyglotta Matritensia 6; Madrid, 1967), 192 and 295, also claims to do this, but unfortunately the Greek text which he prints from Kraeling is not in fact the transcription of 0212 but the pastiche of passages from the canonical Gospels which Kraeling printed next to it to facilitate its analysis.

12 [ιουδαιω]ν και αυτοϲ προσεδεχετο
[την] *υ* β[αϲιλειαν] του̣ θ̅υ̅· ο̣υτοϲ ουκ
[ην ϲυνκατατ]ιθεμ̣εν̣[ο]ϲ̣ τη β̣[ουλη]
15 [ ]..[ ].[

Translation of 0212:

of [Zebed]ee and Salome a[nd] the women
[amongst] those who followed him from
3 [Galil]ee to see the cr(ucified one). Now, it was
[the day] Preparation, Sabbath was dawn-
[ing.] Now as it was becoming evening on the Prep-
6 [aration,] that is the day before the Sabbath, there app-
[roached] a man, a member of the council [be-
[ing,] from Erinmathaia, a city of
9 [Jud]ea, named Jo[seph], a good, right-
[eous man,] being a disciple of Je(sus), but hid-
[de]n for fear of the
12 [Jew]s, and he was expecting
[the] k[ingdom] of Go(d). This one was not
[consent]ing to the c[ounsel]
15 [..]

Commentary on the Reconstruction:

Line 2:
The problem to which we have devoted most attention lies at the beginning of line 2. We have come to the conclusion that Kraeling's reconstruction is to be rejected.[25] He reads:

κ[α]ι̣ α̣ι̣ γ̣υ̣ν̣αικεϲ | [των ϲυ]νακολουθηϲαντων α̣[υτ]ω̣

We prefer:

κ[αι] α̣ι̣ γ̣υ̣ν̣αικεϲ | [εκ τω]ν̣ ακολουθηϲαντων α̣[υ]τω

[25] Kraeling's discussion of the reconstruction of this part of the text is in 'Greek Fragment', 28-30.

This proposal carries an important difference in meaning. Kraeling is aware that [εκ τω]ν represents an alternative to the reconstruction he offers and he says that at first sight this option is 'seemingly the easier':

> It is not so distant from the meaning of Tatian's Lukan source, and is close enough to the versions to provide at least a possible basis for their readings, due allowance being made for the differences of idiom and for the influence of the separate Gospels upon the text.[26]

Nevertheless, he rejects this for two reasons, the first of which is 'Tatian's departure from Luke's συνακολουθέω.'[27] Kraeling explains:

> The only purpose which the departure from Luke's συνακολουθοῦσαι could serve would be to guard against the misconception that Jesus' followers were exclusively women. This is manifestly insufficient to justify the change.[28]

This argument, however, is both overstated and circular. To talk about 'Tatian's Lukan source' and 'departure from Luke's συνακολουθοῦσαι' assumes what needs to be proved. In reconstructing the text of a Gospel harmony, one needs to be open, at each stage, to different possibilities of where the harmonist might be looking.

The point is reinforced by a closer examination of the Synopsis.[29] Kraeling is convinced that from the latter part of the first line to the latter part of the third line, κ[αι] α̣ι̣ γυ̣ν̣α̣ικες [των cυ]νακολουθηcαντων α̣[υτ]ω̣ απο τηc [γαλιλαι]αc ορωcαι τον c̄τ̄ᾱ, the harmonist is following Lk 23:49b-c, καὶ γυναῖκες αἱ συνακολουθοῦσαι αὐτῷ ἀπὸ τῆς Γαλιλαίας, ὁρῶσαι ταῦτα. This conjecture is reasonable not least because both the fragment and the manuscripts of Lk 23:49 have ὁράω whereas both Mt 27:55 and Mk 15:40 have θεωρέω. But even if it is clear that the harmonist is at this point looking at Luke, it is not so clear that he is

---

[26] 'Greek Fragment', 28. When talking about 'Tatian' here, Kraeling is referring to the author of the fragment.

[27] 'Greek Fragment', 28.

[28] 'Greek Fragment', 30.

[29] The parallels are most easy to see in this context in Huck-Greeven, pericope 265.

looking solely at Luke. Both Matthew and Mark use ἀκολουθέω: (αἵτινες ἠκολούθησαν τῷ Ἰησοῦ // αἵ ... ἠκολούθουν αὐτῷ) and it is possible, perhaps even likely, that the harmonist chooses to base his participle, ἀκολουθησάντων according to the proposed reconstruction, on their uncompounded verb rather than on Luke's συνακολουθοῦσαι.[30]

Because Kraeling assumes that the harmonist is following Luke for the section in question, he does not think to consider the use of ἀκολουθέω in both Matthew and Mark. This oversight lends to his reading a plausibility which it would not otherwise have. The presence, therefore, of the uncompounded verb in Mark and Matthew could release us from the circularity of Kraeling's argument, providing at the same time a justification, which he thought was wanting, for reconstructing [εκ τω]ν.

Kraeling's second objection to this reconstruction has a little more weight. He notes that:

> The women mentioned by name in the context were also 'of Jesus' Galilean disciples', in the wider sense of the term, and scarcely deserved being set apart from them.[31]

If we are to reconstruct Ζεβεδαίου καὶ Σαλώμη καὶ αἱ γυναῖκες **ἐκ τῶν** ἀκολουθησάντων αὐτῷ ἀπὸ τῆς Γαλιλαίας, it does indeed look as if the women following from Galilee are a different group from those who, like the mother of the sons of Zebedee and Salome, are named.

It is not difficult, however, to see how this oddity could have arisen. The Synoptics are all different at this point and the harmonist has to make some choices. Matthew mentions γυναῖκες πολλαί (Mt 27:55) and then names some of them (Mt 27:56). Mark mentions γυναῖκες, names some of them (Mk 15:40) and then speaks of ἄλλαι πολλαί who had come up to Jerusalem with Jesus (Mk 15:41). Luke only mentions γυναῖκες and does not name any (Lk 23:49).

The option taken was apparently to give the named women first and then to mention αἱ γυναῖκες. In this respect the Dura fragment is not close to any of the Gospels and the impression of two distinct sets of women may just be an unfortunate consequence of a difficult

---

[30] It is worth noting that Luke himself apparently prefers a different compound in a similar and adjacent context, κατακολουθέω at Luke 23:55.

[31] 'Greek Fragment', 28.

editorial decision. The harmonist appears to have turned first to Matthew and Mark for the names of the women and then to have relied mainly on Luke for the general statement, connecting the two groups with a simple καί.

It is also worth noting that Mark, like the Dura fragment, does mention two distinct groups. Perhaps, then, the harmonist has aligned Mark's ἄλλαι πολλαί with Matthew's and Luke's γυναῖκες and distinguished this group from the named women. In this case, the reconstruction would not be as far from the Gospels, or as odd, as Kracling attempts to make it.

One should avoid, however, placing too much emphasis on this question for our proposed reconstruction. We cannot know how the named women were introduced in the text which preceded the words Ζεβεδαίου καὶ Σαλώμη with which the fragment begins. Moreover, Kraeling's reconstruction itself has to deal with two sets of women, one set of which, 'the wives of those who followed him from Galilee', is unattested elsewhere in the Gospel tradition.

In summary, the proposed reconstruction makes better sense of the data than does the standard reading. To postulate that the harmonist wrote **ἐκ τῶν** ἀκολουθησάντων gives weight to Matthew's and Mark's parallel use of ἀκολουθέω, thus avoiding the circularity of Kraeling's constant appeal to the text of Luke and freeing us from the otherwise unparalleled oddity of introducing wives of those who followed from Galilee.[32]

A palaeographical problem remains. Four letters rather than five seems to be too small a number for the space available. A check on the other lines where (1) clear parchment in the right margin at the end of the previous line is visible and (2) the extant letters begin at the same point vertically in relation to the left margin yields some strange results:

Line number:	3	4	5	6	8	12
Probable number of letters:	7	5	5	4	4	7

[32] Without wishing to prejudge the issue of the authorship of 0212, it might be noted that a reference to the wives of the disciples does not sit easily with the encratism attributed to Tatian, several examples of which have been detected in his Diatessaron (cf. B.M. Metzger, *The Early Versions*, 33-5). Nor would emphasis on marriage be typical of early eastern Christian texts in general.

Examination of the various extant photographs shows that the shape of the fragment varies, although according to Hopkins, the fragment as discovered was 'not badly crumpled'.[33] The straightness of the left margin and the degree to which the lines of writing are distorted from the horizontal vary in proportion: the straighter the margin, the wavier the lines. It is thus impossible to be certain of the exact original dimensions. Neither four nor five letters is out of the question.

Lines 3 and 12:
More difficult is the number of missing letters in lines 3 and 12. Kraeling gives us seven letters in each. Both lacunae contained two *iotas* (unless one posits a different reading), and this fact could help in solving the problem. On the other hand, in line 12 the reconstruction supplies an *omega*. Because of these problems, it has to be asked whether, although we can descry no signs of writing on the parchment after της in line 2 and των in line 11, the first part of each of the words in question was written on the previous line. γα|λιλαιας and ιου|δαιων would both fit much better. This problem cannot be resolved without an examination of the parchment itself, and so in reconstructing the text we have not felt that the evidence permits us to overturn the line division of Kraeling's edition in these lines.

Lines 5-6:
A further problem arises with the words επι̣ τ̣[η π]α̣ρ̣[α|cκευη] (Kraeling επι τ̣[η π]α̣ρ̣[α]c|[κευη]) in lines 5-6. επ is certain. After that the reconstruction is harder. The text of 0212, as presented in the *editio princeps* and in our own reconstruction, is not found in any other Gospel witness. The Gospel parallels require something like ἐπεὶ ἦν παρασκευή (Mk 15:42) or ἐπεὶ παρασκευὴ ἦν (Jn 19:31). It is just conceivable that the remaining ink interpreted as *iota* by the editors is the top of the most vertical part of *epsilon*: the top curve of this letter is, as one would expect, written by the scribe as a separate stroke.[34] Beyond this, we do not profess to be certain of anything.

[33] Hopkins, 106.
[34] Another possibility, but one that is all but impossible to assess given the broken state of the text at this point, is that επι is written for επει. Confusion of ι and ει is a common feature of the texts from Dura (cf. *Final Report*, 47),

But we wonder about the amount of space required for the editors' text, which takes the line well to the right beyond other lines. On the other hand, the more natural line division according to their text would be παρα|σκευη. This would fit better on each line. Our suggestion would allow a little more space for the extra letter in επει, but without a re-examination of the parchment itself it is not possible to reach a conclusion on this matter. Our uncertainty is reflected in our reconstruction.

Lines 10-11:
In line 10, Kraeling reads [το]υ̣, while the *Final Report* could see the initial *tau*, i.e. τ̣[ο]υ̣. More significantly, they disagree over the last letter that is visible in the line. Kraeling read an *alpha*, giving κ̣α̣[τακε|κρυμ]μενος; the *Final Report* has *epsilon*, giving κ̣ε̣|[κρυμ]μ̣ενος. We have preferred the reading of the *Final Report*.

3. *The Nomina Sacra*

1. In line 3, the fragment reads σ̅τ̅α̅, which is the only known occurrence of this abbreviation. It could be argued that it represents σταυρόν or σωτῆρα, but since Kraeling's original edition it has been universally interpreted as σταυρωθέντα, and we see no good reason to disagree with this.[35] Σταυρόω is unique among the *nomina sacra*, since it is the only verb. The difficulty of indicating any augment and the ending leads to some strange results. It should be noted that the form σταυρωθέντα does not occur in the New Testament,[36] so the nearest analogies are other passive forms. In looking for similarities

---

as well as in papyri from Egypt and elsewhere. Cf. F.T. Gignac, *A Grammar of the Greek Papyri of the Roman and Byzantine Periods*, vol. I *Phonology* (Milan, 1976), 189: 'There is a very frequent interchange of ει and ι (whether long or short etymologically) in all phonetic environments throughout the Roman and Byzantine periods'. Examples given include: ἔχι (for ἔχει) PHamb. 9.6 (AD 143-6), BGU 15 i (AD 194); ἐπιδέ (for ἐπειδή) POxy. 1683.17 (late fourth century). If such interchange were to be allowed here, reconstructions in line with the Gospel parallels could be proposed.

[35] In Section 5 (Item 3) below, we reject the theory that σ̅τ̅α̅ is a corruption.

[36] The word does occur, however, in the Gospel of Peter, and the significance of this is discussed below.

to the Dura form, we must analyse the various types of contractions found in different manuscripts.[37] They divide into three groups: ϲτρ-, ϲρ- and ϲτ-. The first group is the largest. In these the *rho* is included in the contraction, as εϲτραν, εϲτρη. This includes use of the symbol ⳨ combining *tau* and *rho*, found regularly in $\mathfrak{P}^{66}$, and $\mathfrak{P}^{75}$. The second form, consisting of ϲρ and the ending (e.g. Lk 14:27 ϲρν for σταυρόν in $\mathfrak{P}^{45}$), does not occur with parts of the verb. Thirdly, there are a few instances of the form without *rho*:

Mk 15:14	ϲτη	= σταυρωθῇ in Codex Bezae
Mk 15:15	ϲτν	= σταύρωσον in Codex Bezae
1 Cor 1:23	εϲτν	= ἐσταυρωμένον in $\mathfrak{P}^{46}$
Gal 5:24	εϲταν	= ἐσταύρωσαν in $\mathfrak{P}^{46}$

In addition to these abbreviations of verbal forms there is also a single example of an abbreviation of the noun without the letter *rho*, which is found in $\mathfrak{P}^{46}$ at Col 1:20 where ϲτου is used for σταυροῦ.

To complete this outline of scribal practice in those early manuscripts which are our concern here, we note that the use of an abbreviation for this verb and noun is by no means universal, and that there are many instances of the word written in full. Examples of this can be found in, amongst others, the second-century witness to

[37] There are three principal sources of information on this subject: Ludwig Traube, *Nomina Sacra: Versuch einer Geschichte der christlichen Kürzung* (Quellen und Untersuchungen zu lateinischen Philologie des Mittelalters 2; Munich, 1907), 118-20: A.H.R.E. Paap, *Nomina Sacra in the Christian Papyri of the First Five Centuries AD: The Sources and Some Deductions* (Papyrologica Lugduno-Batava 8; Leiden, 1959), Chapter 3 and 112-13; J. O'Callaghan, «Nomina Sacra» in *Papyris Graecis Saeculi III Neotestamentariis* (AnBib 46; Rome, 1970), 63-5, 79; See also K. Aland, *Repertorium der griechischen christlichen Papyri.* I *Biblische Papyri. Altes Testament, Neues Testament, Varia, Apokryphen* (Patristische Texte und Studien 18; Berlin/New York, 1976), 427. B.M. Metzger, *Manuscripts of the Greek Bible* (Oxford, 1981), 36f; C.H. Roberts, *Manuscript, Society and Belief in Early Christian Egypt* (Oxford, 1979), 35 n.3; C.H. Turner, 'The *Nomina Sacra* in Early Christian Latin Mss', (*Miscellanea Francesco Ehrle* IV; Rome, 1924), 62-74.

John, 𝔓^{90}, which has been published since the work of Paap and O'Callaghan.[38]

From this necessarily brief survey it should be observed that in none of the papyri and other early witnesses are *nomina sacra* ever produced for words derived from σταυρόω by a process of suspension. They are always produced by contraction. Thus the possibility that $\overline{\text{ϲτα}}$ is an abbreviation for σταυρόν appears to be excluded. Furthermore, the form in 0212 is the type of contraction found elsewhere only on two occasions each in D and in 𝔓^{46}. At Mk 15:13, Codex Bezae has the form $\overline{\text{ϲτρν}}$. These three contractions of D are the only instances in that manuscript where σταυρόω is contracted. The noun is also only contracted in Mark, in the form $\overline{\text{ϲτρ}}$-. The evidence from all the Greek *nomina sacra* in D is that, comparatively late though the manuscript is, it is a partial witness to an early stage in their development.[39] 𝔓^{46} is consistent in preferring the form with *rho*, except on these two occasions. The conclusion to be drawn from this is that the $\overline{\text{ϲτ}}$- form is a primitive contraction that was fairly quickly abandoned in favour of $\overline{\text{ϲτρ}}$-. The Dura fragment, limited though its evidence is, encourages us to conclude that this was the form in the later second or perhaps early third centuries.

2. In line 10, the fragment reads του $\overline{\text{ιη}}$. This suspension is also found in: Pap. Eg. 2 (the so-called 'Fragments of an Unknown Gospel'), in P. Oxy. 17.2070 (a Christian anti-Jewish dialogue copied at the end of the third century), and in P. Oxy. 10.1224, another non-canonical Gospel; it is the form used in 𝔓^{45} for all cases of the noun, in every instance except Mk 9:2 and Lk 14:3; finally, it is also used in 𝔓^{18}, a third- or fourth-century fragment of a roll preserving Rev 1:4-7. The form is likely to be epigraphic in origin, the forms $\overline{\text{ιη}}$ and $\overline{\text{χρ}}$ being common in inscriptions.

3. In line 13 we have $\overline{\text{θυ}}$. This is the unremarkable contracted form used from the beginning of the practice.

---

[38] T.C. Skeat, as P. Oxy. 50.3523, and in W.J. Elliott & D.C. Parker, eds., *The New Testament in Greek IV. The Gospel According to St. John edited by the American and British Committees of the International Greek New Testament Project, Volume One: The Papyri* (NTTS 20; Leiden, 1995).

[39] D.C. Parker, *Codex Bezae. An Early Christian Manuscript and Its Text* (Cambridge, 1992), 102-5. But Parker does not draw attention to the phenomenon which we have just noted: the apparently archaic nature of the abbreviation without *rho*.

The evidence from the Dura fragment supports the accepted chronology of the *nomina sacra*. Conversely, the evidence of the *nomina sacra* shows the Dura fragment to be, so far as we can tell, representative of the scribal conventions of its day.

4. *Is 0212 a Translation from Syriac?*

Given that 0212 was identified as a fragment of Tatian's Diatessaron in its *editio princeps*, it is not surprising that it was immediately seized upon as a crucial piece of evidence in the long-running argument about the original language of Tatian's work: Syriac or Greek. Proponents of the case for Syriac were forced to look for evidence, however meagre, that this was a fragment of a text that had been translated from Syriac. One cannot help but wonder whether this would have been attempted with any other fragment of Greek text found at Dura. But be that as it may, this is clearly an issue that needs to be addressed here.

Are there Syriacisms?

Three readings have been claimed as syriacisms.

1. line 2: Kraeling's text [των συ]νακολουθησαντων α[υ]τω. Plooij argued that this striking reading could be best explained by reference to a hypothetical Syriac *Vorlage*.[40] We have argued that the text should be reconstructed differently, but it is worth granting the possibility and examining his argument. It runs as follows. The Old Syriac (and Peshitta) text of Lk 23:49, the passage drawn upon by the harmonist at this point, reads an unambiguous feminine third person plural perfect (ܐܬܝ; Pesh ܐܬܝ ܗܘܝ[41]), instead of the Greek participle. The corresponding participle in Syriac would have been ܐܬܝܢ. This form, without vowels, is ambiguous. That is, it could represent either the masculine plural (ܐܳܬܶܝܢ) or the feminine plural (ܐܳܬܝ̈ܳܢ) participle.[42] Thus, it is then argued, the hypothetical text

[40] Plooij, *op. cit.*, 475.

[41] The addition of the verb 'to be' adds emphasis, and often needs to be translated in English by a pluperfect.

[42] Plooij, in his transcription of the participle in the hypothetical Syriac text, gives the masculine plural form '*atēn*' (for '*ātên*') instead of the correct

ܢܫ̈ܐ ܐܝܠܝܢ ܕܐܬܝܢ ܥܡܗ would mean 'those women who came with him', whereas by the addition of a single letter we would get ܢܫ̈ܐ ܕܐܝܠܝܢ ܕܐܬܝܢ ܥܡܗ, 'the women of those who came with him'. Such a change in a Syriac *Vorlage* would explain the unexpected reading of the fragment.

The weakness in this argument is, of course, precisely the fact that both the Old Syriac and Peshitta read a perfect, not a participle. In Syriac a participle can indeed be used not only to express the present tense and the immediate future, but also (particularly with the addition of the perfect of the verb 'to be', ܗܘܐ) the durativity, frequentativity, and cursive aspect of past actions.[43] From the context given in 0212, however, 'those who came with him from Galilee to see the crucified one', it is clear that the emphasis is on the travel as a completed action (hence in Greek requiring aorist forms). In Syriac this could only be rendered by the use of a perfect or of a participle plus the perfect of ܗܘܐ, not by a participle alone. Indeed, the two choices available to a Syriac translator are well demonstrated by Mt 27:55 where the Greek αἵτινες ἠκολούθησαν Ἰησοῦ is rendered by the Peshitta with a perfect (ܐܬܝ ܗܘܝ), but by the Old Syriac Sinaitic palimpsest (the Curetonian is not extant) with a participle plus ܗܘܐ: ܐܝܠܝܢ ܕܐܬܝܢ ܗܘܝ ܒܬܪ ܝܫܘܥ ('those who were following/had followed Jesus'). The significance for us is that the addition of ܗܘܝ, a feminine third person plural perfect, does not permit any ambiguity of interpretation. Since the context provided by 0212 would also have required the use of a perfect or participle plus ܗܘܝ, this rules out the possibility that Plooij's hypothetical Syriac *Vorlage* with its unmarked plural participle could ever have existed. It should also be noted that, in any case, the revised reconstruction of the Greek text of 0212 offered above renders the proposal otiose.

---

feminine form '*ātyān*'. It is only the consonantal form that is identical in both cases.

[43] Cf. T. Nöldeke, *Compendious Syriac Grammar* (London, 1904), 211-218; J. Joosten, *The Syriac Language of the Peshitta and Old Syriac Versions of Matthew: Syntactic Structure, Inner-Syriac Developments and Translation Technique* (Leiden, 1996), 114-129.

2. line 8: Ερινμαθαια[ς]; TR = Ἀριμαθαίας. The reading of 0212 is peculiar and without parallel. However, Baumstark suggested[44] that if one presumed the existence of a Syriac *Vorlage* in which the usual Greek form of the name was simply transcribed into Syriac letters, i.e. ܐܪܝܡܬܝܐ, a careless Syriac scribe could easily have corrupted this into ܐܪܢܡܬܝܐ (i.e. replacing the third letter *yodh*, representing *iota*, with a *nun*, the latter being distinguishable from the former only by its slightly greater height). The last step of the process would be for the Greek translator of the harmony to reproduce this new form in Greek letters but (due to the ambiguity of the initial *alaph* which indicates the presence of a vowel, but not its identity) replacing the initial 'a' with an 'e' vowel. This explanation of the word as the product of an inner Syriac corruption is at first sight quite compelling, but it does not stand up to close examination.

First, the proposed transcription of Ἀριμαθαίας as ܐܪܝܡܬܝܐ never occurs in Syriac, where the original semitic form of the place name, ܪܡܬܐ (= רָמָה and הָרָמָתַיִם), is used for every occurrence of the name in all the extant versions of the Gospels, even the Harklean,[45] as well as in the Peshitta Old Testament. The strongest support for the possibility of the existence of a Greek form of the name in an Aramaic text comes from the Christian Palestinian Aramaic version of the Gospels. This version notoriously gives all proper names in their Greek form, and it transcribes Arimathea as ܪܡܐ,[46] ܪܡܬܝܣ,[47] and ܪܝܡܬܝܣ.[48] Only the last of these would even partially support Baumstark, and since (a) this language is quite distinct from Syriac, (b) the manuscripts containing these readings

[44] Baumstark, 'Das griechische "Diatessaron"-Fragment', 249-50.

[45] For general discussions of the relationships of Greek and Syriac proper names in the New Testament cf. P. Schwen, 'Die syrische Wiedergabe der neutestamentlichen Eigennamen', *ZAW* 31 (1911) 267-303; and F.C. Burkitt, 'The Syriac Forms of New Testament Proper Names', *PBA* (1911-12) 377-408.

[46] Mt 2:18. Cf. A.S. Lewis & M.D. Gibson, *The Palestinian Syriac Lectionary of the Gospels* (London, 1899), 257.

[47] Mt 27:57 (Cod. BC); Mk 15:43 (Cod. AB); Jn 19:38 (Cod. ABC). Cf. Lewis & Gibson, *op. cit.*, 214, 9, 207 *bis*.

[48] Mt 27:57 (Cod. A); Mk 15:43 (Cod. C). Cf. Lewis & Gibson, *op. cit.*, 214, 9, 207.

date from the eleventh and twelth centuries, and (c) the version itself can be no earlier than the late fifth or sixth century,[49] its significance is strictly limited.

Secondly, and most importantly, the form Ερινμαθαια[ς] can be satisfactorily explained as a native Greek phenomenon. In his magisterial two-volume grammar of the Greek papyri, Gignac writes as follows of the interchange of *alpha* and *epsilon*:[50]

> This occurs frequently, not only in unaccented syllables where vowel reduction or assimilation are possible factors, but in accented syllables as well, and in various other phonetic conditions, especially before /r/.

He provides numerous examples of this phenomenon from the papyri,[51] and although it is arguable that some of these instances may reflect the specific interference in pronunciation and writing of Coptic/Greek bilingualism, nevertheless he emphasises that 'an interchange of α and ε is found elsewhere in Greek, especially before liquids'.[52] Since the *epsilon* occurs in Ερινμαθαια[ς] before *rho*, in an unaccented syllable, this is entirely consistent with the examples cited by Gignac.

Again, Gignac provides numerous examples from the papyri of the insertion of nasal letters into Greek words, in texts written both before and after 0212, and particularly striking is the frequency with which *nu* appears to be inserted before *mu*.[53]

---

[49] Cf. B.M. Metzger, *The Early Versions*, 77.

[50] F.T. Gignac, *A Grammar of the Greek Papyri of the Roman and Byzantine Periods*, vol. I *Phonology* (Milan, 1976), 278-83.

[51] E.g. in unaccented syllables: τέσσερα (for τέσσαρα) BGU 133.9 part. rest. (AD 144/5), PMich 214.23 (AD 296); ἐγρανομίου (for ἀγορα-) PLond 1168 (iii, 135-8).35 (AD 44); εὐμερῶς (for εὐμαρῶς) PBeattyPanop. 1.231,234,238 etc (AD 298). In accented syllables: βρέκια (for βράκια) PRyl. 627.33 (AD 317-23). Cf. also E. Mayser, *Grammatik der griechischen Papyri aus der Ptolemäerzeit*, Bd. I. *Laut- und Wortlehre* (Leipzig, 1906), 55.

[52] Gignac, 283. At Dura itself there is a single example of this phenomenon, albeit the writing of α for ε: ὀατρανός (for ὀετρανός) Pg. Dura 31.56.

[53] Gignac, 118. E.g. ἐπιγραφονμένου (for ἐπιγραφομένου) PTebt. 397 = MChr. 321.20 (AD 198); ὄμνυνμεν (for ὄμνυμεν) PCairIsidor. 9.9-10 (ca. AD 310); ἐνετιλάνμην (for ἐνετειλάμην) POxy. 1299.10 (4th century); ἔχονμεν (for ἔχομεν) PSI 884.6 (AD 391).

There is thus no reason to seek an explanation for Ερινμαθαια[ς] in the Greek translation of a hypothetical and unattested Syriac transcription of a Greek form of a semitic name. It is simply a Greek word containing two dialectal variants which are well known and widely attested in contemporary Greek texts.

3. line 3: στα. As has already been stated above, this is probably an abbreviation for σταυρωθέντα, although this passive form does not occur anywhere in the New Testament. Baumstark noted[54] that both Syriac words for 'cross', ܙܩܝܦܐ and ܨܠܝܒܐ, can be construed either as nouns or as passive participles/adjectives, and so can be translated 'cross' or 'the crucified one'. He suggested, therefore, that one or other of these words was found in the hypothetical Syriac *Vorlage*, and that this gave rise to the unusual reading in 0212. It should be noted, however, that although the word σταυρωθέντα is not found in the New Testament it does occur in the Gospel of Peter,[55] in the response of the angel in the tomb to Mary Magdalene and her friends: Τὶ ἤλθατε; τίνα ζητεῖτε; μὴ τὸν σταυρωθέντα ἐκεῖνον; ἀνέστη καὶ ἀπῆλθεν· ('Why have you come? Whom do you seek? Not him who was crucified? He has arisen and gone'). Neither here nor in 0212 is it clear whether τὸν σταυρωθέντα is being used as a title (though this is perhaps unlikely) or as a simple description. More significant is the likely provenance of the Gospel of Peter. The main fragment of the text, on parchment, was found in the grave of a monk in Akhmim in Upper Egypt and has been dated to the eighth or ninth century. Two smaller fragments on papyrus, dating to the late second/early third century, were found at Oxyrhynchus.[56] An early date is also indicated by a passage in the *Ecclesiastical History* of Eusebius,[57] where he records that Serapion, Bishop of Antioch c.189-203, wrote a letter to the church in Rhosus, a town on the coast some thirty miles north-

[54] Baumstark, *op. cit.*, 248.

[55] 13.56 in M.G. Mara ed., *Évangile de Pierre* (SC 201; Paris, 1973), 64. Cf. H.B. Swete, *The Akhmîm Fragment of the Apocryphal Gospel of St. Peter* (London, 1893).

[56] POxy 2949, ed. R.A. Coles, in *The Oxyrhynchus Papyri*, XLI, ed. G.M. Browne *et al.*, (London, 1972), 15. Text identified by D. Lührmann, 'POx 2949: EvPet 3-5 in einer Handschrift des 2/3 Jahrhunderts', *ZNW* 72 (1981) 217-26.

[57] E. Schwartz ed., *Die Kirchengeschichte* (= *Eusebius Werke* II.2; GCS 9.2; Leipzig, 1908), VI.12.3-6.

west of Antioch, prohibiting the use of the Gospel of Peter. This suggests that the Gospel of Peter was produced some time before 190, and also, supported by other internal evidence and by its use amongst the Manichees,[58] that it was of West Syrian (rather than Egyptian) origin. Thus the two known occurrences of the term σταυρωθέντα being applied to Jesus are to be found in texts apparently produced in the same region and at a similar date. This evidence of a local and little known Greek textual tradition makes it unnecessary to postulate an underlying Syriac text for 0212.

Does 0212 contain readings derived from a Syriac Vorlage?

1. line 3: ην δε [η ημερ]α. This is from Lk 23:54, where most witnesses read καὶ ἡμέρα ἦν. Plooij first noted[59] that this reading of 0212 (i.e. having the verb before the noun) was also apparently to be found in the Sinaitic Syriac which reads: ܘܗܘ ܗܘ ܝܘܡܐ. He concluded that this agreement in word order was evidence of a translation from a Syriac text. The presentation of this evidence, however, has been rather misleading. Both of the Old Syriac witnesses have the same reading, and in full this is: ܘܗܘ ܗܘ ܝܘܡܐ ܥܪܘܒܬܐ ܗܘܬ ('and the very day Friday/Preparation was').[60] That is, in both cases they have the verb *after* the word for Friday. Thus this argument is unsustainable. In addition, the reading of the fragment is found precisely in D 05. The reading ην δε is also supported by the Vetus Latina (c [*fuit autem*] d r^1 [*erat autem*]) and Cop^{sah} (5 mss). This strongly suggests that the reading of 0212 is simply a second-century Greek reading.

2. line 8: της ι[ουδαι]ας.[61] This is taken from Lk 23:51.[62] All Greek witnesses read τῶν Ἰουδαίων. The reading of the fragment is found in the Old Syriac, Peshitta, Vetus Latina (except a d f), the Latin

---

[58] Cf. W. Sundermann, 'Christliche Evangelientexte in der Überlieferung der iranisch-manichäischen Literatur', *MIO* 14 (1968) 386-405.

[59] Plooij, 475. This is expanded by Petersen, 201.

[60] F.C. Burkitt, *Evangelion da-Mepharreshe: The Curetonian Version of the Four Gospels with the Readings of the Sinai Palimpsest* (2 vols.; Cambridge, 1904), 412, gave the reading of OS[S] as: ܗܘ [ܕܝܢ ܝܘܡܐ] ܥܪܘܒܬܐ ܗܘܬ, but this was corrected by A.S. Lewis, *The Old Syriac Gospels or Evangelion Da-Mepharreshê* (London, 1910), 283.

[61] This suggestion also comes from Plooij, 475.

[62] Not Jn 19:38 as stated by Petersen, 201.

Vulgate, and several Diatessaronic witnesses (Arabic, Fuldensis, Liège). Again, given the widespread versional attestation for this reading, it is clearly impossible to ascribe its presence in 0212 to Syriac influence. We are here again at risk from circular arguments. The reading may in fact be Tatianic. If so, then it may be part of Tatian's base text. If that is so, then it may be independently derived by 0212 from a similar second-century base. It is at any rate clear that the question of Syriac influence cannot be established by this piece of evidence.

3. line 6: προσ[ηλθεν]. This seems to be taken from Mt 27:57, but all Greek witnesses read ἦλθεν. The reading of the fragment finds a parallel in the Sinaitic Syriac reading ܩܪܒ 'he approached'.[63] It should be noted, however, first that Lk 23:52 reads προσελθὼν in the context of Joseph going to Pilate, and second that προσέρχομαι is a favourite Matthaean word which even comes in the immediate context (Mt 27:58). We have again to conclude that the argument lacks substantial foundation.

Against the arguments that have been advanced in favour of the fragment being a translation out of Syriac, we must set out those in favour of its having being composed in Greek.

1. line 13: β[ασιλειαν] τοụ $\overline{\theta\upsilon}$ ('kingdom of God' =Lk 23.51). Both of the Old Syriac witnesses, however, have the distinctive reading: ܠܡܠܟܘܬܐ ܕܫܡܝܐ ('kingdom of heaven').[64] This makes a Syriac original seem unlikely.

2. line 13-14: ọυτος ουκ | [ην συνκατατ]ιθεμẹṿ[ο]ϲ̣ τη β̣[ουλη], ('This one was not | [consent]ing to the c[ounsel]'). As Burkitt noted,[65] this is taken from Lk 23:51, where all the Old Syriac witnesses paraphrase. The Old Syriac Sinaitic and Curetonian manuscripts read: 'this man who did not agree ("equal his mind") with the accusers' (ܗܢܐ ܓܒܪܐ ܕܠܐ ܐܫܘܝ ܪܥܝܢܗ ܥܡ ܐܟ̈ܠ ܩܪܨܐ). Ephrem's commentary on the Diatessaron reads: '(the righteous one) who was not in agreement with the accusers' (ܗܢܐ ܕܠܐ ܐܫܬܘܝ,

[63] The suggestion is from Baumstark, *op. cit.*, 250.

[64] F.C. Burkitt, 'Note on Lk. xxiii 51 in the Dura Fragment', *JTS* 36 (1935) 258-9.

[65] *Ibid.*

ܠܟܚ̈ܠ ܡܪܝܐ).[66] The Arabic Harmony has a similar text: 'was not agreed with the accusers in his plans and actions'.[67] As Burkitt himself stated: 'it is clear that the text of the Fragment here cannot be a retranslation from the paraphrastic Syriac'.

Our conclusion is that there is no linguistic or biblical text-critical evidence which may best be explained by the text's being derived from a Syriac original, or having undergone Syriac influence. Given that there are also readings in 0212 which are quite untypical of the earliest Syriac texts we are compelled to conclude that 0212, and the text it contains, is not a translation from Syriac but was composed in Greek.

5. *The Reconstruction of Tatian's Text of this Passage, and a Comparison with 0212*

In order to determine whether the fragment represents Tatian's Diatessaron, we have to attempt to establish what we consider Tatian's text to have been. In what follows, we have tried to keep separate the recovery of Tatian's order and the recovery of his wording. We have attempted to follow the three basic rules laid down by Petersen:

> (1) To be considered Diatessaronic, a reading should be found in both Eastern and Western branches of the Diatessaronic tradition;
> (2) The reading should not be found in any non-Diatessaronic texts, from which the Diatessaronic witnesses might have acquired it;
> (3) The genre of the sources should be the same. All should represent harmonized 'Lives of Jesus', or traditions (e.g. the Vetus Latina, the Peshitta) which are acknowledged to have come under the influence of the harmonized tradition.[68]

---

[66] 21.20. Cf. L. Leloir, *S. Éphrem Commentaire de l'Évangile Concordant Texte Syriaque (Manuscrit Chester Beatty 709)*, (CBM 8; Dublin, 1963), 222.

[67] Cf. A. Ciasca, *Tatiani Evangeliorum Harmoniae Arabice* (Rome, 1888) 52.26 (p.198): ولم يكن بموافق للتلابين في هوايهم وافعالهم .

[68] Petersen, *Diatessaron*, 373f.

We have been aware of two recurrent problems. The first is the risk of circularity: if the Dura fragment is Tatianic, then it becomes much easier to decide what Tatian's text was. By excluding it we may be ignoring the most important witness to this passage. The second is that it is much harder to establish a continuous text of Tatian than it is to establish his reading in particular instances (not that the latter is easy). In other words, it is easier to demonstrate instances when Tatian deviated from common Gospel readings of the second century than to prove that in certain passages he was following them. For this reason the second of Petersen's criteria seems unnecessarily harsh, and whilst we have preserved it as a useful caveat we have not always felt it possible to adhere to it. Furthermore, because our quest is not only for the original words, but also for the original order, we have limited our witnesses more stringently than Petersen's third criterion allows, to harmonized 'Lives of Jesus' only.

We have used the following witnesses:

1. Eastern: The Arabic Harmony.[69]
   The Persian Harmony.[70]
   [A Syriac Passion Harmony.[71] (= SPH)]
2. Western: The Codex Fuldensis.[72]
   The Liège Harmony.[73]
   The Stuttgart Harmony.[74]
   The Tuscan Harmony.[75]

---

[69] A.-S. Marmardji, *Diatessaron de Tatien. Texte arabe établi, traduit en français....* (Beirut, 1935).

[70] G. Messina, *Diatessaron Persiano* (BibOr 14; Rome, 1951).

[71] As the Appendix 'Évangéliaire diatessarique syriaque' to Marmardji's *Diatessaron de Tatien*, 1*-75*. Associated with the Harklean Version (for bibliographical details, see B.M. Metzger, *The Early Versions*, 20, 74f.) it has now been established that there is no connection between this harmony and the Diatessaron. However, we have considered it prudent to keep an eye on it.

[72] Read from microfilm. The standard edition is E. Ranke, *Codex Fuldensis, Novum Testamentum Latine interprete Hieronymo ex manuscripto Victoris Capuani* (Marburg, 1868).

[73] J. Bergsma, *De Levens van Jezus in het Middelnederlandsch* (De Bibliotheek van Middel-nederlandsche Letterkunde 54, 55, 61; Leiden 1895-98).

[74] Also in Bergsma, *op. cit.*

The Venetian Harmony.[76]
Zacharius Chrysopolitanus (Zachary of Besançon).[77]
The Pepysian Harmony.[78]
The Heliand.[79]

During our examination of these Diatessaronic witnesses we ignored 0212 and its text, and only afterwards compared it with our tentative reconstruction. For the sake of brevity and intelligibility this comparison is here placed after the reconstruction of each item of Tatian's text.

We have identified a number of significant items within the narrative unit corresponding to the text found in 0212, and so we will now examine these in narrative order.

Item 1: *The women's names*

Reconstruction:

1.	'of Zebedee' and Salome	Arabic, [SPH]
2.	'of Zebedee'	Persian, Venetian
3.	Salome and 'of Zebedee'	Liège, Stuttgart, Tuscan
4.	Salome 'of Zebedee'	Fuldensis, Zacharius
5.	*No names*	Pepysian, Heliand

All witnesses, except the Pepysian Harmony and the Heliand, include 'of Zebedee'. The Arabic places it first. The Persian and Venetian have no other name. Whether Salome should be included, and the word's position if it should, is more uncertain. The firm presence of Ζεβεδαιου encourages us to conclude in favour of either 1 or 2.

Comparison with 0212:
The wording agrees with the Arabic (and Syriac Passion Harmony), one of our two choices. So it may be Diatessaronic.

---

[75] V. Todesco, A. Vaccari, M. Vattasso, *Il Diatessaron in Volgare Italiano* (Studi e Testi 81; Vatican, 1938) Part 2.
[76] *Ibid.*, Part 1.
[77] PL 186.11-620.
[78] M. Goates, *The Pepysian Harmony* (Early English Text Society O.S. 157; London, 1922).
[79] O. Behagel, *Heliand und Genesis* (Tübingen, [8]1965). English translation by G.R. Murphy, *The Heliand. The Saxon Gospel* (Oxford, 1992).

Item 2: *The women's journey*

Reconstruction:

1.	And many other women who had gone up with him to Jerusalem (Mk 15:41b)	Arabic
2.	And many other women who had come/gone up with him to Jerusalem	Persian
3.	And many women who had come with him from the land of Galilee to Jerusalem	Liège, Stuttgart, cf. Pepys
4.	et cum esset in Galilaea sequebantur eum	Fuldensis, Zacharius

Note the following points:

1. No witness has 'from Galilee' after the names of the women.
2. No witness has names + 'the women' (Mt 27:55b).
3. In the Arabic and Persian the fact of the women coming from Galilee is noted before the names.

Comparison with 0212:

While the *wording* of the Dura fragment may be Diatessaronic, the *structure* is not. The problem with the wording is that it could have been like Mark: women + names + women.

Item 3: *The women's actions*

Reconstruction:

1.	and they saw that	Arabic
2.	and they saw these things	[SPH]
3.	watched from afar	Persian
4.	stood at a distance and saw this	Liège, Stuttgart
5.	saw these things	Tuscan
6.	haec uidentes	Fuldensis, Zacharius
7.	*Omit*	Venetian, Heliand
8.	saw all these things and published them forth	Pepysian

The common factor seems to be the use of Luke's phrase ὁρῶσαι ταῦτα, which we conclude to have been the text of Tatian.

Comparison with 0212:
0212 agrees with the first word, ὁρῶσαι. Its text has altered the second, ταῦτα, to give its unique ϲ̅τ̅α. The reading of the Dura fragment is not Tatianic. In our opinion, the reading is very unlikely to have been produced by scribal error.[80] What stands is freer than Tatian.

Item 4: *The removal of Christ from the cross*
Reconstruction:
Fuldensis, Pepys, and Zacharius include the passage from Jn 19:31ff here. Apart from the witness of the Arabic, the weight of evidence is that Tatian included the passage here.

Comparison with 0212:
The Dura sequence is not Tatianic.

Item 5: *The day of the week*
Reconstruction:
First, we need to collect the Gospel parallels:

1.	ἦν δὲ ἡ ἡμέρα	Lk 23:54D
2.	σάββατον ἐπέφωσκεν	Lk 23:54 (Mt 28:1)
3.	ὀψίας δὲ γενομένης	Mt 27:57 (Mk 15:42)
4.	ὅ ἐστιν προσάββατον	Mk 15:42 (Lk 23:54D)
5.	καὶ ἦν τῷ σαββάτῳ	Mk 15:42 Sy[c.s]

The Diatessaronic witnesses are as follows:

1.	Mt 27:57	Fuldensis, Tuscan, Venetian, Zacharius, Pepysian, Heliand
2.	Mk 15:42	Arabic, Persian (an indirect witness).

We conclude that Tatian used either Mk 15:42 or Mt 27:57. This is sufficient for present purposes. Note that Luke's order places the time reference after the Joseph story.

[80] Against Merk, *op. cit.*, 237.

Comparison with 0212:
The Dura text combines a number of separate elements:

ην δε [η ημερ]α παραcκευη	Lk 23:54D + Jn 19:31
caββατον επεφω[cκεν]	Lk 23:54 (Mt 28:1)
[ο]ψιαc δε γενομενηc	Mt 27:57 (Mk 15:42)
επι τ[η π]αρ[αcκευη]	The text of 0212 is uncertain here. Mk 15:42 + Jn 19:31 are both possible sources
ο εcτιν προcaββατον	Mk 15:42 (Lk 23:54D)

This is quite different from Tatian, who here does not use Luke. The only question is whether the Dura text could be a revision based upon the Tatianic text. It certainly shows some confusion, which would be compatible with interference. The different phrases are set alongside each other with no attempt at integration. It attempts to put everything into one place. But, while it would be possible to strip out everything except either Mt 27:57 or Mk 15:42, this would seem to be an artificial way of achieving agreement with Tatian. We conclude that the text does not agree with Tatian.

Item 6: *The introduction of Joseph*
Reconstruction:
There are three epithets of Joseph at this point in the texts: that he was rich (Mt 27:57) and noble (Mk 15:43) and a βουλεύτης (Mk 15:43; Lk 23:50). The witnesses differ as follows:

1.	rich	Arabic
2.	rich and a βουλεύτης	Stuttgart[81]
3.	rich and noble and a βουλεύτης	Liège, Venetian, Tuscan, Zacharius

The Persian has the same information as the last, but is aberrant in including it after, rather than before, the place name. The Pepysian also has it in an unusual position.

81 Βουλεύτης is generally rendered in the medieval harmonies as 'that had ten knights to his name', through taking the wrong meaning of the Latin translation *decurio*.

The conclusion, again sufficient for our purposes, is that Tatian began with ἦλθεν ἄνθρωπος πλούσιος from Matthew, and then added either εὐσχήμων βουλεύτης from Mark or βουλεύτης from Luke.

Comparison with 0212:
The Dura text omits the adjective 'rich', and so is not Tatianic. It may also be untatianic in its omission of εὐσχήμων.

***Item 7:** Joseph's name and place of origin*
Reconstruction:
The question is one of order. Both name and place are found in the separated Gospels:

1.	Place then name (= Mt)	Arabic, Liège, Tuscan, Venetian, Fuldensis, [SPH]
2.	Name then place (=Mk-Lk-Jn)	Persian
3.	Omit both	Pepysian

There seem to be no grounds for going against the majority. It appears that Tatian again followed Matthew here.

The Arabic, Liège, Tuscan, Venetian, Heliand (and Syriac Passion Harmony) all include the words 'by name', from Matthew and Luke.

There is then a further question: did Tatian include 'a city of Judaea'? The phrase is based on Lk 23:51, τῶν Ἰουδαίων. The witnesses are divided:

1.	of Judaea	Arabic, Tuscan, Venetian, Zacharius, [SPH]
2.	omit	Persian
3.	uncertain	Liège, Stuttgart, Heliand

The phrase could have been removed from a harmony out of a lack of interest or hostility, and we therefore again follow the majority and conclude that Tatian read it. The change of Luke's text to 'of Judaea' may be the consequence of the political situation in the time of Tatian. With the dispersal of the Jews, the town is simply in a Roman province called Judaea. Another explanation is that it avoids repetition with the words from John 'for fear of the Jews'. Although there is a problem of vulgatization (the majority of Old Latin manuscripts and Sy$^{s.c}$ read 'of Judaea', so that both Eastern and

Western witnesses *could* have been corrupted) we consider it more likely that Tatian had 'of Judaea' rather than 'of the Jews'.

The place name Ἀριμαθαίας appears in various forms:

1.	Rama	Arabic, Persian
2.	Ramta	[SPH]
3.	Arimathia	Zachary (who adds *est Ramatha civitas Elcanae et Samuelis*), Stuttgart
4.	Arimatia	Liège, Venetian
5.	Barimattia	Tuscan
6.	Omit	Pepysian, Heliand

Comparison with 0212:
The Dura text agrees with Tatian in the order – place then name. It also agrees in reading 'of Judaea'. Not surprisingly, none of the witnesses agree with 0212 in its unique writing of Ερινμαθαια[ς].

Item 8: *The description of Joseph*
Reconstruction:
What is then said of Joseph may be divided into five items:

A	he looked for the kingdom of God	Mk 15:43 and Lk 23:51
B	disciple of Jesus	Jn 19:38
C	he hid for fear of the Jews	Jn 19:38
D	he did not consent to their counsel	Lk 23:51
E	a good just man	Lk 23:50

The sequence in the Diatessaronic witnesses is as follows:

1.	E B C D A	Arabic
2.	A E D	Persian
3.	E B C A D	Fuldensis, Liège, Tuscan, Venetian,
4.	C... B D A	Heliand
5.	E... D B C	Pepysian
6.	B E D A C	[SPH]

There seem to be no clear grounds for preferring any of these. If Tatian included them all, then the choice is between the order of the Arabic and that of the majority of Western versions. (It might be noticed that they vary only in the sequence of the last two items, A and D.) Both are remarkable for the fact that in neither of them are D and E, the two certainly Lukan phrases, adjacent to one another.

Comparison with 0212:
The sequence of items in the Dura text is E B C A D. This is the order of the majority of the Western Diatessaronic witnesses, and is close to the order found in the Arabic. This strongly suggests that the order found in 0212 is Tatianic, although we cannot be certain.

Item 9: *He looked for the kingdom of God*
Reconstruction:
It is impossible to determine from the versions whether Tatian drew on Mark (καὶ αὐτὸς ἦν προσδεχόμενος ...) or Luke (ὃς προσεδέχετο ...).

Comparison with 0212:
Dura fuses together Mark and Luke. We cannot determine what Tatian did.

Item 10: *Good, just*
Reconstruction:
The same is true of this phrase. There is some variation in the Greek manuscripts with regard to the presence or absence of καί before both adjectives. Tatian included it in some form. More cannot be said.

Comparison with 0212:
The wording of Tatian cannot be recovered.

Results of the comparison of the reconstruction of Tatian with 0212:
These are the results of this investigation:

Tatianic	7				
Possibly Tatianic	1	8			
Non-Tatianic	2	3	4	5	6
Indeterminable	9	10			

If we break the non-Tatianic items down further, we get:

Non-Tatianic in structure	2	4	5	6
Non-Tatianic in wording	3	5	6	

We confess to having felt some surprise when five out of the eight items on which a conclusion could be reached proved to be non-Tatianic. The bulk of evidence is strongly against the fragment's being a part of Tatian's Diatessaron.

6. *The Greek Text of the Gospels Represented by 0212*

We now turn to examine our fragment as a witness to the Greek text of the New Testament Gospels. We do so by first setting out the evidence in tabular form.

The Dura Text Compared with Manuscripts of the Canonical Gospels[82]

Line	*Text of 0212*	*Matthew*	*Mark*	*Luke*	*John*
1.	[ζεβεδ]αι̣ο̣υ	**M27.56**			
	και cαλωμη		**m15.40**		
	κ[αι]	**M27.55D**	**m15.40**	**L23.49**	
	α̣ι̣			**L23.49**	
				𝔓75 B	
				1241	
	γ̣υ̣ναικες	**M27.55**	**m15.40**	**L23.49**	
2.	[εκ τω]ν̣ ακολουθηcαντων	[M27.55]	[m15.41]	[L23.49]	
	α̣[υ]τω		**m15.41**	**L23.49**	
2-3.	απο της [γαλιλαι]α̣c	**M27.55**		**L23.49**	
				L23.55D	
3.	ορωcαι			**L23.49**	
	τον cτα·				
	ην δε			**L23.54 D**	
				Lvt (c r1)	
4.	[η ημερ]α παραcκευη			L23.54	
	OM. και			L23.54 A	
				CC W al	
				pler	
4-5.	cαββατον επεφω̣[cκεν]			**L23.54**	

[82] Bold indicates a precise agreement. A chapter and verse reference with no manuscripts listed indicates that there is either no variant or no variant which we consider relevant. Square brackets and ordinary type indicate that the same word is used but in another form. M = Matthew and m = Mark.

5.	[ο]ψιαϲ δε γενομενηϲ	**M27.57 exc.A***	[m15.42]		
	επι τ[η]		m15.42?		J19.31?
5-6.	[π]αρ[αϲκευη]		m15.42		J19.31
6.	ο εϲτιν		**m15.42**		
	προϲαββατον		**m15.42** **ℵ B* C**	L23.54 D Lvt (c)	
6-7.	προϲ[ηλθεν]	**M27.58 D lat sy**			
7.	ανθρωποϲ	**M27.57**			
	βουλευτη[ϲ]		**m15.43**	**L23.50**	
7-8.	[υ]παρ[χων]			**L23.50**	
8.	[α]πο	**M27.57**	**m15.43**	**L23.51**	**J19.38**
	ερινμαθαια[ϲ]	M27.57	m15.43	L23.51	J19.38
	π[ο]λεωϲ			**L23.51**	
8-9.	τηϲ [ιουδαι]αϲ			**L23.51 Lvt Lvg Sy$^{s.c}$**	
9.	ονομα	**M27.57 D**		**L23.50 f^1**	
	ιω[ϲηφ]	**M27.57**	**m15.43**	**L23.50**	**J19.38**
9-10.	α[γ]αθοϲ δι[καιοϲ]			**L23.50 B**	
	ων μαθητηϲ τ[ο]υ $\overline{\text{ιη}}$·				**J19.38 exc. B**
10-11.	κε[κρυμ]μενοϲ δε				**J19.38**
11.	δια τον φοβον				**J19.38**
11-12.	των [ιουδαιω]ν				**J19.38**
12.	και αυτοϲ προϲεδεχετο		m15.43	**L23.51 K M Π al**	
13.	[την] β[αϲιλειαν] του $\overline{\text{θυ}}$·		**m15.43 exc. Sy^{s}**	**L23.51 exc. Sy$^{s.c}$**	
	ουτοϲ ουκ			**L23.51**	
14.	ην ϲυνκατατ]ιθεμεν[ο]ϲ τη β[ουλη]			**L23.51**	

Several further points should be noted.

(1) line 1: αι γυναικεϲ. The article is in fact shared with the Arabic and Persian harmonies. But the position of the whole phrase is different. It is therefore the common Greek base which is of interest.

(2) line 3: τον $\overline{\text{ϲτα}}$. It has been proposed by several writers that this unique reading is a corruption of ταῦτα. However, we noted in examining the *nomina sacra* that the form $\overline{\text{ϲτα}}$ is rare. It is therefore unlikely to be the result of a mistake by a copyist: such a slip is conceivable with a common *nomen sacrum*, but not with an unusual one.

(3) line 9: ονομα. At Matthew 27:57 D in fact has τὸ ὄνομα (with 482) against τοὔνομα in other witnesses; at Luke 23:50, ᾧ ὄνομα is

read by 1 118 131 205 209 1582, i.e. by Family 1, against ὀνόματι in other witnesses (this is also found in ℓ55 at Mt 27:57). There is therefore no precise parallel to the anarthrous reading of 0212.

(4) line 12: και αυτοϲ προϲεδεχετο. The witnesses supporting the agreement are almost all Byzantine. 157 is an exception.

(5) lines 13-14: ο̣υτοϲ ουκ | [ην ϲυνκατατ]ιθεμ̣ε̣ν̣[ο]ϲ̣ τη β̣[ουλη]. The positioning of these words (at the end of Lk 23:51) is also found in Sy$^{s.c}$.

It is to be regretted that the surviving piece of 0212 should contain a piece of text so free from significant variation in the manuscripts. However, what we do have shows our witness to have the kind of text we would expect. It shows readings shared with later representatives of quite dissimilar text-types: with 𝔓^{75} B; with D; and with Byzantine witnesses. Here is the evidence taken out of the table:

With B al:

1.	α̣ι̣	**L23.49 𝔓^{75} B 1241**
6.	προϲαββατον	**m15.42 ℵ B* C**
9-10.	α[γ]αθοϲ δι[καιοϲ]	**L23.50 B**

With D:

1.	κ[αι]	**M27.55 D** (but it need not be this parallel)
3.	ην δε	**L23.54 D Lvt (c r^1)**
6-7.	προϲ[ηλθεν]	**M27.58 D lat Sy^s**
9.	ονομα	**M27.57 D** (but, again, it need not be this parallel: we should note the agreement with family 1 only at L23.50)

With Byzantine witnesses:

4.	OM. και	L23.54 A C^C W plcr
12.	και αυτοϲ	m15.43 **K M Π al** (but, again, it need not be this parallel)

Since the passage lacks major variation, the range of agreements is rather striking. Whether this harmony is as old as Tatian's must remain an open question. But on this evidence there is no reason why it should not be. Its base texts show no sign of representing any early recension. It attests the age of some readings found otherwise in less ancient witnesses of the separated Gospels.

7. *Conclusions*

We conclude that 0212 was originally composed in Greek, probably in the latter part of the second century. It is not a part of Tatian's Diatessaron, and so it can shed no light on the origins of the Diatessaron. Since there are no quotations from the Gospel passages corresponding to 0212 extant in Justin, it is also impossible to ascertain whether the fragment might be a copy of Justin's Harmony.[83] Again, whether it is part of a complete harmony or, as Plooij suggested, just a section of a passion harmony cannot be determined.

Its significance is threefold. First, it provides essential, and scarce, information about the theological identity of the early Christian community at Dura-Europos. Second, it is an important witness to the text of the canonical Gospels in the second century. Third, it emphasises the need apparently felt in Syria and Mesopotamia in the second and third centuries for a harmonised text of the Gospels, a need that was to lead to the later success, indeed dominance, in the region of Tatian's Diatessaron. Unfortunately, it also raises an uncomfortable question for students of Tatian's text: how can we be certain that witnesses at present described as 'diatessaronic' are not in fact relics of this, or some other, early harmony? The impact on our methodology could be dramatic.

[83] We have been far from convinced by the arguments of Boismard, *Le Diatessaron*, that the second part of 0212 depends on Tatian but the first part on Justin.

WHERE IS EMMAUS? CLUES IN THE TEXT OF LUKE 24 IN CODEX BEZAE[1]

J. READ-HEIMERDINGER

A number of scholars have drawn attention to the use made by Luke of the Jewish Scriptures, and fresh discoveries continue to be made as more information about the nature and the function of the Scriptures in first-century Judaism becomes known.[2] Scriptural reference is seen not just in the direct quotations which Luke makes but much more in his creative adaptation of texts or groups of texts to produce Midrashic-type narratives which rely on the devices of

---

[1] This examination of variant readings in Lk 24 is more fully developed in a detailed study of the chapter carried out in collaboration with Josep Rius-Camps (CBQ forthcoming). I am grateful for comments made by participants at the Birmingham Colloquium, which have been taken into account in this article.

[2] In addition to the information provided in the introductions to recent editions of intertestamental literature, there have been detailed studies of Jewish exegetical techniques which give an idea of how the first Christians may have used and interpreted Scripture. Among the many contributions to the field, the following may be cited as particularly helpful: the comprehensive, if technical, work by M. Fishbane, *Biblical Interpretation in Ancient Israel* (Oxford: Clarendon, 1987); a collection of studies specifically of targumic techniques, D.R.G. Beattie & M.J. McNamara (eds), *The Aramaic Bible: Targums in their Historical Context* (Sheffield: Sheffield Academic Press, 1994); and, in French, a collection of a more general nature edited by M. Tardieu, *Les Règles de l'Interprétation* (Paris: Le Cerf, 1987). For studies relating to the writings of Luke, see C.A. Kimball, *Jesus' Exposition of the Old Testament in Luke's Gospel* (Sheffield: Sheffield Academic Press, 1994); see also C.A. Evans, 'Luke and the Rewritten Bible: Aspects of Lukan Hagiography', in *The Pseudepigrapha and Early Biblical Interpretation*', J.H. Charlesworth & C.A. Evans (eds), (Sheffield: Sheffield Academic Press, 1993), 170-201; Read-Heimerdinger, 'Acts 8:37: A Textual and Exegetical Study', *The Bulletin of the Institute for Reformation Biblical Studies* 2:1 (1991) 8-13.

traditional Jewish exegesis for their interpretation. He thereby situates the events relating to the life of Jesus (in the Gospel), as indeed those relating to the first communities of his disciples (in Acts), in the stream of the continuing unfolding of the history of Israel.[3]

In the final chapter of his Gospel, there are overt references to the Jewish Scriptures which Luke portrays as made by the resurrected Jesus in order to interpret his Messiahship (vv. 27; 44-7). There is, however, much more to Luke's use of Scripture in his account of Jesus' resurrection appearances than these obvious references. Our study will examine in detail this aspect, and will focus on the central section of the chapter (vv.13-25), where Jesus meets two disciples as they walk from Jerusalem to a village a certain distance away.

One of the indispensable tasks is to establish the text of Luke, for Chapter 24 exists in two main forms, usually described as the Alexandrian text (AT) and the Western text (WT). The WT is often thought of as being characterized by its greater length in Luke-Acts,[4]

---

[3] Cf. B.T. Arnold, 'Luke's Characterizing Use of the Old Testament in the Book of Acts', in *History, Literature and Society in the Book of Acts*, B. Witherington (ed.), (Cambridge: Cambridge University Press, 1996), 300-23; C.A. Evans & J.A. Sanders, *Luke and Scripture: The Function of Sacred Tradition in Luke-Acts* (Sheffield: Sheffield Academic Press, 1993); cf. Evans, 'Luke and the Rewritten Bible', 172-3. R.G. Hall, *Revealed Histories. Techniques for Ancient Jewish and Christian Historiography* (Sheffield: Sheffield Academic Press, 1991), 171-208. Although the exact definition of Midrash is disputed, it can be broadly said to represent the interpretation of events which occur in the history of Israel as a commentary on the divine revelation expressed through the events narrated in the Torah. For a discussion of Midrash in the modern world, see J. Sacks, *Crisis and Covenant* (Manchester: Manchester University Press, 1992), 209-46; cf. Read-Heimerdinger, 'The Seven Steps of Codex Bezae. A Prophetic Interpretation of Acts 12', in Parker & Amphoux, 303-10; 'Barnabas in Acts', in JSNT (1998). The evidence in Luke's writing of a Jewish way of thinking, suggests that he was himself a Jew. This is a possibility which is increasingly being considered, contrary to the traditional view of Luke as a gentile Christian, cf. F. Bovon, 'Studies in Luke-Acts: Retrospect and Prospect', *HTR* 85:1 (1992) 175-96, for a survey of contributions to the debate over Lukan identity.

[4] For the book of Acts, the figure of 10% is usually quoted as the difference in the length of the two texts, based on the calculations of A.C. Clark, see Metzger, *Textual Commentary I*, 260; cf. W. Strange, *The Problem of the Text of*

but in the final chapters of the Gospel the contrary situation exists. The traditional maxim of textual criticism, *lectior brevior potior*, has caused the shorter, so-called Western, form of the text to be regarded with exceptional favour, with the series of longer readings in the AT of the end of Luke's Gospel being labelled by Westcott and Hort as 'Western non-interpolations'.[5] Nevertheless, despite the approval granted to the WT, there has been little sustained analysis of it, most studies of Luke's Gospel being based on the AT. In fact, as has been argued on a number of occasions elsewhere,[6] the WT, unlike the AT, is not a homogenous recension but a collection of witnesses (many of them versions) whose chief resemblance to each other is that they differ in one way or another from the AT. What is often meant by the 'Western text' is consequently a hypothetical reconstruction based on a variety of differing witnesses, most of them versional as opposed to Greek MSS. It is not sound methodology to compare a reconstructed, non-existent text with the AT which can be easily identified by consulting its two main representatives, Codex Sinaiticus (א01, previously א) and Codex Vaticanus (B03). Independent analysis of extended passages in the only Greek witness which consistently differs from the AT in Luke's writings, Codex Bezae (D05), has demonstrated that the text of this manuscript regularly displays a high degree of linguistic and literary consistency. Some studies argue that its readings function together to

---

Acts (Cambridge: CUP, 1992), 213, n.18. The difference is, in fact, somewhat smaller when actual MSS are compared: according to a detailed word count of the extant chapters of Acts, the text of D05 is less than 7% longer than that of B03 and in any case, the additional material only accounts for about one third of the variation between the MSS.

[5] Because of their preference for the MSS of א01 and B03, which they believed to have a 'neutral text' in the NT generally, Westcott & Hort refer to the longer text of the Alexandrian witnesses at the end of Luke as 'Western non-interpolations' which, if nothing else, is an indication of their prejudices. The traditional maxims of *lectio brevior potior* and *lectio difficilior potior*, formulated by G. von Mästricht in 1711 (see L. Vaganay & C.-B. Amphoux, *Introduction to New Testament Textual Criticism* [Cambridge: CUP, 1992], 80-1), are no longer viewed by many textual critics as valid criteria for evaluating readings. See M.W. Holmes, 'Reasoned Eclecticism in New Testament Textual Criticism', in Ehrman & Holmes, 342-3.

[6] See, for example, Vaganay and Amphoux, *An Introduction to New Testament Textual Criticism*, 110.

communicate a particular theological intention on the part of the author.[7] Such results challenge the view that the text of Codex Bezae as it now stands has been formed by successive layers of modification,[8] or that it is the work of a slipshod and whimsical scribe.[9]

By consulting current editions of the Greek New Testament,[10] it is possible to gain some impression of the variation which exists among the manuscripts used for the establishment of the text. This impression, however, is too vague to enable the text of any one manuscript to be reconstructed in detail. All kinds of readings are

---

[7] In addition to his full-scale comparative translation of the two texts of Acts (*Les Deux Actes des Apôtres* [Paris: Gabalda, 1986]), E. Delebecque has published a number of exegetical articles which defend the carefulness of the Bezan scribe and which point to a coherence of meaning in the Bezan text of Acts. E.J. Epp argued that there was an anti-Judaic tendency in Codex Bezae in *The Theological Tendency of Codex Bezae Cantabrigiensis* (Cambridge: CUP, 1966) but his discussion is flawed in so far as it draws on other MSS when Codex Bezae does not support his claims. The commentary on Acts in Catalan by J. Rius-Camps agrees on the homogeneity of Codex Bezae following a more rigorous comparison of the MS with those of the Alexandrian tradition (*Comentari als Fets dels Apòstols*, vols. I-III [Barcelona: Herder, 1992-6], vol. IV forthcoming). A linguistic examination which I carried out using the principles of discourse analysis tends to confirm the uniformity of the language and purpose of Codex Bezae in Acts ('The Contribution of Discourse Analysis to Textual Criticism: A Study of the Bezan Text of Acts', PhD Thesis, University of Wales, 1994). On the consistency of the Bezan text in other books of the New Testament, cf. a study of Matthew's Gospel by C.-B. Amphoux, *L'Evangile Selon Matthieu. Codex de Bèze* (L'Isle-sur-la-Sorgue: Le Bois d'Orion, 1996).

[8] This view is advocated by D.C. Parker, *Codex Bezae. An Early Christian Manuscript and its Text* (Cambridge: CUP, 1994); cf. 'Professor Amphoux's History of the New Testament Text: A Response', *New Testament Textual Research Update* 4 (1996) 41-5. A range of opinions are expressed in the collection of papers from the Lunel Colloquium in France 1994 (Parker & Amphoux).

[9] This has been traditionally the most popular view, see Metzger, *Textual Commentary I, passim*. It is maintained with respect to Acts by M.-E. Boismard and A. Lamouille (*Le texte occidental des Actes des Apôtres: Reconstitution et Réhabilitation*, vol. I [Paris: Éd. Recherche sur les Civilisations, 1985], 11) who regard Codex Bezae as a 'témoin très abâtardi' of the Western text, a text which they otherwise regard as representing the primitive text.

[10] NA^{27} or UBS^{4}.

not cited in the critical apparatus; many are deemed insignificant by the editors and, in any case, limited space makes more frequent citings impractical. Furthermore, successive variant readings which occur within any one passage are generally treated by textual critics as independent instances of variation, with the result that the usefulness of acknowledging them all in a critical edition is not recognized. That said, the larger-scale edition of Luke's Gospel produced by the International Greek New Testament Project displays a comprehensive range of variant readings without being overly restricted by criteria of significance.[11] This edition, together with access to the text of certain manuscripts, means that it is not difficult to step outside the confines of the popular editions in order to make a more exact comparison of some of the different states of the New Testament text which have existed. It is becoming increasingly apparent that the study of manuscripts, as opposed to a string of selected variant readings, is an exercise which yields interesting information and valuable clues as to the history of the text of the New Testament.

What I aim to do here in this study of the central section of the final chapter of Luke's Gospel, is to comment on some readings of the 'short text' as it stands in D05 and to compare them with those of B03, which is essentially the text printed in the NA^{27}/UBS^{4} editions. B03 will be taken as a representative of the AT but variants which arise in the text of ℵ01 will be pointed out. I will seek to indicate reasons for the variation between the two main forms of the text and to consider how Luke's purpose as conveyed by the text in D05 differs from that conveyed by the text in B03.

A Theological Key

The themes which run throughout Luke's narrative in the final chapter of his Gospel – a journey, an encounter with God, and the divine provision of food – are all prominent themes in the earliest stories in the history of the Jewish people as told in the book of Genesis and there are verbal parallels in Lk 24 with several of these stories. Amongst them can be noted the visit by the oaks of Mamre of the three angels to Abraham who offers them bread before they continue with their journey (18:5); and the provision of Hagar with bread and water as she sets off on her wanderings in the wilderness

[11] IGNT, *Luke*.

of Beersheba (21:14). Most striking is the journey of Jacob to Bethel where he had his dream of the ladder between heaven and earth, an episode which will be examined in more detail now to see how it illuminates the underlying theological meaning of the central episode of the resurrection appearances in Lk 24, Jesus' encounter with the two disciples.

The clue to the significance of the Jacob incident is provided by the name given in Lk 24:13 in Codex Bezae to the village for which they were heading, 'Oulammaous'. The text of the verse in each MS reads as follows:

Codex Bezae	*Codex Vaticanus*
ἦσαν δὲ δύο πορευόμενοι ἐξ αὐτῶν ἐν αὐτῇ τῇ ἡμέρᾳ εἰς κώμην ἀπέχουσαν σταδίους ἑξήκοντα ἀπὸ Ἰερουσαλὴμ ὀνομάτι Οὐλαμμαοῦς	Καὶ ἰδοὺ δύο ἐξ αὐτῶν ἐν αὐτῇ τῇ ἡμέρᾳ ἦσαν πορευόμενοι εἰς κώμην ἀπέχουσαν σταδίους ἑξήκοντα ἀπὸ Ἰερουσαλὴμ ᾗ ὄνομα Ἐμμαοῦς

The name 'Oulammaous' is read only by the Greek and Latin sides of Codex Bezae. It is found only once elsewhere in Greek literature, in certain MSS of the LXX version of the story of Jacob's ladder in Gen 28.[12] It is worth looking at the Genesis passage to see the significance of the name there.

After tricking his father into giving him the birthright of Esau, his elder brother, Jacob was fleeing from his brother's anger (Gen 27:18-45). He was on his way from Beersheba to Haran when he stopped at nightfall at a place on the mountain road running north out of Jerusalem. There he dreamed that he saw a ladder reaching to heaven with angels of God ascending and descending on it, or on him.[13] A voice spoke to him and assured him of God's protection and

[12] The form οὐλαμμαύς is read by Codex Alexandrinus and MS 370. Most Greek MSS have a form of the name which retains the 'L' of 'Luz' (οὐλαμλούζ, for example). Eusebius alone reads the exact form of D05 in Lk 24:13, οὐλαμμαούς. A number of versions also have the name in one form or another without any 'L'.

[13] The Hebrew allows for both meanings of the pronoun; it is interpreted in the personal sense in some exegetical traditions. See J.L. Kugel, *In Potiphar's House. The Interpretative Life of Biblical Texts* (Cambridge, Mass./ London:

confirmed that the land on which he rested would be given to him and his descendants and that these would multiply and spread out over the earth. Arising in the morning, Jacob took the stone on which he had placed his head and set it up as a pillar over which he poured oil as a thanksgiving sacrifice. The name of the place which was formerly Luz was now called Beth-El, the house of God. The scene then concludes with Jacob making a vow that if God stays with him and looks after him, providing him with bread and clothing so that he returns safely from his flight, back to his father's house, then the Lord will be his God and the pillar will be God's house; and he willl give a tenth of everything back to God.[14]

In the LXX version of the story, the name 'Oulammaous' is said to be the former name of Bethel (Gen 28:19). Its form depends on a misunderstanding (probably involuntary, but possibly deliberate) of the explanation given in the Hebrew text, that it was 'formerly Luz' (אוּלָם לוּז [ulam luz]).

'Oulammaous' designates, in other words, the place Jacob called Bethel. It is important to be specific about the connotations of the name. Under the divided monarchy, Bethel became the place of opposition to true worship in Jerusalem and represented antagonism to the faithful prophets. It was the religious centre of the rebellious, northern kingdom. If, however, Luke had intended the reference to Bethel to evoke the associations of the place as a centre of idolatry, he could have more straightforwardly used the name 'Bethel'.[15]

Harvard University Press, 1994), 112-20; cf. J. Massonnet, 'Targum, Midrash et Nouveau Testament', in *Les Premières Traditions de la Bible* (Lausanne: Editions du Zèbre, 1996), 67-101 (especially 86-9), who examines the use of this Jacob story in the Gospel of John.

[14] The account as it stands in Genesis looks as if it is made up of several strands, on which see A. De Pury, *Promesse Divine et Légende Cultuelle Dans le Cycle de Jacob*, vol. I-II (Paris: Gabalda, 1975). Luke makes use of elements from different strands of the account which he clearly takes as a whole, despite the apparent discrepancies within it.

[15] C.-B. Amphoux, 'Le Chapitre 24 de Luc et l'origine de la tradition textuelle du Codex de Bèze (D.05 du NT)', *Fil Neotest* 4 (1991) 21-49, thinks that there is an underlying play on words between Bethel (house of God, Temple worship) and Bethlehem (house of bread, represented by Jesus who replaces the cultic practices in the Temple with the breaking of bread, 24:19), see 29-30. This interpretation tends to render Luke's message somewhat complicated and obscure, to conceal the significance of the event,

Instead, he gives the name of the place as 'Oulammaous' which makes an unquestionable connection with the scene of Gen 28 in which Jacob first set a monument to mark the place where God dwelt on earth.

When the two narratives of Lk 24 and Gen 28 are considered side by side, a rich weave of parallels can be noticed. These involve similarities of concepts but also depend in part on the wording of the LXX text. The elements in Lk 24 are concentrated in the central episode of vv.13-35 but the parallels spill over into the preceding and following episodes of the chapter. They can be seen most clearly when the Genesis account is taken step by step:

	Genesis 28	*Luke 24*
v.10	Jacob is going on a journey to flee from his brother	The two disciples are going on a journey, v.13, which is a journey of flight (see below).
v.11	a. the sun sets when he gets to a certain place	a. towards evening, the day declining, as they approach the village, vv.28-9.
	b. he sleeps	b. their eyes are darkened, v.16
v.12	a. he dreams	a. the women said they had had a vision, v.23
	b. the ladder which connects heaven and earth	b. the day of ascension, Jesus goes to heaven, v.51 (not D05), Ac 1:10-11
	c. angels ascending and descending	c. the women had a vision of angels, v.23
v.13	God reveals himself out of heaven to Jacob	Jesus, in resurrected form, communicates with his disciples; he reveals himself from the Scriptures, vv.25-27, 44

whereas in fact Luke's use of coded language rather has the opposite function of *unveiling* deeper meaning. In any case, there would have been no need for Luke to use the singular designation of Bethel, 'Oulammaous', if it were the name 'Bethel' itself which was important. 'Oulammaous' is never used again to refer to Bethel.

v.14	Promise that Jacob will be father of many descendants who will spread to the four corners of the earth	Jesus will order his disciples to go to the ends of the earth, and promises the Holy Spirit, vv.47, 49, cf. Ac 1:4, 8. His twelve apostles represent the twelve sons of Jacob (22:30; Ac 1:17)
v.15	a. God will be always with him (μετὰ σοῦ)	a. Jesus stayed with the disciples (μετ' αὐτῶν), v.29 (twice in D), v.30B
	b. everything God has said will be accomplished	b. the fulfillment of the Scriptures in Jesus, vv.25, 32, 44
v.16	a. Jacob awakens	a. the disciples' eyes are opened, v.31; their mind is opened, v.45
	b. he realizes that the Lord was there	b. they recognize Jesus, vv.31, 35; they realize that he has risen, v.34D
v.17	he is afraid	the disciples gathered in Jerusalem are afraid when Jesus appears, v.37
v.18	he gets up	the two disciples get up, v.33
v.20	he asks for bread and clothing as a sign of the covenant being kept	the taking of the bread from Jesus is the sign which shows them who he is, v.31D (in B, it is the breaking of bread, cf. v.35)

In the B03 text, the clue to the identity of Jesus is in the *breaking* of the bread, commonly taken as a recollection of the 'last supper' of Lk 22. In the D05 text, it is the *taking* of the bread which serves as the sign for the disciples. Long before the distribution of bread became a Christian eucharistic symbol, it was a Jewish sign of hospitality and provision on the part of the master of the household. The D05 text avoids making a connection with Jesus' farewell meal, but enables a wider application of the clue to be made, to God as provider of food, thus establishing a further parallel with Gen 28:20.[16]

[16] In the B03 text, the sign of the bread is presented in a form which links the breaking and the blessing of the bread (v.31 τὸν ἄρτον, where D05 does

The number of resemblances between the text of Gen 28 and Lk 24 is striking, and they are especially close in the Bezan account of the disciples' meeting with Jesus. They suggest that the author is presenting the meeting as a re-enactment of Jacob's encounter with Yahweh at Bethel. This is a reading of the Scriptures which is typically Jewish in that it demonstrates how the recent events concerning Jesus and his followers were already contained within the Torah. It is a use of Scripture which is confined neither to this instance in the writings of Luke nor indeed to Luke as a writer in the New Testament. The question is why the Jacob story is chosen as template in this case.

The reason becomes clearer when the motive for Jacob's journey is taken into consideration. He was fleeing from his brother whom he had just tricked into losing his inheritance due to him as the first-born son. He was running away to save his life.[17] It was during the flight which resulted from such a crime that God came to meet with him. In the traditional teaching which grew up around the Jacob story,[18] certain elements became considerably developed. In particular, great importance is attached to the setting of the sun: God is said to have miraculously advanced the hour of sunset because he wanted to speak with Jacob in private, and even that he

not have the article). This creates an association which is a typically Jewish one, absent from the D05 form of the text. The avoidance of stereotypical expressions and associations is, however, a characteristic which has been noticed in the Bezan text of Acts, where there is a correspondingly more spontaneous and creative use of language, cf. J. (Read-)Heimerdinger and S.H. Levinsohn, 'The Use of the Definite Article Before Names of People in the Greek Text of Acts with Particular Reference to Codex Bezae', *Fil Neotest* 9 (1992) 15-44.

[17] In the lectionary cycle of readings identified by J. Mann (*The Bible as Read and Preached in the Old Synagogue*, vol. I [New York: KTAV, 1940] 226ff), the start of the *Haftarot* connected with the *Seder* which begins at Gen 28:10 is Hos 12:13 (12) where Jacob's flight to Haran is cited because of the reference to the cities of refuge. The associated homily develops the theme of seeking refuge after killing a person in order to escape the avenger of blood. The existence of such traditions illustrates how much the Genesis passage was seen as portraying Jacob in flight when he left Beersheba.

[18] See especially Midrash Rabbah Genesis 28, and Targum Neofiti I of Genesis.

took this action because 'the "Word" was burning to speak with him'.[19]

If Luke uses the Jacob story as a basis for the account of Jesus' resurrection appearance to the two disciples in his Gospel, it would seem that he wishes to portray the journey of the two disciples as a similar journey of flight, to show that they were running away. This interpretation is confirmed by a number of factors which are again more evident in the text of Codex Bezae. First of all, there is a reason for their flight which is to be found in the two-fold betrayal of Jesus which has taken place within the group, that of Judas (Lk 22:3-6, 47-8) and that of Peter (22:54-62). It is of no little interest that in the Bezan text, the betrayal by Judas is a re-enactment of Jacob's betrayal of his brother. In the account of the sign of the kiss which Judas gives to Jesus (22:47-8), the D text of v.47 reproduces the exact wording with which the LXX text relates the betrayal of Esau by Jacob when he goes to claim the blessing from his father (Gen 27:27).[20] The result of this quotation here is that the parallel of the Jacob story is, in fact, already in place by Chapter 24.

While it is true that in the summary which the disciples give to Jesus, they attribute the handing over (παρέδωκαν, the same verb as

[19] TgGen 28:10; cf. v.12. The Targumic text may have an echo in the remark of the disciples in the text of Lk 24:32 B03 (read by most MSS except D05), 'did not our hearts burn within us while he talked with us...?' The presence of the allusion in the non-Bezan text may be an indication that even in there the Jewish traditions of the Jacob story were recognized as behind the Lukan narrative. Cf. v.31 B03 which likewise displays evidence of a Jewish perspective in the association of the blessing and the breaking of the bread (see n.16 above).

[20] καὶ ἐγγίσας ἐφίλησεν αὐτόν. Lk 22:47 D05: καὶ ἐγγίσας ἐφίλησεν τὸν Ἰησοῦν. The other Greek MSS read καὶ ἤγγισεν τῷ Ἰησοῦ φιλῆσαι αὐτόν, which expresses exactly the same idea but in a form which no longer resembles the LXX text of Gen 27:27. Furthermore, the D05 text of Lk 22:47 has the narrator specify that the kiss was a pre-arranged sign. Old Latin and Old Syriac MSS share the Bezan reading. On the one hand, the presence of the reading in a range of MSS can be seen as evidence that it was an early reading which had been randomly adopted by several witnesses. On the other hand, if the Bezan text is viewed as the original text with a peculiarly Jewish perspective, it is possible that it was modified within a short space of time by subsequent Greek editors in order to attenuate the Jewish reminiscences, but not before it had been translated into the languages of neighbouring peoples.

'to betray') of Jesus to the 'chief priests and rulers' (v.20), this needs to be considered in the social context of a profoundly united community who share a corporate sense of responsibility for wrong-doing. The religious authorities represent the people, and in so far as they have sinned by handing the Messiah over to be killed, then the people too have sinned.[21] Even if the two disciples on the road had not played an individual part in the betrayal/handing over of Jesus, there is no doubt about their affinity with those who had done so. The theme of betrayal is an important one which also provides clues about the identity of the two disciples, but that is an aspect of the question which there is not time to develop here.

In fact, the particular word order of the Bezan text in v.13 gives to the sentence which introduces the account of the disciples' journey the sense that they were leaving the group of apostles (the last characters to be mentioned, in v.11 D05) to which they belonged: ἦσαν δὲ δύο πορευόμενοι ἐξ αὐτῶν. Furthermore, the sense of failure and disappointment which comes across in the explanation given by the disciples to Jesus as he walks with them is more acute in the text of D05:

v.19: In place of the nationalistic form Ναζαρηνός, D05 uses Ναζωραῖος, which carries Messianic connotations in Luke's writings.[22] According to the D05 text, the disciples had recognized Jesus as the Messiah, the ruler of Davidic descendance, but he did not fulfil their expectations.

v.21: The hope expressed by D05 is in the past tense: 'we were hoping that he was ...'; ℵ01 has the present for the first verb and both ℵ01 and B03 have the present for the second. In D05, the hope that Jesus would free the nation of Israel has been

---

[21] The tractate of the Mishnah, *Horayoth*, which would have been in existence at least in oral form in the first century, spells out the consequences for Israel when the rulers sin. All the people of Israel are implicated, although it is the rulers alone who have to carry out the steps necessary to obtain forgiveness.

[22] Ναζωραῖος (Messianic form) is the only form found in Acts (2:22; 3:6; 4:10; 6:14; 22:8; 24:5; 26:9), where Jesus is always referred to in a Messianic context. In the Gospel, the only firm reading is of Ναζαρηνός (nationalistic form) at 4:34 (the demoniac in the synagogue). The Messianic form is read elsewhere by ℵ01/B03 at 18:37 (the people to the blind man) and by D05 at 2:39 (by Luke, as a fulfilment of prophecy, cf. Mt 2:23) and here at 24:19. The nationalistic form is read by D05 at 18:37 and by ℵ01/B03 at 24:19.

abandoned because it has apparently come to nothing with the death of the Messiah. It will be rekindled once the resurrection of Jesus is understood (Ac 1:6; 2:36; 3:20-21; 5:31), although abandoned once more in a positive sense by Peter at least.[23]

v.22: The sense of time which has lapsed since his death is accentuated in D05 by the use of 'today is the third day ...' rather than 'this is the third day ...'.[24]

Furthermore, D05 follows the time phrase with the perfect, '... since all these things happened', whereas the AT has the aorist, a difference which cannot be easily brought out in an English translation. The perfect is an aspect which expresses the idea that an event is viewed in its entirety with all the attendant circumstances, so here can be thought of as referring to the death of Jesus together with the betrayal and the trial; the aorist, on the other hand, focuses more narrowly on the event of the crucifixion.[25] The sense of bewilderment is again the greater in D05.

When all these features of variation between the MSS are considered together, it is interesting to note that the focus of interest in the version of the story told by the Bezan text is the inner thoughts and feelings of the disciples. The focus is given by the underlying motif of flight, and is maintained by the insistence on the despair and sadness of the disciples. Their sadness is not dispelled by the meeting with Jesus in D05 (cf. λυπούμενοι in v.33), but their comprehension of recent events begins to change as he explains to them the meaning of the Scriptures. This change is again more subtle and progressive in the Bezan text (cf. the use of a simple verb rather than the perfective compound in the AT in vv. 27, 31, 32; the incomplete

[23] Ac 12:11. Cf. Rius-Camps, *Comentari*, vol. II, on Acts 12.

[24] The wording of both texts in this phrase in unusual, because of the apparently impersonal use of ἄγει. For a discussion of the phrase, and the existence of a comparably unusual expression in the Testimonium in the *Jewish Antiquities* of Josephus, see G.J. Goldberg, 'The Coincidences of the Emmaus Narrative of Luke and the Testimonium of Josephus', *JSP* 13 (1995) 59-77, esp. 68-9.

[25] There has been an ongoing debate for some time now among linguists on the significance of verbal aspect in Greek. For a summary of the current thinking, see R.A. Young, *Intermediate New Testament Greek. A Linguistic and Exegetical Approach* (Nashville, Tennessee: Broadman and Holman, 1994), 105-7.

exposition of Scripture by Jesus in v.27; the adjective 'veiled' rather than 'burning' in v. 32).

In comparison with the version of Codex Bezae, the AT presents a less nuanced account of the meeting between the disciples and Jesus. The interest is more in the fact of the resurrection appearance than on the mental attitude of the disciples, and the encounter is related as a straighforward historical fact. The choice of the name 'Emmaus', a place already known if only because it was referred to as a place of battle in the Maccabean wars (I Macc 3:40, 57; 4:3), sets the scene for an encounter which is envisaged as having only a literal reality and not a spiritual one.

The reference to the distance of the village from Jerusalem, sixty stadia which is equivalent to just over 11 km, gives further weight to the idea that the episode of the disciples' encounter with Jesus was included in Luke's Gospel primarily for its significance as a non-literal event. The place referred to as Emmaus in the first book of Maccabees is much further than sixty stadia from Jerusalem and corresponds more to the hundred and sixty of Codex Sinaiticus, suggesting that the ℵ01 reading has arisen in order to overcome the problem of matching a place known as Emmaus to the given distance from Jerusalem.[26] It could be hoped that the understanding of the village as Bethel would provide a solution to the difficulty of the distance. Bethel, however, is not sixty stadia but more like ninety stadia from Jerusalem!

The implication, that being so, is that the distance mentioned by Luke was not intended to be a literal distance but a symbolic one. Of what is it a symbol? The meaning is found in the first chapter of Acts which develops the Gospel account of the resurrection appearances of Jesus.[27] In Ac 1:12, reference is made to the distance permitted to

---

[26] Other attempts to find a place which fits better with the mention of sixty stadia have not been satisfactory, see I.H. Marshall, *The Gospel of Luke* (Exeter: Paternoster Press, 1978), 892-3.

[27] There a number of close affinities of this nature between the final chapter of Luke and the opening chapter of Acts, which are evidence that the two books are volumes of the same work. The studies which claim the contrary (see, most recently, M.C. Parsons & R.I. Pervo, *Rethinking the Unity of Luke and Acts* [Minneapolis: Augsburg, 1993]; cf. J.B. Green, 'Internal Repetition in Luke-Acts', in B. Witherington, ed., *History, Literature, and Society in the Book of Acts* [Cambridge: Cambridge University Press, 1996], 283-99) do not

be travelled on the sabbath day when the narrative specifies that following the ascension of Jesus, the disciples returned to Jerusalem from the Mount of Olives which was a sabbath's day journey 'near (ἐγγύς)' to the city (ὅ ἐστιν ἐγγὺς Ἰερουσαλὴμ σαββάτου ἔχον ὁδόν). Many commentators point out that the reference to the sabbath day regulation is an anomaly since according to the data given in Luke's Gospel and Acts, the ascension did not take place on a sabbath. The distance detail is, in fact, yet one more instance in Luke's writings of information which has a purpose other than a factual one. The mention that the disciples' return journey to Jerusalem was no longer than a sabbath day's journey can be taken as a deliberate indication that, in their own minds at least, they remained within the sphere of the Jewish law as they returned to the capital city, the seat of religious authority.[28]

The permitted sabbath day journey was 2000 cubits or roughly 1.1 km, that is about six stadia, and this is indeed the distance between the Mount of Olives and the city of Jerusalem.[29] Sixty stadia, in contrast, corresponds to ten times the distance permitted to be travelled on the sabbath. This means that when in the Gospel account of the disciples' flight, they are portrayed as running away from Jerusalem, they intend to travel ten times a sabbath's day journey away (εἰς κώμην ἀπέχουσαν σταδίους ἑξήκοντα ἀπὸ Ἰερουσαλήμ – note the verb ἀπέχουσαν here, in contrast to the unusual use of ἔχον at Ac 1:12, which shows that there it is the idea of closeness rather than distance which is in the author's mind). In the light of what we have seen as the circumstances which prompted their journey, the detail of the distance (given first, even before the name of the village in 24:13) may be taken as a metaphor signifying that they were attempting to get out of the sphere of Jewish law.

Conclusions

The reading of 'Oulammaous', with its significance derived from the Genesis story of Jacob, is consistent with other readings of the text in Codex Bezae. The combination of readings in the Bezan text is so

---

take account of these underlying, non-literal, connections which stand as evidence of conscious authorial links.

[28] Rius-Camps, *Comentari*, vol. I, 60-2.

[29] The distance between Jerusalem and the Mount of Olives is given by Josephus in *War* 5.70 as six stadia and in *Ant.* 20.169 as five stadia.

complex, and they are so closely woven together, that it would hardly have been possible for a later editor to have introduced them into a more simple text. There are, on the other hand, reasons why the name 'Oulammaous' may have been altered. It may be that the name 'Oulammaous' was not recognized as the name of a place, and so it was replaced with a like-sounding substitute name. On the other hand, the name 'Oulammaous' and its connotations may have been only too well recognized. For a later generation of Christians who were no longer so conscious of their origins in Judaism as were the first generation, such rooting of their faith in Jewish tradition can have been a difficulty. The reminiscence of the Jacob story in Judas' kiss is already absent in Chapter 22; it may well be that this further allusion in Chapter 24 was therefore likewise deleted and the indications in the story of the dimension of spiritual history were modified so as to produce a simple, factual account.

It is the more straightforward account which has been handed down to us today, through the successive printed editions of the Greek New Testament. It is one which has been particularly cherished by Christians because of its strong note of joyful hope and because it is unique among the New Testament accounts of the resurrection appearances of Jesus. When the story is read in the version of Codex Bezae, it becomes all the more interesting for the detailed attention which is paid to the state of mind of the disciples, and especially for the richness which is conferred on it by its being rooted in the beginnings of the history of Israel.

LA UTILIZACION DEL LIBRO DE JOEL (JL 2,28-32A LXX) EN EL DISCURSO DE PEDRO (HCH 2,14-21): ESTUDIO COMPARATIVO DE DOS TRADICIONES MANUSCRITAS

J. Rius-Camps

Desde la antigüedad se ha intentado reconstruir el texto original de un autor apoyándose en los mejores manuscritos (rollos, códices, papiros, pergaminos, etc.). La moderna crítica textual ha perfeccionado sus métodos estableciendo una serie de reglas y elaborando los estemas a fin de recomponer los avatares que ha sufrido el texto a lo largo de su transmisión. El Nuevo Testamento no constituye una excepción. Los criterios que se han ido formulando para la reconstrucción del texto parten de una doble hipótesis: la existencia de un texto perfectamente fijado por su autor y la voluntad de los escribas de transmitirlo con la máxima fidelidad. Las fluctuaciones que se aprecian en las variantes textuales serían debidas a errores de copista o a influjos externos al texto. La abundancia de testimonios de diversa procedencia permite adivinar con un alto grado de fiabilidad cuál sería la forma original del texto en cuestión. En nuestro caso, sin embargo, observamos que el texto lucano de los Hechos de los Apóstoles ha llegado hasta nosotros en dos recensiones bastante dispares, la «alejandrina», cuyo máximo representante es el códice Vaticano (B03), y la «occidental», cuyo representante principal es el códice Beza bilingüe (D05, d05). Para la mayoría de editores modernos el texto alejandrino (TA) constituye la base de sus ediciones críticas, salvo en los casos singulares en que una determinada variante se presenta suficientemente avalada por otros códices. El texto occidental (TO), en cambio, ha sido sistemáticamente relegado al aparato crítico, exceptuadas las llamadas «Western non-interpolations» y los casos en que se presenta suficientemente avalado por otros códices, puesto que se considera que las variantes de todo tipo contenidas en él han sido fruto de una revisión posterior, hasta el punto de tildar de «Western interpolations» las frecuentes amplificaciones que presenta respecto al texto alejandrino, habiéndose calculado ese plus en torno a un nueve por ciento. Este fenómeno no es nuevo. En textos pertenecientes al canon judío se presentan igualmente diversas recensiones de un mismo libro. Dicho fenómeno se ha podido valorar con más conocimiento de causa a raíz de los manuscritos descubiertos en Qumrán, donde se han preservado varias copias de un mismo libro con variantes muy significativas respecto al texto hebreo masorético y afines muchas de ellas al texto hebreo que sirvió de base para la traducción de los Setenta.

La existencia de diversas recensiones de un mismo texto bíblico no puede explicarse satisfactoriamente recurriendo a defectos de transmisión debidos a los sucesivos copistas y a circunstancias adyacentes. Para dar con una explicación convincente debería dejarse de lado la hipótesis tradicional de un texto que se ha ido transmitiendo fielmente desde que fue redactado, haciendo recurso a la existencia de un texto «vivo» que se ha ido reformulando y actualizando en el seno de las comunidades judías o cristianas que lo utilizaban, y modificando en consecuencia los criterios de selección de las variantes. La historia de la transmisión del texto adquiere entonces un relieve notable. No cabe duda de que los intentos de reconstruir el original se ven notablemente dificultados por las trazas que las sucesivas generaciones han dejado en el texto al reinterpretarlo según las necesidades que iban surgiendo y la nueva problemática en que estaban inmersas.

A grandes rasgos, debería abandonarse la costumbre inveterada de valorar las variantes una por una, aisladas unas de otras, ya que en la mayoría de los casos están conectadas entre sí y puede muy bien darse el caso que no correspondan a una misma forma de texto. En el caso de los Hechos de los Apóstoles la inmensa mayoría de variantes de tipo «occidental» quedan inexorablemente relegadas al aparato crítico por falta de apoyos manuscritos de peso. Por lo general, las variantes deberían examinarse formando conjuntos o cuantos, de manera que el estudioso que maneja una determinada edición crítica pudiera hacerse una idea cabal de la tendencia que ha presidido la formación de una determinada recensión (alejandrina, occidental, en nuestro caso). Sobre las presuntas tendencias del texto «occidental», el estudio de E.J. Epp se ha convertido en una obra de referencia obligada.[1] De posibles tendencias inherentes a la recensión alejandrina apenas si se habla, ya que se presupone por principio que se trata del texto original de Lucas. A medida, sin embargo, que iba publicando las dos monografías en que presentaba las grandes líneas para un futuro comentario,[2] seguidas de un amplio *Comentario a los Hechos de los Apóstoles* a partir tanto de la recensión alejandrina como de la occidental,[3] pero sobre todo a raíz de la publicación periódica de una serie de notas sobre el texto occidental de los Hechos de los Apóstoles en la revista *Filología Neotestamentaria* de Córdoba (en parte me he servido de la tercera para la redacción del presente artículo),[4] me iba preguntando si era posible identificar alguna que otra tendencia que fuese específica de la recensión «alejandrina».

La cita de Joel contenida en Hch 2,17-21 me brindó la ocasión, pues podía establecer una comparación a tres bandas: 1) el texto de Joel, según la versión de los Setenta (Jl-LXX), 2) la página griega del códice Beza (D05) y 3) el códice Vaticano (B03). En el presente artículo la he ampliado a cinco, incluyendo en la sinopsis 4) la página latina del códice Beza (d05) y 5) el texto de la Vulgata de Jerónimo (vg), quien habría tomado como base – según puede apreciarse en la sinopsis – un texto perteneciente a una familia Vetus Latina, al igual que d05, y lo habría corregido de acuerdo con el texto alejandrino ya en boga en sus comunidades. En la sinopsis he dividido el texto (tanto el griego como el latino) respetando la división en esticos que hacen sentido («sense-lines») del códice Beza. La numeración que

---

[1] *The Theological Tendency of Codex Bezae Cantabrigiensis in Acts* (Cambridge: Cambridge University Press, 1966): citado: *The Theological Tendency*.

[2] Josep Rius-Camps, *El camino de Pablo a la misión de los paganos* (Madrid: Cristiandad, 1984) 326 pp.; *De Jerusalén a Antioquía. Génesis de la iglesia cristiana* (Córdoba: El Almendro, 1989) 390 pp.

[3] Josep Rius-Camps, *Comentari als Fets dels Apòstols* I-III (Barcelona: Facultat de Teologia de Catalunya-Editorial Herder, 1991-1995): citado *Comentari* + vol.

[4] 'Las variantes de la recensión occidental de los Hechos de los Apóstoles': I (Hch 1,1-3): *Fil Neotest* 6 (1993) 59-68; II (Hch 1,4-14): *Fil Neotest* 6 (1993) 219-230; III (Hch 1,15-26): *Fil Neotest* 7 (1994) 53-64; IV (Hch 2,1-13): *Fil Neotest* 7 (1994) 197-208; V (Hch 2,14-40): *Fil Neotest* 8 (1995) 63-78; VI (Hch 2,41-47): *Fil Neotest* 8 (1995) 199-208; VII (Hch 3,1-26): *Fil Neotest* 9 (1996) 61-76; VIII (Hch 4,1-22): *Fil Neotest* 9 (1996) 201-16; IX (Hch 4,23-31): *Fil Neotest* 10 (1997) 99-104.

doy en el margen izquierdo del aparato crítico corresponde a dicha división en esticos. La segunda cifra, colocada entre [ ], sirve simplemente para contabilizar las variantes (en ocho versículos he identificado veinticuatro); si va seguida de la sigla *vl* NR, quiere decir que dicha variante no ha sido reseñada en la última edición de Nestle–Aland (NA^{27}), siendo siete en total las variantes que no figuran en dicho aparato crítico. El análisis abarca 1) el encabezamiento (v. 14a-b), 2) la primera parte del discurso de Pedro, dirigida tanto a los judíos como a los representantes de la humanidad presentes figuradamente en Jerusalén el día de Pentecostés[5] (vv. 14c-16), y 3) la cita de Joel contenida en ella (vv. 17-21).

1. *Encabezamiento del Discurso de Pedro*

Hch 2,14a-b

1 [1] En el TO, el episodio central de la secuencia de Pentecostés (vv. 14-36), donde se contiene la respuesta de Pedro a la doble reacción del auditorio (vv. 12-13),[6] está encabezado mediante la partícula τότε con función *conjuntiva*, función que retiene en Hechos tanto en el TA (20x sobre 21x) como en los numerosos pasajes en que sólo se conserva en el TO (13x sobre 15x, excluidas dos lecturas erróneas).[7] Aquí retiene, además, la partícula δέ en tercera posición, cosa que se ha interpretado en el sentido que el copista de D se

[5] Puede verse mi *Comentari* I 121-128.

[6] Después de comprobar la reacción de toda la asamblea formando un todo compacto, enmarcada por la inclusión formada por los vv. 7a // 12b (en negrita las adiciones o cambios del TO): ἐξίσταντο δὲ καὶ ἐθαύμαζον λέγοντες **πρὸς ἀλλήλους** // ἐξίσταντο δὲ πάντες καὶ διηποροῦντο (**-ρουν**) ἄλλος πρὸς ἄλλον **ἐπὶ τῷ γεγονότι**, Lucas especifica la diversa reacción del grupo judío (J) y del otro grupo que representa a la humanidad (H): **καὶ** λέγοντες· Τί θέλει τοῦτο εἶναι; (H) (v. 12c) – ἕτεροι δὲ διαχλευάζοντες ἔλεγον (**διεχλεύαζον λέγοντες**) ὅτι Γλεύκους **οὗτοι** μεμεστωμένοι εἰσίν (J) (v. 13).

[7] Puede consultarse la parte consagrada a la partícula τότε en la tesis doctoral de J. Read-Heimerdinger, *The Contribution of Discourse Analysis in Textual Criticism* (citado: *The Contribution*), University of Wales 1994, 106-126. El uso de τότε «zur Einführung des zeitlichen Nachfolgenden ("darauf", "da")» no se presenta en el griego clásico (BDR., § 459,2).

habría olvidado de suprimirla.[8] El hecho de encontrarse en tercera posición no hace dificultad, pudiendo llegar a ocupar dicha partícula incluso la sexta posición.[9] En Hch 27,21 (laguna en D d) se presenta la misma construcción, precedida de un genitivo absoluto, obviamente sin δέ: τότε σταθεὶς ὁ Παῦλος; respuestas parecidas encabezadas por τότε en 4,8; 10,21 TO; 10,46 TA; 19,15 TO; 21,13 TA, donde algunos códices añaden también la partícula δέ;[10] 22,27 TO; 23,3; 25,12. La colocación retrasada de la partícula indicaría que «las palabras que la preceden están estrechamente unidas por el sentido».[11] Por otro lado, la concatenación τότε ... δέ podría anticipar que Pedro no se limitará a *responder* a la pregunta formulada por los del primer grupo, interesándose por el fenómeno de la glosolalía (v. 12b), sino que intentará *dejar sin fundamento* la interpretación sesgada de los componentes del segundo grupo que hacían mofa de ello (v. 13). En el TA, en cambio, se marca simplemente la disyunción mediante la partícula δέ.

2 [2] El TO es consecuente con la comprobación hecha al término de la elección de Matías en Hch 1,26, a saber, con la mera *adscripción* de éste al grupo constituido por Jesús para que representaran a Israel, «los Doce apóstoles» (συνεψηφίσθη μετὰ τῶν δώδεκα ἀποστόλων);[12] el TA, a su vez, es consecuente con la plena *integración* de Matías al grupo formado en este momento histórico, tras la deserción y el suicidio de Judas, sólo por «los Once apóstoles» (συγκατεψηφίσθη μετὰ τῶν ἕνδεκα ἀποστόλων). La recensión alejandrina usa la misma expresión, «los Once», que Lc 24,9.33; la occidental califica a «los diez» (cf. Mc 10,41; Mt 20,24) compañeros de Pedro de

---

[8] É. Delebecque, *Les deux Actes des Apôtres* (Paris: Gabalda, 1986), 33; Read-Heimerdinger, *The Contribution*, 109; *The Beginnings of Christianity*. I *The Acts of the Apostles*, III (London, 1926): citado *Beginnings*, p. 14: «By conflation D has both τότε and δέ » (Ropes).

[9] Cf. A. Bailly, *Dictionnaire Grec-Français* (Paris: Hachette, [16]1950) s.v. δέ, y K. Aland, *Vollständige Konkordanz zum griechischen Neuen Testament* I/1 (Berlin-New York: Walter de Gruyter, 1983), s.v. δέ, exponentes «k tertio loco; l quarto loco; m quinto loco».

[10] Τότε ἀπεκρίθη (+δὲ C* 33!) ὁ (- 𝔓[74] B) Παῦλος TA (𝔓[74] ℵ A B C E 33. 36 *pc*); D lee Εἶπεν δὲ πρός ἡμᾶς ὁ Παῦλος.

[11] Bailly, s.v., C III, p. 435 B.

[12] Véase, 'Las variantes de la recensión occidental de los Hechos de los Apóstoles' III, *Fil Neotest* 7 (1994) 62-4.

«apóstoles», como en 1,26 (cf. 1,2), dejando entrever de nuevo que Lucas «no asume el propósito común del grupo de discípulos de erigirse en representantes del nuevo Israel, al no considerar a Matías como miembro integrante de los Doce».[13]

3 [3] El TO precisa que Pedro «alzó *el primero* la voz», poniendo así de relieve su función de portavoz del grupo apostólico (cf. Lc 6,14 D, par. Mt 10,2) y el comienzo de «la enseñanza de los apóstoles» (Hch 2,42), continuadora de la línea didáctica iniciada por Jesús.

[4] El TA confiere un tono solemne, formal (cf. Hch 26,25), al discurso petrino mediante un septuagintismo, un pleonasmo de sabor semitizante: «(alzó la voz) y les *dirigió la palabra,*[14] usando el mismo verbo empleado en el v. 4 para calificar de inspirada la forma como el Espíritu Santo les concedía de expresarse. El TO, en cambio, añade: «y dijo», a secas, sin dicha implicación.

---

[13] *Comentari* I 130. Haenchen rechaza con razón que la prep. σύν del TA se interprete en el sentido de «inclusive», sentido que adquiere en el griego clásico (cf. BDR, § 221): «"einschließlich der Elf", so daß die Nachwahl nicht berücksichtigt wäre (so Preuschen, 13)», E. Haenchen, *Die Apostelgeschichte* [= *AG*], (Göttingen: Vandenhoek et Ruprecht, [5]1965), 141, n.2; le sigue Schneider, quien deduce de ello que el TO lo habría entendido erróneamente en ese sentido: «D* liest (σὺν τοῖς) δέκα ἀποστόλοις, wahrscheinlich weil σὺν τοῖς ἕνδεκα so verstanden wurde, daß Petrus mitgezählt (und Matthias ausgeschlossen) sei», G. Schneider, *Die Apostelgeschichte* [= *AG*] I, (Freiburg-Basel-Wien: Herder, 1980), 261, n.a. Es imprescindible no interpretar apriorísticamente una recensión a partir de otra. En ambas recensiones σύν + dat. es equivalente de μετά+ ac. Sería un contrasentido sostener que el TO entendió la prep. σύν del TA en el sentido que tenía en el griego clásico y que la usó después en el sentido que tomó en el griego helenístico. Delebecque sostiene que «le copiste de D a fait sauter la seconde lettre du chiffre grec abrégé ια' devant l'initiale du mot suivant ἀποστόλοις (haplographie)» (*Les deux Actes*, 33). Sin embargo, ni la página griega (D) ni la latina (d) abrevian aquí la cifra δέκα / *decem*, mientras que sí habían abreviado la cifra .ιβ. / *.xii.* en Hch 1,26. Es aventurado, pues, afirmar que el autor de dicha recensión «either disregarded or was ignorant of the election of Matthias», Metzger, *Textual Commentary I*, 294. Cada recensión debe examinarse por separado.

[14] Cf. F.F. Bruce, *The Acts of the Apostles: The Greek Text* (Norwich: Inter-Varsity Press, [2]1976), 88; M. Zerwick & M. Grosvenor, *A Grammatical Analysis of the Greek New Testament* (Rome: Biblical Institute Press, 1981), 353.

2. *Primera Parte del Discurso de Pedro*

Hch 2,14c

4-5 [5: *vl* NR] La anticipación del adjetivo πάντες (posición predicativa) en el TO contradistingue todavía mejor que en el TA (posición atributiva) los dos grupos a quienes Pedro dirige la salutación inicial: 1) «Hombres judíos», los judíos históricamente presentes en el acontecimiento (J); 2) «y todos los que residís en Jerusalén» sin excepción,[15] los hombres de todas las razas presentes figuradamente en Jerusalén (H) en representación de la entera humanidad (cf. v. 5),[16] los dos grupos, a saber, que han mostrado reacciones encontradas ante el fenómeno de la glosolalía (vv. 12-13). Su posposición en el TA podría dar pie a que se interpretara como si constituyesen un solo grupo.[17] Una doble salutación análoga en Hch 13,16b.26a.

7 [6: *vl* NR] El TO atestigua el uso del activo ἐνωτίζω: «prestad oídos», mientras que el TA lo hace derivar de ἐνωτίζομαι (cf. Jl 1,2 LXX), deponente, hápax en el NT (septuagintismo): «y meteos en vuestros oídos» (lit.). La doble llamada de atención, más marcada en el TO por la ausencia del καὶ copulativo, parece corresponderse a los dos grupos reseñados: 1) τοῦτο ὑμῖν γνωστὸν ἔστω se referiría a «los hombres judíos» (J); 2) ἐνωτίσατε τὰ ῥήματά μου, a «todos los que residís en Jerusalén» (H), en correspondencia con el encabezamiento del libro de Joel (Jl 1,2 LXX), del cual aducirá a continuación el cumplimiento de la profecía: 1) Ἀκούσατε δὴ ταῦτα, οἱ πρεσβύτεροι (= los ancianos/responsables del pueblo de Israel), 2) καὶ ἐνωτίσασθε,

---

[15] Cf. M. Zerwick, *Graecitas biblica Novi Testamenti* (Romae: Pontificio Istituto Biblico, ^{5}1966), § 188; Read-Heimerdinger, *The Contribution*, 74-5.

[16] Recuérdese lo dicho en 'Las variantes de la recensión occidental' IV, 201-2 y mi *Comentari* I, 130.

[17] Así lo entienden Haenchen, *AG*, 141: «*parallelismus membrorum*», y n. 6: «'Jüdische Männer' und 'Bewohner Jerusalems' meint nicht zwei verschiedene Gruppen»; le sigue Schneider, *AG* I, 267, n. 24: «Die doppelte Anrede bezieht sich auf den gleichen Personenkreis (HAENCHEN). Möglicherweise berücksichtigt jedoch die erste ('Jüdische Männer!'), daß auch Nicht-Jerusalemer anwesend sind». En el encabezamiento de la profecía de Joel, en el cual sin duda Lucas se inspira, se presenta una expresión análoga, diferenciándose igualmente dos estamentos: Ἀκούσατε ταῦτα, οἱ πρεσβύτεροι, καὶ ἐνωτίσασθε, πάντες οἱ κατοικοῦντες τὴν γῆν.

πάντες οἱ κατοικοῦντες τὴν γῆν (= los habitantes de la tierra prometida). A los judíos (J) Pedro les pediría una *comprensión correcta* del hecho que acaban de tergiversar (γνωστὸν ἔστω vuelve a presentarse en Hch 4,10; 13,38; 28,[22].28); a los representantes de la humanidad (H) presentes figuradamente en Jerusalén, una *presta atención* (ἐνωτίσατε /-σθε, hapax NT) a fin de que comprendan a fondo el significado del suceso que acaban de presenciar.

Hch 2,15

9 [8] El TO vincula la segunda explicativa a la explicación de Pedro mediante un genitivo absoluto[18] y confiere mucho más realce a la hora «tercia», al colocarla enfáticamente al final de la frase, mientras que el TA la apoya con un segundo γάρ, a modo de inciso parentético,[19] sin poner énfasis en la hora. Habida cuenta de la importancia que Lucas confiere a las diversas «horas» (la hora «sexta», Lc 23,44a; Hch 10,9; «nona», Lc 23,44b; Hch 3,1; 10,3.30) y teniendo presente el pasaje de Mc 15,25 (ἦν δὲ ὥρα τρίτη καὶ ἐσταύρωσαν [ἐφύλασσον D d it sa^{mss}] αὐτόν), la hora en que irrumpió el Espíritu Santo sobre la comunidad coincidiría con la hora en que «crucificaron» a Jesús/en que después de crucificarlo (v. 24 ℵ A C D Θ 0250) «lo custodiaban». La donación del Espíritu vendría a constituir las primicias de su muerte.

Hch 2,16

11 [9] Los nombres de los profetas menores no son mencionados – salvo en el presente pasaje (TA) – en toda la obra lucana: Hch 7,42.48; 13,40; 15,15. Sólo Isaías es mencionado explícitamente: Lc 3,4; 4,17; Hch 8,28.30; 28,25; no así en Lc 20,46; Hch 13,47.

---

[18] Según BDR, § 423, n. 2, los Sinópticos emplean con frecuencia el gen. absoluto: Mc 34x, Mt 51x, Lc 57x + Hch 100x, a los que cabe añadir 24 ocurrencias más en el TO: Hch 1,9; 2,1.15; 3,11.13; 4,18; 9,8 Clark; 10,25; 11,27; 12,21; 13,6.44; 14,19; 15,11; 18,6a.b (una construcción singular de 4 verbos en gen., paralela a la de 13,44-45); 18,[26: error].27; 19,1; 20,4.12. 18; 21,1.27; 26,30 Clark.

[19] Cf. Delebecque, *Les deux Actes*, 201; Schneider, *AG* I, 261, n. d.

3. *Actualización de la Profecía de Joel*

Hch 2,17

12 [10] El TO reinterpreta la profecía de Joel cambiando la dimensión *histórica*, «después de estos (acontecimientos)», a saber, la plaga de la langosta // la invasión de un pueblo extranjero (comparar Jl 1,6 con 2,2.5: cf. 2,25) que presagiaba la llegada inminente de «el día del Señor» (Jl 1,15; 2,1.11; 3[4],14) en que tendría lugar la restauración de Judá (Jl 3[4],1ss), por una anticipación de los tiempos *escatológicos*, «en los últimos días» (cf. Is 2,2), momento en que iba a tener cumplimiento la Promesa que Dios había hecho antaño a Israel. El TA, en cambio, sigue literalmente a Jl 2,28 LXX (3,1 TM). Los editores de NA^{27} se han visto forzados a relegar al aparato crítico la lección de B03, si bien han retenido (sin indicar si hay variantes) el καί inicial de la profecía de Joel (καὶ ἔσται μετὰ ταῦτα), mientras que D05 lo suprime, confiriendo gran solemnidad al cumplimiento de la profecía en los tiempos escatológicos: ἔσται ἐν ταῖς ἐσχάταις ἡμέραις. Ropes, por su cuenta, considera que «This 'Western' reading was apparently drawn from ἐν ταῖς ἡμέραις ἐκείναις, vs 18, which is therefore in consistency omitted».[20] Epp viene a decir lo mismo.[21] Esto no obstante, en las ediciones modernas se hace, sin más, una conflación entre el texto de D05 en el v. 17 y el de B03 que retiene la lección de Jl-LXX en el v. 18.

[11] Tanto una como otra recensión añaden al texto de Jl-LXX un inciso parentético: el TA pone la profecía en boca de «Dios» (con artículo); el TO, en labios de Jesús, «el Señor» resucitado (enfatizado mediante la omisión del artículo), pues es él quien ha derramado su propio Espíritu sobre los presentes (cf. v. 33: ἐξέχεεν, refiriéndose a ἐκχεῶ ἀπὸ τοῦ πνεύματός μου de la profecía, vv. 17.18).

---

[20] *Beginnings* III, 16.

[21] «The first alteration, the change from μετὰ ταῦτα to ἐν ταῖς ἐσχάταις ἡμέραις (perhaps taken over, in D, from *v.* 18), may be only an attempt to adapt the quotation to the present situation» (*The Theological Tendency*, 67).

13 [12] El testimonio aislado de D*, en contra de toda la tradición manuscrita y de Jl-LXX, pone énfasis mediante el plural, «sobre todos los mortales», en la *universalidad* (cf. vv. 5.14 TO).[22]

14-17 [13-14] El TA sigue en todo a Jl 2,28 LXX, entendiendo por consiguiente que «vuestros hijos y vuestras hijas ... vuestros jóvenes ... y vuestros ancianos» se refiere obviamente a los judíos *inmigrantes* de todas las naciones residentes en Jerusalén por las fiestas de Pentecostés, mientras que, con algunos ligeros retoques, entenderá como dicho de los habitantes *autóctonos* lo relativo a «los siervos/las siervas», según se verá a continuación. El TO, en cambio, reinterpreta el pasaje de Joel diferenciando igualmente los dos grupos, pero dejando entender que el primer grupo se refiere a los individuos no-judíos (H),[23] residentes *figuradamente* en Jerusalén en representación de la *entera humanidad* (cuatro miembros dispuestos en forma de cruz siguiendo los cuatro puntos cardinales): *a*) «*sus* hijos» y *b*) «*sus* hijas» (el artículo, en D, ha sido omitido por *homoioteleuton*), en el palo vertical; *c*) «*los* jóvenes» y *d*) «*los* ancianos» (v. 17), en el horizontal, mientras que el segundo grupo lo restringe a los judíos (J) *históricamente* presentes en la escena en representación del *pueblo* de Israel (dos miembros): *a*) «sobre *mis* siervos» y *b*) «sobre *mis* siervas» (v. 18). La repetición de la misma frase, «derramaré parte de mi Espíritu», al principio del primer grupo (v. 17c) y al final del segundo (v. 18a), enmarca y a la vez separa un grupo del otro. A los cuatro miembros del primer grupo se les asignan tres acciones verbales: «profetizarán», «tendrán visiones», «tendrán sueños», mediante las cuales se describe *globalmente* el impacto que tendrá en un futuro próximo la efusión del Espíritu sobre la humanidad (profecía, visión/experiencia consciente, sueño/experiencia inconsciente); a los del segundo grupo no se les asigna ninguna,

---

[22] «This plural form in Codex Bezae leaves no doubt that the D-text intends Peter to say that the promise is to all men, not only to the Jews; the outpouring of the Spirit is upon all races» (*The Theological Tendency*, 69).

[23] Metzger, *Textual Commentary I*, 296: «motivated by the Western reviser's wish to make the prophetic oracle apply to Gentiles and not exclusively to the Jews to whom Peter was speaking»; Schneider *AG* I, 261, n. g: «der D-Text will die Weissagung nicht auschließlich auf Juden bezogen wissen»; véase *Comentari* I, 132-133.

según el TO; el TA, en cambio, añade: «y profetizarán», según se verá a continuación.

16-17 [15-16: *vll* NR] Tanto el TO como el TA invierten el orden de los incisos de Jl-LXX. Según D*, «los jóvenes verán en visión» (lit.) y «los ancianos tendrán sueños»; según el TA, en cambio, «los jóvenes verán visiones» y «los ancianos soñarán sueños», conservando una versión muy cercana a la de Jl-LXX.

Hch 2,18

18 [17: *vl* NR] En los mejores códices de la tradición manuscrita de Jl-LXX, en el encabezamiento de Jl 2,29a figuraba un καί escueto.[24] En la cita de Hch, en cambio, el TO habría añadido el pronombre ἐγώ al primitivo καί de Jl-LXX y, en correspondencia, el pronombre μου después de τοὺς δούλους y τὰς δούλας de Jl-LXX, modificando el sentido original del texto profético («los siervos/las siervas» = los esclavos),[25] puesto en boca de Yahvé, hasta el punto de designar ahora a los israelitas, «mis siervos y mis siervas»: «*yo* mismo sobre *mis* siervos y sobre *mis* siervas derramaré parte de *mi* Espíritu», enfatizando así la donación *personal* del Espíritu a los israelitas, su pueblo, por parte del Señor Jesús (cf. *supra*, v. 17b D: *vl* no. 11). El TA, en cambio, habría añadido la enclítica γε, al tiempo que modificaba igualmente, mediante la adición del pronombre μου, el sentido del texto de Joel en la misma línea. Epp admite como simple posibilidad que «mis siervos» pueda ser tomado para designar a los judíos, pero la rechaza a renglón seguido al asumir sin más la hipótesis de D. Plooij sobre la «anti-judaic tendency» del códice Beza, a quien cita en extenso.[26]

La simple adición de ἐγώ / γε al καί con que daba comienzo en Jl-LXX el segundo miembro del quiasmo (ἐκχεῶ ἀπὸ τοῦ πνεύματός μου ἐπὶ πᾶσαν σάρκα ... // καὶ ἐπὶ τοὺς δούλους ... ἐκχεῶ ἀπὸ τοῦ πνεύματός

[24] καί W* B-א*-V Luc Cat ach sa: καὶ γέ *rell* (en especial, A Q y resto del grupo alejandrino y la recensión hexaplar). En la tradición manuscrita del libro de Joel se observan en el punto donde coinciden Jl y Hch una serie de armonizaciones con el texto de Lucas, siempre de tipo alejandrino (véase el aparato crítico de Ziegler).

[25] Cf. A. Weiser, *Das Buch der zwölf Kleinen Propheten* I (Göttingen, ²1956), 120.

[26] *The Theological Tendency*, 69-70.

μου) refuerza considerablemente la existencia de dos grupos perfectamente diferenciados (en Joel se trataba tan sólo de dos estamentos, el de los hijos y el de los esclavos). Ahora bien, según el TA ambos grupos pertenecen al pueblo de Israel: 1) los judíos venidos de la diáspora *residentes* en Jerusalén por las fiestas de Pentecostés (οἱ υἱοὶ ὑμῶν, αἱ θυγατέρες ὑμῶν, οἱ νεανίσκοι ὑμῶν, οἱ πρεσβύτεροι ὑμῶν) y 2) los judíos *autóctonos* (τοὺς δούλους μου, τὰς δούλας μου). Según el TO, en cambio, 1) el primer grupo representa a toda la *humanidad* (οἱ υἱοὶ αὐτῶν, αἱ θυγατέρες αὐτῶν, οἱ νεανίσκοι, οἱ πρεσβύτεροι), mientras que 2) el segundo grupo lo constituyen los *judíos* históricamente presentes en la escena (τοὺς δούλους μου, τὰς δούλας μου). La estructura concéntrica que se adivinaba en el texto de Jl-LXX se repite en el TO; en el TA aparece una inversión quiástica irregular:

D05	**B03**
Ἔσται ἐν ταῖς ἐσχάταις ἡμέραις, λέγει κύριος,	Καὶ ἔσται μετὰ ταῦτα, λέγει ὁ θεός,
A ἐκχεῶ ἀπὸ τοῦ πνεύματός μου	**A** ἐκχεῶ ἀπὸ τοῦ πνεύματός μου
B ἐπὶ πάσας σάρκας	**B** ἐπὶ πᾶσαν σάρκα,
C καὶ προφητεύσουσιν οἱ υἱοὶ αὐτῶν	**C** καὶ προφητεύσουσιν οἱ υἱοὶ ὑμῶν,
καὶ αἱ θυγατέρες αὐτῶν,	καὶ αἱ θυγατέρες ὑμῶν,
καὶ οἱ νεανίσκοι ὁράσει ὄψονται,	καὶ οἱ νεανίσκοι ὑμῶν ὁράσεις ὄψονται,
καὶ οἱ πρεσβύτεροι ἐνυπνιασθήσονται·	καὶ οἱ πρεσβύτεροι ὑμῶν ἐνυπνίοις ἐνυπνιασθήσονται·
B' καὶ ἐγὼ ἐπὶ τοὺς δούλους μου	**B'** καί γε ἐπὶ τοὺς δούλους μου
καὶ ἐπὶ τὰς δούλας μου	καὶ ἐπὶ τὰς δούλας μου
	ἐν ταῖς ἡμέραις ἐκείναις
A' ἐκχεῶ ἀπὸ τοῦ πνεύματός μου.	**A'** ἐκχεῶ ἀπὸ τοῦ πνεύματός μου,
	C' καὶ προφητεύσουσιν.

20-21 [18-19] Después de que en el encabezamiento de la profecía el TA haya transcrito a la letra simplemente la transición de Jl 2,28 LXX: «Y sucederá después de estos (acontecimientos)»,[27] en el v. 18a sigue fiel a Jl 2,29 LXX: «*en aquellos días* derramaré parte de mí Espíritu», pero añade a continuación: «*y profetizarán*», inciso que de acuerdo con Jl-LXX se había predicado ya de los dos primeros miembros del primer grupo («vuestros hijos y vuestras hijas»), supliendo así la acción verbal que no se predicaba del segundo grupo en Jl-LXX y que se silencia igualmente en D05. El TO, en cambio, elimina la precisión temporal de Jl-LXX (por haberla reinterpretado

[27] Enumeración más completa de los testimonios, con las pequeñas variantes, en UBS⁴, 412.

en clave escatológica al inicio) y se limita a repetir la frase inicial «derramaré parte de mi Espíritu», cerrando así la descripción relativa al segundo grupo con el mismo inciso con que había encabezado el primero. El hecho de insistir el TA en que también los miembros del segundo grupo «profetizarán», al igual que los del primero, indicaría que esta recensión tiene sumo interés en poner en pie de igualdad tanto a los judíos de la diáspora *residentes* en Jerusalén por las fiestas de Pentecostés como a los judíos *autóctonos*. El TO, en cambio, inspirándose en la pauta de Jl-LXX, se limita a constatar que el Señor (Jesús) derramará también su Espíritu sobre los judíos realmente presentes en la escena (J), al igual que sobre toda la humanidad (H).

Hch 2,19
24 [20] El TO elimina la connotación vindicativa, a modo de juicio de Dios apocalíptico, de Jl-LXX. El TA la retiene, a pesar de haber conservado, junto con el TO, las modificaciones introducidas por Lucas (en negrita) en el inciso anterior al texto de Jl 2,30 LXX: καὶ δώσω τέρατα ἐν τῷ οὐρανῷ καὶ ἐπὶ τῆς γῆς, reinterpretando los fenómenos cósmicos en clave de escatología anticipada:[28] καὶ δώσω τέρατα ἐν τῷ οὐρανῷ **ἄνω** καὶ **σημεῖα** ἐπὶ τῆς γῆς **κάτω**.

Hch 2,20
25 [21: *vl* NR] En lugar del futuro segundo ático (μεταστραφήσεται, Jl-LXX y TA), D* prefiere el presente (μεταστρέφεται, ¿presente histórico?), aludiendo quizás al momento de la muerte de Jesús (Lc 23,44), a los fenómenos cósmicos (v. 20a) que han precedido a «el gran día del Señor», indicadores de un profundo cambio de época (cf. Mc 13,24; Lc 21,25).

[28] «The quotation from Jl 2.28-32 (= LXX 3.1-5) is preserved in two forms, represented by codex Vaticanus and by codex Bezae. The former agrees almost exactly with the text of the Septuagint, whereas the latter embodies a series of changes from the Septuagint, most of which make the quotation more suitable for the occasion» (Metzger, *Textual Commentary I*, 295).

27 [22] La construcción de la conjunción πρίν + infinitivo aoristo es la más ordinaria: el TO sigue Jl-LXX; el TA, en cambio, añade la conjunción ἤ, otra construcción posible.[29]

[23] El TA reproduce a la letra el texto de Jl-LXX; el TO elimina la connotación teofánica, «deslumbrante», relativa al día de la parusía del Señor, refiriendo los prodigios y señales que lo hacen ostensible (v. 19) al día de Pentecostés.[30]

Hch 2,21
28 [24: *vl* NR] Con la adición del artículo, el TO hace referencia a la última mención de κυρίου (v. 20), insistiendo de nuevo (recuérdese el cambio de «Dios» por «Señor» del encabezamiento, v. 17b) en que se trata de Jesús resucitado, en su calidad de «Señor», cuyo nombre, al ser invocado, procura la salvación.

Conclusiones

De la colación del texto de Hch con la profecía de Jl-LXX y de la comparación de las dos recensiones entre sí pueden inferirse una serie de conclusiones:

1) El TA concuerda casi a la letra con el texto de los LXX, mientras que el TO depara una serie de cambios redaccionales y de omisiones cambiando ostensiblemente, por lo que hace a la descripción del primer grupo, ὑμῶν (Jl-LXX y TA) por αὐτῶν u omitiendo simplemente ὑμῶν (Jl-LXX y TA) y añadiendo, por lo que respecta al segundo grupo, μου después de τοὺς δούλους / τὰς δούλας (Jl-LXX), adición que comparte con el TA.

2) Ambas recensiones diferencian diáfanamente los dos grupos ya mencionados (vv. 12-13 y 14 TO) y cuya interpelación ha motivado la doble respuesta de Pedro (v. 15 responde a v. 13 y v. 16 a v. 12, con la consiguiente inversión quiástica): «derramaré parte de

[29] Cf. Bailly, s.v. πρίν. En la edición crítica de Jl-LXX (Ziegler) la conjunción ἤ se presenta también en algunos códices esporádicos (W[?] *lII*-613 130'-239 106 Tht.Bas.N).

[30] Lucas presenta aquí, por primera vez, su típica hendíadis τέρατα καὶ σημεῖα: ver *Comentari* I, 133-4.

mi Espíritu sobre todo(s los) mortal(es)» (v. 17c), los judíos procedentes de la diáspora (TA) / los no-judíos (TO) // «sobre mis siervos y mis siervas derramaré parte de mi Espíritu» (v.18a), los judíos autóctonos (TA) / históricamente presentes (TO).

3) El TA deshace la perfecta estructura concéntrica que acabamos de observar en el TO (**A** ἐκχεῶ ἀπὸ τοῦ πνεύματός μου / **B** ἐπὶ πᾶσας σάρκας / **C** καὶ προφητεύσουσιν... / **B'** καὶ ἐγὼ ἐπὶ τοὺς δούλους μου... / **A'** ἐκχεῶ ἀπὸ τοῦ πνεύματός μου), al retener la expresión temporal ἐν ταῖς ἡμέραις ἐκείναις de Jl-LXX y repetir, por su cuenta y riesgo, la expresión inicial καὶ προφητεύσουσιν, formando una más bien irregular inversión quiástica: **A** ἐκχεῶ ἀπὸ τοῦ πνεύματός μου / **B** ἐπὶ πᾶσαν σάρκα / **C** καὶ προφητεύσουσιν... / **B'** καί γε ἐπὶ τοὺς δούλους μου... / **A'** ἐκχεῶ ἀπὸ τοῦ πνεύματός μου / **C'** καὶ προφητεύσουσιν.

4) El TA conserva la referencia de Jl-LXX al juicio de Dios apocalíptico, mientras que el TO elimina la connotación vindicativa «sangre, fuego y nubes de humo».

5) El TA reproduce a la letra el texto de Jl-LXX por lo que hace a la connotación teofánica, «deslumbrante», relativa al día de la parusía del Señor; el TO refiere los prodigios y señales que hacen ostensible el día del Señor al día de Pentecostés.

El hecho indiscutible de que el TA armoniza con el texto de Jl-LXX[31] (a excepción de los ligeros retoques ya señalados relativos al segundo grupo), presentando por consiguiente – por lo menos por lo que hace a la cita de Joel – una versión menos elaborada que la conservada por el TO, deja entrever cierta tendencia de la recensión alejandrina a *historicizar* la escena de Pentecostés en detrimento de la presencia *figurada* de toda la humanidad en la anti-Babel que se desprende del TO. Las tendencias armonizadoras presuponen una época en que el texto ya ha sido definitivamente fijado y que, por consiguiente, las citas explícitas de textos sagrados no pueden estar alteradas.

---

[31] «Toutes les variantes du TA par rapport au TO sont des harmonisations sur la Septante» (M.É. Boismard – A. Lamouille, *Le Texte Occidental des Actes des Apôtres. Reconstitution et Réhabilitation* [Paris: Éditions Recherche sur les Civilisations, 1984] II, 12). Ropes oscilaba todavía: «In some cases manifestly, and probably in all, the departures in D from the LXX-text ... may be the work of the original author, and the agreement of the B-text with the LXX may have been effected by an editor ... Equally possible, however, is the view that the author copied exactly ... and that the modifications are due

Teniendo presentes todos estos datos, podríamos preguntarnos si la tendencia aquí observada en el TA no es sino un caso particular de una tendencia mucho más generalizada de dicha recensión en el libro de los Hechos de los Apóstoles tendente a *historicizar los hechos* en detrimento de su primitivo género literario, el género «evangelio», género que compartía con el primer volumen, mientras uno y otro (Lc-Hch) estaban editorialmente ensamblados. En el primer volumen Lucas habría propuesto el modelo de Jesús cuya realización pensaba comprobar en la vida de las primeras comunidades. La adición de Ἰουδαῖοι en Hch 2,5 podría haber participado ya de esa tendencia historicizante del TA, dando a entender que todos los presentes en Pentecostés eran *judíos*, ya sea de la diáspora, ya autóctonos. La *Vorlage* del códice Bezae (D d) – sólo la lección original del Sinaítico y algunos testimonios esporádicos[32] han preservado la lección primitiva – se habría dejado influenciar en Hch 2,5 por esta «solución» salomónica al problema de una presencia masiva de la humanidad en Jerusalén por la fiesta de Pentecostés. (Obsérvese que Ἰουδαῖοι se encuentra en D05 al final del estico.) Una vez cambiado el registro, al TA no le habrían interesado muchos de los retoques introducidos libremente por Lucas en el texto de Jl-LXX y se habría limitado a armonizar las citas con el texto de Joel considerado ya como sagrado.

Por lo que respecta a la página latina, d05 sigue de cerca la griega (D05), pero se aparta del modelo en siete ocasiones,[33] por influencia sin duda de la recensión alejandrina, influencia que – según puede apreciarse en el aparato crítico – se puede comprobar igualmente en las sucesivas correcciones del códice Beza.[34] Jerónimo

to the customary freedom of the paraphrastic 'Western' reviser» (*Beginnings* III 16-17).

32 En 'Las variantes de la recensión occidental' IV 201-202 la ausencia de Ἰουδαῖοι en ℵ* ℓ844 ph vg^ms me llevó a conjeturar que ésta podría ser la lección primitiva tanto del TA* como del TO* originales. La tendencia armonizadora del TA recién detectada me inclina ahora a asignarla sólo al TO*.

33 Se aparta del modelo (entre [ ] el número de la variante) en los vv. 14a [1], 15b [8], 17c [12], 17e [15], 17f [16], 20a [21], 20c [22].

34 Se puede consultar mi contribución al Coloquio de Lunel, 'Le substrat grec de la version latine des Actes dans le Codex de Bèze', en Parker & Amphoux, 271-295.

corrigió asimismo la versión latina antigua, de la cual se sirvió de base – como se puede comprobar igualmente en la sinopsis – introduciendo las variantes propias de la recensión alejandrina (B03), recensión que en tiempos de Jerónimo había ganado ya la partida a la recensión occidental.[35]

Sinopsis

Jl 2,28-32 LXX (3,1-5 TM)

Καὶ ἔσται μετὰ ταῦτα
ἐκχεῶ ἀπὸ τοῦ πνεύματός μου ἐπὶ **πᾶσαν σάρκα**,
καὶ προφητεύσουσιν οἱ υἱοὶ **ὑμῶν**
15 καὶ αἱ θυγατέρες **ὑμῶν**,
καὶ οἱ πρεσβύτεροι **ὑμῶν ἐνύπνια** ἐνυπνιασθήσονται,
καὶ οἱ νεανίσκοι **ὑμῶν ὁράσεις** ὄψονται·
καὶ ἐπὶ τοὺς δούλους
καὶ ἐπὶ τὰς δούλας
20 **ἐν ταῖς ἡμέραις ἐκείναις**
ἐκχεῶ ἀπὸ τοῦ πνεύματός μου.
καὶ δώσω τέρατα ἐν τῷ οὐρανῷ
καὶ ἐπὶ τῆς γῆς,
αἷμα καὶ πῦρ καὶ ἀτμίδα καπνοῦ·
25 ὁ ἥλιος **μεταστραφήσεται** εἰς σκότος
καὶ ἡ σελήνη εἰς αἷμα
πρὶν ἐλθεῖν ἡμέραν κυρίου τὴν μεγάλην **καὶ ἐπιφανῆ**.
καὶ ἔσται πᾶς, ὃς ἂν ἐπικαλέσηται τὸ ὄνομα κυρίου,
σωθήσεται.

[35] Solamente se aparta de B03 en los vv. 14b [3], 15b [8], 17a [10: si bien conserva el *et* inicial], 17b [11] y 20c [22].

Ac 2,14-21 D05

Τοτε σταθεις δε ο πετρος
συν τοις **δεκα αποστολοις**
επηρεν **πρωτος** την φωνην αυτου και **ειπεν**·
Ανδρες Ιουδαιοι και **παντες**
5 **οι κατοικουντες Ιερουσαλημ**,
τουτο υμιν γνωστον εστω,
ενωτισατε τα ρηματα μου·
ου γαρ ως υμεις υπολαμβανετε
ουτοι μεθυουσιν, **ουσης ωρας της ημερας τριτης**,
10 αλλα τουτο εστιν το ειρημενον
δια του προφητου·
Εσται εν ταις εσχαταις ημεραις – λεγει **κυριος** –,
εκχεω απο του πνευματος μου επι **πασας σαρκας**,
και προφητευσουσιν οι υιοι **αυτων**
15 και ⟨αι⟩ θυγατερες **αυτων**,
και οι νεανισκοι **ορασει** οψονται,
και οι πρεσβυτεροι ενυπνιασθησονται·
και **εγ⟨ω⟩** επι τους δουλους μου
και επι τας δουλας μου
20
εκχεω απο του πνευματος μου.
και δωσω τερατα εν τω ουρανω ανω
και σημεια επι της γης κατω·

25 ο ηλιος **μεταστρεφεται** εις ⟨σ⟩κοτος
και η σεληνη εις αιμα
πριν ελθειν ημεραν κυριου την μεγαλην.
και εσται πας, ος αν επικαλεσηται το ονομα **του** κυριου,
σωθησεται

Ac 2,14-21 B03

Σταθεὶς δὲ ὁ Πέτρος
σὺν τοῖς **ἕνδεκα**
ἐπῆρεν τὴν φωνὴν αὐτοῦ καὶ **ἀπεφθέγξατο αὐτοῖς**·
Ἄνδρες Ἰουδαῖοι καὶ
5 **οἱ κατοικοῦντες Ἰερουσαλὴμ πάντες**,
τοῦτο ὑμῖν γνωστὸν ἔστω
καὶ ἐνωτίσασθε τὰ ῥήματά μου·
οὐ γὰρ ὡς ὑμεῖς ὑπολαμβάνετε
οὗτοι μεθύουσιν, **ἔστιν γὰρ ὥρα τρίτη τῆς ἡμέρας**,
10 ἀλλὰ τοῦτό ἐστιν τὸ εἰρημένον
διὰ τοῦ προφήτου **Ἰωήλ**·
Καὶ ἔσται μετὰ ταῦτα – λέγει **ὁ θεός** –
ἐκχεῶ ἀπὸ τοῦ πνεύματός μου ἐπὶ **πᾶσαν σάρκα**,
καὶ προφητεύσουσιν οἱ υἱοὶ **ὑμῶν**,
15 καὶ αἱ θυγατέρες **ὑμῶν**,
καὶ οἱ νεανίσκοι **ὑμῶν ὁράσεις** ὄψονται,
καὶ οἱ πρεσβύτεροι **ὑμῶν ἐνυπνίοις** ἐνυπνιασθήσονται·
καί **γε** ἐπὶ τοὺς δούλους μου
καὶ ἐπὶ τὰς δούλας μου
20 **ἐν ταῖς ἡμέραις ἐκείναις**
ἐκχεῶ ἀπὸ τοῦ πνεύματός μου, **καὶ προφητεύσουσιν**.
καὶ δώσω τέρατα ἐν τῷ οὐρανῷ ἄνω
καὶ σημεῖα ἐπὶ τῆς γῆς κάτω,
αἷμα καὶ πῦρ καὶ ἀτμίδα καπνοῦ·
25 ὁ ἥλιος **μεταστραφήσεται** εἰς σκότος
καὶ ἡ σελήνη εἰς αἷμα
πρὶν **ἢ** ἐλθεῖν ἡμέραν κυρίου τὴν μεγάλην **καὶ ἐπιφανῆ**.
καὶ ἔσται πᾶς, ὃς ἂν ἐπικαλέσηται τὸ ὄνομα κυρίου,
σωθήσεται.

Ac 2,14-21 d05

Cum stetisset autem Petrus
cum **decem apostolis**
et eleuauit **primus** uocem suam et **dixit**:
Viri Iudaei et **omnes**
5 **qui inhabitant Hierusalem**,
hoc uobis notum sit,
ausilate uerbis meis.
non enim sicut uos suspicamini
hii ebrii sunt, **est enim hora tertia diei**,
10 sed hoc est quod dictum est
per prophetam:
Erit in nouissimis diebus – dicit **dominus** –,
effundam spiritum meum super **omnem carnem**,
et prophetabunt fili **eorum**
15 et filia⟨e⟩ **eorum**,
et iuuenes **uisiones** uidebunt,
et seniores **somnia** somniabunt:
et **ego** super seruos meos
et super ancillas meas
20
effundam spiritum meum.
et dabo prodigia in caelo susum
et signa in terra deorsum:

25 sol **conuertetur** in tenebris
et luna in saguine,
prius quam ueniat dies domini magnus.
et erit omnis quicumque inuocauerit nomen domini
saluus erit.

Ac 2,14-21 vg (B03)

Stans autem Petrus
cum **undecim**
levavit **primus** vocem suam et **locutus est eis**:
Viri Iudaei et
5 **qui habitatis Hierusalem universi**,
hoc vobis notum sit
et auribus percipite verba mea.
non enim sicut uos aestimatis
hii ebrii sunt, **cum sit hora diei tertia**,
10 sed hoc est quod dictum est
per prophetam **Iohel**:
Et erit in novissimis diebus – dicit **dominus** –,
effundam de spiritu meo super **omnem carnem**,
et prophetabunt fili **vestri**
15 et filiae **vestrae**,
et iuvenes **vestri visiones** videbunt,
et seniores **vestri somnia** somniabunt:
et **quidem** super servos meos
et super ancillas meas
20 **in diebus illis**
effundam de spiritu meo **et prophetabunt**.
et dabo prodigia in caelo sursum
et signa in terra deorsum,
sanguinem et ignem et vaporem fumi:
25 sol **convertetur** in tenebras
et luna in saguinem,
antequam veniat dies domini magnus **et manifestus**.
et erit omnis quicumque invocaverit nomen domini
salvus erit.

Aparato Crítico

v.14a-b	1	[1] Τοτε D sy^{p} mae: om. B d *rell*
	2	[2] δεκα αποστολοις D* d: ενδεκα B (D^{E} d$^{E?}$) *rell*
	3	[3] πρωτος D* (προτερον E) d p^{c} w vg^{ms} mae: om. B D$^{s.m.}$ *rell* |
		[4] ειπεν D d it (sy): απεφθεγξατο αυτοις B *rell*
v.14c	4-5	[5: *vl* NR] παντες οι κατοικουντες Ιερουσαλημ D d sy^{p}: 2 3 4 1 B *rell*
	7	[6: *vl* NR] και (Jl 1,2 LXX) B *rell*: om. D d |
		[7] ενωτισατε D* (d): -σασθε (Jl 1,2 LXX) B *rell*
v.15	9	[8] ουσης ωρας της ημερας τριτης D* lat; Ir^{lat} GrElv Aug Hes Cass: εστιν γαρ ωρα τριτη της ημερας B D^{A} d sy^{p} *rell*
v.16	11	[9] Ιωηλ ℵ A B C E Ψ 076^{vid} 096 sy^{p} *rell*: om. D d r; Just Ir^{lat} Rebapt Hil GrElv Aug
v.17	12	[10] Εσται εν ταις εσχαταις ημεραις D d sy bo; Ir^{lat} Hil Aug (Και [εσται κτλ.] ℵ A E I P 028. 81. 462 vg; Mac Chr): Και εσται μετα ταυτα (= Jl-LXX) B 076 sa^{mss} (+ εν ταις εσχαταις ημεραις C 467. 1319; Theoph) |
		[11] κυριος D E 242. 467. 1845 d latt sa bo^{mss}; Ir^{lat} Rebapt Hil Chr Aug GrNys PassPerp JacEd : ο θεος B *rell*
	13	[12] πασας σαρκας D*: πασαν σαρκα (= Jl-LXX) B D^{A} d *rell*
	14-17	[13] αυτων ... αυτων D d gig r; Rebapt Hil GrElv PassPerp: υμων ... υμων (= Jl-LXX) B *rell* |
		[14] υμων ... υμων (= Jl-LXX: con inversión del orden de los incisos) B *rell*: om. D (E) d (p*) r; Rebapt GrElv PassPerp
	16-17	[15: *vl* NR] ορασει D*: -σεις (= Jl-LXX) B D^{A} d *rell* |
		[16: *vl* NR] ενυπνιοις (= Jl-LXX: ενυπνια/-νιοις) B D^{B} d *rell*: om. D*
v.18	18	[17: *vl* NR] εγ<ω> D* d: γε B D^{D} *rell*: om. Jl-LXX
	20-21	[18] εν ταις ημεραις εκειναις (= Jl-LXX) $\mathfrak{P}^{74}$ ℵ A B

		C E Ψ 076 (sy^{p}) *rell*: om. D d gig r ro* vg^{mss}; Just Didache Rebapt Aster Prisc Did Hier |
		[19] και προφητευσουσιν 𝔓^{74} ℵ A B C E Ψ 076 *rell*: om. (Jl-LXX) D d p*; Tert Rebapt Prisc PassPerp Hier
v.19	24	[20] αιμα και πυρ και ατμιδα καπνου (= Jl-LXX) 𝔓^{74vid} ℵ A B C E Ψ 076 *rell*: om. D d it; Prisc
v.20	25	[21: *vl* NR] μεταστρεφεται D*: -αφησεται (= Jl-LXX) B D$^{A.B}$ d *rell*
	27	[22] (πριν) η B 076. 1739 *M* d: om. (Jl-LXX) ℵ A C D E Ψ 33. 81. 88. 383. 453. 463. 876. 915. 1108. 1175. 1505. 1611. 1891 *al* vg |
		[23] και επιφανη (= Jl-LXX) 𝔓^{74} A B C E P 076 vg sy^{p}: om. ℵ D d gig r; Prisc
v.21	28	[24: *vl* NR] του (κυριου) D*: om. (= Jl-LXX) B D$^{s.m.}$ *rell*

English Summary:

The Use Made of the Book of Joel (2:28-32a) in Peter's Speech (Acts 2:14-21): A Comparison of Two Manuscript Traditions

(Numbers in brackets refer to *vll* in critical apparatus; WT = Western MSS; AT = Alexandrian text)

V.14a [1] The position of δε in WT in third place is not a problem; it is found even in fifth place. [2] The number of the apostles given as ten (D) rather than as eleven (AT) is indicative of Luke's view in WT in Acts 1 that the choosing of a replacement for Judas was inappropriate.

V.14b [3] πρωτος WT: Peter is viewed as spokesman for the apostles and his speech as the first among others not cited.

The quotation from the book of Joel occurs in the first part of the exposition of Peter's speech, which is addressed to the representatives of the nations as well as to Jews (the second part, vv.22-35, is addressed specifically to Israelites). The presence of the Gentiles at the outpouring of the Holy Spirit (cf. v.5, where ℵ01 omits Ιουδαιοι), is to be understood as a literary fiction superimposed by Luke on a historic event, the gathering of the Jews in Jerusalem for the festival of Pentecost, in order to make the point that the Holy Spirit is given to all people.

Whereas Peter reproduces the LXX text of Joel with little alteration according to AT, in the WT he adjusts the prophecy to apply it more exactly to the event which has just occurred. The changes have the effect of demonstrating that the Holy Spirit is for the nations as well as for the Jews. The universal nature of the gift of the Spirit is less explicit in the AT. According to a variety of MSS, Peter further uses the prophecy of Joel to interpret the present situation as belonging to the last days, an era which has already commenced with the coming of the Spirit.

V.14c The presence of two separate groups is clearer in D: [5] position of παντες [6] omission of και. Joel 1:2 (cf. 2:1) likewise mentions the two groups as distinct.

V.15 [8] The third hour is underlined in WT: it is the hour of the crucifixion, cf. Mk 15:25.

V.16 [9] Apart from this mention of Joel in AT, Luke does not specify the names of the prophets except for Isaiah.

V.17 [10] 'After this' = AT = Joel LXX; *vl* 'in the last days' presents the coming of the Spirit as a realized eschatological event (cf. 'in those days' = AT v.18 = Joel LXX; W. MSS omit the time indication in line with the alteration made here).

[11] WT = 'the Lord', meaning that Jesus is seen as speaking in Joel's prophecy (confirmed v.33, all MSS) i.e. the prophecy is actualized to show a realization of the divine status of Jesus.

[12] D: πασας σαρκας; [13] WT: αυτων x 2; and [14] WT: omission υμων x 2, are indications of the gift of the Spirit to all nations, which permits a contrast to be established with the Jews in v.18 WT.

V.18 By the qualification of 'servants' with 'my', Peter reinterprets Joel's prophecy, distinguishing between two moments in time: a) the outpouring of the Spirit on the whole of humanity, b) the outpouring on the Israelites.

The absence in WT of the time specification [18] (cf. v.14c) together with the absence of the repeated 'they will prophesy' [19], allow a typically Lukan concentric structure to emerge in D, which presents the two groups of people in parallel:

A I will pour out my Spirit
B on all mortals
C they will prophesy... see visions... dream dreams
B' even on my male servants and my female servants
A' I will pour out my Spirit

Vv.19-20 WT: the arrival of the Spirit is a sign of the last times which loses something of its awesome aspect by the omission in the quotation from Joel of [20] 'blood, fire and columns of smoke' and [23] 'terrible/splendid' to qualify the Lord; these omissions enable the re-interpretation of Joel's prophecy of the end-times as a reference to the present time to be made more easily.

V.21 The universal application of Joel's prophecy is apparent, in all texts, in Peter's omission of the second half of Joel 2:32 where the prophecy is restricted to the Jews.

Conclusions

The almost literal quotation of the Joel text in the AT leaves the reader with the impression that the point of Peter's speech is that the outpouring of the Spirit has been foreseen in the Jewish Scriptures. In the WT, Peter has a different purpose for quoting Joel. Using the prophecy addressed to the remnant of Israel as a guide, he creatively constructs a new prophecy: that which has just taken place among the community of Jewish disciples is nothing other than the first fruits of the outpouring of the Holy Spirit which is destined for all people.

There is no need to see the universalism of the WT as a later trait of a predominantly Gentile church, since Jesus himself according to Luke's Gospel had already shown how the gospel is for all nations. On the other hand, the free use of Joel could well have been felt to be a difficulty which prompted a closer harmonization between the text of Acts and that of Joel LXX in the AT. The revised text loses the nuances of Peter's theological message by substituting a more straightforward historical account.

Out of 24 *vll*, 7 are not mentioned in the apparatus of NA[27]. The full critical apparatus shows that it is Codex Bezae (D05) which is consistently different from the AT – it is the only MS to testify to every reading which is different from ℵ01 or B03. The Vulgate follows the AT, except on four occasions [3.8.10.11] when it follows D05.

INDEX OF BIBLICAL CITATIONS

INDEX OF MODERN AUTHORS

NOTES

NOTES

NOTES

NOTES

NOTES